Liz Hocking Mary Bowen

English World

Teacher's Guide 4

MACMILLAN

Macmillan Education
Between Towns Road, Oxford OX4 3PP
A division of Macmillan Publishers Limited
Companies and representatives throughout the world

ISBN 978-0-230-02474-8

Text © Liz Hocking
Design and illustration © Macmillan Publishers Limited 2009

First published 2009

All rights reserved; no part of this publication may be reproduced, stored in a retrieval system, transmitted in any form, or by any means, electronic, mechanical, photocopying, recording, or otherwise, without the prior written permission of the publishers.

Designed by Anthony Godber
Page layout by Wild Apple Design
Illustrated by Heather Allen, Beth Aulton, Juliet Breese, Chantal Kees, Andy Keylock, Gustavo Mazali, Philip Pepper, Chris Petty, Gary Rees, Mark Ruffle and Barbara Vagnozzi.
Cover design by Oliver Design

The authors and publishers wish to thank the following for permission to reproduce their photographs:
Alamy/Krebs Hanns (bl); Clark Wiseman/www.studio-8.co.uk (t);
Getty Image/Stone/Andy Rouse (tl: Photolibrary Group (br)

The publisher would like to thank the following for their participation in development of this course:
In Egypt - Inas Agiz, Salma Ahmed, Hekmat Aly, Suzi Balaban, Mohamed Eid, Bronwen El Kholy, Mostafa El Makhzangy, Hala Fouad, Johnathan French, Nashaat Nageeb Gendy, Hisham Howeedy, Saber Lamey, Heidi Omara, Maha Radwan, Amany Shawkey, Christine Abu Sitta, Ali Abdel Wahab
In Russia - Tatiana Antonova, Elena Belonozhkina, Galiana Dragunova, Irina Filonenko, Marina Gaisina, Maria Goreetaya, Oksana Guzhnovskaya, Irina Kalinina, Olga Kligerman, Galina Kornikova, Lidia Kosterina, Sergey Kozlov, Irina Larionova, Irina Lenchenko, Irina Lyubimova, Karine Makhmuryan, Maria Pankina, Anna Petrenkova, Elena Plisko, Natalia Vashchenko, Angelika Vladyko.

All the photographs which are reproduced in the facsimilies in this book are credited in English World PB4

Printed and bound in Malaysia

2014 2013 2012
10 9 8 7 6 5 4 3

Contents

Introduction 5
English World components 6
Classroom lessons 8
Teaching the course 9
Unit structure 10
Using the Teacher's Guide 11
Scope and Sequence 12
Posters 14
PB pages 4–5 17

Teacher's Notes

Welcome Unit 18
Unit 1 26
Unit 2 38
Unit 3 50
Revision 1, Project 1 62
Portfolio and Diploma 1: Units 1, 2 and 3 64
Answers to Check-ups Units 1, 2 and 3 65
Unit 4 66
Unit 5 78
Unit 6 90
Revision 2, Project 2 102
Portfolio and Diploma 2: Units 4, 5 and 6 104
Answers to Check-ups Units 4, 5 and 6 105
Unit 7 106
Unit 8 118
Unit 9 130
Revision 3, Project 3 142
Portfolio and Diploma 3: Units 7, 8 and 9 144
Answers to Check-ups Units 7, 8 and 9 145
Unit 10 146
Unit 11 158
Unit 12 170
Revision 4, Project 4 182
Portfolio and Diploma 4: Units 10, 11 and 12 184
Answers to Check-ups Units 10, 11 and 12 185
Games 186
Word list: alphabetical 188
Word list: Unit by unit 190
Grammar Practice Book Answer Key 192

Introduction

English World is a 10-level course designed for children and young people learning English as a first foreign language. They begin at the first stages of language learning and progress year by year towards a high level of competency in written and spoken English.

In the lower levels, grammar and vocabulary are introduced at a steady pace and then practised and recycled systematically. This approach is designed to give all learners, whether they have daily exposure to English or not, a sound knowledge of structures and meaning, and the ability to use language actively from the start.

The methodology of the course encourages communication in the classroom, backed up by a wide variety of practice exercises to reinforce reading and writing skills. It aims to give learners confidence in speaking natural English fluently and in writing with accuracy and appropriately for the purpose. The course offers not only essential activities in the key language skills but also includes practice of study skills which assist children in developing their proficiency as individual learners.

Teachers will find this course practical and useable because:

- the methodology is clear and easy to follow
- teaching materials are provided so that extensive preparation is not required
- step-by-step guidance is given for every lesson
- built-in flexibility makes the course appropriate for a variety of different teaching situations
- grammar is presented clearly and taught actively to build confidence and develop accuracy
- classroom activities, including songs, games and rhymes, are designed to engage children whilst developing their skills in reading, writing, listening and speaking
- each level begins with a Welcome Unit that revises the previous year's work.

English World 4 components

Pupil's Book

The Pupil's Book has 12 units. One unit can be taught in about two weeks.

The Pupil's Book begins with a Welcome Unit which revises the main grammar from the previous year.

CD/cassette

All Pupil's Book dialogues, reading texts, listening activities, songs and rhymes are recorded.

Dictionary

The Dictionary gives new vocabulary for each unit and helps with the practice of dictionary skills.

Grammar Practice Book

Further grammar exercises practise classroom and Workbook learning.

Workbook

Workbook exercises practise every language skill taught in the Pupil Book.

Teacher's Guide

The Teacher's Guide gives step-by-step notes for each lesson.

Posters

Twelve posters introduce new vocabulary in context.

PDFs on the website

Downloadable PDFs provide further support material and printable resources.

DVD

The teacher's DVD contains model classroom lessons, material for interactive whiteboard use and test material.

Pupil's Book

The Pupil's Book has twelve units. A single unit requires eight teaching sessions and is designed to be covered over a two-week period. All units consistently cover the key skills of reading, writing, speaking and listening, underpinned by the firm foundation of the grammar syllabus. These elements are clearly presented in the book so that teachers have a clear objective for every lesson. A variety of well-illustrated stories, information texts, dialogues, songs and poems have been written to attract and motivate young learners.

Welcome Unit

Pupil's Book 4 begins with the Welcome Unit which revises the key grammar and vocabulary that children learned in Pupil's Book 3.

CD/cassette

All reading texts, dialogues, listening comprehension activities, songs and rhymes are included on CD/cassette, allowing children to listen again and practise as an independent activity at home.

Dictionary

For level 4 the new vocabulary is presented unit by unit using a combination of illustrations, definitions and example sentences. The dictionary is designed to introduce children to the skills they will eventually need when using a standard dictionary. The words in each unit are in three classes: *key words* that children should learn as they go through the unit; *extension words* that children can learn to broaden their vocabulary; *special words* that chidren need to understand for the unit topic only and should not be expected to learn and remember.

Workbook

All the work covered in the Pupil's Book is reinforced by exercises in the Workbook. These are designed to be introduced and explained by the teacher and to be completed independently, either in the classroom or for homework. They allow children to work at their own pace and give teachers the opportunity to see what children can achieve when working alone.

Grammar Practice Book

Further exercises to consolidate classroom learning accompany every unit. These have been written for children to work on alone, at their own pace and level of ability.

Posters

Twelve posters, one for each unit, accompany the course. These play a central part in the teaching of new vocabulary. Words are introduced with illustrations allowing the class to focus on them and understand them before they begin the reading text where the words are used in context.

DVD

The DVD gives teachers advice on how to present lessons and shows a model lesson being taught. It contains ready-made tests and questions for building custom-made tests.

It contains material from the course in a format designed for use on an interactive whiteboard. Although this material is also found in the books, using a whiteboard extends the opportunities for whole-class teaching and interaction.

Teacher's Guide

Each step of every lesson is supported by notes for teachers. These are arranged around facsimile pages of the learners' books, so that teachers can see quickly and easily how the student material is intended to be used. The guide also contains suggestions for warm-ups for every lesson, answers to Pupil's Book activities and Workbook exercises, a list of classroom games and suggestions for different ways of carrying out the revision projects

Classroom lessons

Lesson 1 Poster; Reading

An illustrated poster introduces new vocabulary in context.

The Pupil's Book contains fiction and non-fiction texts on a variety of topics. Each unit begins with a different kind of text, chosen to interest young readers and illustrated to help their understanding.

Examples of the target grammar for the unit are in the reading text.

Lesson 2 Reading comprehension and vocabulary

A variety of activities help children to understand the reading texts.

Different tasks with new words reinforce vocabulary learning.

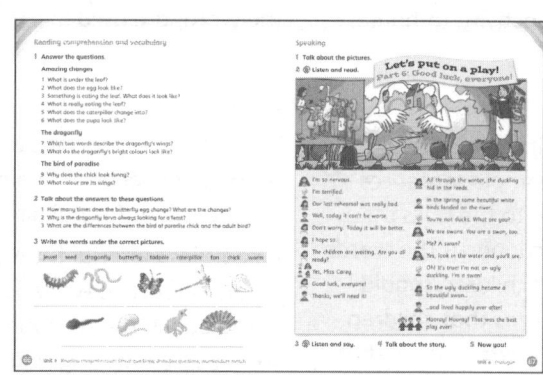

Lesson 3 Speaking and Study skills

Children listen to a dialogue, then practise and act the dialogue.

Lesson 4 Grammar

Session 1 Grammar structure
The first target grammar structure is presented with a clear model.

Children practise actively in class.

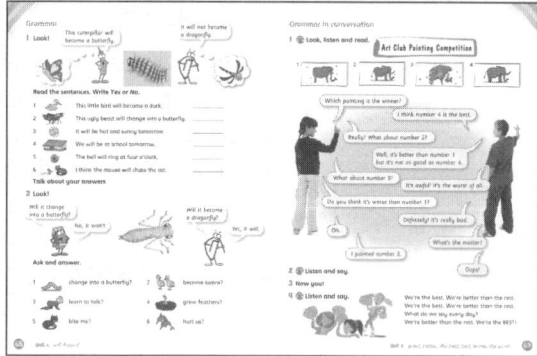

Session 2 Grammar in conversation
The second target grammar structure, often used in daily speech, is presented in a dialogue.

A song or a rhyme reinforces the language.

Lesson 5 Listening, Phonics and Use of English

Children listen for gist and for detail in a listening comprehension activity.

Children listen to English phonemes and practise them in a rhyme.

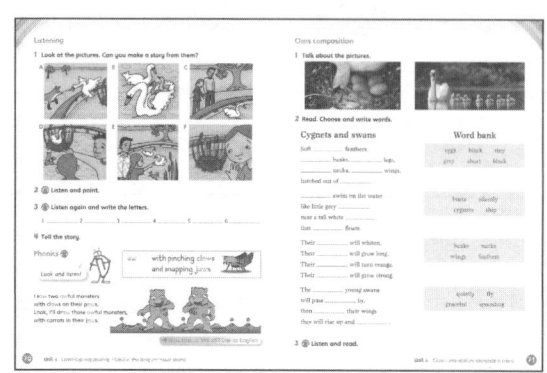

Lesson 6 Writing

Session 1 Class composition
The teacher leads the class in composing a piece of writing.

Session 2 Writing preparation, Composition practice
These exercises are done using Workbook pages in class.

Teaching the course

Lesson 1 Poster, Reading

Poster: key new vocabulary is shown on the poster in context to help children learn and remember. Flashcards can be used to help in teaching and learning new words

Reading text: children practise and develop their reading skills through different kinds of fiction and non-fiction texts. These texts have been chosen as models of the kinds of writing that children need to learn how to write themselves; the variety in the Reading lessons helps children to recognise the ways in which texts differ.

New words are included in Dictionary 4 and this may be used in any lesson for children to check or find meanings.

Learning new words

In the Unit word list on pages 190–191, twenty words are shown (in bold) for each unit. All children should understand and learn these words by the end of the unit. Children should also understand words in normal type. If possible, they should learn these as an extension task during the unit or when the unit is revised. If you wish, divide up the words for each unit and give children short lists of words to learn after every lesson. Suggested short lists for this purpose are available from the English World website and on the DVD.

Alternatively, as there are fewer new words to learn in Units 9–12, children could revise and learn the extension words from earlier units as they approach the end of the book.

Words in grey type are needed for understanding in the units in which they appear only. Children do not need to learn them.

Note: children should understand all the words in each unit and use their dictionaries to help them. They should only be tested on the spelling of words that they have studied in Phonics but not every word in this list.

Lesson 2 Reading comprehension and vocabulary

The text is read again, then children do a variety of tasks which help them to understand the text thoroughly.

Vocabulary activities help and test understanding; they develop word skills and practise dictionary skills.

Workbook exercises practice additional reading comprehension skills.

Lesson 3 Speaking and Study skills

This lesson helps children to continue developing as fluent English speakers with natural intonation and good pronunciation:

- the teacher introduces new words
- children listen to a dialogue and look at the picture which illustrates the dialogue
- children repeat the dialogue
- children follow the dialogue in their books
- groups of children may act the dialogue.

The dialogues tell two stories, centring on the activities of a group of lively child characters. Learners follow each story over six units.

The classroom session is supported by Study skills exercises in the Workbook. These introduce children to dictionary skills and other thinking skills which help children to become constructive learners.

Lesson 4 Grammar

This lesson is taught in two teaching sessions:

(1) Grammar structure: formal structures that children need for reading and writing English are presented with a clear model and practised actively by the class.

(2) Grammar in conversation: other structures that are common in everyday speech are presented in the form of a dialogue that children can repeat and learn.

Language is then practised less formally in a song or a rhyme.

Both sessions in the classroom are supported by written Workbook exercises.

Lesson 5 Listening, Phonics and Use of English

A variety of listening comprehension activities help children to learn to listen for detail, for specific information and for gist.

The different phonemes in English are presented through levels 1–4. Children hear each sound and practise it through class activities and rhymes which help them to develop good pronunciation.

A Workbook page for classroom teaching presents the rules for writing English correctly.

Workbook exercises practise the spelling of words containing the target phoneme.

Lesson 6 Writing

Technical and composition skills are taught in two teaching sessions:

(1) Class composition: the teacher leads the session and helps children to suggest ideas for the required piece of writing. This is always the same type of text as the one studied in Lesson 1 and this helps children to learn to write for different purposes. The teacher guides the class in composing sentences and does the work of writing on the board before children write.

(2) Writing preparation, Composition practice: children practise aspects of written English that they need for their composition, such as punctuation, word choice and making notes, then, with some teacher support, they compose a piece of independent writing following the model they produced in the first session.

Revision activities

After every Workbook unit there are two Check-up pages of grammar revision. The first page practises the structures; the second page gives learners the opportunity to do a longer piece of writing focussing on the target grammar structure.

After every three Pupil's Book units there is a Revision page for oral practice in the classroom and a Project page which allows children to make their own choices for content and illustration when writing about a given topic.

Games

Classroom and group games are a useful and motivating method of reinforcing learning. A list of simple games using resources supplied with the course are found on pages 186–187.

Assessment

The Workbook Check-up pages along with the Pupil's Book revision activities and projects should give teachers some measure of individual and class progress. In addition, the course includes resources to help learners and teachers record progress and they are intended to encourage children in their learning.

Portfolio and Diploma pages

The Portfolio and Diploma pages at the back of the Workbook are each child's own record of progress and achievement. They are not designed as a formal test.

The Portfolio page is intended for assessment by the learner. Work covered every three units is presented on the page. The learner decides how much of the work he or she feels confident about and marks parts of the page accordingly.

The teacher checks the page with the learner. When the teacher is satisfied that the assessment is accurate, the learner completes the token tasks on the Diploma page and receives stickers. This marks the satisfactory completion of three units.

These pages can be removed from the Workbook and included in a portfolio of work.

Creating a portfolio

During the year, teachers may help children to select their best work to put in their personal portfolio. This work can accompany the portfolio pages from the Workbook as part of the record of individual achievement. Much of the work will be in written form, as compositions, projects, grammar exercises, spellings or tests. Where appropriate, children make neat copies of their best work for inclusion in the portfolio.

Work in other forms may be included, for example, recordings of individual or group reading, speaking, acting or singing. Photographs of performance work or of large posters/friezes may also be included as a record of activities.

All children should keep portfolios, whether or not their work is regularly of a high standard. The portfolio encourages children to take pride in their best work, and increases confidence in reaching for a higher standard. Over a period of a year, it shows how the learner has progressed in a variety of tasks and activities.

Formal tests

Teachers may wish to carry out some formal testing, and tests for use after every three units are supplied on the website and on the DVD. These tests include tasks that children are likely to meet in formal examinations. DVD users are able to create their own tests to suit different purposes by using the bank of questions supplied in the test-builder section.

Unit structure

Teaching sessions	Classroom lessons		*Workbook* (or other homework task)
1	Lesson 1	Poster, Reading	(Dictionary: vocabulary)
2	Lesson 2	Reading comprehension and vocabulary	*Reading comprehension and vocabulary*
3	Lesson 3	Speaking	*Study skills*
4	Lesson 4	Grammar	
		Session 1: Grammar structure	*Grammar structure*
5		Session 2: Grammar in conversation	*Grammar in conversation*
			(Grammar Practice Book)
6	Lesson 5	Listening, Phonics, *Use of English (WB)*	*Phonics*
			(Grammar Practice Book)
	Lesson 6	Writing	
7		Session 1 Class composition	(Grammar Practice Book)
8		Session 2: *Writing skills; Composition practice (WB)*	(Check-up pages)

10 Teaching the course / Unit structure

Using the Teacher's Guide

The notes for each lesson are arranged over two pages of the Teacher's Guide.

Lesson Summary box
- explains lesson aim and specific targets
- lists key language and structures
- lists materials needed for the lesson and any preparation.

Warm-ups are suggested for every teaching session.

Pupil's Book page facsimile shows the material to be taught in the classroom lesson.

Detailed notes explain each step of the lesson.

Workbook page facsimile shows the practice exercises.

Notes to Workbook practice exercises give suggestions for preparing the class to complete them independently for homework.

Resource box contains text questions, extra teaching notes, answers to PB and WB exercises and audioscripts.

Time division chart suggests how teaching sessions could be divided.

Grammar Practice Book and other additional homework tasks are suggested when appropriate.

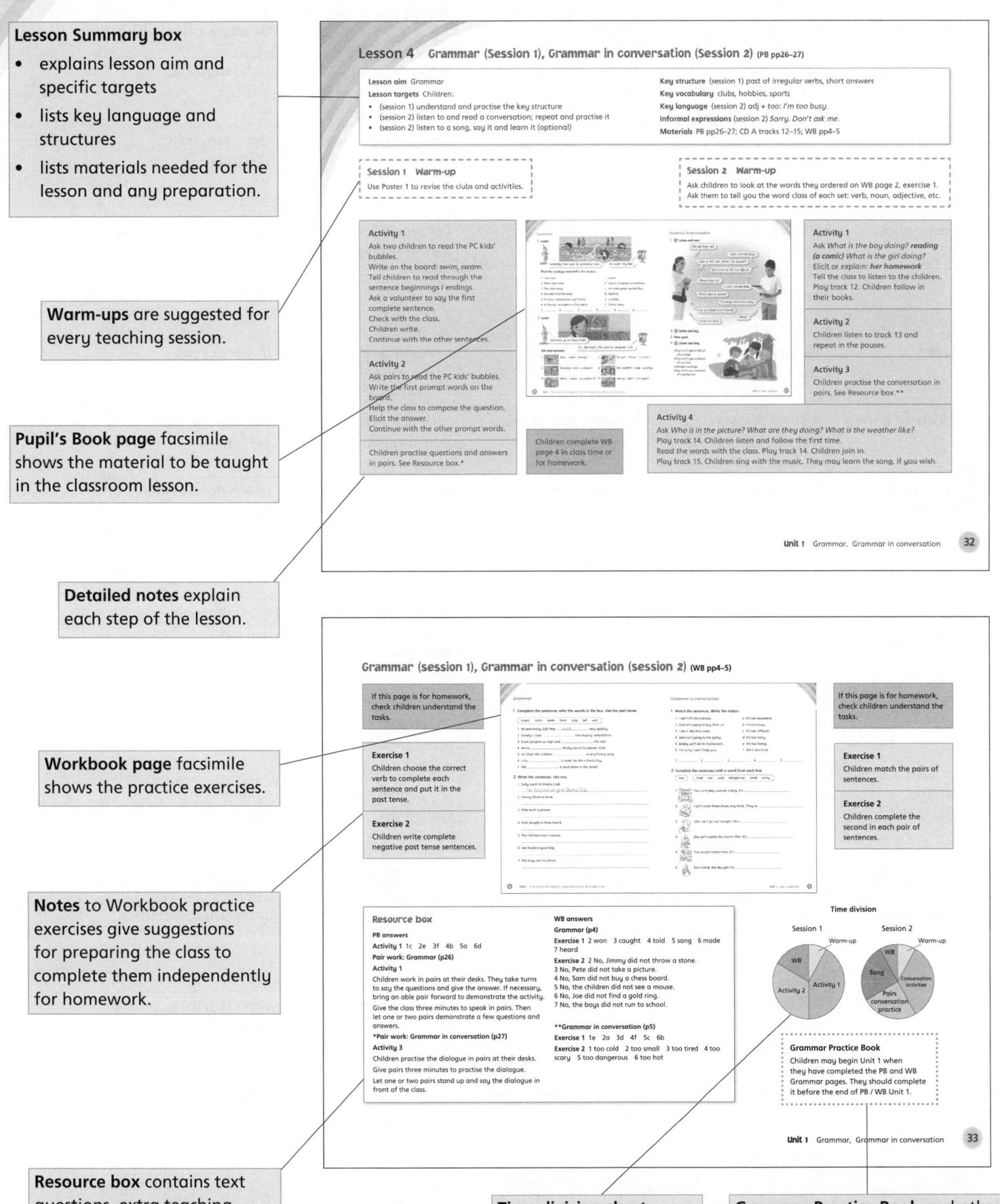

Scope and Sequence

Unit	Poster	Reading	Lexis	Speaking (dialogue)	Study skills (WB)
1	School clubs	*School clubs are fun!* text type: email, descriptions of events	school clubs, hobbies and sports	*Let's put on a play!* Part 1: Come and join the Drama Club!	dictionary skills; odd one out
2	In the theatre	*Red Riding Hood* text type: a traditional tale with a clear beginning, middle, end	theatre, the stage	*Let's put on a play!* Part 2: The script	dictionary skills; alphabetical order
3	Water birds	*Birds of the oceans and lakes* text type: information with labels and captions	the nature of birds	*Let's put on a play!* Part 3: The costumes	sorting; dictionary skills
	Revision				
4	Crafts	*Making things we use* text type: description of a process	crafts, tools and products	*Let's put on a play!* Part 4: Everything's falling down	dictionary skills; sequencing
5	All about a show	*A dance festival* text type: first person recount	posters, programmes and tickets	*Let's put on a play!* Part 5: The final rehearsal	alphabetical order; definitions
6	Changes in nature	*Amazing changes* text type: poems	life stages of insects and animals	*Let's put on a play!* Part 6: Good luck, everyone!	matching; dictionary skills
	Revision				
7	People of the world	*Old customs in the modern world* text type: information	parts of the world; land, sea and ocean	*The golden mask of Chapichapi* Part 1: Who's that man?	dictionary skills; odd one out
8	The Incas	*A message for the Inca king* text type: a story with a strong setting	Inca wealth, soldiers and weapons	*The golden mask of Chapichapi* Part 2: Jewels of the Incas	self-correction; spelling; sorting
9	Chinese inventions	*We use these every day* text type: information and description	early technology	*The golden mask of Chapichapi* Part 3: In the Chinese room	alphabetical order; definitions
	Revision				
10	Space travel	*Space pioneers* text type: biography	space exploration and space crafts	*The golden mask of Chapichapi* Part 4: A journey into space	dictionary skills; sorting
11	Life in the north	*The Sami people* text type: information and description of a person's appearance	clothing and equipment for a cold climate	*The golden mask of Chapichapi* Part 5: Where are Alfie's sandwiches?	dictionary skills; spelling; definitions
12	A desert oasis	*The lost city* text type: an adventure story with a strong opening	desert geography and features	*The golden mask of Chapichapi* Part 6: The Egyptian room	alphabetical order; definitions
	Revision				

Scope and Sequence

Grammar	Grammar in conversation	Listening	Phonics	Language skills (WB)	Writing
Pete went to Swimming Club. He swam very fast. A girl threw a ball.	I'm too busy. You're too noisy. It's too difficult.	identifying; listening for gist and detail	oo cook	contractions	an email to a friend
She was walking in the forest. Was she carrying a basket? Were the birds singing?	I could buy an ice cream but I couldn't buy a CD.	sequencing	u bull	reporting clause in direct speech	a story with a clear beginning, middle and end
This game is more expensive than that one but the other game is the most expensive.	You're as old as me but you're not as clever as me.	gist and detail; giving an opinion	ea head	conjunctions *because* and *so*	information with labels and captions
Revision					
When it started to rain, the children ran into the house.	Is there something in your pocket? No, nothing, look!	identifying	y = ee lady	plural of nouns ending f, fe	describing a process
While Lucy was sleeping, Andy was playing the trumpet.	You must choose either the cat or the dog.	listening for gist and detail	oi oil	time phrases	text for a poster and a programme
This caterpillar will become a butterfly. It will not become a dragonfly.	This one is better but this is the best. This is worse but that's the worst of all.	identifying; sequencing	aw claw	apostrophe for possession	completing a rhyming poem
Revision					
There's lots of snow. There are a lot of yaks. There isn't much sand. There aren't many birds.	You should get up earlier. You shouldn't go to bed late.	following a description	ew new	pronouns, back referencing	factual information
Is anybody in the bathroom? No, there isn't anybody there.	Turn left at the theatre. Walk straight on. Turn right at the park.	identifying dialogues; listening for gist and detail	air chair are rare	punctuating direct speech	continuing a story with a strong setting
If it snows tomorrow, we'll make a snowman.	Shall we take a picnic? Let's take sandwiches. How about chocolate?	sequencing	igh high	subject, verb, object word order	information and description
Revision					
There are a few cakes. There is a little juice. How much water is there?	It's not big enough. It's not heavy enough.	listening for gist and detail	ph photogragh	importance of a verb in a sentence	biography
Grandpa has painted the door. The children have picked some flowers.	They might score three goals. They might not win.	listening for detail	ch school	subject and object pronouns	description of a person's appearance
A tourist is a person who visits places on holiday.	What do you call a person who builds bridges?	sequencing; listening for detail	c city	punctuating exclamations, questions	a story with a strong opening
Revision					

Scope and Sequence

Posters

All poster vocabulary is on the teacher's DVD and the website and may be printed out for making into word cards for classroom use.

1 School clubs
school clubs, hobbies and sports

swimming club	basketball team	coach	chess pieces
computer club	football team	captain	animation
chess club	choir	referee	
drama club	orchestra		

2 In the theatre
theatre, the stage

| stage | curtain | light | scenery |
| props | costume | actor | script |

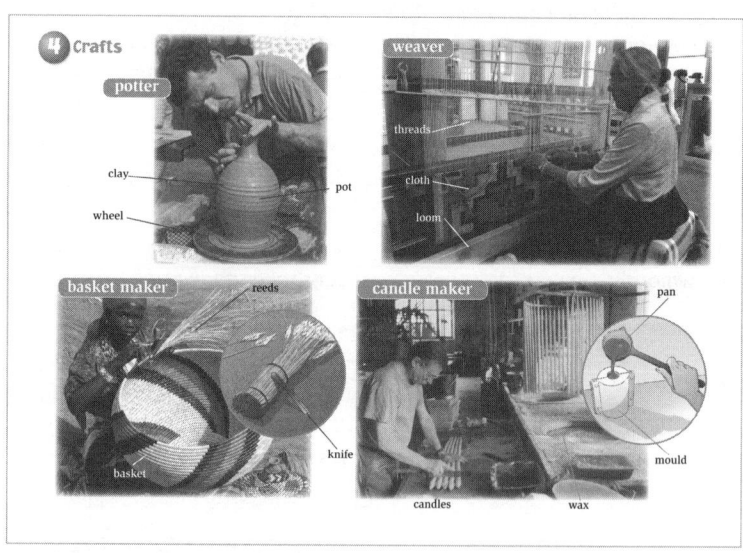

3 Water birds
the nature of birds

swan	albatross	beak
duck	penguin	wing
goose	gull	feather

4 Making things we use
crafts, tools and products

clay	threads	reeds	wax
pots	loom	basket	candles
wheel	cloth	knife	mould
			pan

14 Posters

5 All about a show
posters, programme and tickets

| poster | programme | ballet | character |
| date | cover | show | performer |

6 Changes in nature
life stages of insects and animals

caterpillar	chick	tadpole
butterfly	bird of paradise	frog
dragonfly	cygnet	

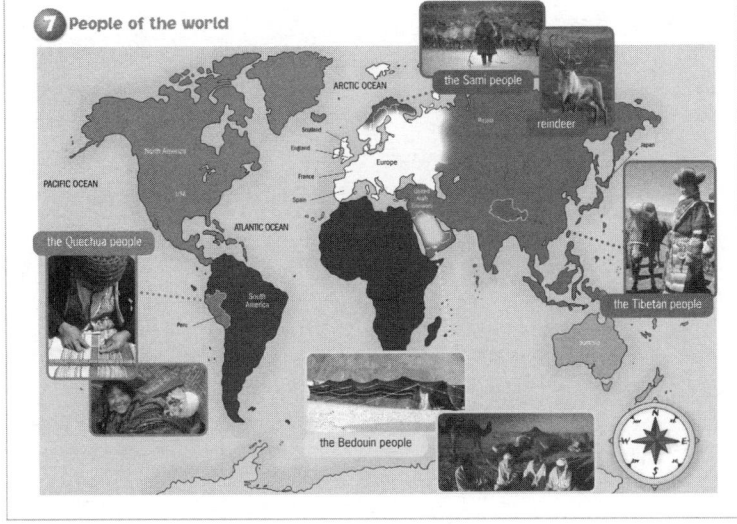

7 People of the world
parts of the world; land, sea and ocean

North America	Atlantic Ocean	Peru
South America	Pacific Ocean	reindeer
Europe	Arctic Ocean	
Asia		

8 The Incas
Inca wealth, soldiers and weapons

sword	headdress	messenger	palace
shield	collar	guard	throne
spear	tunic		

Posters   15

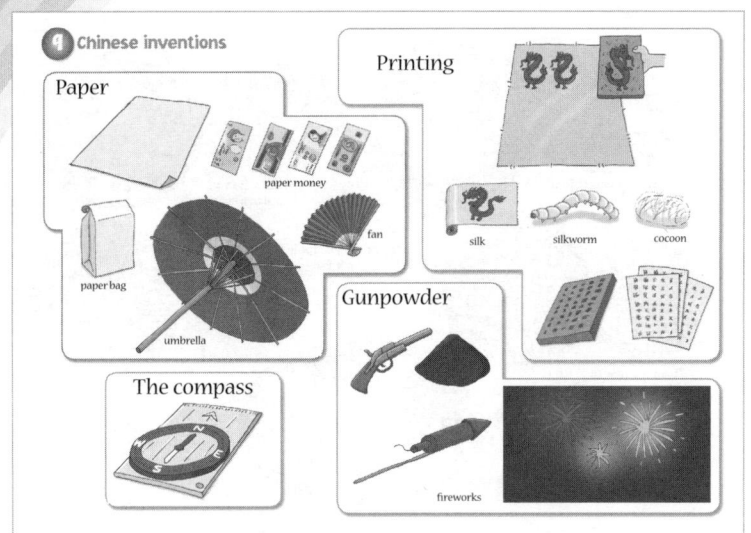

9 Chinese inventions
early technology

compass   cocoon   fan
gunpowder   silk
printing   silkworm
fireworks

10 Space travel
space exploration and spacecrafts

planet   astronaut   space craft   parachute
satellite cosmonaut   space engineer
orbit   commander

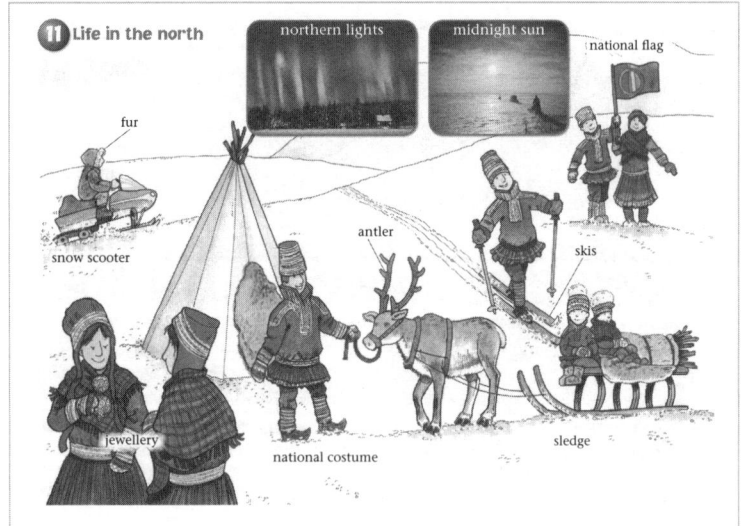

11 Life in the north
clothing and equipment for a cold climate

antler   ski
fur   sledge
national costume   snow scooter

12 A desert oasis
desert geography and features

sand dune   tourist   4x4   souvenir
ruins   archaeologist camel train date palm
oasis

16 Posters

PB pages 4–5

Give children a moment to look at these pages. They should remember the children and their teacher from level 3.

Ask the class if they can tell you anything about them. What did they do? Where did they go?

Explain that the Pencil Case Kids will help them with some of their learning tasks again.

Meet the characters

Welcome Unit: PB pages 6–7

Activity 1

Let different children tell you the names of each child character and their teacher in turn. Play CD A track 1. Children listen and follow in their books.

Track 1

Max: Do you remember us?
Molly: Hello again!
Alfie: Hi!
Lulu: Hi!
Miss Carey: It's nice to see you again.

Activity 2

Ask about each picture: *What time is it? Who is in the picture? What is he / she / are they doing? What else can you see?* If it has not already been named, ask the class if they can guess the name of the horse. Play track 2. Children listen and point to the pictures in turn and the people and objects as they are mentioned.

Track 2

Picture 1 Yesterday afternoon Alfie was in the kitchen. It was quarter past two. A sandwich and some grapes were on the table in front of him. Alfie was hungry!

Picture 2 Lulu was in the garden. It was half past three. What was in the box? A pretty little kitten.

Picture 3 It was four o'clock. Max and Molly were at the farm. Henry the horse was in the field. Molly had some food for him in her hand. Max was on the gate.

Picture 4 Miss Carey was not at the farm. She was at school. She was in the classroom. There were books on the desk. There were some pretty flowers, too. What time was it? It was quarter past four.

Activity 3

Ask a pair to read the bubbles. If you wish, ask other pairs to read again or ask the whole class to repeat. Continue in the same way with the rest of the activity: ask a pair to ask the same questions about Lulu and the others repeat. Alternatively, let the class work in pairs taking turns to ask the questions. Go around listening to them as they work.

Activity 4

Ask a pair to read the bubbles. Class repeats. Ask another pair to ask about the horse and the stable. Help children to compose the question corrects. Class repeats. Continue in the same way with the rest of the activity. Alternatively – or as well – let children work in pairs. Go around listening to them as they ask the questions and answer.

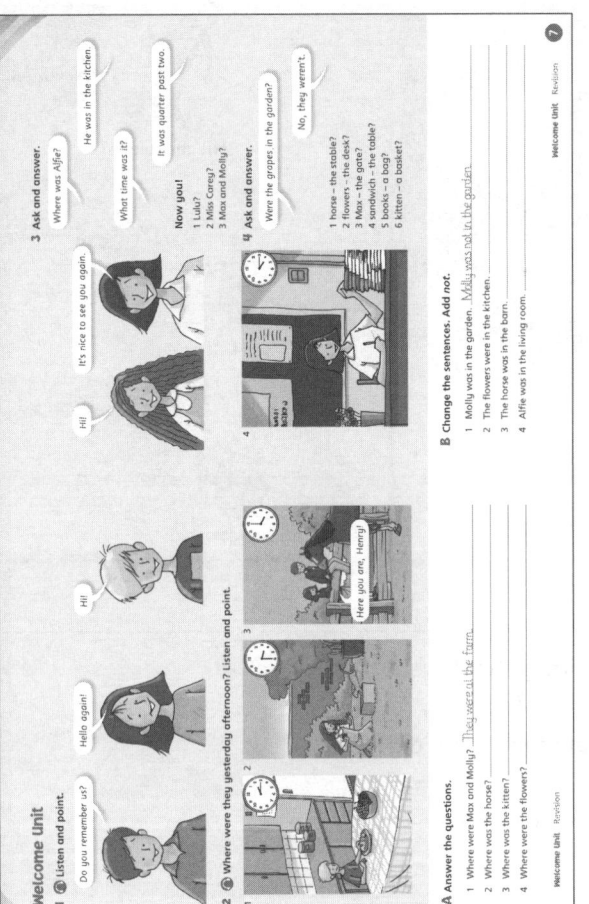

Activity A

Read the example with the class. Children answer the questions in complete sentences. Check answers by asking volunteers to read out their sentences. Other children listen and check their own work.

Activity B

Read the example with the class. Children write negative sentences following the model. Remind them to use the full forms: *was not* and *were not*. Remind them that in speaking we generally use the short forms: *wasn't* and *weren't*.

Welcome Unit pp6–7   18

PB pages 8-9

Activity 1

Give children a moment or two to look at the pictures. Explain that the boy's name is Sam.

Ask *Who else is in the story? Sam's dad What has Sam got? a bike*

Play CD A track 3. Children listen and point to each picture as they hear the story.

Track 3

Sam found an old bike in the street. He wanted a bike so he picked it up and pushed it to his house. The bike was very dirty so he washed it with hot water. Sam's Dad walked over. "I've got some red paint," he said. "Do you want it?" "Yes, please," said Sam.

Sam painted the bike. It looked great!

The next day Sam jumped onto the bike and went along the road. His Dad went with him. They came to a hill. The bike started to go faster. Sam laughed. "This is great!" he said.

"Stop!" shouted Dad. But the bike didn't stop. It went faster and faster and faster. "Help!" shouted Sam.

What do you think happened?

Ask children to suggest what happened next. If children are not sure how to express their ideas, help them to form sentences. Alternatively, ask, e.g. *Did Sam fall off his bike? Did the bike stop? Did Sam's dad catch the bike and help Sam?* Find out how many children agree with the different ideas.

Activity 2

Ask a child to read the first sentence. Ask if the statement is true or false. Elicit an answer. See if the rest of the class agrees. Continue with the other statements. Ask a volunteer to correct any statements that the class agrees are false.

Activity 3

Ask a pair to read the bubbles. Tell the class to look at the words for number 1. Ask a volunteer to read them out.

Ask another to say the complete question. Class repeats. If the class seems unsure, write it on the board. Class reads. Ask for the answer. Continue with the other sentences.

Activity 4

Ask who can tell you the story. Ask a volunteer to say what happened in picture 1. Encourage children to speak without trying to remember exactly what they heard on the audio. Help them to say sentences with correct grammar but encourage them to say what happened using different words, as long as they make sense.

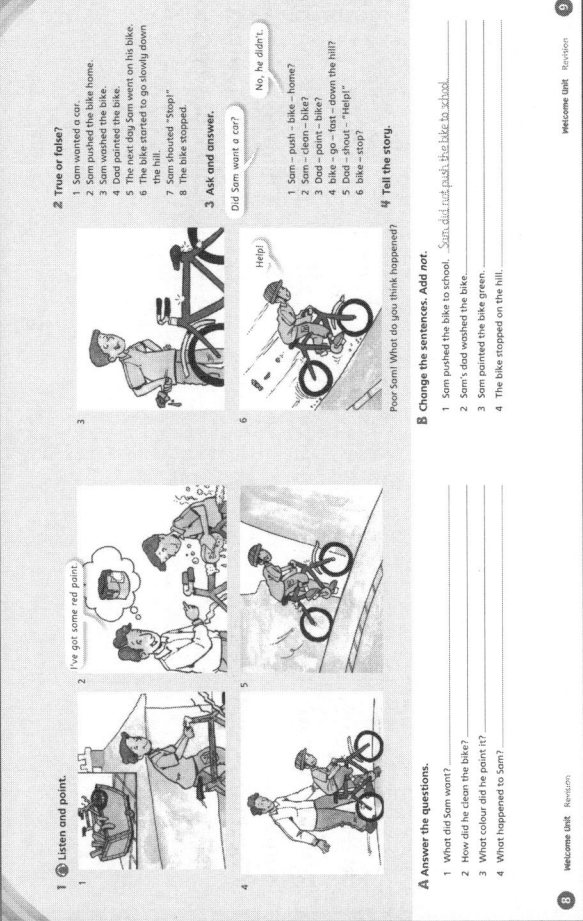

Activity A

Children answer the questions in complete sentences.

To check answers, ask different children to read their sentences. Other children listen and check their work.

Activity B

Read the example with the class. Children write negative sentences using the full form. Check answers together in the usual way.

Welcome Unit pp8-9

PB pages 10–11

Activity 1

Give children time to look at the pictures. Ask *Who is in this story? Max, Lulu, Alfie and Molly.* Ask if anyone can say what the story is about. Listen to a few suggestions then play CD A track 4. Children listen and point to each picture as they hear the events described.

Track 4

On Saturday Alfie, Molly, Lulu and Max were at the mall. Alfie and Max wanted to buy CDs at the music shop. Lulu wanted to go to the book shop. Molly went with her.

In the book shop Lulu found a very good story book and she bought it.

There was an old lady in the book shop. She put her bag on the floor. Suddenly a boy came up and took her bag. Molly saw him.

The boy ran out of the shop with the bag. Lulu and Molly ran after him. "Stop!" they shouted. "Stop, thief!"

The boy ran up some stairs. He ran very fast. Suddenly the girls saw Alfie and Max at the top of the stairs. "Alfie! Max! Stop that boy!"

Alfie and Max caught the boy. The old lady was very happy.

Ask *How did the children help the old lady? They caught the boy.*

Activity 2

Ask a volunteer to read the first statement. Elicit the correct sentence. Check with the class that it is correct. Continue with the other sentences.

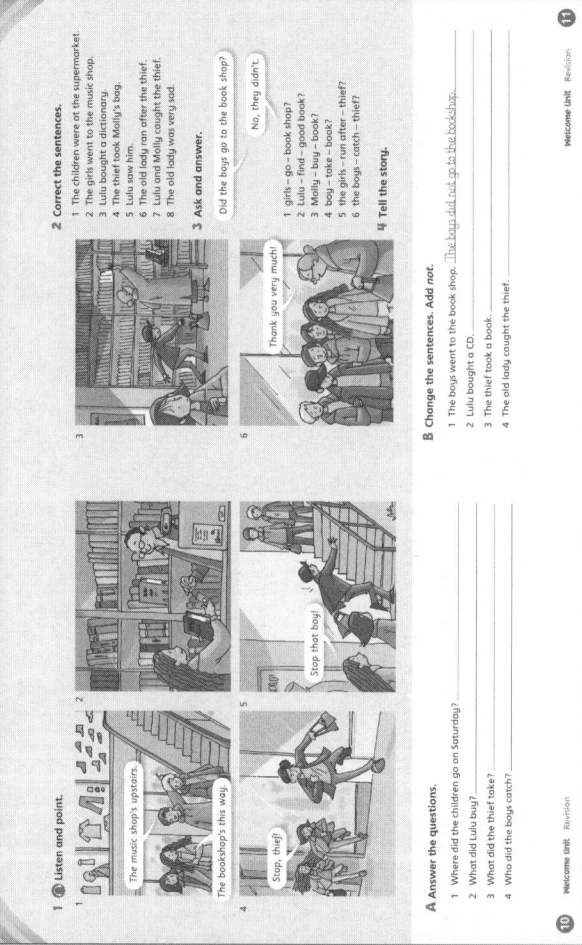

Activity 3

Ask a pair to read the question and answer.

Tell children to work with a partner. They practise asking the question and answering. Give them a short time to do this.

Ask different pairs to say their question and answer. If they have difficulty, go through the rest of the activity with the class working all together, repeating a correct model.

Alternatively, continue in the same way, asking different pairs to say their question and answer each time.

Activity 4

Let different children tell each part of the story, using the pictures to help them. Give them lots of encouragement for speaking without reading words from the page.

Activity A

Children answer the questions using complete sentences.

Check answers together.

Activity B

Read the example with the class. Children write negative sentences using the full form. Go around monitoring as they work.

Check answers together.

Welcome Unit pp10–11

PB pages 12–13

Activity 1

Ask volunteers to read out the names of the children.

Ask other volunteers to read the speech bubble for each one.

Ask children to say as much as they can about what each person is wearing. Encourage them to give detail, e.g. *Ben is wearing a big grey and blue hat. It is tall.*

Ask the class what animals they can see. Ask about size and colour.

Activity 2

Let a volunteer read the questions for number 1. Tell children to look at the speech bubbles again to find the answer or check. Elicit the answer. Make sure the rest of the class agrees. Continue with the other questions.
For 8 and 9, ask children to give reasons for their choices.

Activity 3

Ask a pair to read the speech bubbles. Ask the class if they agree with the statement.

Ask a child to read the first word. Ask a volunteer to say the question. Help as necessary. Elicit an answer. Check the rest of the class agrees.
Continue in the same way with the other words.

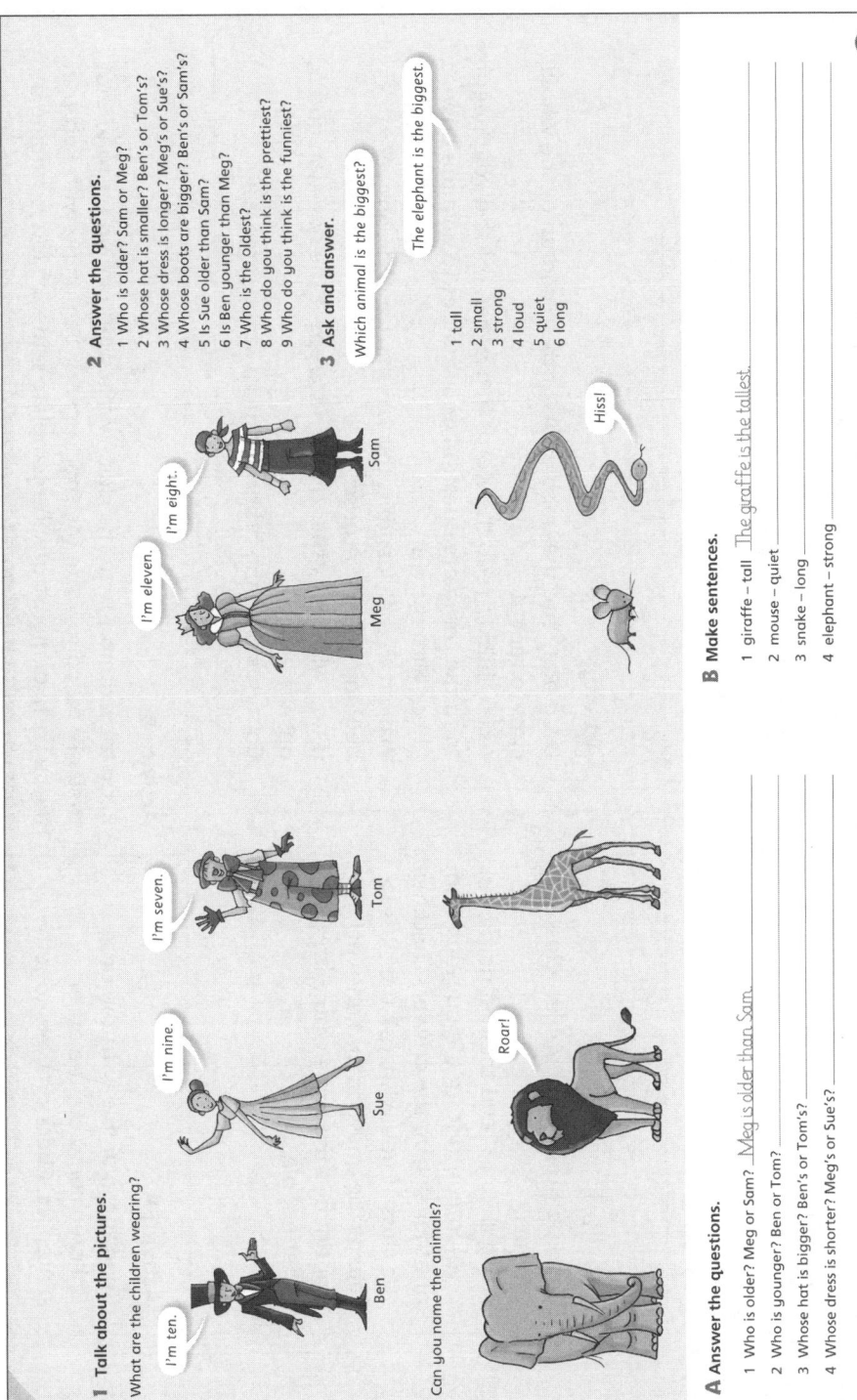

Activity A

Read the example with the class. Remind them of the *-er* ending when talking about two people or things. Children write the other three sentences. Check answers together in the usual way.

Activity B

Read the example with the class. Remind them of the *-est* ending when talking about more than two things. Children write complete sentences. Check answers together.

Welcome Unit pp12–13   21

PB pages 14–15

Activity 1

Give children a few moments to look at the picture.

Ask volunteers to read out the names of all the people.

Ask questions about each person, e.g.
What is Miss Sweet doing? *sitting on a seat*
What is Mr Brown doing? *walking with his dog*
What is Ed carrying? *a football*
Where are Nina and Billy? *in the car*
Where is Jess? *outside the house*
Where are Penny and Jenny going? *to the Sports Club*

Ask other questions if you wish.

Play CD A track 5. Children listen and point to the people as they hear them mentioned.

Track 5

It's a lovely sunny day. Billy and Nina are in the car with their mum and dad. They are going to the beach. Billy and Nina love swimming in the sea. Their sister, Jess, isn't going to the beach. She's staying at home. She's going to watch TV.

Jenny and Penny are going to the Sports Club. They're going to play tennis. They like playing tennis very much. Ed doesn't like playing tennis. He likes playing football. He's going to play football in the park with his friends.

Can you see Mr Brown and his little dog? Mr Brown likes walking with his dog.

Can you see Miss Sweet? She's watching the birds. She loves watching the birds.

Activity 2

Ask volunteers to read out the questions. Ask other children to answer.

Check that the class agrees with the answer.

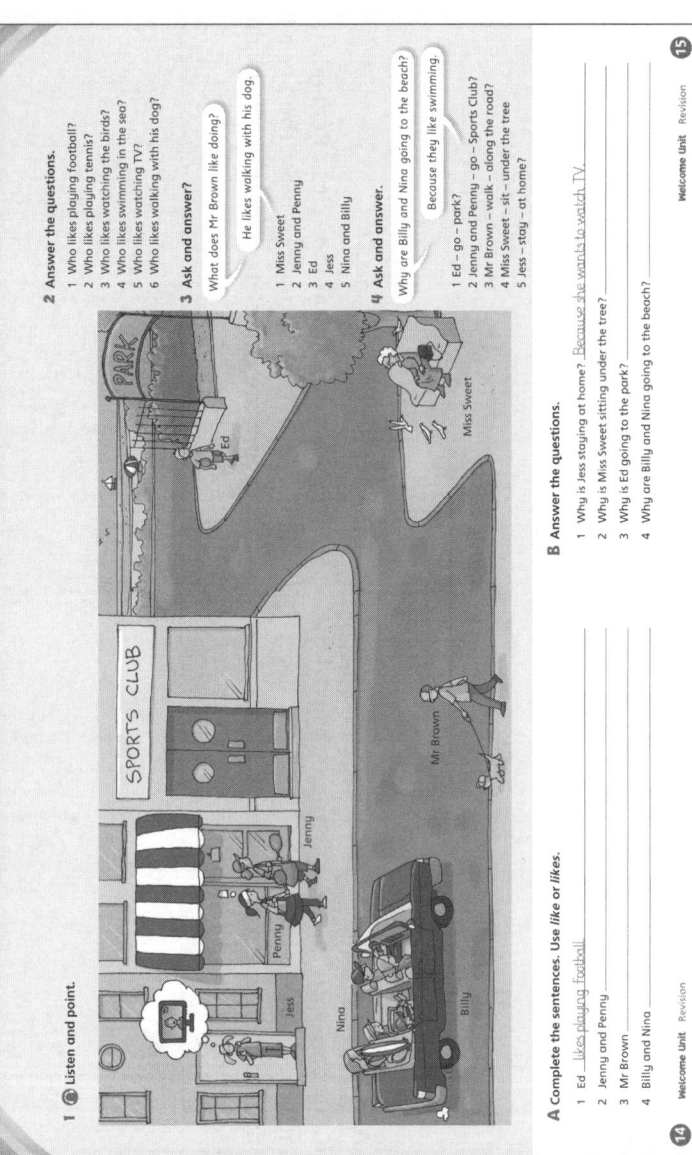

Activity 3

Let a pair read the bubbles. Class repeats.

Ask a child to read the first name. Ask a volunteer to form the question and another to give the answer. Check with the class. If you wish, ask the class to repeat the question and answer. Continue in the same way with the other people.

Activity 4

Let a pair read the bubbles. Ask other children or the whole class to repeat.

Ask a child to read the words in number 1. Ask a volunteer to form the complete question and another to give the answer. Check with the class.

Explain to the class that this is a short spoken answer, beginning with *Because*.

If you wish, ask other children to repeat the question and answer.

Continue with the other questions in the same way.

Activity A

Read the example with the class. Children complete the other sentences. Check answers together.

Activity B

Read the example with the class. Make sure they understand that they are asked to write the short answer beginning with *Because*. If you wish, demonstrate the complete sentence *Jess is staying at home because she wants to watch TV*. Children write short answers. Check them together.

Welcome Unit pp14–15

PB pages 16–17

Activity 1

Give children a moment to look at the picture.

Ask *Who is in the picture? Where are they?*

Ask the class what food they can see. Let them name anything they can. Let volunteers read the bubbles.

Play CD A track 6. Children listen and point to the people and objects as they hear them mentioned.

Track 6

Yesterday Alfie, Lulu, Molly and Max went to the beach with Miss Carey.

They had a picnic on the sand. They had chicken and sandwiches. Alfie didn't like his sandwich. There was some sand in it.

They had juice to drink but there wasn't any water. There weren't any ice creams but there was some fruit. There were some cakes, too. It was a delicious picnic!

Activity 2

Ask two children to read the bubbles. If necessary, remind them *There was some…* for items they cannot count. *There were some…* for items they can count.

Let volunteers say the sentences for each word. Class repeats.

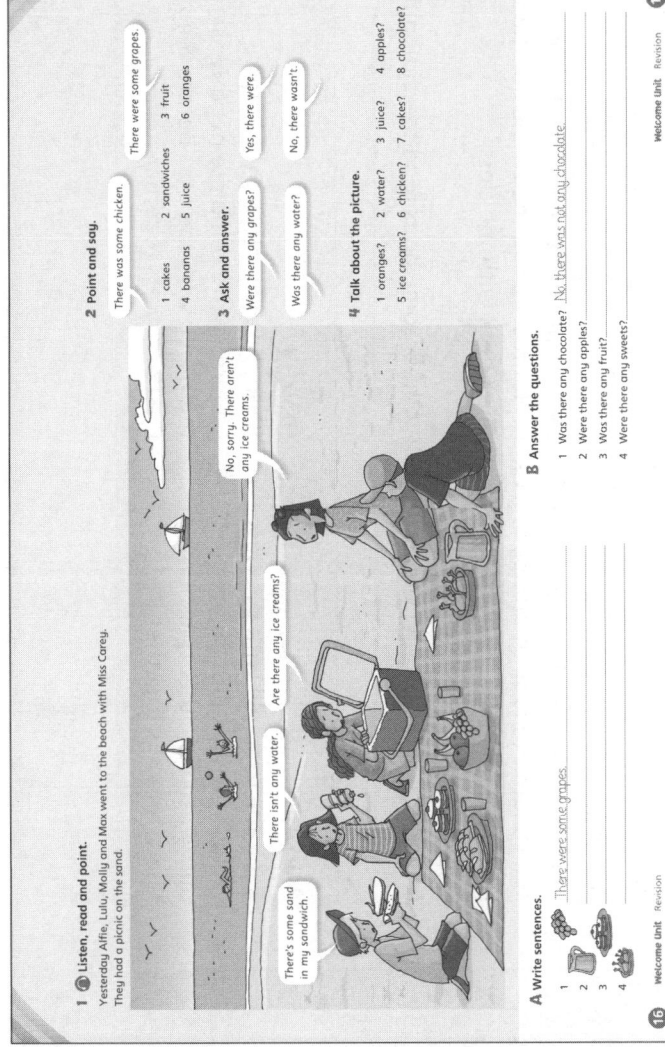

Activity 3

Ask two pairs to read the bubbles.

Ask different children to read out the eight words. Let a volunteer form the question for number 1. Check with the class that it is correct.

Ask other children or the whole class to repeat. Elicit the short answer. Check with the class that it is correct.

Continue with the other words.

Activity 4

Ask children to tell you as much as they can about things and people in the picture, e.g. *Alfie doesn't like his sandwich. Why? Because there is some sand in it.*

If children do not mention other parts of the picture, ask questions, e.g. *How many people are in the water? What are they doing?*

Activity A

Read the example with the class.

Check that children recognise the items in the pictures. Make sure they understand that chicken refers to chicken meat rather than the pieces of chicken, so it is singular as meat cannot be counted.

Children write the sentences. Check answers together.

Activity B

Read the example with the class.

Children write complete negative sentences. Go through this orally before children write if you wish. Check answers together.

Welcome Unit pp16–17

PB pages 18–19

Activity 1

Give children a few moments to look at the pictures.

Explain that the story is about a boy called Toby. Ask *Who is in the story with Toby? his mum*

Play CD A track 7. Children listen and follow in their books.

Track 7

Voice: Toby is going to start at a new school tomorrow.
Mum: You must go to bed early.
Toby: Yes, Mum.
Mum: You must get up early.
Toby: OK, Mum.
Mum: You mustn't be late.
Toby: No, Mum.
Mum: What are you going to wear?
Toby: A T-shirt, jeans and trainers.
Mum: You mustn't wear jeans.
You mustn't wear trainers.
You must wear nice clothes.
Toby: OK, Mum.
I'm not going to like this school.
Mum: Don't worry! It's going to be fine.

Activity 2

Ask volunteers to read the questions and elicit answers. Check with the class if the answers are correct.

Tell children to look back at the speech bubbles to check.

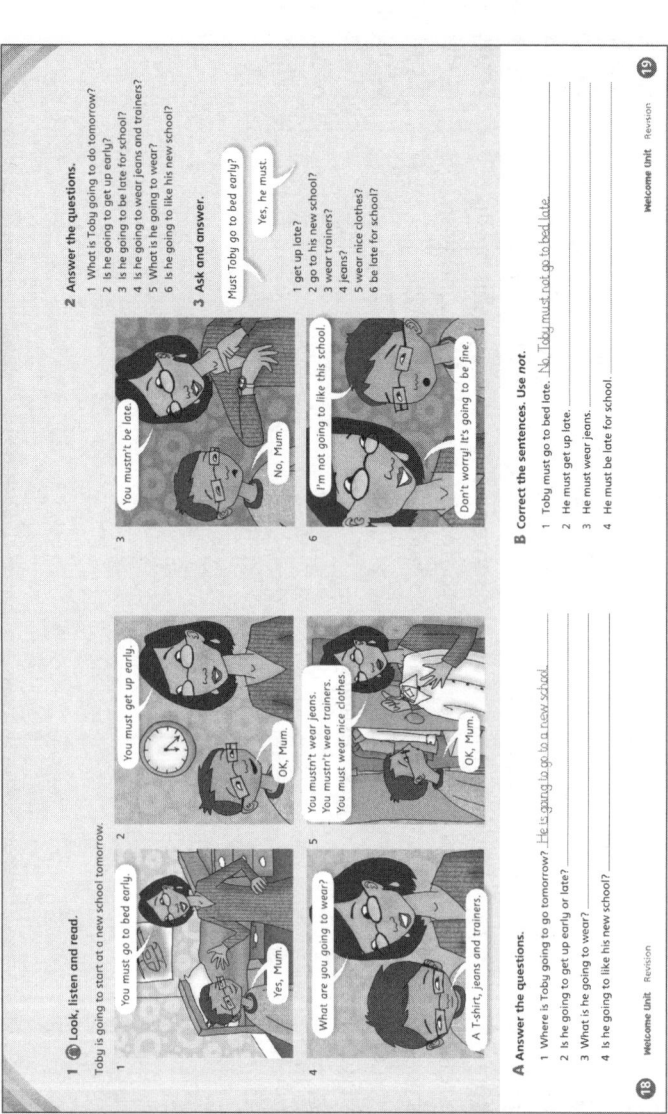

Activity 3

Ask a pair to read the question and answer. Other pairs or the whole class repeat. Tell children to look at number 1. Ask a volunteer to say the whole question. Class repeats if you wish. Elicit the short answer. Check with the class.

Continue with the other questions.

If your class is confident, you may wish to hear some pairs read the dialogue.

Activity A

Read the example with the class.
Children write full sentences in answer to the other questions.
Check answers together.

Activity B

Read the example with the class.
Children write complete negative sentences. Go through this orally with the class before they write, if you wish.
Check answers together.

Welcome Unit pp18–19

PB pages 20–21

Activity 1

Give children a few moments to look at the picture.

Ask *Who can you see?* Children should be able to name Miss Carey and the child characters.

Ask *Where are they? at the station*

Ask children if they can name anything else in the picture. They may recognise: platform, train, kiosk, luggage, suitcase, bag.

Encourage the class to say anything else that they can.

Activity 2

Play CD A track 8. Tell children to listen and point to the characters as they hear them speak.

Track 8

Voice:	Number 1
Lulu and Molly:	Are these our tickets?
Miss Carey:	Yes, they're yours.
Voice:	Who's speaking?
Voice:	Number 2
Max:	This suitcase is mine!
Voice:	Who's speaking?
Voice:	Number 3
Alfie:	Is that our train? Is it ours?
Voice:	Who's speaking?
Voice:	Number 4
Porter 1:	Is this their luggage?
Porter 2:	Yes, it's theirs.
Voice:	Who's speaking?

If you wish, let volunteers read the speech bubbles to the rest of the class.

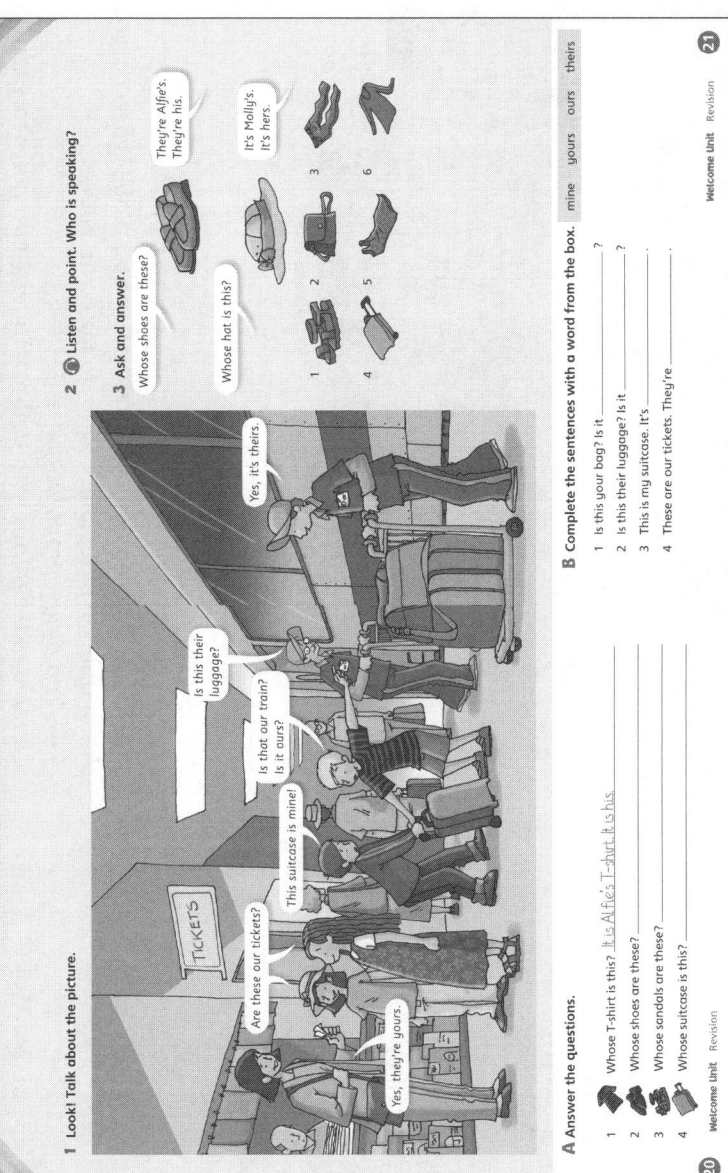

Activity 3

Ask two pairs to read the bubbles.

Ask children to say what the objects are in pictures 1–6.

Give the class a moment to find all the clothing in the main picture.

Ask a volunteer to ask the question about picture 1 *Whose sandals are these?* Elicit the answer *They are Molly's. They are hers.*

Continue with the other pictures.

Activity A

Read the example with the class.

Make sure children can identify the objects in the other small pictures and find them in the main picture.

Children write two sentences about each picture, following the model.

Check answers together.

Activity B

Explain that one word from the box completes each sentence.

If you wish, go through this activity orally with the class before they write.

Check answers together.

Welcome Unit pp20–21

School clubs

Lesson 1 Poster 1, Reading

Lesson aim Reading
Text type Emails
Lesson targets Children:
- read, understand and practise new vocabulary on the poster
- read, understand and practise reading the emails
- answer oral comprehension questions

Key structure past simple of irregular verbs
Key language too + adj: *I was too tired.*
Key vocabulary school clubs, hobbies, sports
Materials PB pp22–23; WB p2; poster 1; CD A track 9; Dictionary 4; word cards for poster vocabulary (see Poster 1 below or list on p14)
Preparation Make word cards; listen to CD A track 9

Warm-up

Ask children *What do you do after school? What do you do at the weekend?*

Poster 1

1 Point to the poster. Read out the title. Give the class a moment or two to look.

2 Point to the pictures. Name the activity and any other words with it. Show the word card/s. Class reads and says the word/s.

Make sure children understand the following words. Use the definitions and example sentences as necessary to ensure understanding:

animation   using lots of drawings to make cartoon films
           My favourite *animation* film is Pinocchio by Walt Disney.
coach   a person who trains people in sports
           Our basketball *coach* helps us and we play well now.
orchestra a group of people who play music together
           The school *orchestra* has ten trumpet players.

Cover the words on the poster if you wish. Point to the activities, objects and people at random. Class names them.

3 Ask the class if they do any of the sports. Ask *When do you play? Do you play in a team? Is the team at school or at a club?*

4 Ask if any children play music. *What do you play? When do you play? Ask if anyone plays chess. Who do you play with? Ask Who plays computer games? Can you make things with your computer? Can you draw pictures? Can you make pictures from other pictures?*

Unit 1 Reading

Reading (PB p22–23)

1 Give children time to look at the pictures. Read the title. Ask what activities they can see. *choir, computers, swimming, chess* Ask them to look at the texts. *What are they?* **emails**

2 Play track 9. Children listen and follow in their books.

3 Read one paragraph or section of the text at a time.
Use Dictionary 4 to help you to explain new words as necessary.
Help children to find new words. Make up extra sentences for new words if you wish.

4 Ask questions about each paragraph or a section of the text. See Resource box. Ask extra questions if you wish.

5 Give reading practice around the class. Ask individuals, groups or the pairs to read sentences or paragraphs.
Play track 9 again.

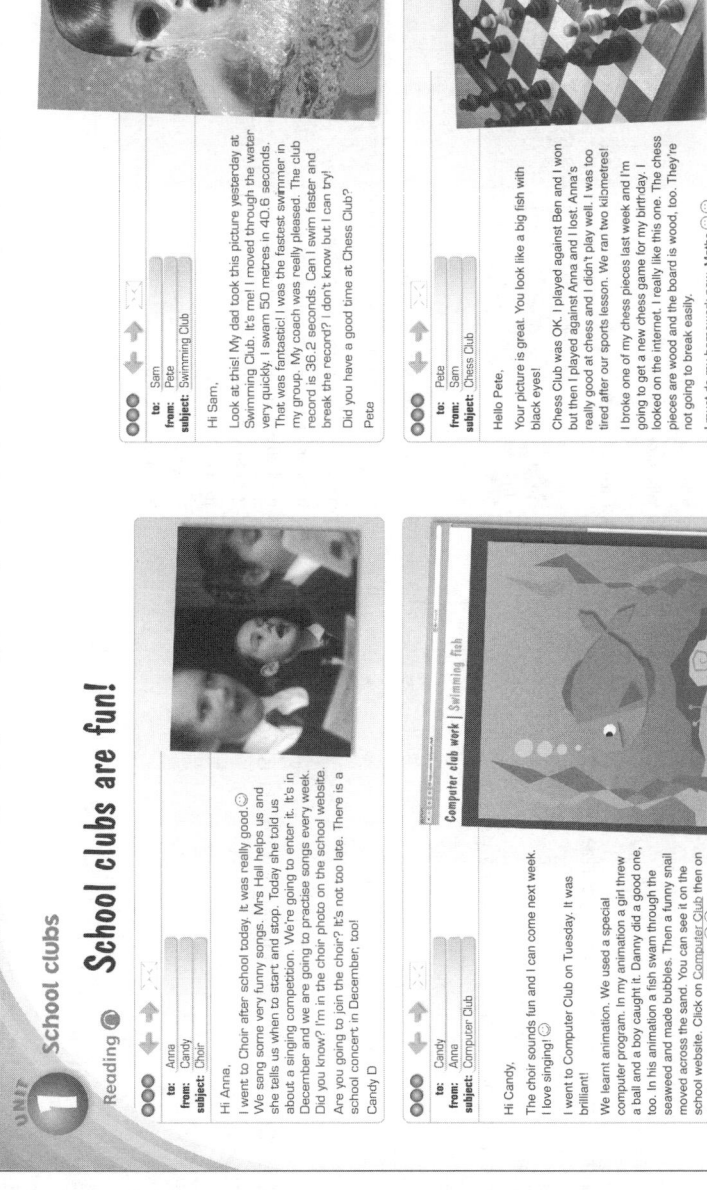

Resource box

Text questions

What kind of songs did the choir sing? **funny songs**
When is the competition? **in December**
When is the concert? **in December**
Is it too late for Anna to join? **no**
When was Computer Club? **Tuesday**
What was in Anna's animation? **a girl, a boy, a ball**
What was in Danny's? **fish, snail, bubbles, seaweed, sand**

Who took the photo of Pete? **his dad**
How far did Pete swim? **50 m**
In how many seconds? **40.6**
What does Pete look like in the photo? **a fish with big black eyes**
How many games did Sam play at Chess Club? **two**
What did he break last week? **a chess piece**
How far did Sam run in sports? **2 km**
Which subject does Sam like a lot? **Maths**

Homework task

Children learn selected vocabulary from Unit 1, Dictionary 4.
See unit word list on pp190–191 for key words, extension words and words for understanding only.

Time division

Warm-up
Poster
Reading
Dictionary home task

Unit 1 Reading 27

Lesson 2 Reading comprehension and vocabulary (PB p24)

Lesson aim Reading comprehension; vocabulary

Lesson targets Children re-read *School clubs are fun!* then:
- (PB) answer *Who…?* questions
- match words to pictures; match words to definitions
- (WB) complete a cloze text and answer questions about it
- write numbers in sentences

Key structure past simple of irregular verbs

Key language *too* + adj: *I was too tired.*

Words vocabulary from Lesson 1

Materials PB p24; CD A track 9 (optional); WB p2; Dictionary 4

Warm-up

Write or put up some irregular verbs that children already know, e.g. *go, see, sit, take, put, come.* Children tell you the past tenses.

Read again

Remind children of *School clubs are fun!*
Play track 9 or read the text to the class. Children listen and follow in their books.

Activity 1

Ask the first question. Elicit an answer. Tell children they should look back to the text and check their answer to find it.
Ask the rest of the class if the answer given was correct. If there is disagreement, ask the whole class to look back and find the sentence where the answer is.
Continue with the other questions.

Activity 2

Ask a volunteer to read out the words in the box.
Children look at the pictures. Ask what the first one is. Check with the class that the answer is correct. Children write. Continue with the other pictures.

Activity 3

Ask a volunteer to read out the words.
Tell children to read all the sentences silently. Give them a minute or two. Children open their dictionaries at Unit 1.
Ask a volunteer to read the first definition in the PB. Ask for the answer. Tell children they may check in their dictionaries before they answer.
Check with the class if the answer is correct. Refer to the dictionary, if necessary. Continue with the other definitions.

Reading comprehension and vocabulary

1 Name the person.
1 Who went to Choir today?
2 Who helps at Choir?
3 Who can come to Choir next week?
4 Who did a good animation of a fish?
5 Who swam very fast?
6 Who was really pleased?
7 Who looks like a fish?
8 Who played chess against Sam and lost?
9 Who is a good chess player?
10 Who was too tired?

2 Match. Write the word.   seaweed   board   chess pieces   bubbles   snail

1   2   3   4   5

3 Read. Write the correct word.
club   coach   choir   referee   captain   orchestra   team

1 a group of people singing together
2 a group of people playing music together
3 a group of people playing a game together
4 a group of people doing something together
5 the leader of a team
6 he keeps the rules of the game
7 he helps people in sports

Unit 1 Reading comprehension and vocabulary: *Who?* questions; word/picture/definition match

Unit 1 Reading comprehension and vocabulary

28

Reading comprehension and vocabulary (WB p2)

If children are doing this page for homework, make sure they understand the tasks. You may wish to read the text in exercise 1 with the class as preparation. Advise them to have their dictionaries with them for the first exercise

Exercise 1
Children read and complete the text using the words in the box.

Exercise 2
Children answer the questions. Remind them to use short answers.

Exercise 3
Children complete the statements.

UNIT 1

Reading comprehension and vocabulary

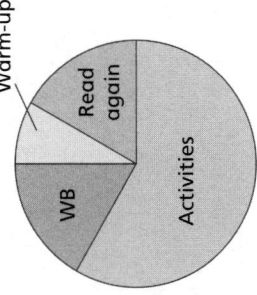

1 Read and complete the dialogue. Use the words in the box.

| animation | join | move | click | website |
| try | practise | program | internet |

Anna told Molly about animation.
"Look," said Anna, "This is how it works.
You use a computer p_____ to put a picture on your screen. That is a _____.
You use the program to make the picture m_____ then it is easier."
"Is it difficult?" asked Molly.
"It is difficult at first," said Anna. "You must p_____ then it is easier."
"Can I see your animation on the i_____?"
"Yes, you can," answered Anna. "Go to the school w_____.
C_____ on Computer Club. Then click on Anna's funny fish."
"Can I j_____ the Computer Club?" asked Molly.
"Yes, you can," said Anna. "Come next week. You can t_____ animation, too."
"Great!" said Molly.

2 Answer the questions. Write short answers.
1 Who goes to Computer Club?
2 What is the title of Anna's animation?
3 Where can you see Anna's animation?
4 Who is going to go to Computer Club next week?

3 Write the numbers.
1 There are ____ seconds in a minute.   2 There are ____ minutes in an hour.
3 There are ____ hours in a day.   4 There are ____ days in a week.

unit 1 Literal questions; time; cloze

Resource box

PB answers
Activity 1 1 Candy 2 Mrs Hall 3 Anna 4 Danny 5 Pete 6 the coach 7 Pete 8 Ben 9 Anna 10 Sam
Activity 2 1 chess pieces 2 snail 3 bubbles 4 board 5 seaweed
Activity 3 1 choir 2 orchestra 3 team 4 club 5 captain 6 referee 7 coach

WB answers
Exercise 1 program, move, animation, practise, internet, website, Click, join, try
Exercise 2 1 Anna 2 Anna's funny fish 3 on the internet 4 Molly
Exercise 3 1 60 2 60 3 24 4 7

Time division

Warm-up / Read again / WB / Activities

Unit 1 Reading comprehension and vocabulary

Lesson 3 Speaking (PB p25) Study skills

Lesson aim Speaking, (WB) Study skills

Lesson targets Children:
- listen to a dialogue; listen and repeat the dialogue
- understand the story and answer oral questions
- read and act the dialogue
- (WB) practise dictionary skills; finding the odd one out

Informal everyday language *Come in! Really? What about me? Sorry.*

New words *put on, come in, play, act, excellent, kindergarten, daughter*

Materials PB p25; CD A tracks 10, 11; WB p3; Dictionary 4

Preparation Listen to CD A track 10 before the lesson

Warm-up

Play a word game. Give children a letter, e.g. *b*. Teams have one minute to write down all the words they can think of beginning with that letter.

Activity 1

Children look at PB page 25. Read the title. Read the title of Part 1. Ask *Who is in the picture?*
Tell children to cover the dialogue text and look at the picture.
Play track 10. Children listen.

Activity 2

Children open their books and look at the dialogue. Play track 10 again.
Children listen and follow.
Check children understand the new words. Use the dictionary if you wish.

Activity 3

Children close books. Play track 11. Children listen and repeat in the pauses.
Encourage them to use the same expression and intonation.

Activity 4

Ask questions to check understanding of the story. See Resource box.

Activity 5

Children act the dialogue without their books if possible. They should be used to this activity from *English World 3*.
Encourage children to remember their lines as much as possible and to speak without reading their lines word by word if they are using their books to help them.
Let at least one group act the dialogue while the class listens and follows.

Unit 1 Speaking 30

Study skills (WB p3)

The exercises on this page give practice in dictionary skills (putting words in alphabetical order) and finding the odd one out in a list of words. Children should be able to do this work independently once the tasks have been explained.
Remind them that the alphabet is at the top of the page to help them or for them to check their work.

Exercise 1

Children write the words in alphabetical order.
Remind them to look at the first letter of each word.

Exercise 2

Children find the odd one out. If they find it difficult, tell them to check definitions in their dictionaries. They should think of the reason why the odd one is odd to help them check their own answer.

Study skills

a b c d e f g h i j k l m n o p q r s t u v w x y z

1 (abc) **Write the words in the correct order.**

1	picture	club	music	group
	club	group	music	picture
2	swim	move	throw	catch
3	ugly	good	funny	beautiful
4	internet	choir	snail	fish
5	took	went	said	found

2 Circle the odd one out.

1	football	basketball	(chess)	swimming
2	choir	orchestra	team	coach
3	Tuesday	December	Thursday	Sunday
4	brilliant	fast	great	fantastic
5	snail	fish	shark	whale

Unit 1 Dictionary skills: odd one out

Resource box

Story questions
Who is going to join the Drama Club? **Alfie**
Which children are already in the Drama Club? **Lulu, Molly, Max**
Who is a good actor? **Alfie**
What is the play? **'The Ugly Duckling'**
Who is it for? **the kindergarten**
What parts are Lulu, Max and Molly playing? **Lulu is the beautiful swan, Max is the kind man, Molly is the kind man's daughter**
What is Alfie going to be? **The ugly duckling**

WB answers

Exercise 1 2 catch, move, swim, throw 3 beautiful, funny, good, ugly 4 choir, fish, internet, snail 5 found, said, took, went
Exercise 2 2 coach 3 December 4 fast 5 snail

Time division

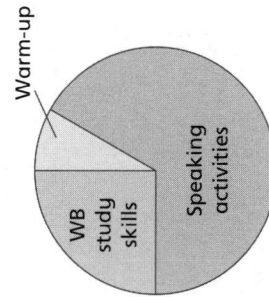

Unit 1 Study skills

Lesson 4 Grammar (Session 1), Grammar in conversation (Session 2) (PB pp26–27)

Lesson aim Grammar

Lesson targets Children:
- (session 1) understand and practise the key structure
- (session 2) listen to and read a conversation; repeat and practise it
- (session 2) listen to a song, say it and learn it (optional)

Key structure (session 1) past of irregular verbs, short answers

Key vocabulary clubs, hobbies, sports

Key language (session 2) adj + *too*: *I'm too busy.*

Informal expressions (session 2) *Sorry. Don't ask me.*

Materials PB pp26–27; CD A tracks 12–15; WB pp4–5

Session 1 Warm-up

Use Poster 1 to revise the clubs and activities.

Activity 1
Ask two children to read the PC kids' bubbles.
Write on the board: *swim, swam.*
Tell children to read through the sentence beginnings / endings.
Ask a volunteer to say the first complete sentence.
Check with the class.
Children write.
Continue with the other sentences.

Activity 2
Ask pairs to read the PC kids' bubbles.
Write the first prompt words on the board.
Help the class to compose the question.
Elicit the answer.
Continue with the other prompt words.

Children practise questions and answers in pairs. See Resource box.*

Session 2 Warm-up

Ask children to look at the words they ordered on WB page 2, exercise 1.
Ask them to tell you the word class of each set: verb, noun, adjective, etc.

Activity 1
Ask *What is the boy doing? reading (a comic) What is the girl doing?*
Elicit or explain: *her homework*
Tell the class to listen to the children.
Play track 12. Children follow in their books.

Activity 2
Children listen to track 13 and repeat in the pauses.

Activity 3
Children practise the conversation in pairs. See Resource box.**

Activity 4
Ask *Who is in the picture? What are they doing? What is the weather like?*
Play track 14. Children listen and follow the first time.
Read the words with the class. Play track 14. Children join in.
Play track 15. Children sing with the music. They may learn the song, if you wish.

Children complete WB page 4 in class time or for homework.

Unit 1 Grammar, Grammar in conversation

Grammar (Session 1), Grammar in conversation (Session 2) (WB pp4–5)

If this page is for homework, check children understand the tasks.

Exercise 1
Children choose the correct verb to complete each sentence and put it in the past tense.

Exercise 2
Children write complete negative past tense sentences.

If this page is for homework, check children understand the tasks.

Exercise 1
Children match the pairs of sentences.

Exercise 2
Children complete the second sentence in each pair of sentences.

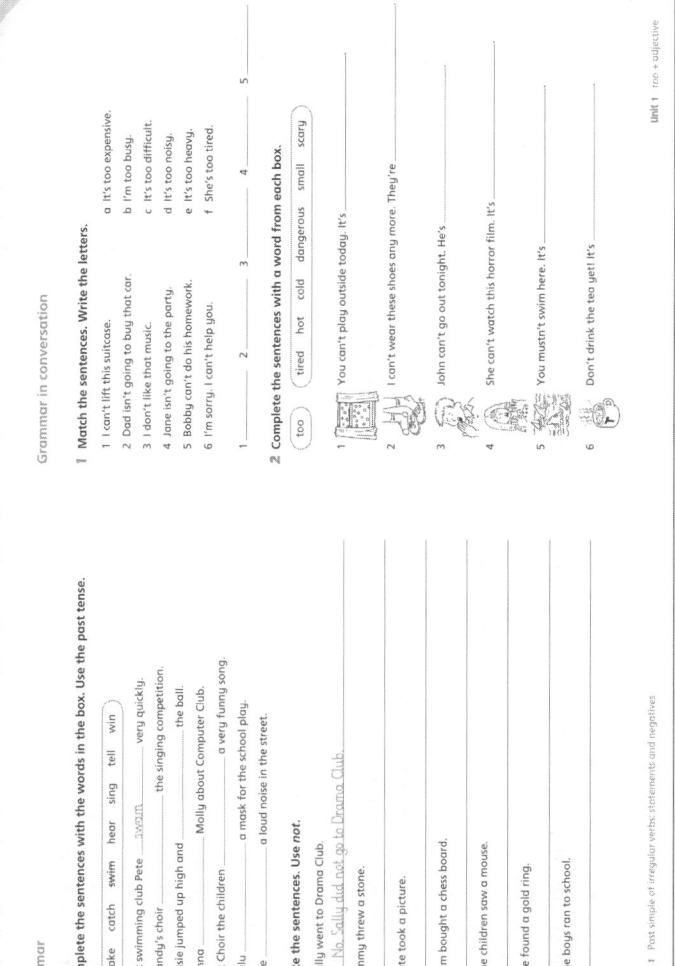

Time division

Session 1 — Warm-up, Activity 1, Activity 2, WB

Session 2 — Warm-up, Conversation activities, Pairs conversation practice, Song, WB

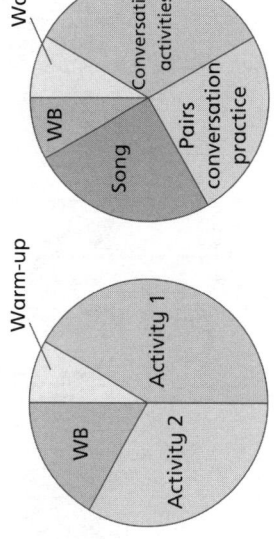

Grammar Practice Book
Children may begin Unit 1 when they have completed the PB and WB Grammar pages. They should complete it before the end of PB / WB Unit 1.

Resource box

PB answers
Activity 1 1c 2e 3f 4b 5a 6d
Pair work: Grammar (p26)
***Activity 2**
Children work in pairs at their desks. They take turns to say the questions and give the answer. If necessary, bring an able pair forward to demonstrate the activity. Give the class three minutes to speak in pairs. Then let one or two pairs demonstrate a few questions and answers.

****Pair work: Grammar in conversation (p27)**
Activity 3
Children practise the dialogue in pairs at their desks. Give pairs three minutes to practise the dialogue.
Let one or two pairs stand up and say the dialogue in front of the class.

WB answers
Grammar (p4)
Exercise 1 2 won   3 caught   4 told   5 sang   6 made   7 heard
Exercise 2 2 No, Jimmy did not throw a stone.
3 No, Pete did not take a picture.
4 No, Sam did not buy a chess board.
5 No, the children did not see a mouse.
6 No, Joe did not find a gold ring.
7 No, the boys did not run to school.

Grammar in conversation (p5)
Exercise 1 1e 2a 3d 4f 5c 6b
Exercise 2 1 too cold   2 too small   3 too tired
4 too scary   5 too dangerous   6 too hot

Unit 1 Grammar, Grammar in conversation

Lesson 5 Listening, Phonics (PB p28) Use of English

Lesson aim Listening, spelling and pronunciation, Use of English (WB)

Lesson targets Children:
- listen to children describing objects and identify them
- listen for specific words
- practise saying, reading and spelling words with oo
- (WB) learn about when to use contractions in writing

Key structure and language from Unit 1

Target words cook, book, look, took, wood, good, wool, hook

Materials PB p28; CD A tracks 15, 16, 17; WB pp6–7

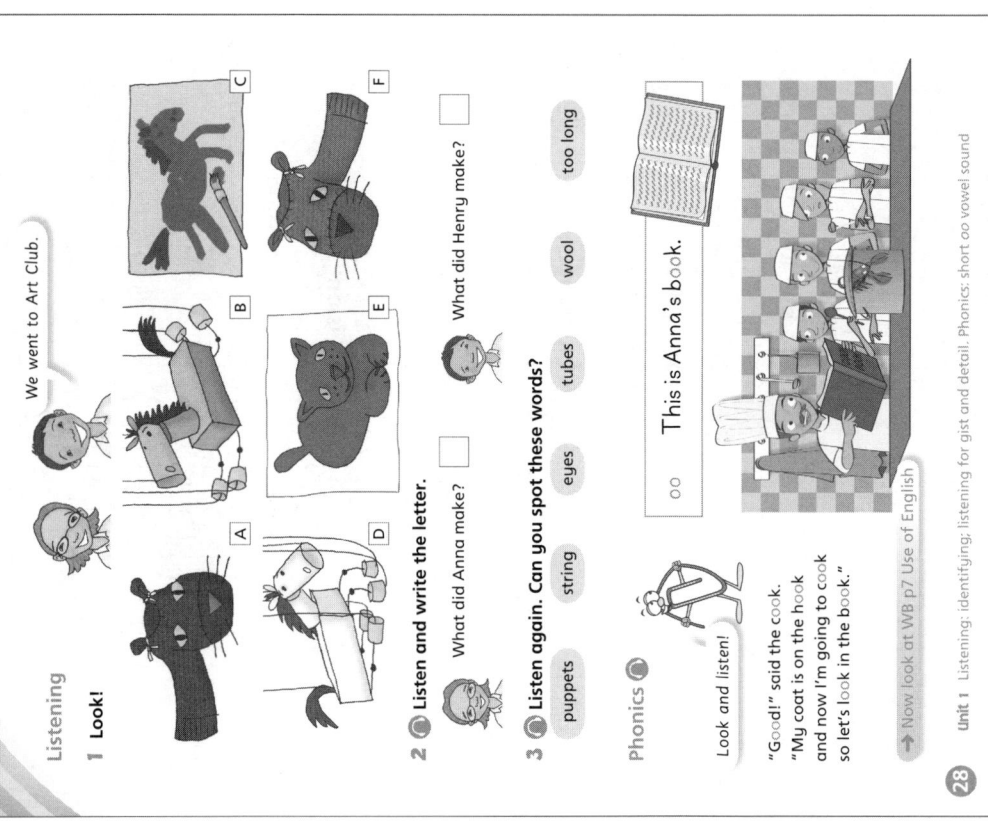

Warm-up
Sing the song about working from PB page 27, track 15.

Listening

Activity 1
Ask a volunteer to read the bubble. Give children a moment to look at each picture. Ask what is in each one. Explain that these are things that some children made at Art Club. Say *There are two different animals in the pictures. What are they? cats and horses*

Activity 2
Play track 16. Children listen. Some children may be able to write both letters the first time. Be prepared to play the track again for children to listen or check. Check the answers together.

Activity 3
Ask one or more volunteers to read the words to the class. Class follows in their books. Tell them they are going to hear the children talking again. This time, they must listen out for the words they have just read. When they hear one of the words, they put their hands up.

Phonics
Point out the box. Tell children to follow in their books and repeat in the pauses. Play the first part of track 17. Make sure children repeat accurately. Play the end of track 17. Children listen and follow. Children say the rhyme. They may learn it if you wish.

Children open their WBs at page 6. The phonics page can be completed for homework. If it is for homework, make sure they understand the tasks.

Phonics, Use of English (WB pp6–7)

Remind the class of the sound oo and *book*.

Write the two sentences on the board. Class reads.

Exercise 1

Children complete the words and write the words. Remind them to read the words out.

Go through the presentation with the class. Write words on the board as necessary.
Children write full forms. Check answers together.

Exercise 2

Children write the words under the correct pictures.

Go through the different use of forms in speaking and writing.
Ask children to read out sentences.
Make sure children understand that in speaking, short forms are used most of the time.

Exercise 3

Children complete the sentences using words from exercise 1, making changes as necessary.

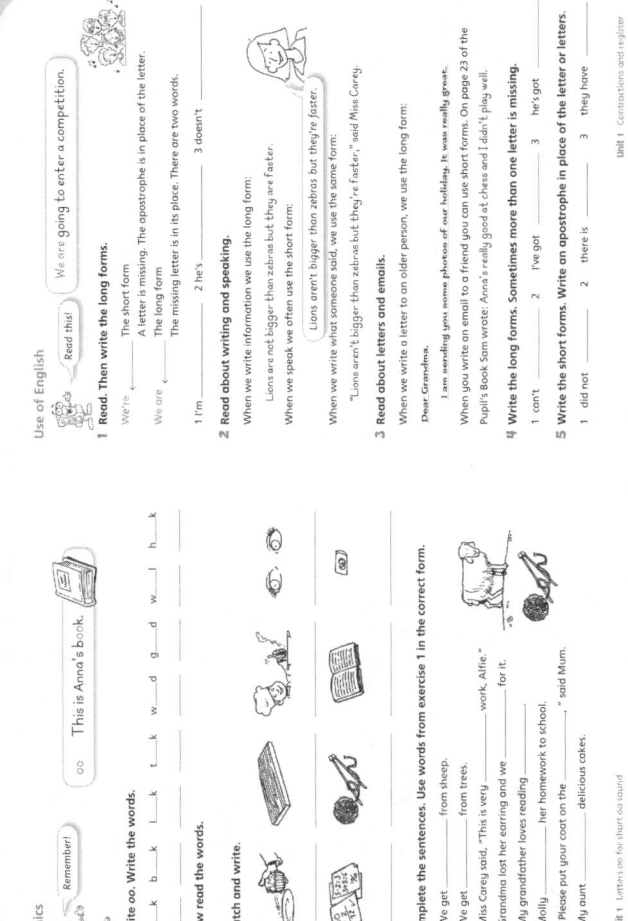

Exercise 3

Go through the information with the class and the examples.
Explain to the class that in their own writing (apart from emails, direct speech and speech bubbles) they should use the long form.
Children practise the long and short forms.

Exercises 4 and 5

Children practise the long and short forms.

Resource box

PB answers Activity 2

Audioscript (CD A track 16) Listening activities 2–3 (PB p28)

Anna: Art Club was really good this week. We made puppets. I used an old sock, coloured paper and string. I put the string round the top of the sock. I pulled it tightly and made two ears. I cut out green paper for its eyes and I used black paper for its nose. My puppet was a red cat.

Henry: I made a puppet, too, but I didn't use a sock. I used a box, tubes, paper and wool. I made a brown horse. I cut out black paper for its eyes and I made a tail from black wool. At first the tail was too long so I cut the wool and made it shorter.

WB answers

Phonics (p6)

Activity 2 took, wood, cook, look, good, wool, book, hook

Activity 3 1 wool 2 wood 3 good 4 looked 5 books 6 took 7 hook 8 cooks/cooked

Use of English (p7)

Exercise 1 I am, he is, does not

Exercise 4 cannot, I have got, he has got

Exercise 5 didn't, there's, they've

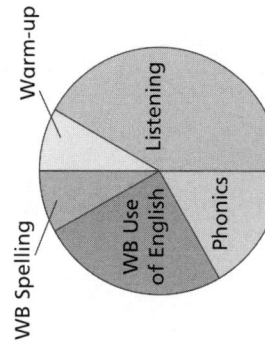

Time division

Unit 1 Phonics, Use of English

Lesson 6 Class composition (Session 1) (PB p29) Writing preparation, Composition practice (Session 2)

Lesson aim Writing

Lesson targets Children:
- (session 1) compose and write an email with teacher support
- (session 2) (WB) practise vocabulary; make notes about a school club
- (session 2) (WB) write an email about a school club

Key structure and language from Unit 1

Key vocabulary sports

Materials PB p29; WB pp8–9

Session 1 Warm-up

Hold a short class discussion about emails: *Do you send emails? Who do you send to? family? friends? How often? Do you like sending emails? Why?*

Class composition

Activities 1 and 2

1 Children look at the picture. Ask a child to read the sentences. Ask the questions. Elicit complete answers. Write notes on one side of the board, e.g. *sat next to Josh – played a trumpet – Josh played a flute – conductor, Mr Grey – going to be a Music Club concert, October – going to be fun.*

2 Ask other questions to help the class write Anna's email, e.g. *Does Anna like Music Club? the trumpet? How many children are in the orchestra? What is Mr Grey like? friendly? fun? kind? What will the children do before the concert? practise* Ask any other questions you wish. Note all the answers on the board.

Activity 3

1 Explain you are going to write Megan's email to Anna together. Ask how Megan begins *Hi Anna*. Write it on the board. Ask a child to read the beginning of the first sentence. Write it on the board. Explain you are writing as Megan so must use *I / we*.

2 Help the class to suggest complete sentences using the notes on the board. Use as many notes as necessary to produce a piece of model writing to match the ability of your class. It is not necessary to use every idea in the notes. Different classes will produce different lengths and qualities of work. Encourage the class to work to their best level.

3 When the email is finished ask one or two volunteers to read it to the class. Erase the complete writing from the board. If you wish, leave some or all of the notes on the board. Children write the complete email in their books. Some children will be able to write more than others. Remind the class that the questions in activity 2 can help them, too.

Class composition

Green Park School
Music Club Concert
Tuesday 25th October, 6.30

1 Read.
Megan went to Music Club after school.
She played in the orchestra.
In the evening she sent an email to Anna.

2 Look at the pictures. Think about these questions.
Who did Megan sit next to? What instrument did she play?
What did Josh play? Who was the conductor?
What is going to happen in October? Is it going to be fun?
Who is in the picture on the poster?

3 Write Megan's email.
Hi Anna.
After school today I went to

Unit 1 Class composition: an email to a friend including a personal recount of events

Unit 1 Class composition

36

Writing preparation, Composition practice (WB pp8–9)

Session 2 Warm-up

Do the *Word mix* game (see Games, page 187).

Exercise 1

Children complete this alone or in pairs. Check answers together.

Exercises 2 and 3

Children work alone or in pairs. Set a time limit. Check answers.

Exercise 4

A child reads the first two sentences. Children fill in the gaps for either Sam or Candy. They can choose what day they like and names for the captains. They decide on the goals / points each team scores and whether Sam and Candy were on the winning teams or not.

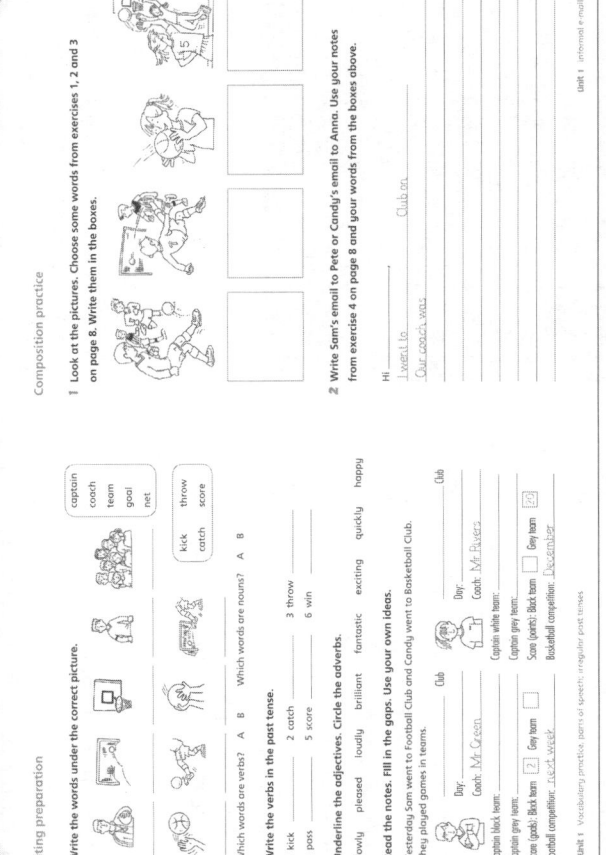

Exercise 1

Children write words for the football game or the basketball game, whichever they did in exercise 4 on page 8.
They should be able to write at least one verb that matches each action and one adjective or adverb for each picture.

Exercise 2

Children use the notes from exercise 4 on page 8 to begin their email. Encourage children to add sentences by using the words and pictures in exercise 1.
Go around helping.

When they have finished or before the end of the lesson, ask different children to read all or some of their emails to the class. Children's work should vary according to their own ideas and ability. The example shows the range that can be expected in a mixed-ability class.

Homework task

Children complete Check-up 1, WB p10. For answers, see p65

Resource box

Class composition example writing (p29)
Hi Anna,
After school today I went to Music Club. I played in the orchestra. I sat next to Josh. I played my trumpet and Josh played his flute. There were a lot of children in the orchestra today. Mr Grey was the conductor. He is very nice. We are going to play in a concert in October. We are going to practise our music every week. It is going to be fun. I am sending the poster for the concert. Can you see who is in the picture? It is my friend [class chooses a name].
Are you going to come to the concert?
Megan

WB answers (p8)
Exercise 1 A: coach, goal, net, captain, team; B: throw, kick, catch, score; verbs: B; nouns: A
Exercise 2 1 kicked 2 caught 3 threw 4 passed 5 scored 6 won
Exercise 3 adverbs: slowly, loudly, quickly; others are adjectives

Composition practice example writing (p9)
I went to Basketball Club on …. Our coach was Mr Rivers. I was in the white team. Our captain was …. The grey team captain was …. We won the game. The score was … (Most children will be able to add, e.g.) It was very exciting. I scored 3 points. I ran quickly and I caught the ball. I threw it into the net. (Able children will add extra information, e.g.) In December we're going to enter the … competition. I'm going to be in the team / play in the match. I'm very happy / pleased.

Time division

Session 1

Class composition writing in books | Class composition teacher-led board writing | Warm-up

Session 2

Warm-up | Writing preparation | Composition practice

Portfolio

Children may make neat copies of their emails. If possible, let them key them into a real email account and print them out.

Unit 1 Writing preparation, Composition practice

2 In the theatre

Lesson 1 Poster 2, Reading

Lesson aim Reading
Text type A traditional story
Lesson targets Children:
- read, understand and practise new vocabulary on the poster
- read, understand and practise reading the story
- answer oral comprehension questions

Key structure past continuous statements: *The sun was shining.*
Key language *could, couldn't: At first she could see nothing.*
Key vocabulary *countryside; traditional characters*
Materials PB pp30–31; WB p12; poster 2; CD A track 18; Dictionary 4; word cards for poster vocabulary (see Poster 2 below or list on p14)
Preparation Make word cards; listen to CD A track 18

2 In the theatre

[Poster labels: scenery, actor, costume, Red Riding Hood, prop, the Wolf, stage, light, curtain, script]

Warm-up

Ask children *Do you know any plays? Write titles on the board. Do you sometimes watch plays? Where?*

Poster 2

1 Point to the poster. Read out the title. Give the class a moment or two to look.

2 Point to the objects and people on the poster. Read the word. Show the word card/s. Class reads and says the word/s.
Make sure children understand the following words. Use the definitions and example sentences as necessary to ensure understanding:

light   a light that shines on the actors on the stage
             When the curtains opened, the *lights* went on.
prop   object an actor uses on stage
             Lily is Red Riding Hood and her *prop* is a basket.
scenery   objects like trees and houses that are on stage for a play
             This paper beanstalk is *scenery* for 'Jack and the beanstalk'.

3 Cover the words on the poster if you wish. Point to the objects and people at random. Class names them.

4 Ask the class if they know the story of Red Riding Hood. Point her out if they do not.
Ask *What does the wolf look like in this picture? Is the costume good? Does he look scary or funny?*

5 Ask *What is on the scenery? trees*
Where are the actors now? in the wood
What are Red Riding Hood's props? a basket and flowers
Has the wolf got any props? no

Unit 2 Reading

38

Reading (PB pp30–31)

1 Children look at the pictures.
Read the title. If children know this story ask them to name the people in it: *Red Riding Hood, her mother, her father, her grandmother, the wolf.* If they do not know it, ask them to say what they can see in the pictures.

2 Play track 18. Children listen and follow in their books.

3 Read one paragraph or section of the text at a time.
Use Dictionary 4 to help you to explain new words as necessary.
Help children to find new words. Make up extra sentences for new words if you wish.

4 Ask questions about each paragraph or a section of the text. See Resource box.

5 Give reading practice around the class.
Ask individuals, groups or the class to read sentences or paragraphs.
Play track 18 again.

UNIT 2 In the theatre

Reading — Red Riding Hood

Red Riding Hood lived in the forest. Her father was a woodcutter. Every day he cut and chopped wood in the forest. One morning, Red Riding Hood's mother said to her, "Here is a cake and a bottle of fruit juice. Take them to Grandmother but don't talk to anyone on the way."

Red Riding Hood put on her red cloak with a hood and set off through the forest. The sun was shining and the birds were singing. The forest was beautiful and Red Riding Hood soon forgot her mother's words. She put down her basket and picked some pretty blue flowers.

Just then a wolf came along the path. He saw Red Riding Hood and he stopped beside her.

"Good morning, my dear. Where are you going today?" he asked.

"Oh! Good morning," answered Red Riding Hood politely. "I am going to my grandmother's house. She lives all alone at the edge of the wood. I am picking these flowers for her."

"You are a kind girl," said the wolf in a friendly voice. "Look! There are some lovely yellow flowers over there."

"Oh yes," said Red Riding Hood. "Thank you."

The wolf disappeared into the forest and Red Riding Hood picked an enormous bunch of flowers.

At last she came to her grandmother's house. She knocked on the door and went in.

The curtains were closed and at first she could see nothing. It was too dark. She felt a little scared but she was a brave girl and she did not run away. Then she saw Grandmother sitting up in her bed. She was wearing her pretty pink shawl and she had her big white nightcap on her head but she looked very strange.

Red Riding Hood said, "Oh, Grandmother, you have enormous ears."
"I can hear you with these ears," said her grandmother.
Red Riding Hood said, "Oh, Grandmother, you have enormous eyes."
"I can see you with these eyes," said her grandmother.
Red Riding Hood said, "Oh, Grandmother, you have a huge nose."
"I can smell you with this nose," said her grandmother and her big nose twitched a little.
Red Riding Hood said worriedly, "Oh, Grandmother, you have lots of big, shiny, white teeth!"
"I can eat you with these big, shiny, white teeth," roared her grandmother and she leapt out of the bed.
It was the wolf!
"Help!" screamed Red Riding Hood.

Suddenly, the door opened and her father stood in the doorway with his sharp, heavy axe. At once, the wolf jumped out of the window and ran away. He was not brave at all.
A sound came from the cupboard. They opened the door and there was Grandmother! She was frightened but safe and they never saw the wolf again.

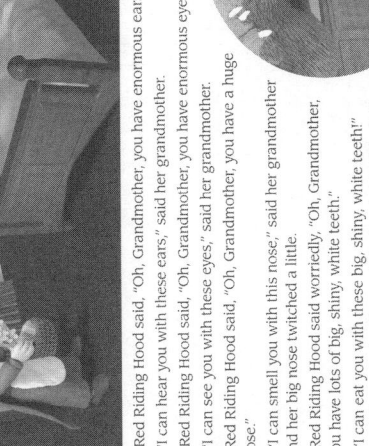

unit 2 Reading: a traditional story

Resource box

Text questions

Where did Red Riding Hood live? *in the forest*

What was her father? *a woodcutter*

What did he do? *he chopped wood*

What did Red Riding Hood put on? *her red cloak with a hood*

What did she soon forget? Why? *her mother's words; it was sunny and she picked flowers*

What did the wolf show Red riding Hood? *lovely yellow flowers*

Why was it dark in the house? *the curtains were closed*

What was Grandmother wearing? How did she look? *a shawl, nightcap; very strange*

What was strange about Grandmother's ears, eyes, nose and teeth? *they were all very big*

Who saved Red Riding Hood? *her father*

What did the wolf do? *he ran away*

Homework task

Children learn selected vocabulary from Unit 2, *Dictionary 4*.
See unit word list on pp190–191 for key words, extension words and words for understanding only.

Time division

(Poster, Warm-up, Dictionary home task, Reading)

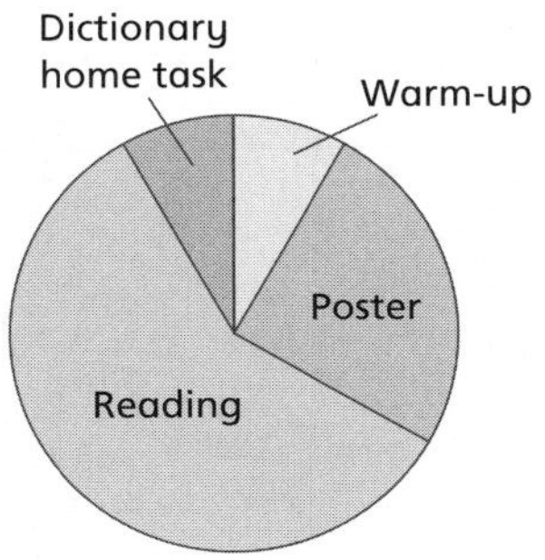

Lesson 2 Reading comprehension and vocabulary (PB p32)

Lesson aim Reading comprehension; vocabulary

Lesson targets Children re-read *Red Riding Hood*, then:
- (PB) answer literal questions; discuss inferential questions
- match adjectives to people; match words to definitions
- (WB) order sentences from the story
- complete a cloze exercise

Key structure past continuous statements: *The sun was shining.*

Key language *could, couldn't: At first she could see nothing.*

Words vocabulary from Lesson 1

Materials PB p32; CD A track 18 (optional); WB p12; Dictionary 4

Warm-up

Do a *Noun chain* on the board (see Games, page 187).

Read again

Remind children of *Red Riding Hood*.
Play track 18 or read the text to the class. Children listen and follow.

Activity 1

Ask the first question. Tell children they should look back at the text to check their answer or to find it. Elicit an answer.
Ask the rest of the class if the answer given was correct. If there is disagreement, ask the whole class to look back and find the sentence where the answer is.
Continue with the other questions.

Activity 2

Discuss each question and hear their ideas. Help them to express them in English. There is a variety of answers for most of these questions. Ask extra questions as appropriate.
Encourage children to make suggestions. Children write.

Activity 3

Ask who each word describes. Check the text as necessary. Children write.

Activity 4

Children match words and definitions. They may check in their dictionaries.
Check answers together.

Reading comprehension and vocabulary

1 Answer the questions.
1. What did Red Riding Hood take to her grandmother?
2. How did Red Riding Hood speak to the wolf?
3. Why didn't Red Riding Hood run away when she was scared?
4. What was Grandmother wearing in bed?
5. Why was Red Riding Hood worried?
6. Why did the wolf run away?
7. Where was Red Riding Hood's grandmother?

2 Talk about the answers to these questions.
1. Why did Red Riding Hood's mother say "Don't talk to anyone on the way?"
2. Why did the wolf show Red Riding Hood the yellow flowers?
3. What good things did Red Riding Hood do in the story?
4. Did she do anything wrong? What?

3 Write the words next to the people they describe.

| polite | friendly | frightened | kind | strange | safe | brave | worried |

4 Match the word to the definitions. Check in your dictionary.

| scream | disappear | forget | leap | set off |

1 to begin on a journey _____   2 to not remember _____   3 to shout loudly _____
4 to go out of sight _____   5 to do a high jump _____

Unit 2 Reading comprehension and vocabulary: literal and deductive questions; definitions

Unit 2 Reading comprehension and vocabulary

Reading comprehension and vocabulary (WB p12)

If children are doing this page for homework, make sure they understand the tasks. You may wish to read the text in exercise 1 with the class as preparation.

Exercise 1
Children order the sentences by referring to the picture sequence.

Exercise 2
Children complete the sentences using the words in the box.

Resource box

PB answers

Activity 1 1 a cake and a bottle of fruit juice
2 politely 3 because she was a brave girl
4 a pink shawl, a big white nightcap 5 because Grandmother's teeth were very big, shiny and white 6 because he was not brave at all
7 in the cupboard

Activity 2 Possible answers: 1 There was a wolf in the forest and the wolf was dangerous; She wanted Red Riding Hood to be safe; She wanted Red Riding hood to take the cake and fruit juice quickly.
2 He wanted to get to Grandmother's house before Red Riding Hood.
3 She took the things to Grandmother. She picked flowers for her. She was polite to the wolf. She didn't run away, she was brave.
4 Children might say: She forgot her mother's words.

Activity 3 Red Riding Hood: polite, kind, brave
The wolf: friendly, strange
Grandmother: frightened, safe

Activity 4 1 set off 2 forget 3 scream
4 disappear 5 leap

WB answers

Exercise 1 a8 b5 c7 d10 e2 f3 g9 h1 i4 j6

Exercise 2 1 anyone 2 Just 3 nothing
4 doorway 5 voice 6 Suddenly 7 beside

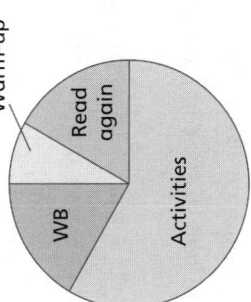

Reading comprehension and vocabulary

1 Look at the pictures. Put the sentences in the correct order.

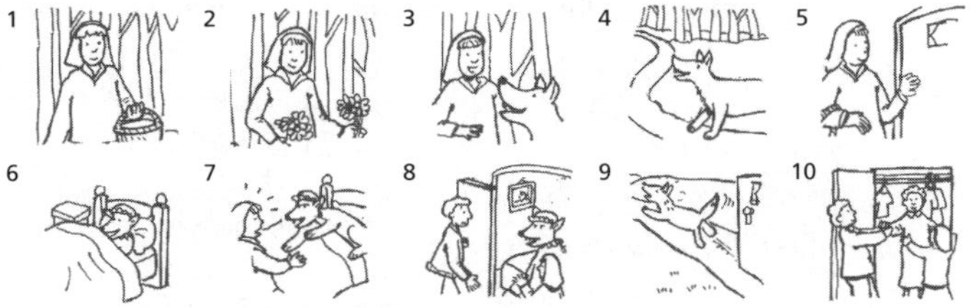

a The woodcutter opened the door.
b Red Riding Hood arrived at her grandmother's house.
c The wolf leapt out of the bed.
d The grandmother was frightened but safe.
e She picked some flowers in the forest.
f The wolf stopped and talked to Red Riding Hood.
g The wolf ran away.
h Red Riding Hood was taking a cake and some juice to her grandmother.
i The wolf disappeared into the forest.
j Red Riding Hood's grandmother looked very strange.

2 Complete the sentences with words from the box.

| voice |
| suddenly |
| nothing |
| just |
| anyone |
| beside |
| doorway |

1 'Is _____ at home?' asked the wolf.
2 _____ then they heard a strange sound.
3 Red Riding Hood could see _____ in the room.
4 The woodcutter was standing in the _____.
5 The wolf had a strange _____.
6 _____ the wolf leaped out of the bed.
7 Red Riding Hood stood _____ the bed.

unit 2 Sequencing a story; cloze

Time division

- Warm-up
- Read again
- WB
- Activities

Unit 2 Reading comprehension and vocabulary

41

Lesson 3 Speaking (PB p33) Study skills

Lesson aim Speaking, (WB) Study skills

Lesson targets
- listen to a dialogue; listen and repeat the dialogue
- understand the story and answer oral questions
- read and act the dialogue
- (WB) practise dictionary skills

Informal everyday language *Wow! Oh no!*

New words theatre and stage; copy, photocopier, work (function) button, thousand, press

Materials PB p33; CD A track 19; WB p13; Dictionary 4

Preparation Listen to CD A track 19 before the lesson

Warm-up
Remind the class of *Let's put on a play!*
Ask the class to tell you what happened in the first part.

Activity 1
Children look at PB page 33. Read the title of Part 2. Ask the class what they think all the paper is for (remind them of the words on the poster): **the script**
Tell children to cover the dialogue text and look at the picture.
Play track 19. Children listen.

Activity 2
Children open their books and look at the dialogue. Play track 19 again. Children listen and follow.
Check children understand the new words. Use Dictionary 4 if you wish.

Activity 3
Play track 20. Children listen and repeat in the pauses. Encourage them to use the same expression and intonation.

Activity 4
Ask questions to check understanding of the story. See Resource box.

Activity 5
Children act the dialogue without their books if possible.
Encourage children to remember their lines as much as possible and to speak without reading their lines word by word.
If possible, let two groups act in front of the class or read from their places.

Study skills (WB p13)

The exercises on this page practise dictionary skills.
Children should be able to do this work independently once the tasks have been explained.
They should have their dictionaries to check spelling in exercise 2.

Exercise 1
Children find the word in the wrong place. They draw the arrow to the correct place.

Exercise 2
Children write the words correctly.

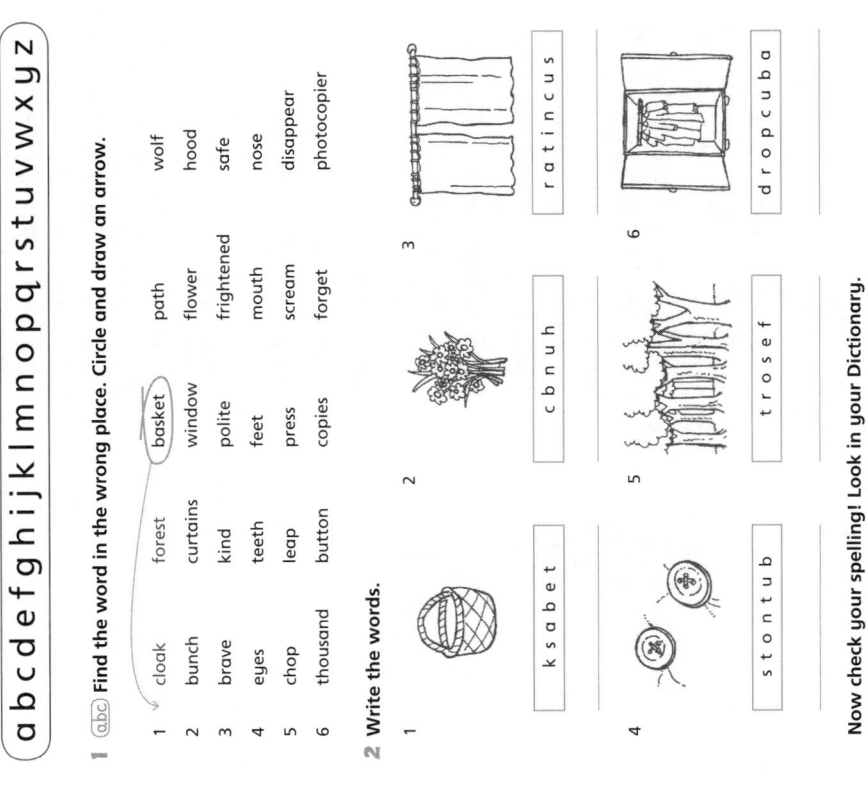

Resource box

Story questions
Where are the children going to perform the play? in the school theatre
What are they going to wear? costumes
What are they going to have? scenery and props
What do they need now? copies of the script
How many copies do they need? ten
How many copies is the machine making? one thousand and ten

WB answers (p13)
Study skills
Exercise 1 2 bunch → curtains window → flower hood
3 brave → kind polite → frightened safe
4 eyes → teeth feet mouth → nose
5 chop → leap press scream → disappear
6 eyes → thousand button copies forget → photocopier
Exercise 2 1 basket 2 bunch 3 curtains 4 buttons 5 forest
6 cupboard

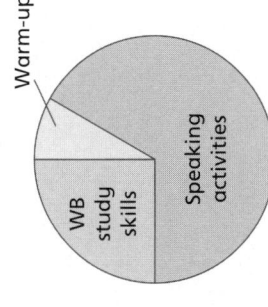

Time division: Warm-up, WB study skills, Speaking activities

Unit 2 Study skills

Lesson 4 Grammar (Session 1), Grammar in conversation (Session 2) (PB pp34–35)

Lesson aim Grammar

Lesson targets Children:
- (session 1) understand and practise the key structure
- (session 2) listen to and read a conversation; repeat and practise it
- (session 2) listen to a song, say it and learn it (optional)

Key structure (session 1) past continuous, statements and questions

Key vocabulary from Lesson 1

Key language (session 2) could, couldn't

Informal expressions (session 2) Time's up! Guess what?

Materials PB pp34–35; CD A tracks 21–24; WB p14–15

Session 1 Warm-up

Play an *Action verb* game to practise the present continuous (see Games, page 186).

Activity 1

Ask two children to read the PC kids' bubbles. Write *was walking* on the board. Point out the structure: past tense of *to be* + verb + *ing*. Let volunteers read each sentence. Ask what is wrong. Other children give correct sentences.

Activity 2

Ask pairs to read the PC kids' bubbles. Write the first prompt words on the board. Help the class to compose the question. Elicit a short answer. Continue with the other prompt words.

Children practise questions and answers in pairs. See Resource box.*

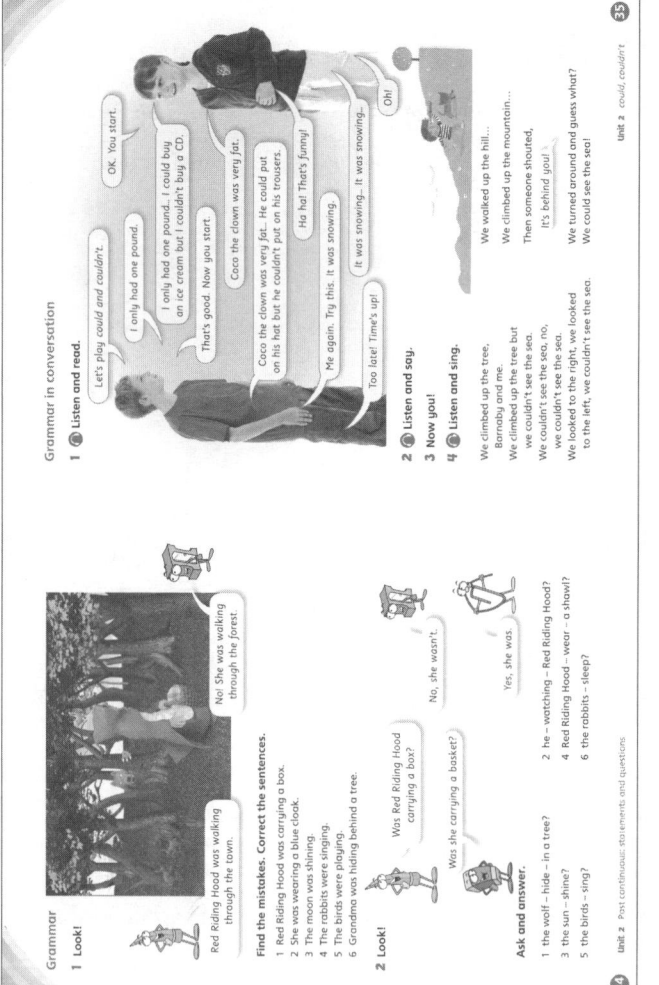

Session 2 Warm-up

Play *I spy* (see Games, page 187 using poster 2.

Activity 1

Point out the boy and girl. Explain they are playing a word game.
Tell the class to listen to them.
Play track 21. Children follow in their books.

Activity 2

Children listen to track 22 and repeat in the pauses.

Activity 3

Children practise the conversation in pairs. See Resource box.**

Activity 4

Ask *Who and what can you see in the picture?*
Play track 23. Children listen and follow the first time.
Read the words with the class.
Play track 23. Children join in.
Play track 24. Children sing with the music. They may learn the song, if you wish.

Children complete WB page 14 in class time or for homework.

Unit 2 Grammar, Grammar in conversation

Grammar (Session 1), Grammar in conversation (Session 2) (WB pp14–15)

If this page is for homework, check children understand the tasks.

Exercise 1
Remind children of the structure of the past continuous. Point out the example.

Exercise 2
Children write complete negative sentences. Point out the *Remember!* box. Revise the negative structure if necessary.

If this page is for homework, check children understand the tasks.

Exercise 1
Remind the class of the structure:
could / could not + verb

Exercise 2
Point out the example. Do one or two orally if you wish before children complete the exercise.

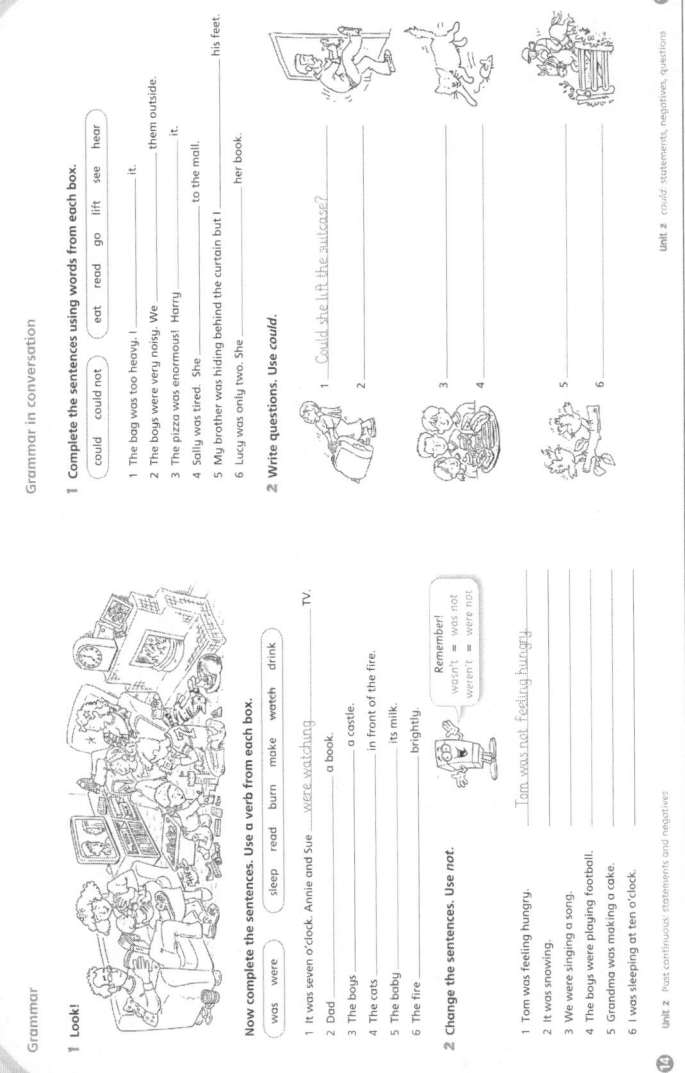

Time division

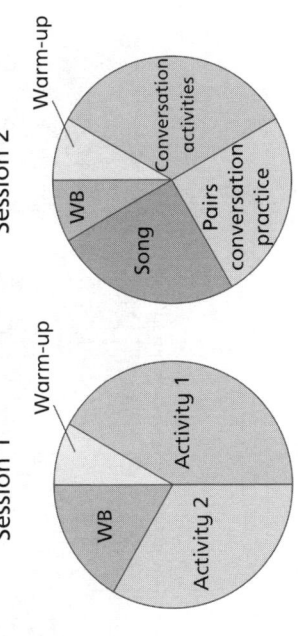

Session 1 — Warm-up, WB, Activity 2, Activity 1

Session 2 — Warm-up, Conversation activities, Pairs conversation practice, Song, WB

Grammar Practice Book
Children may begin Unit 2 when they have completed the PB and WB Grammar pages. They should complete it before the end of PB / WB Unit 2.

Resource box

PB answers (p34)
Activity 1 (correct phrase in each sentence given)
1 carrying a basket   2 red cloak   3 The rabbits   5 The birds   6 The wolf

*Pair work: Grammar (PB p34)

Activity 1
Children work in pairs at their desks. They take turns to say the questions and give the short answer. If necessary, bring an able pair forward to demonstrate the activity. Give the class three minutes to speak in pairs. Then let one or two pairs demonstrate a few questions and answers.

**Pair work: Grammar in conversation (PB p35)

Activity 3
Children practise the dialogue in pairs at their desks.

Encourage children to play the game. They must think of one thing for *could* and another for *couldn't*. The idea of the game is to make the two things part of the same situation, like the children in the book, joining two sentences with *but*.

Give pairs three minutes to practise the dialogue.

Let one or two pairs stand up and say their conversations. Less able children may say the dialogue in the book.

WB answers

Grammar (p14)

Exercise 1 2 was reading   3 were making   4 were sleeping   5 was drinking   6 was burning

Exercise 2 2 It was not snowing.   3 We were not singing a song.   4 The boys were not playing football.   5 Grandma was not making a cake.   6 I was not sleeping at ten o'clock.

Grammar in conversation (p15)

Exercise 1 1 could not lift   2 could hear   3 could not eat   4 could not go   5 could see   6 could not read

Exercise 2 2 Could he open the door?   3 Could they eat the cakes?   4 Could it catch the mouse?   5 Could they fly?   6 Could they jump over the gate?

Unit 2   Grammar, Grammar in conversation

Lesson 5 Listening, Phonics (PB p36) Use of English

Lesson aim Listening, spelling and pronunciation, Use of English (WB)

Lesson targets Children:

- try to sequence pictures to make a story
- listen to the story and identify the correct picture
- practise saying, reading and spelling words with short *u*
- (WB) learn about reporting clauses in direct speech

Key structure and language from Unit 2

Target words *bull, put, push, pull, full*

Materials PB p36; CD A tracks 24–26; WB pp16–17

Warm-up

Sing the seeking song from PB page 35, track 24.

Listening

Activity 1

Children look at the pictures. Ask what they think the story is.
Encourage children to say what the wolf did and what Grandma did.

Activity 2

Tell the class they are going to hear the story. Play track 25. Children listen and point to the pictures.

Activity 3

Play track 25 again. Children write the letters of the pictures in order.
Be prepared to play the track again for children to listen or check.

Activity 4

Encourage children to tell the story in their own words. If necessary, prompt them, e.g. *What was happening in picture E? picture C? What did the wolf do in picture A?*, etc. Let a volunteer try to tell the whole story.

Phonics

Point out the box. Tell children to follow in their books and repeat in the pauses. Play the first part of track 26. Make sure children repeat accurately.
Play the end of track 26. Children listen and follow.
Children say the rhyme. They may learn it, if you wish.

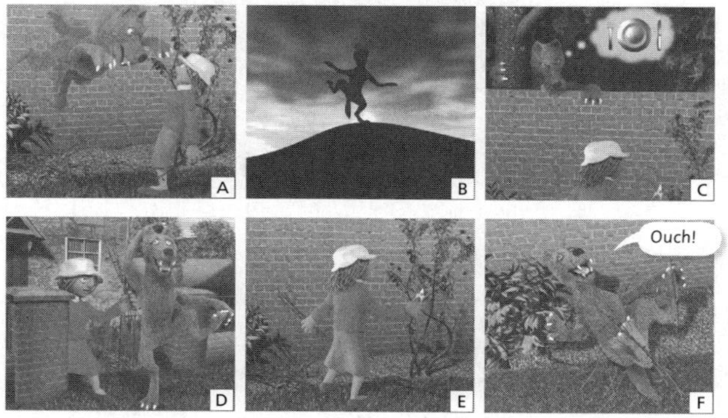

Children open their WBs at page 16. They may complete the Phonics page for homework.
If it is for homework, make sure they understand the tasks.

Listening

1 Look at the pictures. Can you make a story from them?

2 Listen and point.

3 Listen again and write the letters.

1 ____ 2 ____ 3 ____ 4 ____ 5 ____ 6 ____

4 Tell the story.

Phonics

u The bull is strong.

Look and listen!

Put, push, pull. Put, push, pull.
Put on your boots, push open the gate.
Pull the bull, through the gate.
Put, push, pull. Put, push, pull.

→ Now look at WB p17 Use of English

Use of English

Move on to WB page 17.

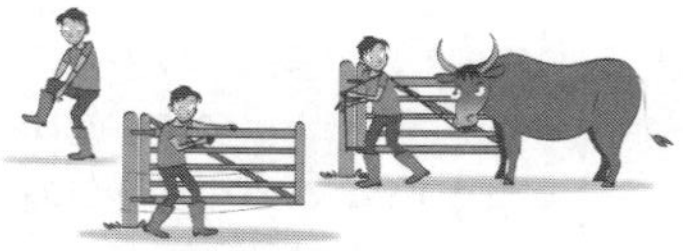

Phonics, Use of English (WB pp16–17)

Remind the class of the sound *u* and *bull*.

Exercise 1
Children complete and write the words. Remind them to read them.

Exercise 2
Children complete the sentences.

Exercise 3
Children write their own sentences. If they cannot think of ideas, tell them to look through Units 1 and 2 for ideas.

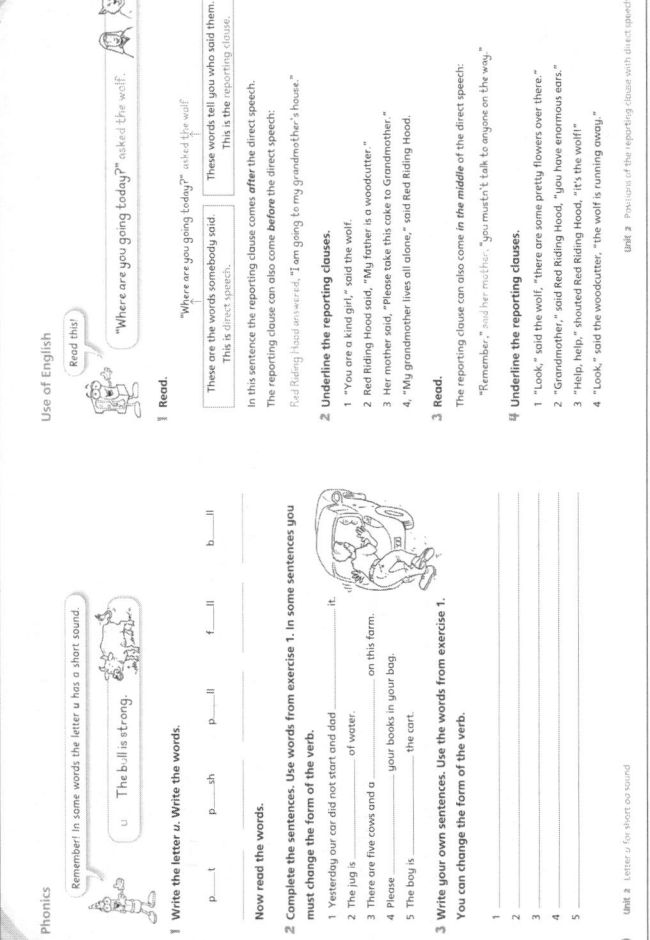

Write the sentence on the board. Class reads.

Exercise 1
Go through the presentation with the class. Write sentences on the board as necessary.
Ask volunteers to underline reporting clauses.

Exercise 2
While children underline in their books, write the sentences on the board. Volunteers underline and other children check.

Exercise 3
Write the sentence. Let a volunteer underline.

Exercise 4
Do the same as for exercise 2.

Resource box

PB answers
Audioscript (CD A track 25) **Listening activities 2–3** (PB p36)
It was a lovely day and the sun was shining. Grandma was in her garden. She was cutting her rose tree. She was wearing thick gloves because the rose tree had long, sharp thorns.

Grandma didn't see the wolf. He was hiding behind a tree and he was watching her. "What a nice Grandma!" he said quietly.

Suddenly the wolf leapt over the garden wall. Grandma was very frightened.

The wolf landed on the long, sharp thorns. They went into his feet. "Ouch!" he screamed.

"Go away, you horrible animal!" shouted Grandma. She was very brave.

The wolf hopped away as fast as he could. "Ouch! Ouch! My feet hurt!" he said. "She wasn't a nice Grandma!"

Activity 3 1E 2C 3A 4F 5D 6B

WB answers
Phonics (p16)
Exercise 2 1 pushed 2 full 3 bull 4 put 5 pulling

Use of English (p17)
Exercise 2 1 said the wolf
2 Red Riding Hood said
3 Her mother said
4 said Red Riding Hood

Exercise 4 1 said the wolf
2 said Red Riding Hood
3 shouted Red Riding Hood
4 said the woodcutter

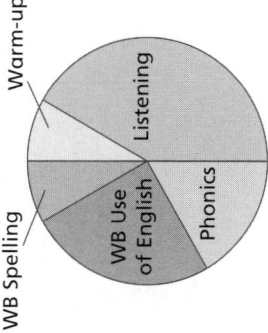

Time division
Warm-up
Listening
Phonics
WB Use of English
WB Spelling

Unit 2 Phonics, Use of English   47

Lesson 6 Class composition (Session 1) (PB p37) Writing preparation, Composition practice (Session 2)

Lesson aim Writing

Lesson targets Children:
- (session 1) compose a traditional story with teacher support
- (session 2) (WB) practise past tense verbs and prepositions for the composition
- (session 2) (WB) write a traditional story independently using prompt words

Key structure and language from Unit 2
Key vocabulary verbs used to tell a traditional story
Materials PB p37; WB pp18–19; CD A track 14

Session 1 Warm-up

This task shows children how a story is divided into a beginning, middle and end. Write up *Beginning, Middle, End*. Help the class to divide *Red Riding Hood*, e.g.
beginning *Red Riding Hood went to see her grandmother. She met a wolf in the woods and she talked to him.*
middle *Red Riding Hood arrived at her grandmother's house but when she saw her grandmother she thought she was strange.*
end *Red Riding Hood's father came into the cottage The wolf ran away. Her father opened a cupboard. Grandmother was safe inside.*
Explain to the class that stories have a clear beginning, middle and end.

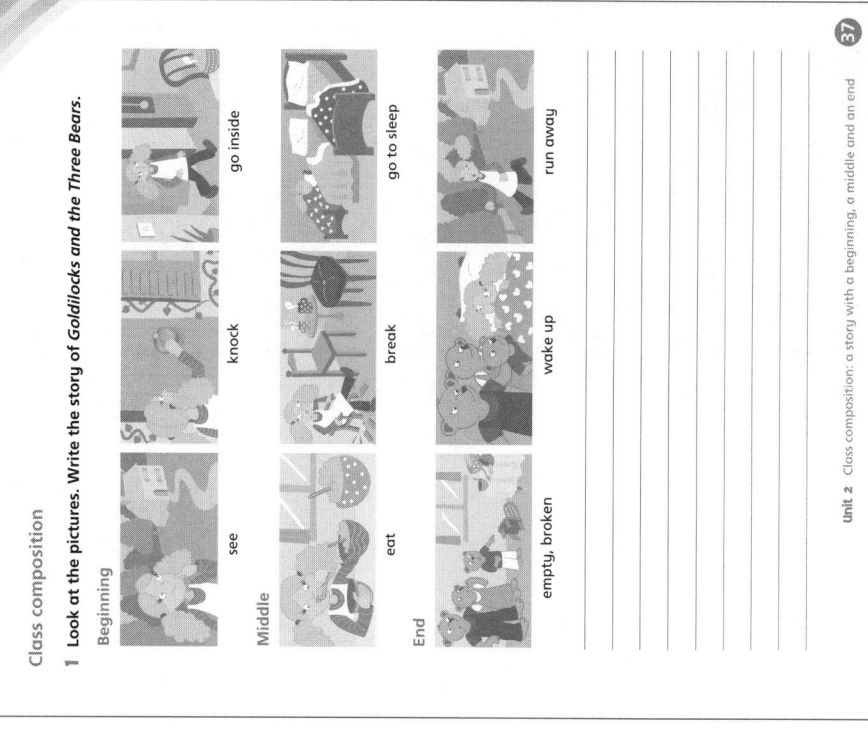

Class composition

1 Look at the pictures. Write the story of *Goldilocks and the Three Bears*.
Beginning — see, go inside
Middle — eat, break, knock, wake up
End — empty, broken, run away, go to sleep

Class composition

Activity 1

1 Ask the class questions about each picture, e.g. picture 1: *Where was Goldilocks walking? What did she see?* Tell them to make notes for each section of the story.

2 Help the class to compose three paragraphs from the notes and prompt phrases. Let them add as much detail as they can think of from the pictures. The story can be more or less detailed depending on the ability of your class. Some children may suggest direct speech. Include this a few times if they do.

3 When the writing is completed on the board ask different children to read a paragraph. After each one, ask *Can we make the story better? Does it need more adjectives? Does it need any adverbs?* Make any changes that you and the class agree to.

4 Erase the writing from the board. Children write the story in their books. Remind them to use the pictures and prompt words to help them. Make sure they realise they do not need to include the words *Beginning, Middle, End* in their stories.
Tell the class they may add in extra ideas of their own if they wish. They should continue on paper or in copy books if they need more space.

Their written versions may be simpler than what was on the board, but encourage them to write in as much detail as they can.
Children's writing will vary according to ability. The example writing suggests the range that could be expected.

Unit 2 Class composition

Writing preparation, Composition practice (WB pp18–19)

Session 2 Warm-up

Sing the working song on PB page 27, track 14.

Exercises 1 and 2

Children complete these working alone or in pairs. Set a time limit. Check answers together.

Exercise 3

Read the paragraph to the class.

Exercise 4

1 Explain that the pictures on page 19 tell the story of the race between the hare and the tortoise.

2 Children look at the pictures and read the words above them. Check understanding, e.g. *Who was in the race? a hare and a tortoise*
Which animal was winning at first? the hare
What did the hare do? He slept.
Who won the race? the tortoise

3 Remind the class that the story has a beginning, a middle and an end. They must write a paragraph for each of these.
They can use the pictures, the words above the pictures and words on page 18 to help them.

4 Children write the story. They should be able to write three paragraphs of four or five sentences. Some children will write very simple sentences. Other children will be able to write more.

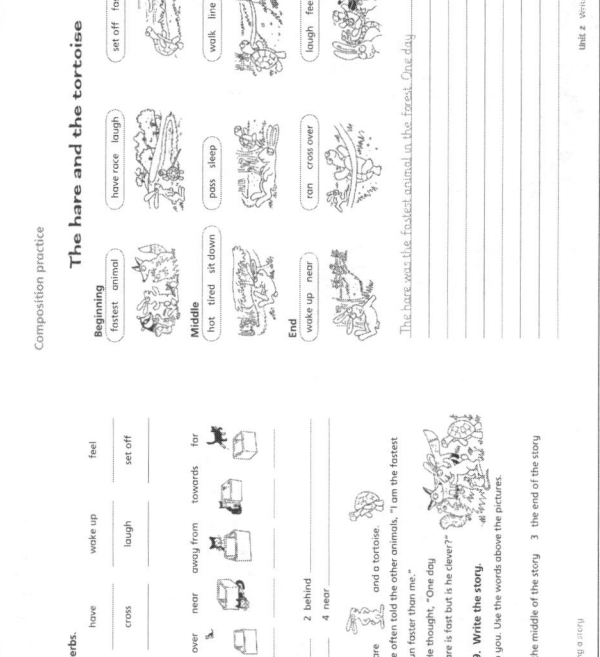

5 Go around helping and monitoring as they work. If necessary, children complete the story in their copy books. When they have finished or at the end of the lesson, ask one or two children to read some or all of their work to the class.

Homework task

Children complete Check-up 2, WB p20. For answers, see p65

Time division

Session 1

- Class composition writing in books
- Class composition writing in teacher-led board writing
- Warm-up

Session 2

- Writing preparation
- Composition practice
- Warm-up

Portfolio

Children may make neat copies of their stories and illustrate them.

Resource box

Class composition example writing (p37)

Simple narrative (see p65 for a narrative with more detail)

Goldilocks saw a little house. She knocked on the door. She went inside.
She ate the food in the smallest bowl. She broke the smallest chair. She went to sleep in the smallest bed.
The bears saw the empty bowl and the chair. They saw Goldilocks. Goldilocks woke up. She saw the bears and then she ran away.

WB answers

Composition practice example writing (p19)

The hare was the fastest animal in the forest. One day the tortoise and the hare had a race. The hare laughed at the tortoise. They set off. The hare ran very fast and the tortoise walked very slowly.
The hare was hot and tired. He sat down under a tree. The tortoise passed the hare. The hare was sleeping. The tortoise walked slowly towards the line.
The hare woke up. He saw the tortoise. The tortoise was near the line. The hare ran fast but the tortoise crossed the line first. The other animals laughed and the hare felt very silly.

Unit 2 Writing preparation, Composition practice

3 Water birds

Lesson 1 Poster 3, Reading

Lesson aim Reading

Text type Information with labels and captions

Lesson targets Children:
- read, understand and practise new vocabulary on the poster
- read, understand and practise reading the information
- answer oral comprehension questions

Key structure comparative and superlative of longer adjectives

Key language comparison: *not as beautiful as; as strong as*

Key vocabulary *birds, nature*

Materials PB pp38–39; poster 3; CD A track 27; Dictionary 4; word cards for poster vocabulary (see poster 3 below or list on p14)

Preparation make word cards; listen to CD A track 27

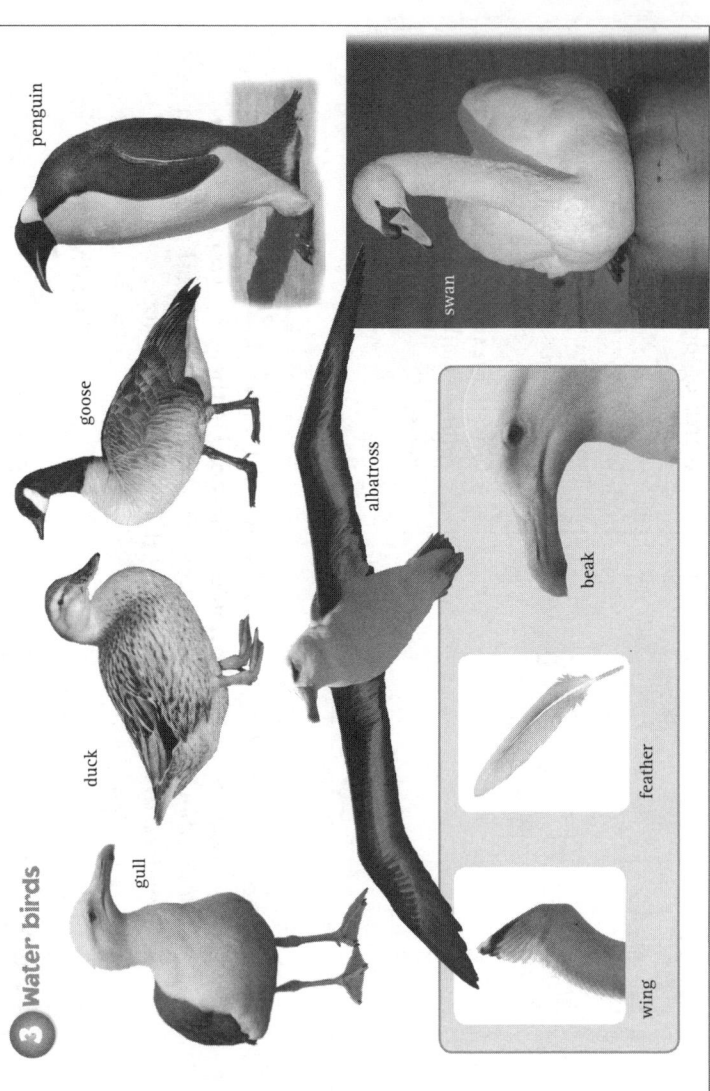

3 Water birds

Warm-up

Ask different children what their favourite animals are. Ask why they like them.

Poster 3

1 Point to the poster. Read out the title. Give the class a moment or two to look.

2 Point to the birds and parts of birds. Read the word. Show the word card/s. Class reads and says the word/s.
Make sure that children understand that these words are the names of different kinds of birds: *albatross, goose, gull, penguin*. Encourage the class to repeat the words accurately.
Cover the words on the poster if you wish.
Point to the birds and parts at random. Class names them.

3 Ask if anyone has a bird at home. Ask what kind of bird it is. *Does it live in a cage? Who looks after it?*

4 Ask *Do know anything about any of these birds. Where do they live? What can they do?*

5 Ask *Do you know any stories about any of these birds?* Children should be able to mention 'The ugly duckling'.

Reading (PB pp38–39)

1. Give children time to look at the pictures. Read the title. Ask which birds they can see on these pages.

2. Play track 27. Children listen and follow in their books.

3. Read one paragraph or section of the text at a time. Use *Dictionary 4* to help you to explain new words as necessary. Help children to find new words. Make up extra sentences for new words if you wish.

4. Ask questions about each paragraph or a section of the text. See Resource box. Ask other questions if you wish.

5. Give reading practice around the class. Ask individuals, groups or the class to read sentences or paragraphs. Play track 27 again.

Homework task

Children learn selected vocabulary from Unit 3, *Dictionary 4*. See unit word list on pp190–191 for key words, extension words and words for understanding only.

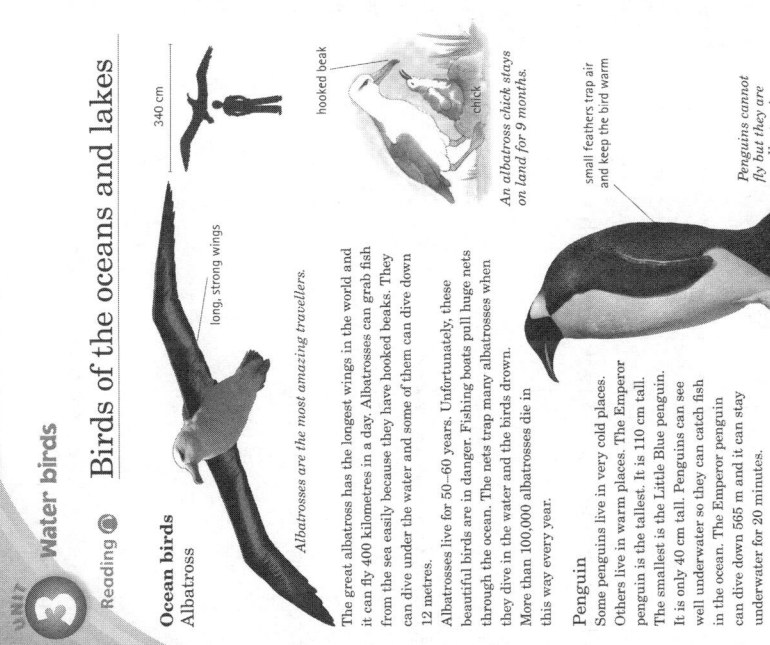

Resource box

Text questions

How far can an albatross fly in a day? **400 km**

What do albatrosses eat? **fish**

How long do albatross chicks stay on land? **9 months**

Why are the albatrosses in danger? **Fishing nets trap them and they drown.**

How many drown every year? **more than 100,000**

What is the tallest penguin? **the Emperor penguin**

What is the smallest penguin? **the Little Blue penguin**

How do a penguin's feathers keep it warm? **They trap air.**

How many eggs does a mother swan lay? **4–7**

What are a swans feet like? **webbed**

Where do swans live? **rivers and small lakes**

Where do geese live? **on farms; near water**

What is a baby goose called? **a gosling**

Time division

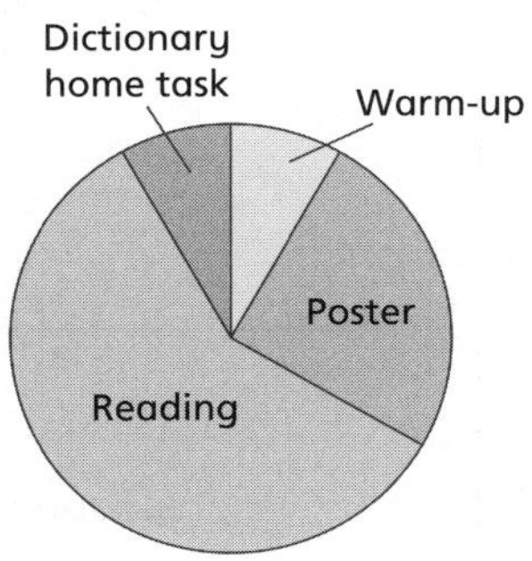

(pie chart: Poster, Warm-up, Dictionary home task, Reading)

Unit 3 Reading

Lesson 2 Reading comprehension and vocabulary (PB p40)

Lesson aim Reading comprehension; vocabulary

Lesson targets Children re-read *Birds of oceans and lakes* then:
- (PB) multiple choice; personal response questions
- identify verbs and nouns; match to meanings and pictures
- (WB) identify nouns and adjectives
- match descriptions to pictures; match words to definitions

Key structure comparative and superlative of longer adjectives

Key language comparison: *not as beautiful as*; *as strong as*

Words vocabulary from Lesson 1

Materials PB p40; CD A tracks 24, 27 (optional); WB p22; Dictionary 4

Warm-up

Sing the seeking song from PB page 35, track 24.

Read again

Remind children of *Birds of oceans and lakes*.
Play track 27 or read the text to the class. Children listen and follow in their books.

Activity 1

Give children a few minutes to read all the sentences.
Read the first sentence with the choice of answers. Tell children they should look back at the text to check their answer or to find it. Elicit an answer.
Ask the rest of the class if the answer given was correct.
If there is disagreement, ask the whole class to look back and find the sentence where the answer is.
Continue with the other sentences. Encourage children to scan the text to check.

Activity 2

Children give their own answers to questions 1 and 2. Encourage them to say as much as they can.
Ask for suggestions to the answer for 3.

Activity 3

Children read and circle. Check answers together.
Ask a volunteer to read the first definition. Ask for the word. Tell children to look in their dictionaries if they need to. Check the answer together. Children write.
Children write the nouns under the pictures. Check answers together.

Reading comprehension and vocabulary

1 Circle the correct numbers and words.
1 In one day an albatross can fly **4** / **40** / **400** kilometres.
2 Albatrosses can grab fish easily because they have hooked **beaks** / **feet** / **wings**.
3 Albatrosses are in danger because of fishing **lines** / **nets** / **boats**.
4 An Emperor penguin can dive down **5.65** / **56.5** / **565** metres.
5 Water birds have webbed feet so they can **fly** / **swim** / **run** quickly.
6 A baby swan is a **chick** / **cygnet** / **gosling**.
7 The plural of *goose* is *goose* / *gosling* / *geese*.

2 Think about the answers to these questions.
1 Which bird is the most beautiful? Why?
2 Which bird is the most interesting? Why?
3 Can we help the albatrosses? How?

3 Underline the verbs. Circle the nouns

trap   lay   beak   twig   dive   branch   net   die   toe   lake   drown

Write the correct verb next to each definition.
1 to go head first into water _____
2 to catch _____
3 to stop living _____
4 to die in water _____
5 to make an egg come out _____

Write the correct noun under each picture.

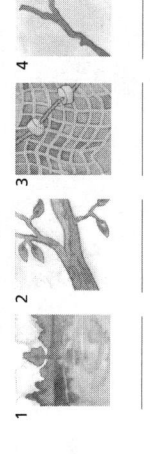

1 _____ 2 _____ 3 _____ 4 _____ 5 _____ 6 _____

40 Reading comprehension and vocabulary: multiple choice; personal response; definitions

---

Unit 3 Reading comprehension and vocabulary

Reading comprehension and vocabulary (WB p22)

If children are doing this page for homework, make sure they understand the tasks.

Exercise 1
Children read and circle.

Exercise 2
Children underline the correct answer.

Exercise 3
Children name the birds in the pictures and match descriptions to pictures.

Exercise 4
Children write the words. Tell them they may check their ideas in the dictionary as they complete the exercise.

UNIT 3 Reading comprehension and vocabulary

1 Circle the words for birds.

albatross   webbed   penguin   goose   hooked   gull
geese   wild   chick   graceful   gosling   cygnet

2 Look at the words that are not circled. What are they? Underline A, B, C or D.

A verbs   B adverbs   C adjectives   D nouns

3 Write the name of the bird.

a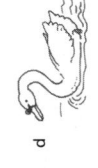
b
c
d

Now match the description to the picture. Write the letter.

1 It is usually white and it is a graceful bird. It has a long neck and it lives on lakes and rivers. It builds an enormous nest near the water. Picture _____
2 It can dive and it can swim fast. It has webbed feet. It can see well under water and it catches fish. It is black and white. It can live in a cold place. Picture _____
3 It has strong white wings and it is a beautiful bird. It has a hooked beak. It is in danger because fishing nets can trap it. Picture _____
4 It has a long neck. It can fly and it can swim. It is a wild bird and it lives on lakes and rivers. You can also find this bird on farms. Picture _____

4 Match the words in the box with the definitions. Write the words. You may check in your dictionary.

| lake |
| skin |
| adult |
| parent |
| danger |

1 something that can kill or hurt a person or animal _____
2 water with land all round it _____
3 the outside covering of a person's or animal's body _____
4 a grown-up person or animal _____
5 a mother or father _____

Unit 3 Identifying parts of speech; matching; definitions

22

Resource box

PB answers
Activity 1 1 400 2 beaks 3 nets 4 565 5 swim 6 cygnet 7 geese

Activity 2 1, 2 children's own answers
3 children may suggest: smaller nets; no fishing in the ocean; no fishing in part of the ocean

Activity 3
1 dive 2 trap 3 die 4 drown 5 lay
1 lake 2 branch 3 net 4 twig 5 beak 6 toe

WB answers
Exercise 1 1 albatross, penguin, goose, gull, geese, chick, gosling, cygnet
Exercise 2 C adjectives
Exercise 3 a goose b albatross c penguin d swan;
1d 2c 3b 4a
Exercise 4 1 danger 2 lake 3 skin 4 adult 5 parent

Time division

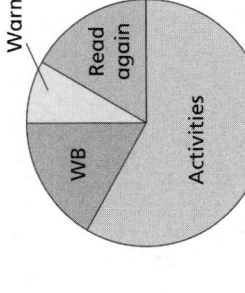

Warm-up, Read again, Activities, WB

Unit 3 Reading comprehension and vocabulary   53

Lesson 3 Speaking (PB p41) Study skills

Lesson aim Speaking, (WB) Study skills

Lesson targets Children:
- listen to a dialogue; listen and repeat the dialogue
- understand the story and answer oral questions
- read and act the dialogue
- (WB) practise dictionary skills

Informal everyday language *Come and see! Here you are. Oh dear! What next?*

New words *put on, much, ridiculous, disaster, fit*

Materials PB p41; CD A tracks 28, 29; WB p23; Dictionary 4

Preparation Listen to CD A track 28 before the lesson

Warm-up
Ask children if they can remember what happened in the last part of *Let's put on a play!* Ask *What went wrong?*

Activity 1
Children look at PB page 41. Read the title of Part 3. Ask *What are the children doing wearing costumes*
Tell children to cover the dialogue text and look at the pictures. Play track 28. Children listen.

Activity 2
Children open their books and look at the dialogue. Play track 28 again.
Children listen and follow.
Check children understand the new words. Use Dictionary 4 if you wish.

Activity 3
Children close their books. Play track 29. Children listen and repeat in the pauses. Encourage them to use the same expression and intonation.

Activity 4
Ask questions to check understanding of the story. See Resource box.

Activity 5
Children act the dialogue without their books if possible.
Encourage children to speak without reading their lines word by word if they have their books with them.
If they are reading from their places, encourage them to look up and turn towards the other characters when they speak.

Unit 3 Speaking

Study skills (WB p23)

The exercises on this page practise sorting and dictionary skills. Children should be able to do this work independently once the tasks have been explained.

Exercise 1
Children draw lines to the number of legs then write the animals in the correct list.

Exercise 2
Children order the words alphabetically.

Resource box

Story questions
What is Molly wearing in the play? *a dress*
What is Lulu's costume? *a swan with an orange beak*
What is wrong with Molly's dress? *It's too long.*
What is wrong with Max's hat? *It's too small.*
What is wrong with Alfie's feet? *They're too big.*
What has Lulu not got? *any wings*

WB answers
Study skills
Exercise 1 No legs: snake, whale, shark; Two legs: baby, penguin, goose; Four legs: wolf, horse, lion; Six legs: butterfly, dragonfly; Eight legs: spider
Exercise 2 1 albatross duck gull penguin swan
2 beak eggs feather nest wing
3 catch dive fly jump swim

Time division

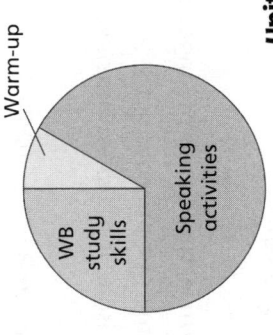

Warm-up / WB study skills / Speaking activities

Study skills

1 How many legs? Draw lines.

0 2 4 6 8

Now write the words.

No legs:
Two legs:
Four legs:
Six legs:
Eight legs:

2 Write the words in the correct order.

1	gull	swan	albatross	duck	penguin
2	wing	feather	beak	nest	eggs
3	fly	swim	dive	jump	catch

a b c d e f g h i j k l m n o p q r s t u v w x y z

Unit 3 Sorting; dictionary skills

Unit 3 Study skills

55

Lesson 4 Grammar (Session 1), Grammar in conversation (Session 2) (PB pp42–43)

Lesson aim Grammar

Lesson targets Children:
- (session 1) understand and practise the key structure
- (session 2) listen to and read a conversation; repeat and practise it
- (session 2) listen to a riddle, say it and learn it (optional)

Key structure (session 1) comparative, superlative of longer adjectives

Key vocabulary adjectives from this and previous units

Key language (session 2) comparison: *as old as, not as clever as*

Informal expressions *Me, too.*

Materials PB pp42–43; CD A tracks 30–32; WB pp24–25

Session 1 Warm-up

Bring three children forward of different heights. Arrange them in order. Ask *Who is the tallest? Who is the smallest?*

Activity 1

Children look at the pictures. Ask a child to read the prices. Ask a pair to read the PC kids' bubbles. Write up *expensive* and *more expensive*. Ask a child to read the adjectives in the box. Point to the first two pictures. Say *This flower is beautiful. This flower is more beautiful.* Help the class make statements about the other objects.

Activity 2

Ask a child to read the bubbles. Write them on the board. Explain the rule for using longer adjectives to compare two things and more than two.

Help the class to compose three sentences about the three objects in each row. See Resource box.*

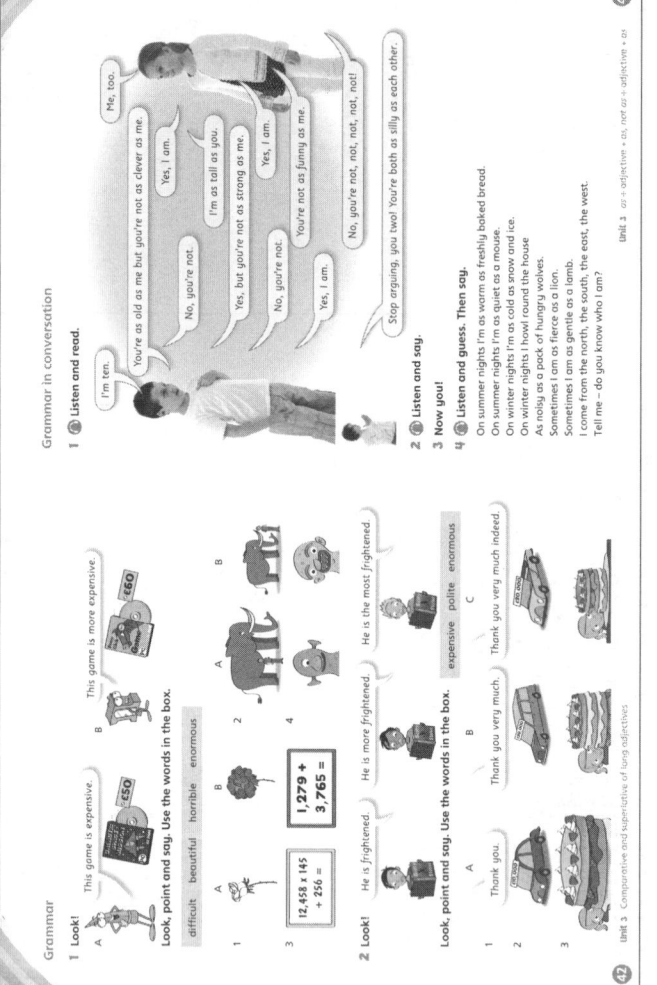

Session 2 Warm-up

Play *Simon says* (see Games, page 186).

Activity 1

Point out the boy and girl. Tell the class to listen to them. Play track 30. Children follow in their books.

Activity 2

Children listen to track 31 and repeat in the pauses.

Activity 3

Children practise the conversation in pairs. See Resource box.**

Activity 4

Play track 32. Children listen and follow. Read the words with the class. Help with any new words. Ask if they know what the answer is: *the wind*. Play track 32 again. They may learn this riddle if you wish.

Children complete WB page 24 in class time or for homework.

Grammar (Session 1), Grammar in conversation (Session 2) (WB pp24–25)

If this page is for homework, check children understand the tasks.

Exercise 1
Children write sentences comparing two things.
Go through this orally first if you wish.

Exercise 2
Children arrange the words to make sentences using the superlative form of longer adjectives.

If this page is for homework, check children understand the tasks.
Check they are able to form the structure correctly.

Exercises 1 and 2
Go through these sentences orally first if you wish.

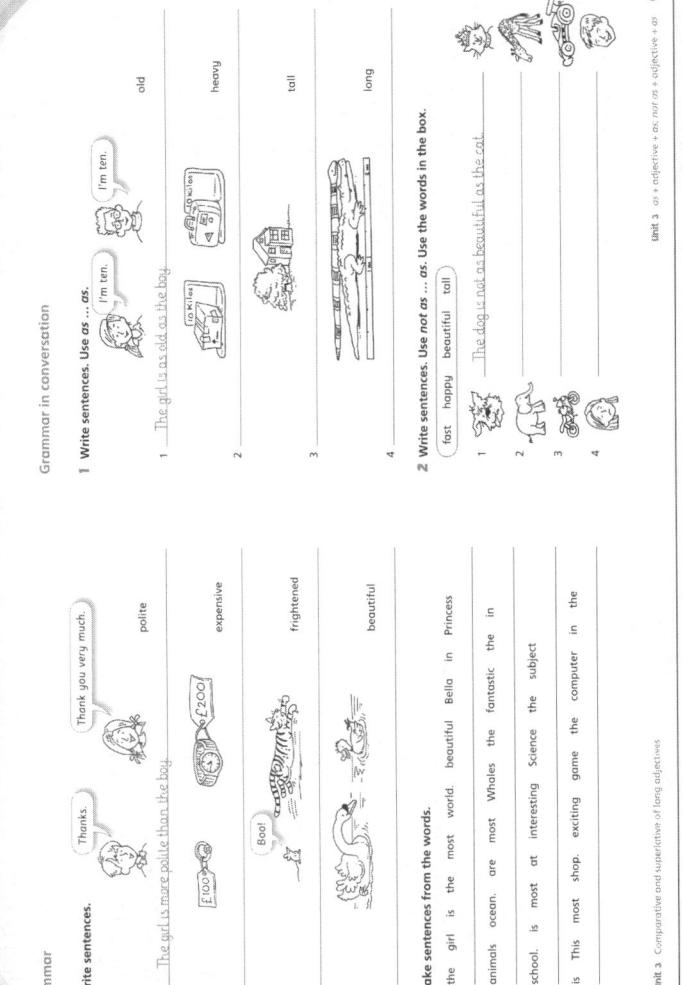

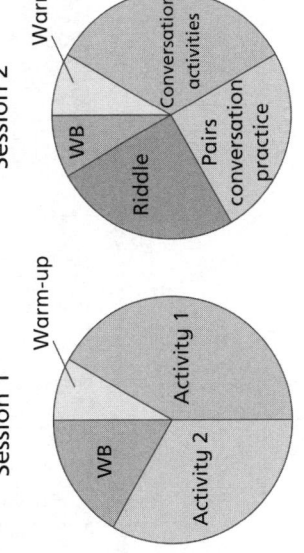

Time division

Session 1 — Warm-up, Activity 1, Activity 2, WB

Session 2 — Warm-up, Conversation activities, Pairs conversation practice, Riddle, WB

Grammar Practice Book
Children may begin Unit 3 when they have completed the PB and WB Grammar pages. They should complete it before the end of PB / WB Unit 3.

Resource box

PB answers

Pair work: Grammar (p42)

Activity 1
Children work in pairs at their desks. They take turns to point and make two statements about each set of pictures.

***Activity 2**
Children take turns to point and make three statements. You may wish to practise this with some pairs in front of the class before other children work in pairs at their desks.

Pair work: Grammar in conversation (p43)

****Activity 3**
Children practise the dialogue in pairs at their desks. Give pairs three minutes to practise the dialogue.
Let one or two pairs stand up and say the dialogue or act it in front of the class. Encourage them to speak with expression.

WB answers

Grammar (p24)

Exercise 1 2 The watch is more expensive than the ring.
3 The cat is more frightened than the mouse.
4 The swan is more beautiful than the duck.

Exercise 2 1 Princess Bella is the most beautiful girl in the world.   2 Whales are the most fantastic animals in the ocean.   3 Science is the most interesting subject at school.   4 This is the most exciting computer game in the shop.

Grammar in conversation (p25)

Exercise 1 2 The box is as heavy as the bag.
3 The tree is as tall as the house.
4 The snake is as long as the crocodile.

Exercise 2 1 The dog is not as beautiful as the cat.
2 The elephant is not as tall as the giraffe.
3 The motorbike is not as fast as the car.
4 The girl is not as happy as the boy.

Unit 3 Grammar, Grammar in conversation

57

Lesson 5 Listening, Phonics (PB p44) Use of English (WB pp26–27)

Lesson aim Listening, spelling and pronunciation, Use of English (WB)

Lesson targets Children:
- listen to descriptions of birds and identify them in photographs
- listen for specific information; give personal opinions about birds
- practise saying, reading and spelling words with short *e*
- (WB) learn about conjunctions *because* and *so*

Key structure and language from Unit 3

Target words *head, bread, spread, thread, feather, weather*

Materials PB p44; CD A track 34; WB pp26–27

Warm-up
Say the poem from PB page 43, track 32.

Listening

Activity 1
Read the words in the box to the class. Ask *What are these?* Elicit **birds**. Ask *Which birds do you know?* Children know *swan* and *penguin*. They should remember *eagle* from level 2. *Flamingo* and *peacock* are new.
Tell them to listen to descriptions of all the birds.
Play track 33. They write the names as they listen. Pause for them to write if necessary.
Check answers together.

Activity 2
Ask a volunteer to read out the questions.
Play track 33 again. Children listen and write the answers.
Be ready to play the track again if necessary. Check answers together.

Activity 3
Children give their views. Encourage them to say as much as they can.

Phonics
Point out the box. Tell children to follow in their books and repeat in the pauses.
Play the first part of track 34. Make sure children repeat accurately.
Play the end of track 34. Children listen and follow.
Children say the poem. They may learn it, if you wish.
Children open their WBs at page 26. They may complete the Phonics page for homework. If it is for homework, make sure they understand the tasks.

Listening

1 Listen and write the names.

swan   flamingo   eagle   penguin   peacock

2 Listen again and answer the questions.
1 Which birds live in, on or near water?
2 Which bird eats small animals?
3 Which bird lives in the mountains?
4 Which bird cannot fly?

3 What do you think? Say why.
1 Which bird is the most beautiful?
2 Which bird is the most graceful?
3 Which bird is the strongest?
4 Which bird is the funniest?
5 Which bird do you like the best?

Phonics
Look and listen!

ea   The swan's head is white.

In the cold winter weather
Wind blows the swan's feathers.
Head under its wing,
It is waiting for spring.

44 unit 3 Listening: identifying; listening for gist and detail. Phonics: the short *ea* vowel sound

→ Now look at WB p27 Use of English

Use of English
Move on to WB page 27.

Phonics, Use of English (WB pp26–27)

Remind the class of the sound *ea* and *head*.

Exercise 1 Children complete the words, write the whole words and read them.
Exercise 2 Children write the words under the correct picture.
Exercise 3 Children complete the sentences.

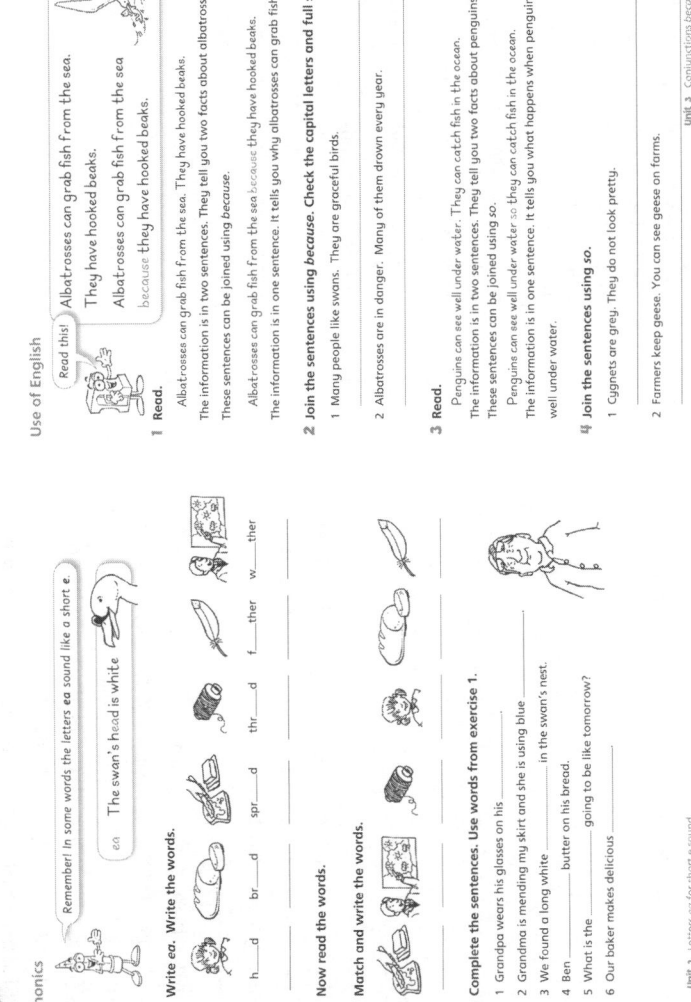

Write the three sentences on the board. Class reads.

Exercise 1 Go through the presentation with the class.
Exercise 2 Children suggest how to join the sentences. Write them on the board. Children write in their books.
Exercise 3 Write the sentences on the board and give the explanation.
Exercise 4 Children suggest how to join the sentences. Write them on the board. Children write in their books.

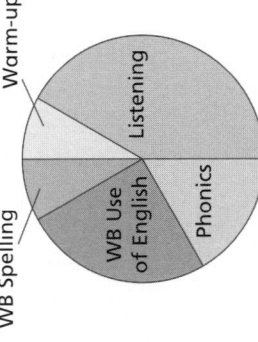

Time division

WB Spelling, Warm-up, Listening, Phonics, WB Use of English

Resource box

Audioscript (CD A track 33) **Listening activity 2** (PB p44)
The swan is a large white bird with a long neck and an orange beak. It lives on lakes and rivers. It is very graceful.

The flamingo is also a water bird. It has a large hooked beak and very long legs. Its feathers are pink and white. It lives in warm countries.

The eagle lives in the mountains. It has a sharp beak and strong claws. It catches small animals.

The penguin lives in and near the sea. It is an excellent swimmer but it cannot fly. Its feathers are black and white. It lives in cold or warm places.

The peacock is a very beautiful bird. It has an amazing long tail. Its feathers are green and blue and gold. They shine in the sun.

PB answers

Activity 1 1 eagle 2 peacock 3 penguin 4 flamingo 5 swan
Activity 2 1 the swan, the flamingo, the penguin 2 the eagle 3 the eagle 4 the penguin

WB answers

Phonics (p26)
Exercise 2 spread weather thread head bread feather
Exercise 3 1 head 2 thread 3 feather 4 spreads 5 weather 6 bread

Use of English (p27)
Exercise 2 1 Many people like swans because they are graceful birds. 2 Albatrosses are in danger because many of them drown every year.
Exercise 3 1 Cygnets are grey so they do not look pretty. 2 Farmers keep geese so you can see geese on farms.

Unit 3 Phonics, Use of English

Lesson 6 Class composition (Session 1) (PB p45) Writing preparation, Composition practice (Session 2)

Lesson aim Writing

Lesson targets Children:
- (session 1) write a paragraph about gulls with teacher support, using notes
- (session 2) (WB) make notes about ducks using information in pictures
- (session 2) (WB) label a picture; write a paragraph using notes and labels

Key structure and language from Unit 3

Key vocabulary birds and nature

Materials PB p45; WB pp28–29; poster 3

Session 1 Warm-up

Put up poster 3. Make statements about the birds and children guess which bird it is, e.g. *This bird is white. It swims on lakes and rivers.* **swan** *This bird lives in the Antarctic. It can swim well underwater.* **penguin** Do the same with the parts of the bird, e.g. *Some birds use this to catch fish.* **beak**

Class composition

Activity 1

Give children a minute or two to look at the picture. Ask a volunteer to read out the words in the box.
Children label the picture.

Activity 2

Ask one or more volunteers to read out the notes. Remind the class that these are not complete sentences.

Activity 3

1 Help the class to use the notes to write two paragraphs about gulls. The first paragraph is about where gulls live, their nests and eggs. The second paragraph is about what they eat and where they go to find food.

2 Ask volunteers to read each paragraph when it is completed and both paragraphs are on the board. Tell the class to look at the writing. Ask if there are any details missing that they could add in. Put in any good detail the class can suggest, e.g. the colour of the eggs. When any extra details have been added in, ask volunteers to read the two paragraphs again.
Erase the writing from the board. Children write in their books. Remind them that they have the notes to help them. If necessary they should continue the writing in their copy books.

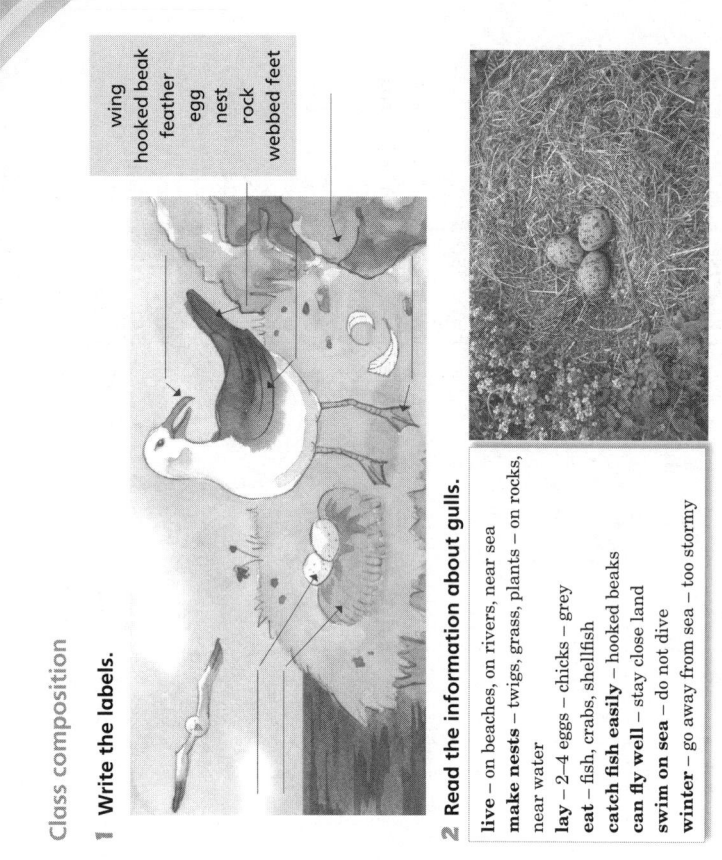

Class composition

1 Write the labels.

wing
hooked beak
feather
egg
nest
rock
webbed feet

2 Read the information about gulls.

live – on beaches, on rivers, near sea
make nests – twigs, grass, plants – on rocks, near water
lay – 2–4 eggs – chicks – grey
eat – fish, crabs, shellfish
catch fish easily – hooked beaks
can fly well – stay close land
swim on sea – do not dive
winter – go away from sea – too stormy

3 Write about gulls.

Unit 3 Class composition: information with labels and pictures

Writing preparation, Composition practice (WB pp28–29)

Session 2 Warm-up

Class names as many birds as they can in one minute.

Exercise 1

Children look at the pictures. Talk with the class about the ducks and what they do. Ask questions as appropriate, e.g. *Where do ducks live? How do they make nests?*, etc.

Exercise 2

Children write notes about ducks using the pictures to help them. Give them a time limit. While they work, write the exercise on the board. Check answers together.

The exact notes may vary a little, but children should have more or less the same information to help them write on page 29.

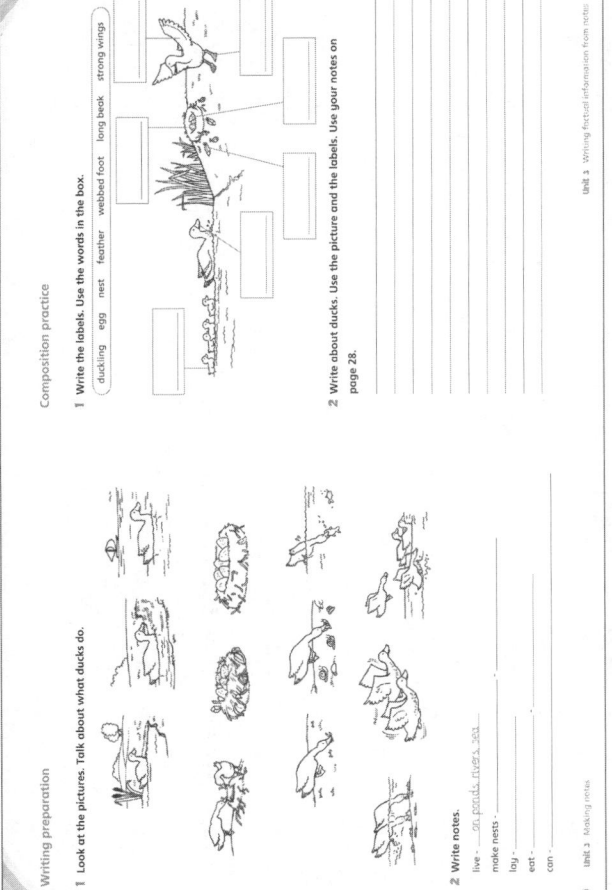

Exercise 1

Children label the picture. They should do this independently.

Exercise 2

Children write about ducks. Encourage them to write two paragraphs: paragraph 1 – where ducks live, their nest and eggs; paragraph 2 – what they eat and where they go to find food. If children forget about paragraphing, one paragraph is acceptable: correct paragraphing will come with practice. Remind the class to use the notes on page 28 and the picture and labels on this page to help them with ideas for writing.

Go around helping and monitoring. When they have finished, or before the end of the lesson, ask one or more children to read their paragraphs to the class.

Homework task

Children complete Check-up 3, WB p30. For answers, see p65.

Resource box

Class composition example writing (p45)

Gulls live on beaches and on rivers near the sea. They make nests from twigs, grass and plants. They build their nests on rocks or in plants near the water. The mother gulls lay 2–4 eggs. The chicks are grey. Gulls eat fish, crabs and shellfish. They can fly well but they have hooked beaks. They can catch fish easily because they have hooked beaks. They can fly well but they stay close to land. They can swim on the sea but they do not dive underwater. In winter they go away from the sea because it is too stormy.

WB answers (p28)

Exercise 2 make nests from twigs, grass, plants – near water;
lay – 4–6 eggs;
eat grass, snails – weed, fish;
can – fly, land on water, swim and put heads underwater

Composition practice example writing (p29)

Ducks live on ponds and rivers. Some ducks live on the sea. They make nests from twigs, grass and plants. They build their nests near the water. The mother duck lays 4–6 eggs. A baby duck is a duckling. Ducks have long beaks. They eat grass and snails. They can put their heads under the water. They catch fish and they eat plants under the water. Ducks have strong wings so they can fly well. They can land on the water.

Time division

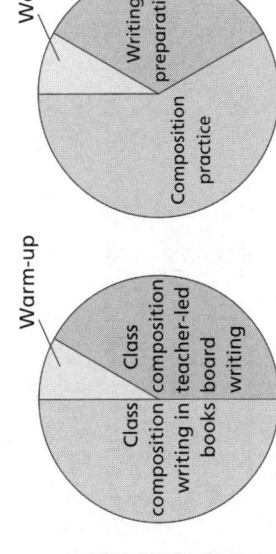

Session 1 — Class composition writing in books / Class composition teacher-led board writing / Warm-up

Session 2 — Composition practice / Writing preparation / Warm-up

Portfolio

Children may make neat copies of their work. Encourage them to add pictures and to label them.

Unit 3 Writing preparation, Composition practice

Revision 1, Project 1

Activity 1

Children look at the pictures for a moment. Explain they show different school clubs yesterday.

Ask a volunteer to read out the names under the small pictures at the top of the page.

Ask one or more children to read out the names of the children in the other two pictures.

Activity 2

Ask *What clubs were there yesterday?* Children name the eight clubs.

Ask about the children at the top of the page, e.g. *What did Pete do? He went to swimming club. What did he do at swimming club? He swam in the pool.*

Ask about the computer club, e.g. *What did the children do? They made an animation. What was in the animation? What birds were there?* Children name the three birds: *albatross, swan, penguin.*

Ask *Which bird did Andy / Meg / Freddy have in his/her animation?*

Extra activities

Class games

Play in teams. Make statements, e.g. *She went to Music Club.* Children name the person: *Molly*

The first team to answer correctly wins a point.

Use these statements or any others of your own:

In his animation there was a penguin. **Freddy**
She sang in the choir. **Anna**
His hat was too small. **Max**
He went to Chess Club. **Tom**
His head fell off. **Alfie**
She put swans in her animation. **Meg**
She threw a basketball. **Amy**
He swam very fast. **Pete**
Her dress was too long. **Molly**
Her costume was too big. **Lulu**
He kicked a football. **Sam**
His trousers were too short. **Max**
His animation had an albatross in it. **Andy**

Pair work

Children take turns to point to a person on the page. Their partner makes a statement about the person.

Revision 1

1 Look and read the names.

Pete Anna Tom Candy Sam Amy

Andy Meg Freddy Lulu Molly Max Alfie

2 Think about these questions. Talk about the children.

What clubs were there yesterday? What did Pete do? What did the other children do?
Look at the Computer Club. What birds were in the animations?
Look at the Drama Club. Where were the children? What were they doing?
What were their costumes like?
Whose costume was too big? too small? too long? too short?
Who looked the most ridiculous?

 Revision

Ask about the Drama Club.
Use the questions on the page and ask any others of your own.

My club

In this project children write about any club they go to.
If some children do not go to a club at all, they may choose one of the clubs from PB page 46.

Activity 1

Talk with the class about the clubs that they go to.
Write the names of the clubs on the board.
Ask different children who go to a club what they do there.
Children write their answer to one or both of the questions.

Activity 2

Explain the task to the class. Make sure all children have chosen a club.
Go through the questions with the class.
Encourage them to answer these questions in their writing and to add in any other information they can.

All children should be able to complete this project working at their own level. Depending on your class, you may wish them to write on paper, in a book, or to make a poster with their writing stuck onto it with a picture.
Encourage them to use their dictionaries to find words they need and to check spelling.

Activity 3

Children draw or find a picture to illustrate their writing. If some children go to a school club, there may be photographs of these activities already or some could be taken.

Activity 4

Children present their work to the rest of the class. They read out their writing and show their pictures.
Display all the work if possible and encourage children to read each other's work.

Project 1: My club

1 Answer these questions.

Do you go to a club in school? What is it?
Do you go to a club out of school? What do you do there?

2 Write about your school club or another club.

Write what you did there last week.
or
Choose one of the clubs on page 46. It is your club. You went last week. Say what you did.

Think about these questions:
What happened? Was it fun? Was it difficult?
What could you do? What couldn't you do?
Were your friends there? Who was there?

3 Draw a picture of what you did or find a photograph of your club.

4 Talk about your club.

I go to Basketball Club. Last week we practised. We threw balls at the goal. It wasn't easy. I could not score a goal. Then we played a game. I was in the red team. My friend, Jenny was in the red team too. We... Jenny took this picture at Basketball Club on Wednesday. We practised again and it was fun. I scored...

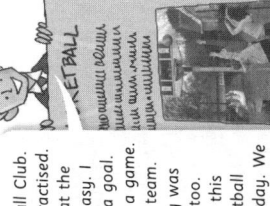

I go to Music Club and I play in the orchestra. Last week we practised... Then we played ... I sat next to my friend... She played ... It was ... This is a picture of the orchestra. You can see...

Project 47

Summary box

Lesson aim Revision

Lesson targets Children:
- talk about school clubs and what different children did
- write and draw about a club that they go to, or a club they have read about in the PB
- read out their work to the class

Resource box

Portfolio

If you wish, this project may be included in children's portfolio of written work.

Before starting Unit 4 you may wish children to complete PDF test 1.

Project 1

Portfolio 1 and Diploma 1: Units 1-3

1. When children have completed all the work in Units 1–3, they turn to page 129 in their Workbook.

2. This page allows children to make their own assessment of what they have learned in English.

Vocabulary
Tell children to tick each box only when they are confident that they know the words in each category.

Grammar
Children tick the boxes when they are confident of the tenses and structures.

Make sure they realise this means all the work you have done, not just the sentences on this page.

Phonics
Children tick the boxes when they can read and spell the words accurately.

3. Check through the completed Portfolio page with each child. Some children may take a little longer to feel confident with the work that has been covered. It is not necessary for the whole class to tick everything on this page before moving on to Unit 4.

1. When children are confident with all the elements of the work on page 129, they may complete the Diploma page.

2. This contains a representative task from each field of work. This page is not a formal test. Children should complete it in their own time, working carefully and steadily.

3. Children receive a sticker for each task completed and one more when they have finished the page.

4. These pages may be taken out of the Workbook and kept in children's individual portfolios of work along with a few examples of children's best work from Units 1–3.

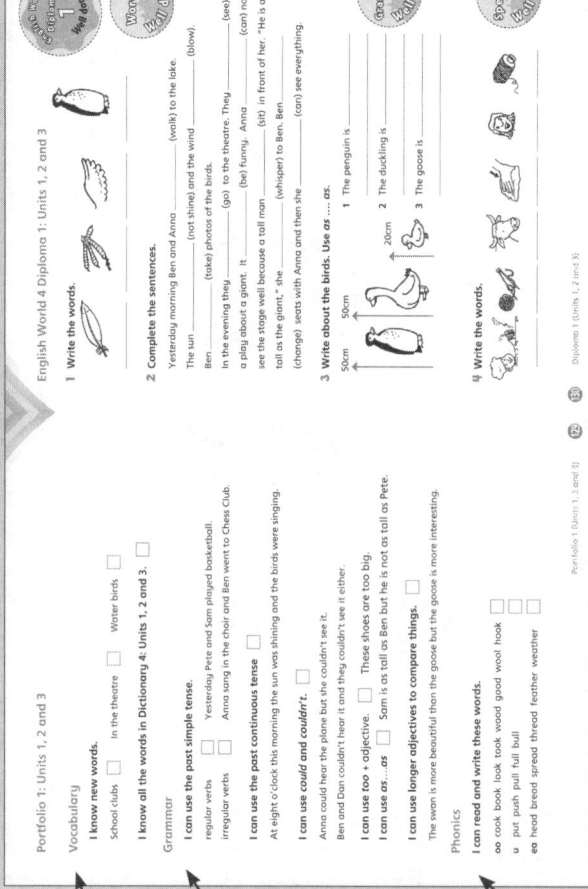

4. Tell children who are not entirely confident (even if they have ticked everything on the page) to spend extra time learning key words for Units 1–3. They should use pages 1–7 of the Dictionary to help them learn and revise.

Completed Diploma 1

Exercise 1 feather, claw, wing, penguin
Exercise 2 walked, wasn't shining, was blowing, took, went, saw, was, could, was sitting, whispered, changed, could
Exercise 3 1 as tall as the goose 2 not as tall as the penguin/goose 3 as tall as the penguin
Exercise 4 cook, wool, bull, push, head, thread

Answers to Check-ups: Units 1–3

Check-up 1 WB pp10–11

Exercise 1
1 took
2 found
3 caught

Exercise 2 2 Did Sam win the race?
2 What did they hear?
3 What did you / we sing?

Exercise 3 1 No, the teacher did not tell a story.
2 No, Mum did not make a cake.
3 No, John did not swim fast.

Exercise 4 1 too heavy
2 too scary
3 too big

Exercise 5 Children write a paragraph of continuous writing. They use the questions to help them write. Encourage able children to add as much detail into their stories as they can (examples in brackets).

Exercise 6 Example writing: Ben and Tom went to the sports shop. Ben bought a football. Later the boys went to the park. Ben threw the ball to Tom. (The ball went up high.) Tom did not catch the ball. The boys ran after the ball. (They ran quickly.) They were too late. They saw the ball in the river (They could not get the ball.) Ben was very angry.

Check-up 2 WB pp20–21

Exercise 1
1 were singing
2 was smiling
3 was raining
4 were eating

Exercise 2 1 Were the children playing?
2 What was Grandma wearing?
3 How were the boys feeling?

Exercise 3 1 No, it was not snowing.
2 No, the people were not laughing.
3 No, Grandpa was not sleeping.

Exercise 4 1 could not watch
2 could see
3 could hear
4 could not pick up

Exercise 5 Children write a paragraph of continuous writing. They use the questions to help them write. Encourage able children to add as much detail into their stories as they can (examples in brackets).

Exercise 6 Example writing: It was a hot day yesterday. The sun was shining (brightly). The children were playing on the beach / sand. Mum was sitting under an umbrella (a huge umbrella). The little boy was crying because he wanted an ice cream. (Mum said, "No, you can't have an ice cream.") Dad was standing in the water / sea. He could see a boat. The boat was sailing towards an island (a very small island).

Check-up 3 WB pp30–31

Exercise 1 1 as old as Tom.
2 as pretty as Pam.
3 as expensive as the ring.

Exercise 2 2 The snake is more dangerous than the cat.
3 The boy is more frightened than the girl.

Exercise 3 2 Sum B is the most difficult.
3 The elephant is the most enormous.

Exercise 4 Children use the questions that they read in Activity 4 to help them write a paragraph about the monsters.

Exercise 5 Example writing: Igg is tiny. Ugg is more enormous than Igg. Ogg is the most enormous. Igg is as polite as Ogg. Ugg is more polite than Igg and Ogg. Igg is the most horrible monster.

4 Crafts

Lesson 1 Poster 4, Reading

Lesson aim Reading

Text type a description of a process

Lesson targets Children:
- read, understand and practise new vocabulary on the poster
- read, understand and practise reading the descriptions
- answer oral comprehension questions
- practise reading the text

Key structure Time clause with *When…*

Key language *Candle light makes everything* look *pretty.*

Key vocabulary crafts, tools and products

Materials PB pp48–49; poster 4; CD A track 24, 35; Dictionary 4; word cards for poster vocabulary (see poster 4 below or list on p14)

Preparation make word cards; listen to CD A track 35

Warm-up

Sing the seeking song from PB page 35, track 24.

Poster 4

1 Point to the poster. Read out the title. Give the class a moment or two to look.

2 Point to the people and objects on the poster. Read the word. Show the word card/s. Class reads and says the word/s.

Make sure children understand the following words. Use the definitions and example sentences as necessary to ensure understanding:

basket maker	a person who makes baskets
	A *basket maker* uses reeds.
candle maker	a person who makes candles
	A *candle maker* uses string.
clay	very hard soil
	You can make *clay* into different shapes.
loom	a wood square or rectangle with strong threads from top to bottom
	A weaver makes cloth on a *loom*.
mould	a shape you can use to make another shape the same
	Candles often come from the same *mould*.
potter	a person who makes pots
	Potters work in every country in the world.
weaver	a person who weaves cloth
	Some *weavers* make mats.

Cover the words on the poster if you wish. Point to the people and objects at random. Class names them.

---

4 Crafts

weaver — threads, cloth, loom

potter — pot, clay, wheel

candle maker — pan, mould, candles, wax

basket maker — reeds, knife, basket

3 Ask if children have any of these things at home: pots, baskets, candles. Do they have anything that a weaver made on a loom, e.g. a special mat or rug?

4 Ask *What do we use these things for?* *We put water, plants and food in pots. We carry things in baskets. We light candles and we have mats and rugs in our homes.*

5 Ask *Can you make any of these things?* Do you know how people make them? Find out if children know anything about these crafts.

Unit 4 Reading

Reading (PB pp48–49)

1. Give children time to look at the pictures. Read the title. Ask what things they can name in the pictures.

2. Play track 35. Children listen and follow in their books.

3. Read one paragraph or section of the text at a time.
Use *Dictionary 4* to help you to explain new words as necessary.
Help children to find new words. Make up extra sentences for new words if you wish. In particular, explain *coil* and *pinch*. Point out the pictures of the coil pots and the pinch pots.

4. Ask questions about each paragraph or a section of the text. See Resource box.

5. Give reading practice around the class. Ask individuals, groups or the class to read sentences or paragraphs. Play track 35 again.

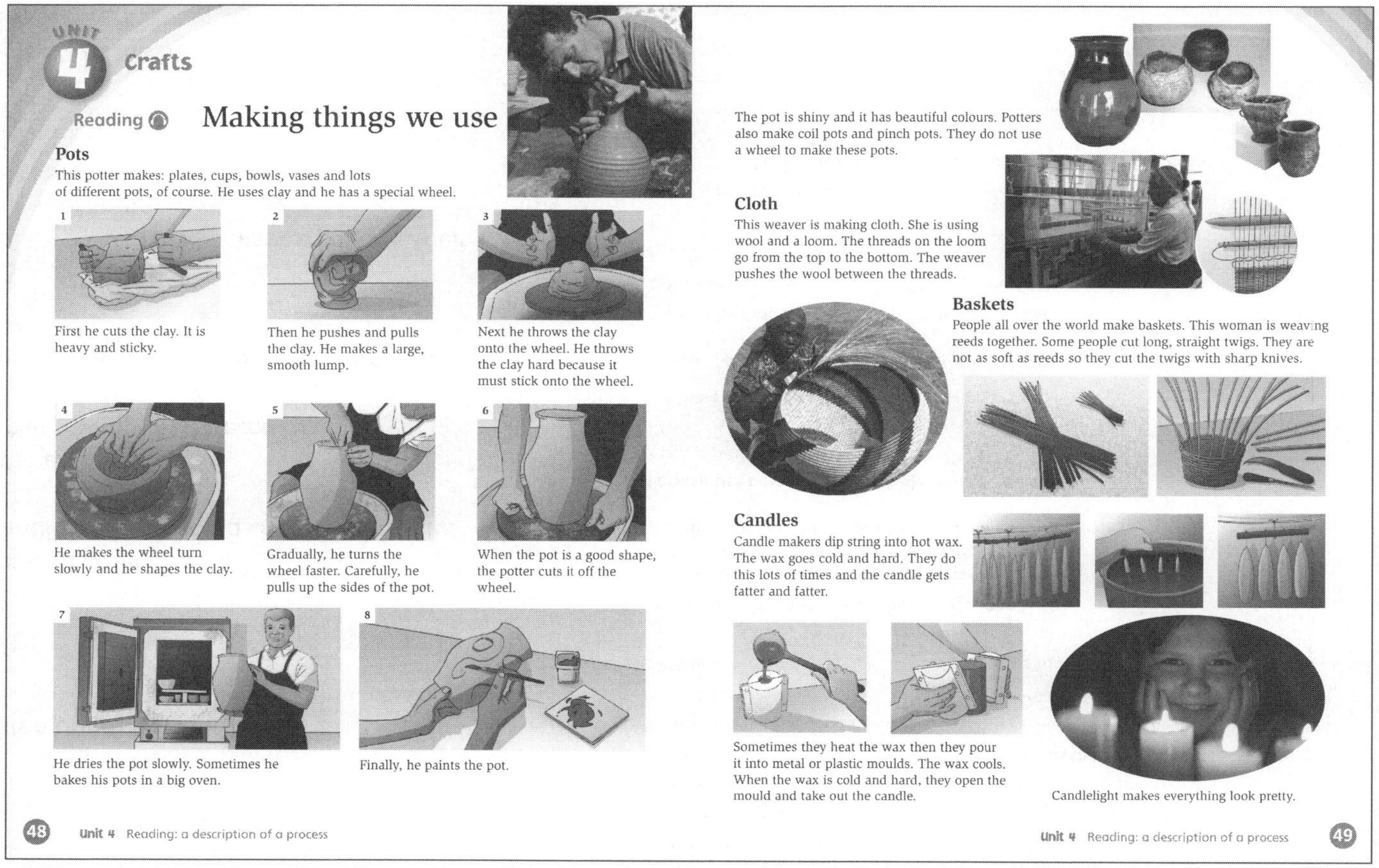

Homework task

Children learn selected vocabulary from Unit 4 *Dictionary 4*.
See unit word list on pp190–191 for key words, extension words and words for understanding only.

Unit 4 Crafts

Reading — Making things we use

Pots

This potter makes: plates, cups, bowls, vases and lots of different pots, of course. He uses clay and he has a special wheel.

1 First he cuts the clay. It is heavy and sticky.

2 Then he pushes and pulls the clay. He makes a large, smooth lump.

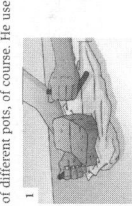
3 Next he throws the clay onto the wheel. He throws the clay hard because it must stick onto the wheel.

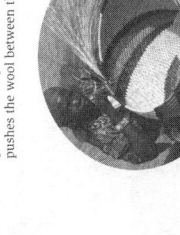
4 He makes the wheel turn slowly and he shapes the clay.

5 Gradually, he turns the wheel faster. Carefully, he pulls up the sides of the pot.

6 When the pot is a good shape, the potter cuts it off the wheel.

7 He dries the pot slowly. Sometimes he bakes his pots in a big oven.

8 Finally, he paints the pot.

The pot is shiny and it has beautiful colours. Potters also make coil pots and pinch pots. They do not use a wheel to make these pots.

Cloth

This weaver is making cloth. She is using wool and a loom. The threads on the loom go from the top to the bottom. The weaver pushes the wool between the threads.

Baskets

People all over the world make baskets. This woman is weaving reeds together. Some people cut long, straight twigs. They are not as soft as reeds so they cut the twigs with sharp knives.

Candles

 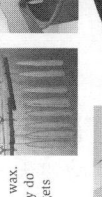  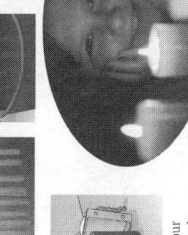

Candle makers dip string into hot wax. The wax goes cold and hard. They do this lots of times and the candle gets fatter and fatter.

Sometimes they heat the wax then they pour it into metal or plastic moulds. The wax cools. When the wax is cold and hard, they open the mould and take out the candle.

Candlelight makes everything look pretty.

48 Unit 4 Reading: a description of a process

49 Unit 4 Reading: a description of a process

Resource box

Text questions

What things does the potter make? **plates, cups, bowls, vases, pots**
What does he use? **clay**
What is clay like? **heavy and sticky**
Where does he throw the clay? **onto the wheel**
What does he do when the pot is a good shape? **He cuts it off the wheel.**
Does he bake the pot? **sometimes**
What is the weaver using? **wool, a loom**
Which way do the threads on a loom go? **from the top to the bottom**
What is the basket maker using? **reeds**
What else can she use? **twigs**
Do candle makers use hot or cold wax? **hot**
What happens to the wax? **It goes cold and hard.**
How do candle makers use a moulds? **They pour hot wax in them. When the wax is cold they open them and take out the candle.**

Time division

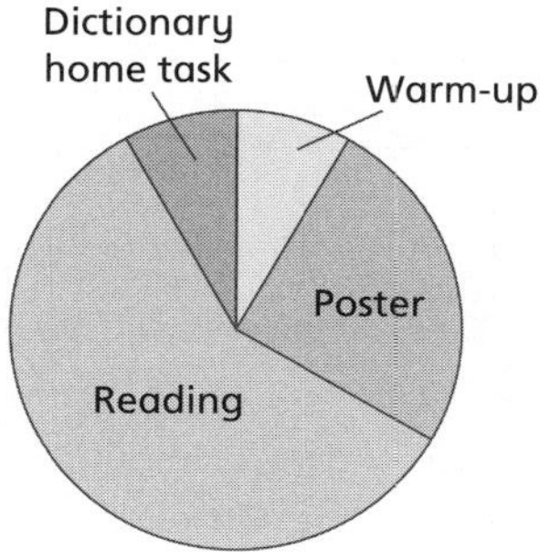

(pie chart: Warm-up, Poster, Reading, Dictionary home task)

Unit 4 Reading 67

Lesson 2 Reading comprehension and vocabulary (PB p50)

Lesson aim Reading comprehension; vocabulary

Lesson targets Children re-read *Making things we use*, then:
- (PB) match sentence beginnings and endings
- give personal response; complete a cloze activity
- (WB) match tools and materials to people
- match descriptions to pictures

Key structure Time clauses with *When...*
Key language *Candlelight makes everything look pretty.*
Words vocabulary from Lesson 1
Materials PB p50; CD A track 35 (optional); WB p32; Dictionary 4

Warm-up

Put up poster 4. Ask the class *Which craft do you think is the most difficult? Why?* Ask for views. After getting as many views as possible, take a class vote. Make sure everyone responds.

Read again

Remind children of *Making things we use*.
Play track 35 or read the text to the class. Children listen and follow in the PB.

Activity 1

Give children a few minutes to read all the beginnings and endings silently.
Tell them to look at the first beginning and find the ending. They should check back to the text during this activity.
Ask a volunteer to read the first beginning and add the ending.
Check the answer with the class. Children go back to the text again if necessary.
Children match all the sentences.
If you wish, they may write the complete sentences in their workbooks as a homework task.

Activity 2

Children discuss the questions in pairs or small groups. Give them a time limit to decide their answers. Find out what the class view is. Ask for reasons for their views.
Children write down which objects they have. Ask for some answers.

Activity 3

Children look at the pictures. Ask a child to read the words in the box.
Children read the first sentence. Ask a child to say the complete sentence.
Check with the class. Children write.

Reading comprehension and vocabulary

1 Read the sentence beginnings. Find the correct ending on the right.

1 The potter uses clay and ____
2 First ____
3 Next he throws ____
4 He throws the clay hard because ____
5 He makes the wheel turn slowly ____
6 Gradually, ____
7 Carefully, ____
8 When the pot is a good shape ____
9 He dries the pot ____
10 Finally, ____

a he pulls up the sides of the pot.
b the potter cuts it off the wheel.
c the clay hard onto the wheel.
d slowly.
e and he shapes the clay.
f he paints the pot.
g he cuts the clay.
h he has a special wheel.
i it must stick onto the wheel.
j he turns the wheel faster.

2 Talk about the answers to these questions.
1 Which craft on pages 48–49 is the most useful? Why?
2 Which object is the most beautiful? Why?
3 Do you have any of the objects in your home? Which ones?

3 Choose the best word to complete each sentence.

| cools | heats | gradually | finally | pours | dips |

1 The candle maker ____ the wax in a big pan.
2 The candle maker ____ the long candles many times.
3 ____ the candles get fatter.
4 He ____ hot wax into a mould.
5 The wax in the mould ____ and goes hard.
6 ____ the candle maker opens the mould and takes out the candle.

50

Unit 4 Reading comprehension and vocabulary: beginning/end sentence match; personal response

Reading comprehension and vocabulary (WB p32)

If children are doing this page for homework, make sure they understand the tasks. Children should be able to read exercise 2 independently but if you have weak readers you may wish to read the text with the class as preparation.
Remind them to have their dictionaries with them to help them complete the exercises.

Exercise 1
Children write the jobs under the correct picture first.
They read the list of objects and write them under the correct job.

Exercise 2
Children match the descriptions to the pictures.

UNIT 4

Reading comprehension and vocabulary

1 What do these people do? Write the correct job under each picture.

a basket maker   b potter   c weaver   d candlemaker

What things do they use? Write these words under the correct person.

| oven | loom | twigs | wheel | wax | reeds |
| mould | threads | clay | wool | knife | string |

2 Read and match. Write the letters.

a   b   c   d

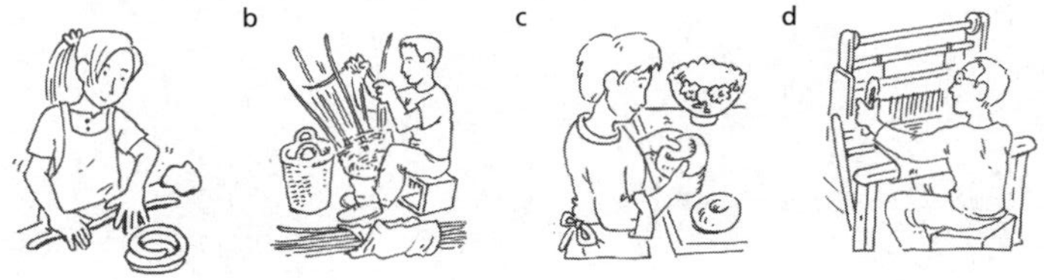

1 This woman is using a lump of clay. She is pinching the clay to make the sides of a pot. The finished pot is called a pinch pot. Picture ___
2 This woman is using a long, thin piece of clay. She is coiling the clay round and round. The finished pot is called a coil pot. Picture ___
3 This man is using wool on a loom. He is weaving a piece of cloth. Picture ___
4 This man is using long, thin twigs. He is making a tall basket. Picture ___

32 Unit 4 Sorting; matching

Time division

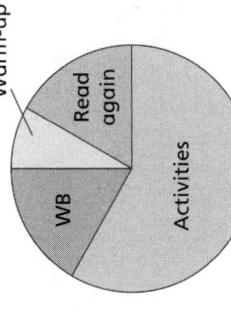

Warm-up, Read again, Activities, WB

Resource box

PB answers
Activity 1 1h 2g 3c 4i 5e 6j 7a 8b 9d 10f
Activity 3 1 heats 2 dips 3 Gradually 4 pours 5 cools 6 Finally

WB answers
Exercise 1 picture 1 candlemaker: wax mould string; picture 2 weaver: loom threads wool; picture 3 potter: oven wheel clay; picture 4 basket maker: twigs reeds knife
Exercise 2 1c 2a 3d 4b

Unit 4 Reading comprehension and vocabulary 69

Lesson 3 Speaking (PB p51) Study skills

Lesson aim Speaking, (WB) Study skills

Lesson targets Children:
- listen to a dialogue; listen and repeat the dialogue
- understand the story and answer oral questions
- read and act the dialogue
- (WB) practise dictionary skills, sequencing

New word reeds

Materials PB p51; CD A tracks 36, 37; WB p33; Dictionary 4

Preparation Listen to CD A track 36 before the lesson

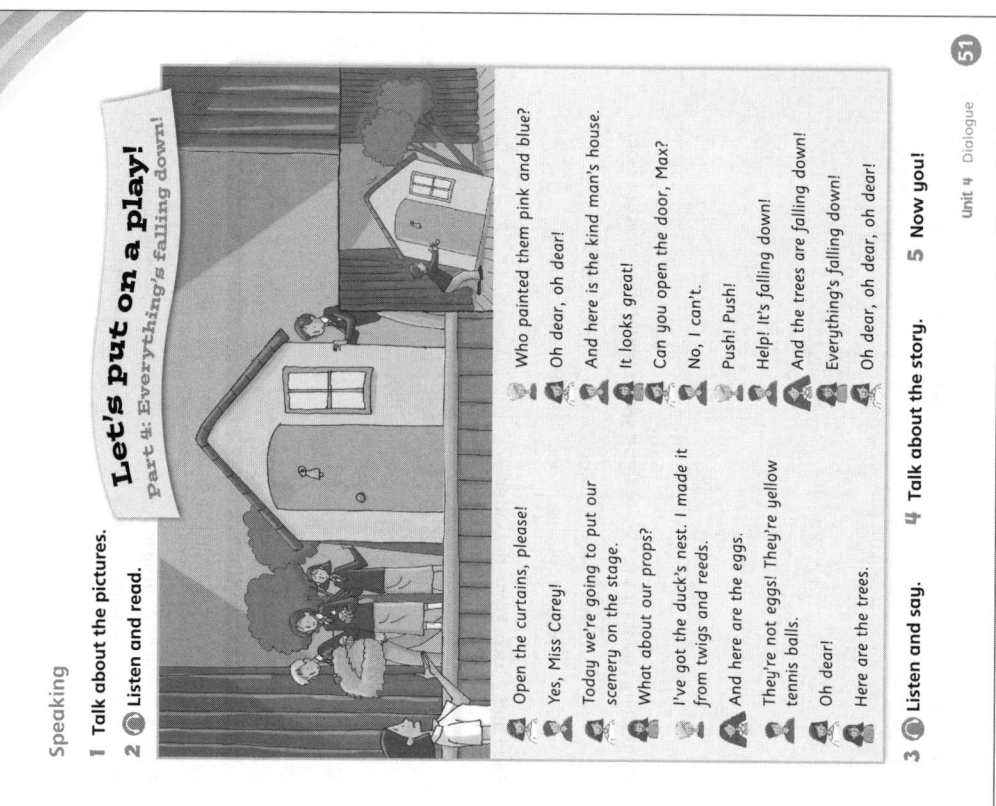

Warm-up

Ask children *What went wrong in the last part of 'Let's put on a play!'?* *The costumes did not fit the children.* Ask if they can remember what was wrong with all the costumes. Let the class look back at Part 3 to check.

Activity 1

Children look at PB page 51. Read the title of Part 4. Ask *What are the children doing?* Children suggest what is happening. Tell children to cover the dialogue text and look at the picture. Play track 36. Children listen.

Activity 2

Children open their books and look at the dialogue. Play track 36 again. Children listen and follow.
Check children understand the new words. Use Dictionary 4 if you wish.

Activity 3

Children close their books. Play track 37. Children listen and repeat in the pauses. Encourage them to use the same expression and intonation.

Activity 4

Ask questions to check understanding of the story. See Resource box.

Activity 5

Children act the dialogue. Encourage them not to use their books if they can manage without them. If children enjoy this activity, let more than one group act it out.

Unit 4 Speaking

70

Study skills (WB p33)

The exercises on this page practise dictionary and sequencing skills.
Children should be able to do this work independently once the tasks have been explained.
You may wish to demonstrate one or two sets of words beginning with the same letter.
Explain the task in exercise 2 so that children understand how to approach it.

Exercise 1
Children order the words. Make sure they understand that the second letter of the word tells them the order.
Remind them they have the alphabet at the top of the page to help them.

Exercise 2
Children look at the pictures first. Tell them to read all the sentences before they try to order the pictures.
When they have read the sentences they number the pictures and re-order the sentences to make a story that matches the pictures.
Tell them to read the story through to make sure it makes sense.

Study skills

a b c d e f g h i j k l m n o p q r s t u v w x y z

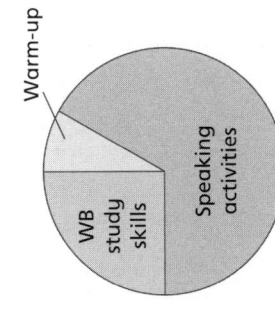

Look at the second letter!

1 Put the words in the correct order.

1	crab	clay	car
	car	*clay*	*crab*
2	pot	play	party
3	blue	box	basket	bike
4	nice	nasty	number	nose
5	fish	four	fly	fast	friend

2 Put the pictures in the correct order. Write the number.

Now read the sentences. Write them in the correct order in your copy book.
She looked at the baskets. Then she went to the market and bought some fruit.
She went inside and bought a big basket. Then she walked home. Mrs Green was outside the basket maker's shop. She put it in the basket.

Unit 4 Dictionary skills; sequencing

Resource box

Story questions
Talk about what was wrong with the scenery:
Did [x] make a good duck's nest? **yes**
*Were the eggs good props? **No, because they were tennis balls.***
*What was wrong with the trees? **They were pink and blue.***
*What was wrong with the kind man's house? **Max couldn't open the door.***
*What happened to all the scenery? **It fell down.***

WB answers
Exercise 1 2 party play pot   3 basket bike blue box   4 nasty nice nose number   5 fast fish fly four friend

Exercise 2 2 2 4 1 3
Mrs Green was outside the basket maker's shop. She looked at the baskets. She went inside and bought a big basket. Then she went to the market and bought some fruit. She put it in the basket. Then she walked home.

Time division

Warm-up / WB study skills / Speaking activities

Unit 4 Study skills

Lesson 4 Grammar (Session 1), Grammar in conversation (Session 2) (PB pp52–53)

Lesson aim Grammar

Lesson targets Children:
- (session 1) understand and practise the key structure
- (session 2) listen to and read a conversation; repeat and practise it
- (session 2) listen to a song, say it and learn it (optional)

Key structure (session 1) Time clauses with *When…*

Key vocabulary general vocabulary

Key language (session 2) *Is there something in your pocket?*

Informal expressions Aha!

Materials PB pp52–53; CD A tracks 38, 39, 40; WB pp34–35

Session 1 Warm-up

Ask around the class *What did you do when you got home yesterday?* Elicit, e.g. *I did my homework. I watched TV. I played with my friend*, etc.

Activity 1
Children look at the pictures. Ask what the weather is in each one. Ask two children to read the PC kids' bubbles. Write the second sentence on the board. Class reads. Volunteers read the sentences. Children match and write.

Activity 2
Ask a child to read the example. Children read the other sentences. Ask for suggestions for a second sentence for each one. Write them on the board. Help the class to rewrite the pairs into one sentence as in the example. Class reads.

Children write their own sentences in pairs. See Resource box.*

Children complete WB page 34 in class time or for homework.

Session 2 Warm-up

Repeat the grammar Warm-up from session 1. This time children begin their answers *When I got home yesterday, I…*

Activity 1
Elicit or explain that the girl is pretending to be the teacher. Tell the class to listen to the children. Play track 38. Children follow in their books.

Activity 2
Children listen to track 39 and repeat in the pauses.

Activity 3
Children practise the conversation in pairs. See Resource box.**

Activity 4
Point out the two boys. Ask *Are they talking or arguing?* Listen to children's ideas. Tell them they will find out in the song. Play track 40. Children listen and follow the first time.

Read the words with the class. Play track 40 again. Children listen and follow the first time. Read the words with the class. Play track 40 again. Children join in. Play track 41. Children sing with the music. They may learn the song, if you wish.

Unit 4 Grammar, Grammar in conversation

Grammar (Session 1), Grammar in conversation (Session 2) (WB pp34–35)

If these pages are for homework, check children understand the tasks.

Exercise 1
Children read and match.

Exercise 2
Children write single sentences. Remind them of the comma after the time clause. Write the example sentence on the board but omit the comma. Ask a volunteer to put the comma in.

Exercise 1
Go over the main rules: *something* for positive statements; *anything* for negative statements and questions; *everything* when the meaning is all the things. Note: *something* can sometimes be used in questions when a positive answer is expected.

Exercise 2
Children complete the sentences using the words in brackets.

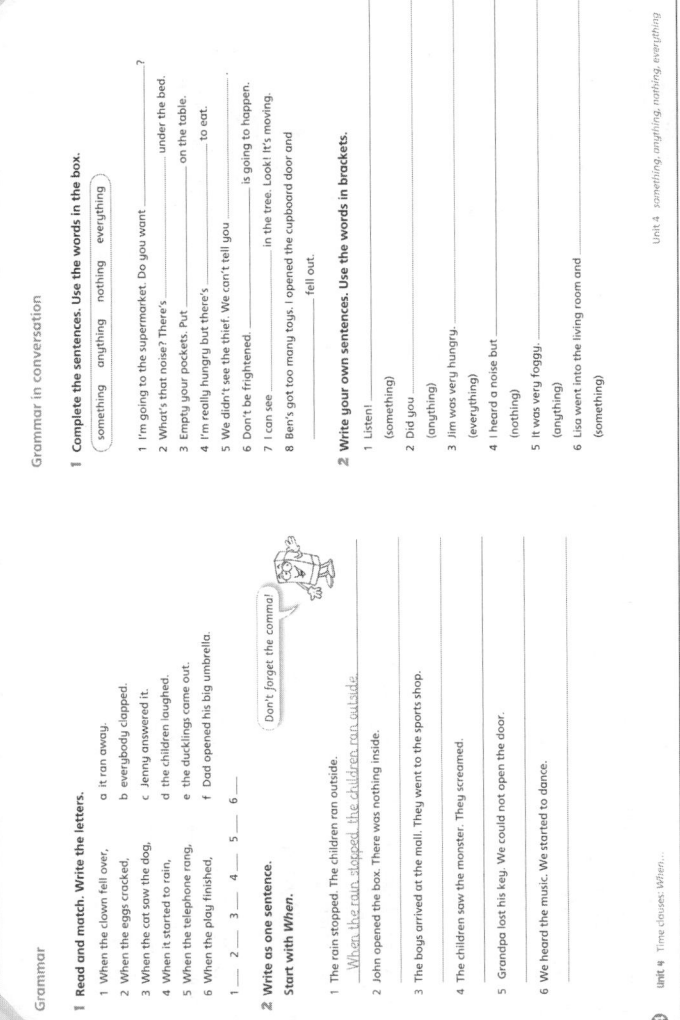

Resource box

PB answers (p52)
Activity 1 1C 2A 3D 4B
***Pair work: Grammar (p52)**
Activity 2 Children work in pairs. They write their own second sentence for at least one first sentence. They make the two sentences into one beginning with the *When* time clause.
Give children a short time to do this. Check pairs' work around the class by asking them to read out their two sentences then the single sentence.
Go over the structure again if children find this hard. Use the Warm-up sentences: *When I got home yesterday, I watched TV.*
****Pair work: Grammar in conversation (p53)**
Activity 3 Children practise the dialogue in pairs at their desks. Give pairs three minutes to practise the dialogue. Let one or two pairs stand up and say it in front of the class.

WB answers
Grammar (p34)
Exercise 1 1d 2e 3a 4f 5c 6b
Exercise 2 2 When John opened the box, there was nothing inside.
3 When the boys arrived at the mall, they went to the sports shop.
4 When the children saw the monster, they screamed.
5 When Grandpa lost his key, we could not open the door.
6 When we heard the music, we started to dance.
Grammar in conversation (p35)
Exercise 1 1 anything 2 something 3 everything 4 nothing 5 anything 6 Nothing 7 something 8 everything
Exercise 2 example answers
1 Did you hear something? / I heard something. 2 Did you see / hear anything? 3 He ate / wanted everything on the plate. 4 I saw / could see nothing. 5 We couldn't see anything. 6 saw / heard / found something.

Time division

Session 1
Warm-up
WB
Activity 2
Activity 1

Session 2
Warm-up
Conversation activities
Pairs conversation practice
Song
WB

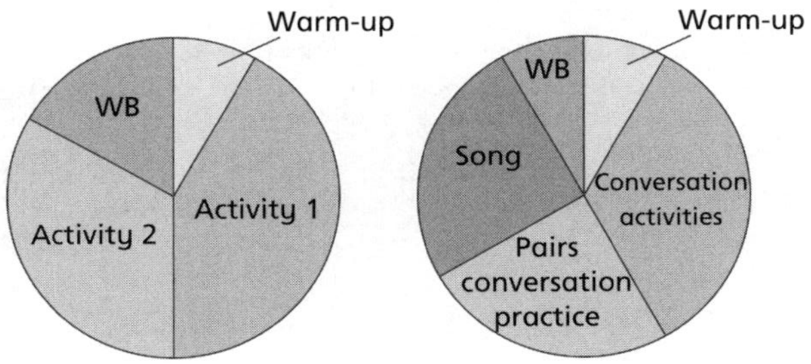

Grammar Practice Book
Children may begin Unit 4 when they have completed the PB and WB Grammar pages. They should complete it before the end of PB / WB Unit 4.

Unit 4   Grammar, Grammar in conversation   73

Lesson 5 Listening, Phonics (PB p54) Use of English

Lesson aim Listening, spelling and pronunciation, Use of English (WB)

Lesson targets Children:

- listen to descriptions of objects and actions and identify them in order
- practise saying, reading and spelling words with y sounding *ee*
- (WB) learn about spelling rules for the plural of nouns ending f, fe

Key structure and language from Unit 1

Target words *heavy, sticky, very, lady, baby, lolly*

Materials PB p54; CD A tracks 40, 42, 43; WB pp36–37

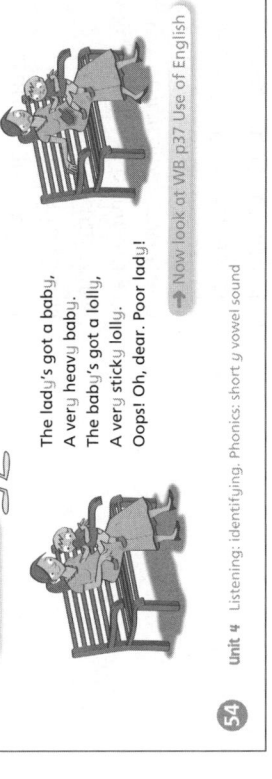

Warm-up

Sing the 'doing better' song from PB page 53, track 40.

Listening

Activity 1

Children look at the pictures for a few moments. Ask them to name some of the things they can see.
Play track 42. Children listen and point to the pictures as they hear the things mentioned.

Activity 2

Play track 42 again. Children listen and write the letter of each picture in the order they hear it described. Be ready to play the track again for children to listen once more or check.
To check answers, ask what the word spelled by the letters is: *beautiful*.

Phonics

Point out the box. Tell children to follow in their books and repeat in the pauses. Play the first part of track 43. Make sure children repeat accurately.
Play the end of track 43. Children listen and follow.
Children say the rhyme. They may learn it, if you wish.

Children open their WBs at page 36. They complete the Phonics page now or for homework. If it is for homework, make sure they understand the tasks.

Use of English

Move on to WB page 37.

Listening

1 Look, listen and point.

E U U I T B A L F

2 Listen again and write the letters.

1 2 3 4 5 6 7 8 9

What's the word?

Phonics

Look and listen!

y Clay is heavy and sticky.

The lady's got a baby,
A very heavy baby.
The baby's got a lolly,
A very sticky lolly.
Oops! Oh, dear. Poor lady!

→ Now look at WB p37 Use of English

54 Unit 4 Listening: identifying. Phonics: short y vowel sound

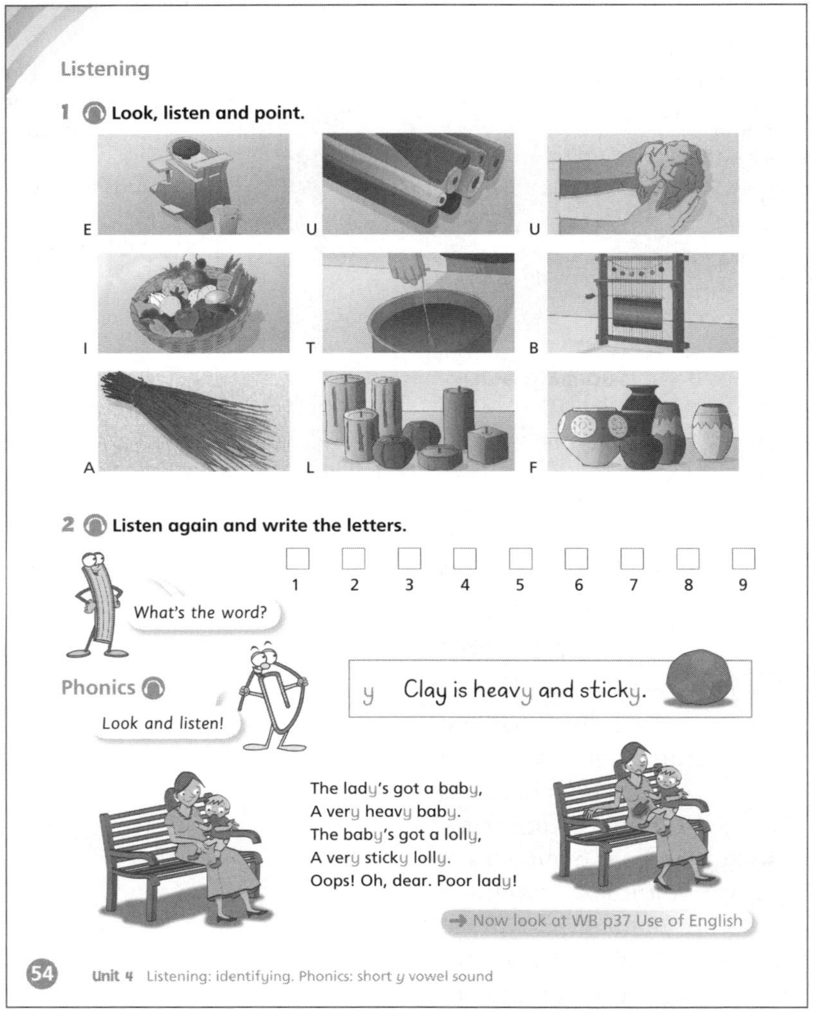

Phonics, Use of English (WB pp36–37)

Remind the class of the sound *y* and *heavy*.

Write the example sentences on the board. Class reads.

Exercise 1
Children complete and write the words.

Go through the presentation with the class. Write the nouns on the board. Ask children to underline the *-fe* and *-ves* endings.

Exercise 2
Children read the clues and complete the crossword.

Children write the plurals. Check answers together. Children correct any mistakes they have made.

Exercise 3
Children write a sentence of their own for each word. Encourage them to write interesting sentences.

Children write four sentences of their own. Encourage them to write interesting sentences. Ask several children to read out their work.

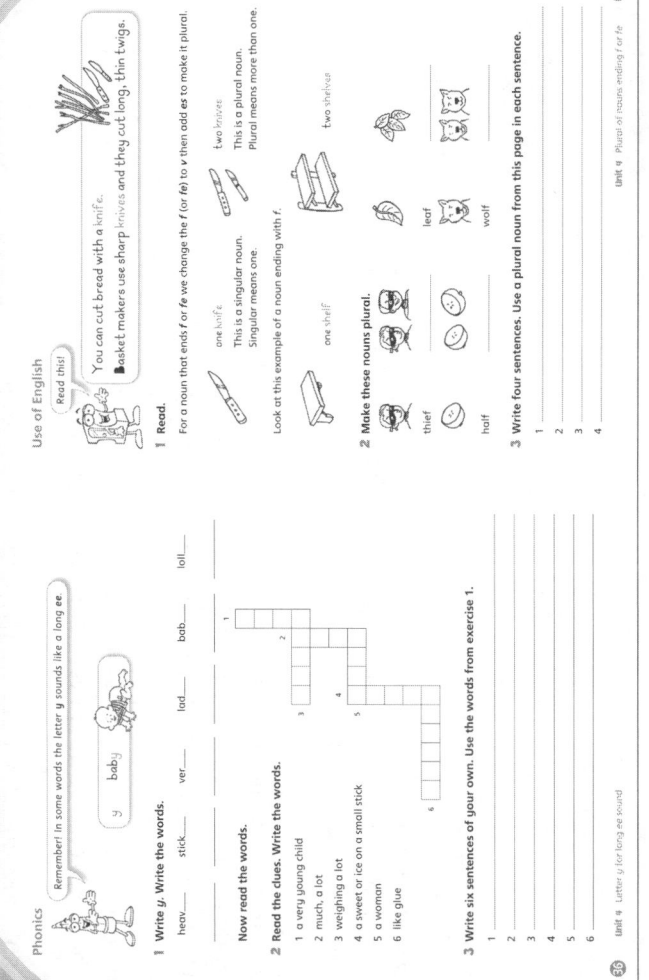

Resource box

Audioscript (CD A track 42) **Listening activities 1–2** (PB p54)
- Number 1: This machine is a loom. A weaver is going to make cloth on it.
- Number 2: This is a wheel. A potter is going make clay pots on it.
- Number 3: These are reeds. Who is going to use these? A basket maker is going to make baskets from them.
- Number 4: Look at the hands. They're holding something heavy and sticky. It's wet clay. These are the potter's hands.
- Number 5: The candle maker is holding a long string. He's dipping it into hot wax. He takes it out and the wax cools. When the wax on the string is hard, he dips it in again. He's making a candle.
- Number 6: The basket maker made this basket from twigs and reeds. Is there anything in the basket? Yes. It's full of fruit and vegetables.
- Number 7: The potter made these pots on his wheel. When they came out of the oven, he waited for them to cool. Then he painted them in bright colours. There's nothing in them. They're empty.
- Number 8: The weaver made this beautiful cloth on her loom. She used wool.
- Number 9: The candle maker made these candles. Some are big and some are small. What can you do with tiny candles? Put them on a birthday cake!

PB answers
1B 2E 3A 4U 5T 6I 7F 8U 9L

WB answers
Phonics (p36)
Exercise 2 1 baby 2 very 3 heavy 4 lolly 5 lady 6 sticky

Use of English (p37)
Exercise 2 thieves leaves halves wolves

Time division

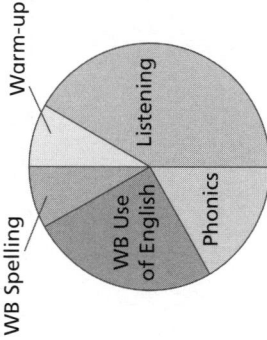

Warm-up, Listening, Phonics, WB Use of English, WB Spelling

Unit 4 Phonics, Use of English 75

Lesson 6 Class composition (Session 1) (PB p55) Writing preparation, Composition practice (Session 2)

Lesson aim Writing

Lesson targets Children:
- (session 1) describe an illustrated process with word prompts and teacher support
- (session 2) (WB) practise verbs and order words for describing a process
- (session 2) (WB) write a description of a process independently

Key structure and language from Unit 4

Vocabulary potter's materials, tools and method

Materials PB p55; WB p38–39

Session 1 Warm-up

Play *What's missing?* (see Games, page 187) with verb word cards, e.g. *cut, pull, push, roll, coil, make, dry, paint.*

Class composition

Activity 1

1 Point out the photo in the middle of the page. Explain that the potter made these pots too, but he made them in a different way. Ask a volunteer to read the short paragraph at the top of the page.

2 Tell the class to look at the pictures and read the words silently. Ask one or more volunteers to read the words aloud to the class.

Activity 2

1 Read the question to the class. Remind them that they must describe what the potter does when he makes a coil pot. They must describe each action. Tell the class to look at the first picture. Ask *What does the potter do first?* Let a volunteer make a sentence using the prompt words and describing the first step in the process. Prompt a full sentence if the child does not suggest one.

2 Continue with the other pictures. Remind children of the order words on the board. Prompt them to use these words as appropriate. They do not have to be used exactly as shown in the example writing. Make sure children understand that only *First* and *Finally* have fixed positions.

3 When all the actions have been described, ask a volunteer to read the sentences. Children look at the pictures and listen. Ask the class *Is the writing clear? Does it tell you what the potter does?*
Ask if any words or sentences could be better. Discuss any changes with the class. Make changes that you and the class agree are improvements. When the class is satisfied with the composition, ask a volunteer to read it a final time.
Erase the writing from the board. Children write the composition in their books.

Writing preparation, Composition practice (WB pp38–39)

Session 2 Warm-up

Do an *Action mime* with the verbs in exercise 1 (see Games, page 186).

Exercise 1

A child reads the verbs. Do this exercise with the class or let them work independently then check answers together.

Exercises 2

Do this exercise with the class. Write the words on the board. Ask the questions. Volunteers circle. Check with the class. Children circle in their books. Read out the last sentence.

Exercise 3

Children look at the pictures and read the gapped sentences. Make sure they understand that they must use the words from exercise 2 to complete the sentences. Children work independently. Check answers together.

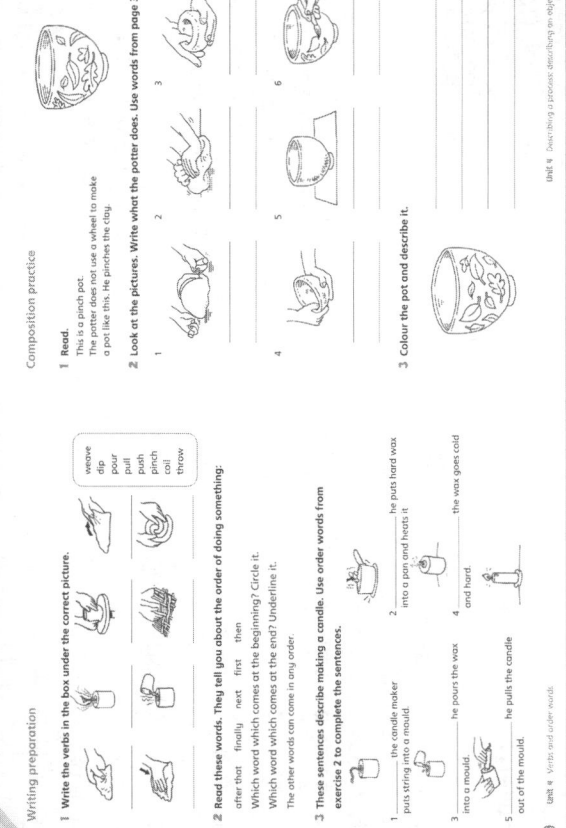

Exercise 1

A volunteer reads the sentences to the class. Ask *Does the potter use a wheel? What does he do?*

Exercise 2

Children write sentences. Remind them to use the order words in exercise 2 on page 38 and that all the verbs they need are on the same page.

Exercise 3

Children colour the pot and write sentences to describe its shape and colour.

Go around helping and monitoring as they write. Make sure the class understands for pictures 1–6 they must write clear, simple sentences that describe what the potter does. For the last picture, they may describe the pot in any way they choose – colour, size, what it looks like, etc.

Homework task

Children complete Check-up 4, WB p40. For answers, see p105.

Time division

Session 1

- Class composition
- Class composition writing in books
- Class teacher-led board writing
- Warm-up

Session 2

- Warm-up
- Writing preparation
- Composition practice

Portfolio

Children may make neat copies of their WB compositions.

Resource box

Class composition example writing (p55)

First the potter cuts the clay.
Then he makes it into a smooth shape.
Next he rolls the clay. He makes a long, thin shape.
He coils the clay round and round.
Gradually, he makes the shape.
After that he dries the pot slowly.
Finally, he paints it.
The pots are round. They are not tall. They are blue.

WB answers (p38)

Exercise 1 pinch, dip, throw, pull, push, pour, weave, pull
Exercise 2 beginning: first; end: finally
Exercise 3 First, (any order for the next three words) the, next, after that, finally

Composition practice example writing

Exercise 2 1 First the potter cuts the clay. 2 Then he pulls and pushes the clay. 3 Next he pinches the clay. 4 Gradually, he makes the shape. 5 After that, he dries the pot slowly. 6 Finally, he paints it.
Exercise 3 This pinch pot is round. There are big and small leaves on the pot. They are… [description to match the colouring done by the child].

Unit 4   Writing preparation, Composition practice

5 All about a show

Lesson 1 Poster 5, Reading

Lesson aim Reading

Text type a first person recount

Lesson targets Children:
- read, understand and practise new vocabulary on the poster
- read, understand and practise reading personal recounts
- answer oral comprehension questions

Key structure time clause: *While* + past continuous

Key language *either... or*

Key vocabulary publicity and information for a show

Materials PB pp56–57; poster 5; CD B track 1; Dictionary 4; word cards for poster vocabulary (see poster 5 below or list on p15)

Preparation Make word cards; listen to CD B track 1

Warm-up
Play the *Word chain* game (see Games, page 187).

Poster 5

1 Point to the poster. Read out the title. Give the class a moment or two to look.

2 Explain that the pictures are of information for a show. Point out and name the poster, the programme and the tickets.
Explain that this information is about a ballet. Use the dictionary to help explain any new words.
Make sure children understand the following words. Use the definitions and example sentences as necessary to ensure understanding:

cover   the front of an object that has something inside it
            The programme cover has a dancer on it but the CD cover has a huge mouse.
nutcracker a tool for opening nuts
            Dad used the nutcracker and he broke the nut.
Russian   from Russia
            Natalia lives in England but her grandmother is Russian.

3 Point out and read all the labels around the picture of the poster for the ballet. Make sure children can see what is on the ballet poster: place, date, time, etc. You may wish to bring children closer for this part of the lesson.

4 Do the same with the programme. Make sure children can see what the labels on it are pointing to.
If possible, show children a real poster and programme from a performance of something in school or elsewhere.

5 If children in your class have been in a school show, ask them *Were there posters for the show? What was on them? Was there a programme? What was in the programme?*
If there is a school show happening soon, talk about the poster for the show and what is on it.

Unit 5 Reading 78

Reading (PB pp56–57)

1 Give children time to look at the pictures. Read the title. Ask them to name anything they can.
Ask if they can guess what any of the characters in the photos or pictures are.

2 Play CD B track 1. Children listen and follow in their books.

3 Read one paragraph or section of the text at a time.
Use Dictionary 4 to help you to explain new words as necessary.
Help children to find new words. Make up extra sentences for new words if you wish.
The following words are not in the dictionary. Check that children understand them:

Arabian	from Arabia
Chinese	from China
dancer	a person who dances
Japanese	from Japan
Spanish	from Spain

If you wish, make up sentences using the words and write them on the board or ask volunteers/groups to make up sentences.

4 Ask questions about each paragraph or a section of the text. See Resource box.

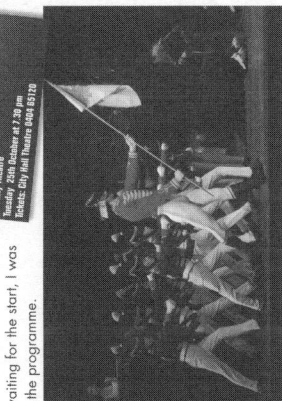

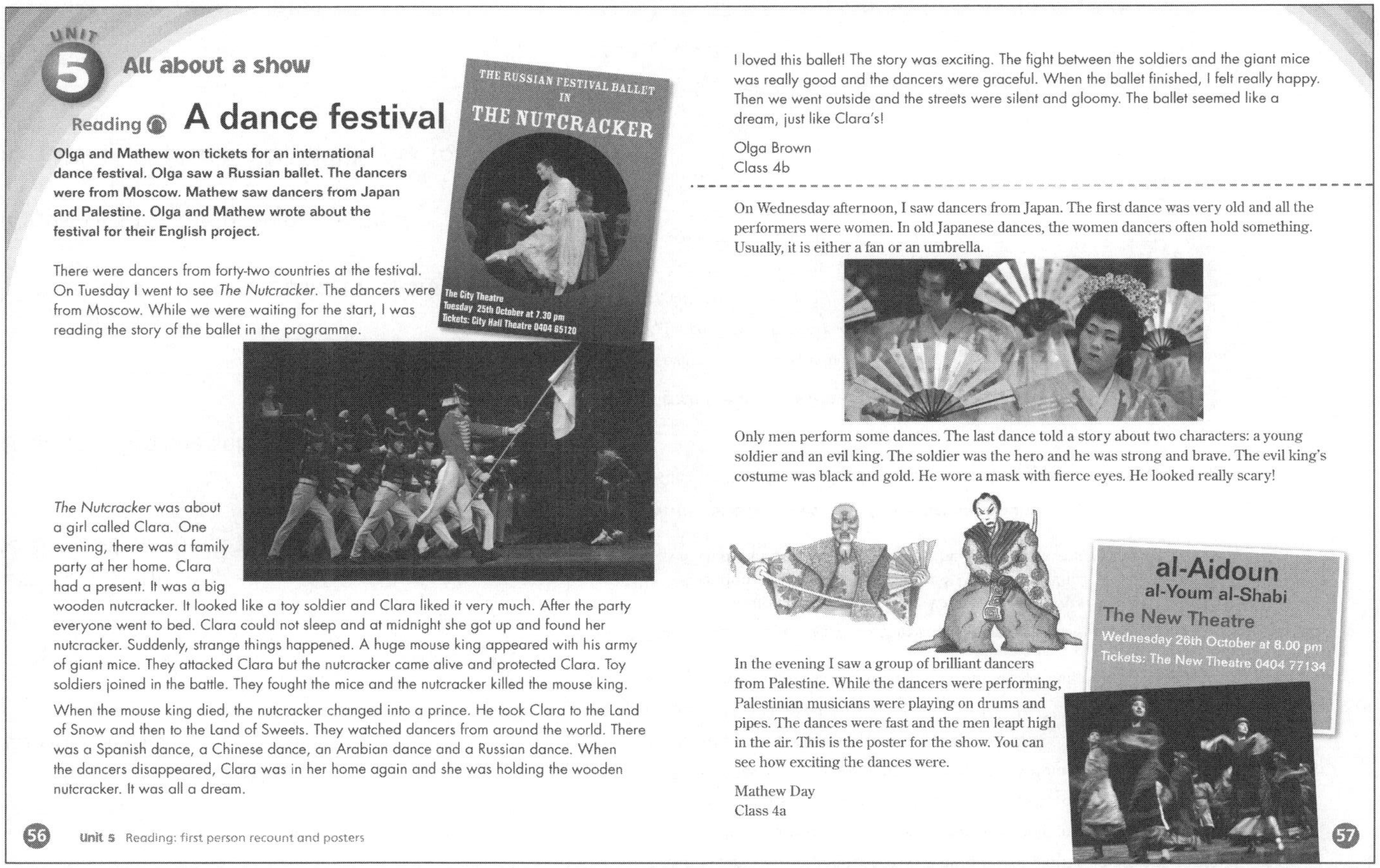
UNIT 5 All about a show

Reading A dance festival

Olga and Mathew won tickets for an international dance festival. Olga saw a Russian ballet. The dancers were from Moscow. Mathew saw dancers from Japan and Palestine. Olga and Mathew wrote about the festival for their English project.

There were dancers from forty-two countries at the festival. On Tuesday I went to see *The Nutcracker*. The dancers were from Moscow. While we were waiting for the start, I was reading the story of the ballet in the programme.

The Nutcracker was about a girl called Clara. One evening, there was a family party at her home. Clara had a present. It was a big wooden nutcracker. It looked like a toy soldier and Clara liked it very much. After the party everyone went to bed. Clara could not sleep and at midnight she got up and found her nutcracker. Suddenly, strange things happened. A huge mouse king appeared with his army of giant mice. They attacked Clara but the nutcracker came alive and protected Clara. Toy soldiers joined in the battle. They fought the mice and the nutcracker killed the mouse king.

When the mouse king died, the nutcracker changed into a prince. He took Clara to the Land of Snow and then to the Land of Sweets. They watched dancers from around the world. There was a Spanish dance, a Chinese dance, an Arabian dance and a Russian dance. When the dancers disappeared, Clara was in her home again and she was holding the wooden nutcracker. It was all a dream.

I loved this ballet! The story was exciting. The fight between the soldiers and the giant mice was really good and the dancers were graceful. When the ballet finished, I felt really happy. Then we went outside and the streets were silent and gloomy. The ballet seemed like a dream, just like Clara's!

Olga Brown
Class 4b

On Wednesday afternoon, I saw dancers from Japan. The first dance was very old and all the performers were women. In old Japanese dances, the women dancers often hold something. Usually, it is either a fan or an umbrella.

Only men perform some dances. The last dance told a story about two characters: a young soldier and an evil king. The soldier was the hero and he was strong and brave. The evil king's costume was black and gold. He wore a mask with fierce eyes. He looked really scary!

In the evening I saw a group of brilliant dancers from Palestine. While the dancers were performing, Palestinian musicians were playing on drums and pipes. The dances were fast and the men leapt high in the air. This is the poster for the show. You can see how exciting the dances were.

Mathew Day
Class 4a

56 Unit 5 Reading: first person recount and posters 57

THE RUSSIAN FESTIVAL BALLET
IN
THE NUTCRACKER
The City Theatre
Tuesday 25th October at 7.30 pm
Tickets: City Hall Theatre 0404 65120
al-Aidoun
al-Youm al-Shabi
The New Theatre
Wednesday 26th October at 8.00 pm
Tickets: The New Theatre 0404 77134

5 Give reading practice around the class. Ask individuals, groups or the class to read sentences or paragraphs. Play track 1 again.

Homework task

Children learn selected vocabulary from Unit 5 *Dictionary 4*.
See unit word list on pp190–191 for key words, extension words and words for understanding only.

Resource box

Text questions

*Why were Olga and Mathew at the dance festival? **they won tickets***

*There were dancers from how many countries? **forty-two***

*What was the Nutcracker about? **a girl called Clara***

*When did Clara get up? **midnight***

*What did the army of mice do? **attacked Clara***

*Who protected Clara? **the nutcracker***

*Where did the nutcracker prince take Clara? **Land of Snow, Land of Sweets***

*Who was in the first Japanese dance? **women***

*What do they usually hold? **a fan or an umbrella***

*What was the last dance about? **a young soldier and an evil king***

*What did the dancers from Palestine do? **leapt high in the air***

Time division

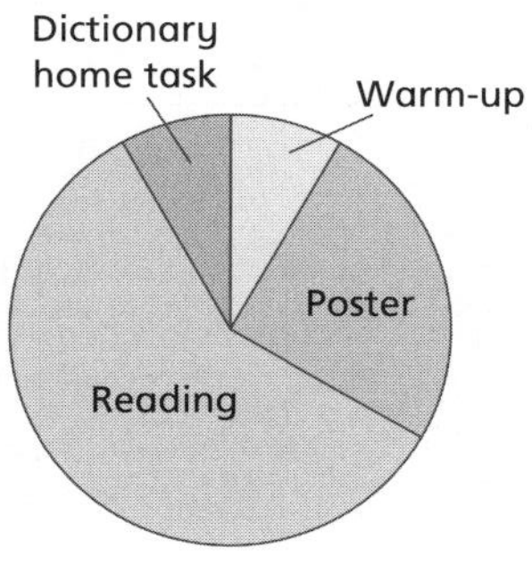

Dictionary home task
Warm-up
Poster
Reading

Lesson 2 Reading comprehension and vocabulary (PB p58)

Lesson aim Reading comprehension; vocabulary

Lesson targets Children re-read *A dance festival*, then:
- (PB) find the incorrect words in statements and correct
- answer inferential questions
- make adjectives from nouns; write descriptive phrases
- (WB) order sentences; match words to pictures and definitions

Key structure time clause: *While* + past continuous
Key language *either ... or*
Words vocabulary from Lesson 1
Materials PB p58; CD B track 1 (optional); WB p42; Dictionary 4

Warm-up

Put up poster 5. Ask children what they can remember about the story of *The Nutcracker* ballet. Cover the story on the programme if children are close enough to read it but leave the character names visible.
If necessary, ask e.g. *What was the girl called? What present did she have?*, etc.

Read again

Play track 1 or read the text to the class. Children listen and follow.

Activity 1

Point out the example. Ask a volunteer to read the next statement. Elicit an answer. Tell children they should look back to the text to check their answer or to find it.
Ask the class if the answer given was correct.
If there is disagreement, ask the whole class to look back and find the sentence where the answer is. Continue with the other questions.

Activity 2

Children look back at paragraph 1 on page 57. Tell them to read it through quickly. Elicit answers.
Tell children to look back at Mathew's report. Elicit suggestions for the answer. Remind children they must give reasons for their answers.
Children give their own responses. Encourage as many children as possible to speak. Ask for reasons for their choice.

Activity 3

Children form the adjectives. Refer them to the text to check.

Reading comprehension and vocabulary

1 Read. In each sentence one word is wrong. Underline it. Write the correct word.

1 Olga saw an English ballet. _Russian_
2 Clara's present was a wooden toy soldier. ___
3 A huge mouse king appeared with his army of giant soldiers. ___
4 When the mouse king died, the nutcracker turned into a soldier. ___
5 The prince took Clara to the Land of Ice. ___
6 On Wednesday evening, Mathew saw dancers from Japan. ___
7 The first dance told a story about two characters. ___
8 The evil king looked very funny. ___
9 In the evening, musicians played on trumpets and pipes. ___

2 Talk about the answers to these questions.

1 What did Olga like in *The Nutcracker* ballet? Find three things.
2 Which dancers do you think Mathew liked best? Why?
3 Which dance do you think sounds the most interesting? Why?

3 Write the adjectives from these proper nouns.

Russia   Arabia   England   Spain   China   Japan   Palestine

Russian ___

4 Match the nouns with adjectives. Write the phrases.

1 evil   a streets   ___
2 fierce   b nutcracker   ___
3 gloomy   c eyes   ___
4 brave   d king   _evil king_
5 wooden   e hero   ___

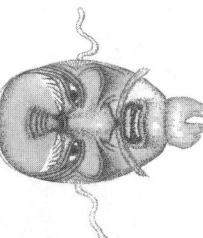

58

Activity 4

Children match and write phrases. Remind them to check in their dictionaries or in the text.

Unit 5 Reading comprehension and vocabulary

Reading comprehension and vocabulary (WB p42)

If children are doing this page for homework, make sure they understand the tasks. You may wish to read the text in exercise 1 with the class as preparation.

Exercise 1
Children read and order the sentences. They may need to check back to the text.

Exercise 2
Children match the nouns and pictures.

Exercise 3
Remind children to look in their dictionaries if they need to, to check for correct matching of words and definitions.

UNIT 5

Reading comprehension and vocabulary

1 Read the sentences from The Nutcracker. Number them in order.

a Strange things happened.
b The prince took Clara to the Land of Snow and the Land of Sweets.
c When the dancers disappeared, Clara was at home.
d At midnight she looked for her nutcracker.
e Clara had a toy nutcracker.
f The nutcracker came alive and fought the mouse king.
g A mouse king appeared with his army of giant mice.
h When the mouse king died, the nutcracker turned into a prince.
i They saw dancers from different lands.
j They attacked Clara.

Now write out the complete story in your copy book. Read it.

2 Match.

mask   midnight   ballet   programme   dream

1   2   3   4   5

3 Match the words in the box with the definitions. Write the words.

disappear   attack   the start   suddenly   perform   turn into

1 the beginning
2 all at once
3 to fight against someone
4 to change from being one thing to being another thing
5 to go from sight
6 to act, sing, or dance while people watch

Unit 5 Sentence order; matching words to pictures and definitions

---

Resource box

PB answers

Activity 1 2 soldier, nutcracker 3 soldiers, mice 4 soldier, prince 5 Ice, Snow 6 evening, afternoon 7 first, last 8 funny, fierce 9 trumpets, drums

Activity 2 1 Olga liked: the story – it was exciting; the fight between the soldiers and the giant mice was good; the dancers were graceful. 2 Mathew says the dancers from Palestine were brilliant and the dances were exciting, so he probably liked these dancers the best.

Activity 3 Arabian English Spanish Chinese Japanese Palestinian

Activity 4 2 fierce eyes 3 gloomy streets 4 brave hero 5 wooden nutcracker

WB answers

Exercise 1 a3 b8 c10 d2 e1 f6 g4 h7 i9 j5

Exercise 2 1 programme 2 dream 3 midnight 4 ballet 5 mask

Exercise 3 1 the start 2 suddenly 3 attack 4 turn into 5 disappear 6 perform

---

Time division

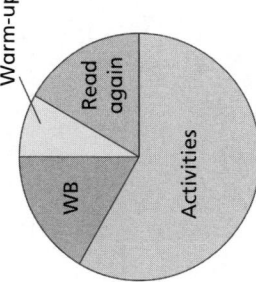

Warm-up, Read again, Activities, WB

Unit 5 Reading comprehension and vocabulary

Lesson 3 Speaking (PB p59) Study skills

Lesson aim Speaking, Study skills (WB)

Lesson targets Children:
- listen to a dialogue; listen and repeat the dialogue
- understand the story and answer oral questions
- read and act the dialogue
- (WB) practise dictionary skills and definitions

Informal everyday expressions *I can't wait! Here we go. It certainly was.*

New words *final, rehearsal, excited, begin, switch on, loud, hour, terrible, certainly, on time, forgot, fell off, disaster, total*

Materials PB p59; CD B tracks 2, 3; WB p43; Dictionary 4

Preparation Listen to CD B track 2 before the lesson

Warm-up
Ask the class to say what happened in Part 4 of *Let's put on a play! What was wrong? What happened?* Let children look back if they cannot remember.

Activity 1
Children look at PB page 59. Read the title of Part 5. Ask *What is happening in the picture? Miss Carey is talking to the children.* Tell children to cover the dialogue text and look at the picture. Play track 2. Children listen.

Activity 2
Children open their books and look at the dialogue. Play track 2 again. Children listen and follow.
Check children understand the new words. Use the dictionary if you wish.

Activity 3
Children close their books. Play track 3. Children listen and repeat in the pauses. Encourage them to use the same expression and intonation.

Activity 4
Ask questions to check understanding of the story. See Resource box.

Activity 5
Children act the dialogue without their books if they can.
If children have their books encourage them to speak out clearly and to look at the book as little as possible.

Unit 5 Speaking

Study skills (WB p43)

The exercises on this page practise dictionary skills.
Children should be able to do this work independently once the tasks have been explained.

Exercise 1
Children number the words. Remind them they can use the alphabet at the top of the page to check their work

Exercise 2
Children order the letters to write the words. Remind them to use their dictionaries to check.

Resource box

Story questions
When are the children going to perform the play? **tomorrow**
Which children are coming to see it? **the kindergarten children**
Is there going to be another rehearsal? **No, this is the last rehearsal.**
What happened when the music came on? **It was too loud.**
What did Max do? said Molly's words **Lulu**
Who forgot their words? **Lulu**
What happened to the house? **It fell down.**
Was it a good rehearsal? **No.**
What was it? **a disaster**

WB answers
Exercise 1 2 – 2 3 1 4 6 5
3 – 1 3 2 6 4 5
4 – 3 2 1 4 6 5
5 – 2 4 3 5 6 1
6 – 4 5 2 3 1 6
Exercise 2 1 army 2 ballet 3 midnight
4 nutcracker 5 silent 6 wooden

Study skills

a b c d e f g h i j k l m n o p q r s t u v w x y z

1 Number the words in the correct order.

1	ballet ___	dancer _2_	soldier ___	king _3_	nutcracker ___	mice _4_
2	Chinese ___	English ___	Arabian _6_	Japanese ___	tickets ___	Russian ___
3	curtain ___	music ___	lights ___	costume ___	poster ___	stage ___
4	mask ___	drums ___	graceful ___	programme ___	umbrella ___	scenery ___
5	evil ___	sleep ___	fast ___	huge ___	strange ___	brave ___
6	perform ___	hold ___	hold ___	leap ___	dance ___	watch ___

2 Read the definitions and write the words. Use the letters in brackets.

1 a large group of soldiers _____ (m y r a)
2 a kind of dancing _____ (l a t l e b)
3 12 o'clock at night _____ (t h i n d i g m)
4 you open nuts with this _____ (r u n t r a c e c k)
5 very, very quiet _____ (t e l i n s)
6 made of wood _____ (n e d o w o)

Now check your answers in your Dictionary.

Unit 5 Dictionary skills

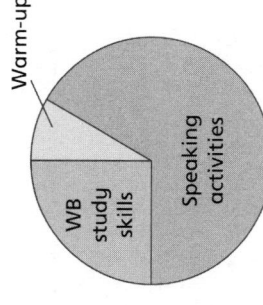

Time division

Warm-up
WB study skills
Speaking activities

Unit 5 Study skills

Lesson 4 Grammar (Session 1), Grammar in conversation (Session 2) (PB pp60–61)

Lesson aim Grammar

Lesson targets Children:
- (session 1) understand and practise the key structure
- (session 2) look at a the pictures in a quiz game
- (session 2) listen to children doing the quiz; repeat and do the quiz

Key structure (session 1) time clause: *While* + past continuous

Key vocabulary (session 1) leisure activities

Key language (session 2) *either … or*

Informal expressions (session 2) *Let's see.*

Materials pp60–61; CD B tracks 4, 5; WB pp44–45

Session 1 Warm-Up

Write countries on the board, e.g. *Japan, China, Arabia, Russia, Spain, Palestine*. Children tell you the adjectives.

Activity 1
Children look at the picture. Ask three children to read the PC kids' bubbles. Write up the third sentence. Class reads. Children look at the pictures. Volunteers read the sentences. Children match and write. Check answers.

Activity 2
Ask a child to read the example. Children read the other sentences. Ask for suggestions for a second sentence for each one. Write them on the board. Help the class to rewrite the pairs into one sentence as in the example. Class reads.

Children write their own sentences in pairs. See Resource box.*

Session 2 Warm-up

Play an *Action mime* to practise *While* + past continuous (see Games, page 186).

Activity 1
Children look for a moment. Explain this is a quiz in a magazine.

Activity 2
Point out the boy and girl. Explain they are doing the quiz. Tell the class to listen to the children. Play track 4. Children follow in their books.

Activity 3
Children listen to track 5 and repeat in the pauses.

Activity 4
Children do the quiz in pairs. See Resource box.**

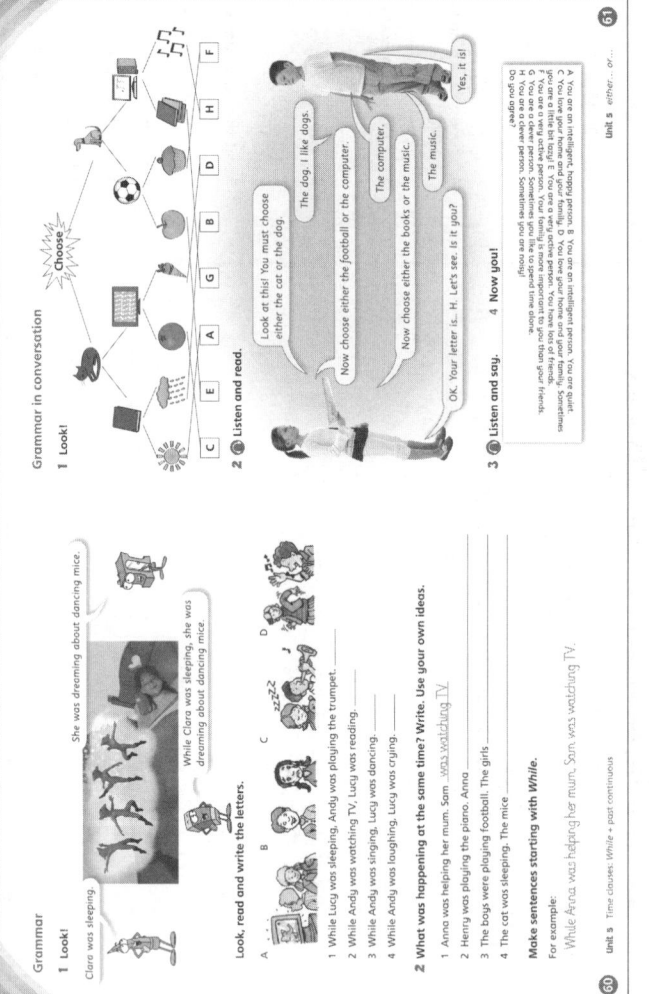

Children complete WB page 44 in class time or for homework.

Unit 5 Grammar, Grammar in conversation

Grammar (Session 1), Grammar in conversation (Session 2) (WB pp44–45)

If this page is for homework, check children understand the tasks.

Exercise 1
Children match the time clauses to the main clauses.

Exercise 2
Children write sentences using the structure.
Write the example on the board and point out the comma at the end of the time clause.

If this page is for homework, check children understand the tasks.

Exercise 1
Children complete the sentences. Point out the example.

Exercise 2
Children complete the dialogue.
Let pairs read it. Others listen and check.

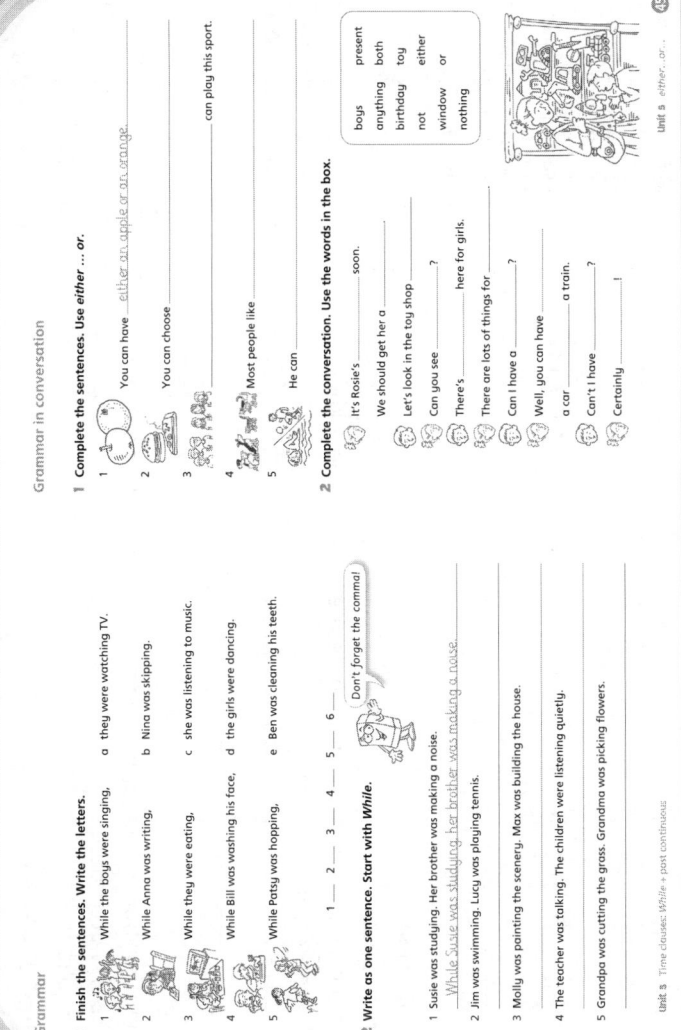

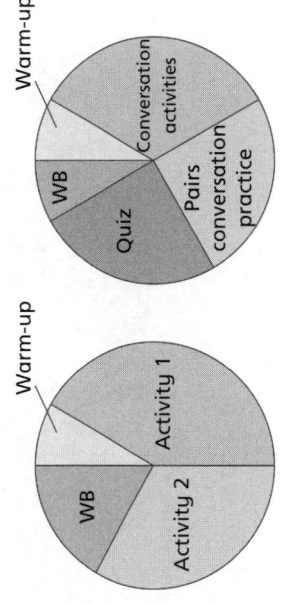

Time division

Session 1 — Warm-up, Activity 1, Activity 2, WB

Session 2 — Warm-up, Conversation activities, Pairs conversation practice, Quiz, WB

Grammar Practice Book

Children may begin Unit 5 when they have completed the PB and WB Grammar pages. They should complete it before the end of PB / WB Unit 5.

Resource box

PB answers (p60)
Activity 1 1C 2A 3D 4B
*Pair work: Grammar (p60)

Activity 1
Children work in pairs. They write their own second sentence for at least one first sentence in Activity 2. They make the two sentences into one beginning with the *While* time clause.

Give children a short time to do this. Check pairs' work around the class by asking them to read out their two sentences then the single sentence.

Go over the structure again if children find this hard.

**Pair work: Grammar in conversation (p61)

Activity 4
Children do the quiz themselves in pairs. They take turns to tell their partner what to choose. Then they find the letter and turn the book upside down to see what the key says. Give pairs a few minutes to do the quiz.

Go around listening to them as they work. Remind them to say *Choose either the… or the…* Let one or two pairs stand up and do the quiz in front of the class while the others listen.

WB answers

Grammar (p44)
Exercise 1 1d 2c 3a 4e 5b
Exercise 2 2 While Jim was swimming, Lucy was playing tennis.
3 While Molly was painting the scenery, Max was building the house.
4 While the teacher was talking, the children were listening quietly.
5 While Grandpa was cutting the grass, Grandma was picking flowers.

Grammar in conversation (p45)
Exercise 1 2 either a pizza or a burger 3 Either girls or boys 4 either dogs or cats 5 either play football or go swimming
Exercise 2 birthday, present, window, anything, nothing, boys, toy, either, or, both, not

Unit 5 Grammar, Grammar in conversation

Lesson 5 Listening, Phonics (PB p62) Use of English

Lesson aim Listening, spelling and pronunciation, Use of English (WB)

Lesson targets Children:
- talk about scenes from different plays
- listen to a recount of a rehearsal; answer gist and detailed questions
- practise saying, reading and spelling words with *oi* sounding *oy*
- (WB) learn about prepositions in time phrases

Key structure and language from Unit 5

Target words *join, coin, soil, boil, oil, coil, voice*

Materials PB p62; CD A track 32; CD B tracks 6, 7; WB pp46–47

Warm-up

Children say the riddle from PB page 43, CD A track 32. Ask volunteers to read one or two lines each, or let the whole class say the poem if they learned it.

Listening

Activity 1
Children say which plays these scenes are from: 'The ugly duckling' and 'Jack and the beanstalk'. Ask what each scene shows. Encourage children to tell you as much as they can about what happens in each story.

Activity 2
Children listen to track 6 and answer the questions. They should be able to answer these on the first listening.

Activity 3
Ask one or more children to read out the questions. Play track 6 again. Children circle the correct person. To check answers, ask different children to read each questions and name the person. Check the class agrees. Play the track again to check if necessary.

Phonics

Point out the box. Tell children to follow in their books and repeat in the pauses. Play the first part of track 7. Make sure children repeat the sound accurately.
Play the end of track 7. Children listen and follow.
Children say the rhyme. They may learn it, if you wish.
Children open their WBs at page 46. They complete the Phonics page now or for homework. If it is for homework, make sure they understand the tasks.

Listening

1 Talk about the pictures.

2 Listen.
1 What was the name of the play?
2 Was it the first performance or the final rehearsal?

3 Read the questions. Listen again and circle the right person.
1 Who switched on the lights?   Miss Carey / Max / Molly / Alfie / Lulu
2 Who started the music?   Miss Carey / Max / Molly / Alfie / Lulu
3 Who shouted?   Miss Carey / Max / Molly / Alfie / Lulu
4 Who forgot the nest?   Miss Carey / Max / Molly / Alfie / Lulu
5 Who forgot her words?   Miss Carey / Max / Molly / Alfie / Lulu
6 Who fell down?   Miss Carey / Max / Molly / Alfie / Lulu
7 Whose head fell off?   Miss Carey / Max / Molly / Alfie / Lulu
8 Who laughed?   Miss Carey / Max / Molly / Alfie / Lulu

Phonics
Look and listen!

oi   The toy soldiers joined in the battle.

Join in the song,   dig the soil,   coil the rope,   boil the oil.

→ Now look at WB p47 Use of English

Unit 5 Listening: understanding a narrative; listening for gist and detail. Phonics: *oi* vowel sound

Use of English

Move on to WB page 47.

Phonics, Use of English (WB pp46–47)

Remind the class of the sound *oi* and *join*.

Write the sentence on the board. Class reads.

Exercise 1
Children complete the words and write them.

Go through the presentation with the class. Write sentences and phrases on the board as appropriate. Ask volunteers to underline prepositions and/or phrases in example sentences.

Exercise 2
Children write the words under the correct picture.

Exercise 3
Children complete the sentences using the target words.

Exercise 2
Children complete the exercise referring back to the information and the examples in exercise 1. Children work alone. Check answers together.

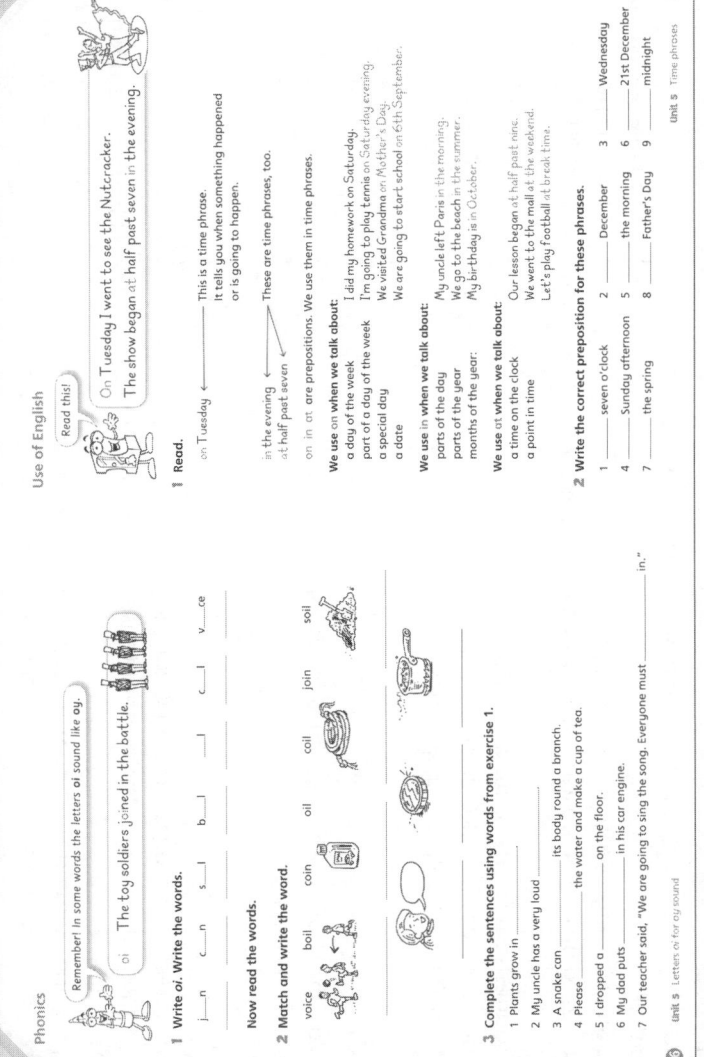

Resource box

Audioscript (CD B track 6) Listening activities 2–3 (PB p62)
It was time for the final rehearsal. Lulu, Molly and Max were excited but Alfie was worried. "I can't remember my words," he said.

The stage was dark. Max switched on the lights and Molly started the music. "It's too loud," shouted Miss Carey. The curtains opened and there was the river, the reeds, the trees and a little house on the right. But where was the nest? "Alfie! Where is your nest?" shouted Miss Carey. "Sorry!" said Alfie. He ran onto the stage and put the nest on the river bank.

The rehearsal was a disaster! Alfie didn't forget his words but Lulu forgot hers. Max said Molly's words and Molly said Lulu's words. The little house fell down and Lulu fell down, too. Poor Alfie! He was the ugly duckling and his head fell off!

"That was terrible!" said Miss Carey, but she wasn't angry. She laughed. "The play's going to be great," she said. "Just wait and see!"

WB answers (p46)

Exercise 2 join, oil, coil, voice, coin, boil

Exercise 3 1 soil 2 voice 3 coil 4 boil 5 coin 6 oil 7 join

Use of English (p47)

Exercise 2 1 at 2 in 3 on 4 on 5 in 6 on 7 in 8 on 9 at

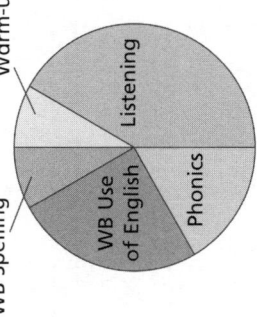

Time division

Unit 5   Phonics, Use of English

Lesson 6 Class composition (Session 1) (PB p63) Writing preparation, Composition practice (Session 2)

Lesson aim Writing

Lesson targets Children:
- (session 1) design a poster and write a programme for a show with teacher support
- (session 2) (WB) write and design a poster for a show independently
- (session 2) (WB) write and design a programme for a show independently

Key structure and language from Unit 5

Vocabulary publicity and information for a show

Materials PB p63; WB pp48–49; poster 5

Session 1 Warm-up

Put up poster 5. Ask what things are on it: *poster, programme, tickets*.
Ask *What information do the poster and programme give?*

Class composition

Activity 1

Ask a child to read the first two sentences. Read out the task.
Draw a poster on the board as on the PB page.
Help the class to complete the information that is needed, e.g. the name of the group, etc. Ask the class for ideas. Choose the best one together.
Ask about the name of the play – *'The ugly duckling'*. Write it on the board.
Ask for suggestions for one or more pictures to go on the poster. Write up several ideas for children to choose from.
Encourage children to think of sensible suggestions for the day, time, etc.
Remind them that the show is taking place in school for a KG class.
Give the class time to note the ideas in their Pupil's Books or copy books

Activity 2

Children draw their own posters on a large sheet of paper. They may finish this work for homework, or in pairs or groups in class time if you wish.

Activity 3

Help the class to complete the programme. Read the programme on poster 5.
Explain that in a programme, the story of the play is told in the present tense because it is always the same and the actors perform it many times.
Ask children to suggest ideas for a story outline. Remind them that they cannot tell the whole story in detail. Help them to tell the main points in five or six short sentences. Explain that they do not need to say exactly what happens at the end.
List the characters on the second page. Children suggest names for the performers.

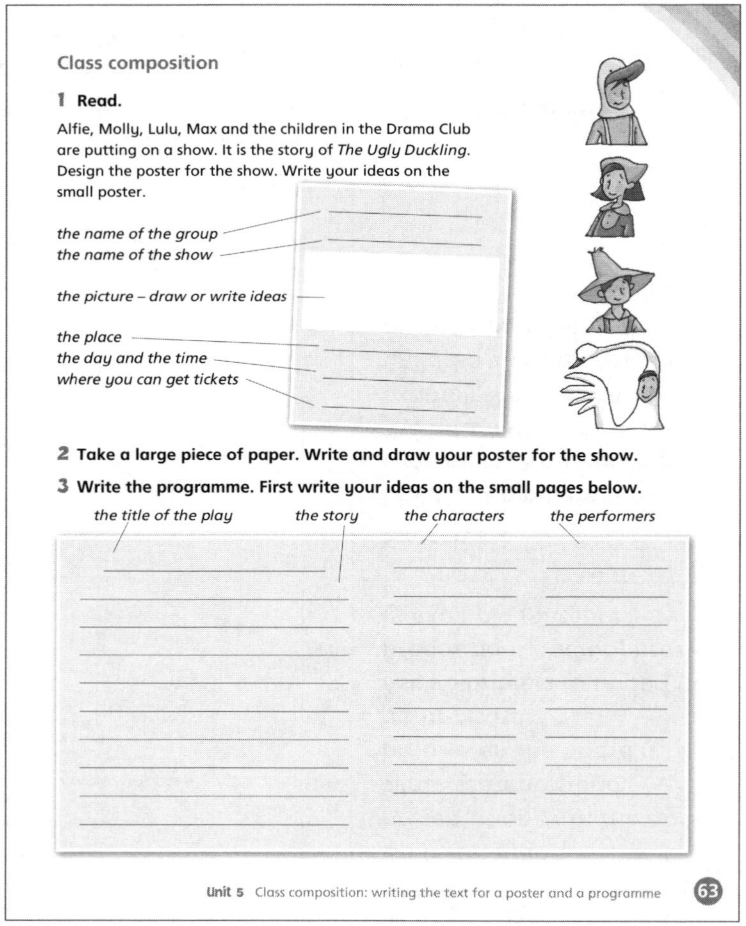

Class composition

1 Read.

Alfie, Molly, Lulu, Max and the children in the Drama Club are putting on a show. It is the story of The Ugly Duckling. Design the poster for the show. Write your ideas on the small poster.

- the name of the group
- the name of the show
- the picture – draw or write ideas
- the place
- the day and the time
- where you can get tickets

2 Take a large piece of paper. Write and draw your poster for the show.

3 Write the programme. First write your ideas on the small pages below.
- the title of the play
- the story
- the characters
- the performers

Children use a large piece of paper folded in half to make their own programme. Remind them of the front cover. Let the class check what is on the programme on Poster 5 to give them ideas. Children may begin this work in class and finish for homework if you wish.

Writing preparation, Composition practice (WB pp48–49)

Session 2 Warm-up

List all the plays and stories children can name.

1. Children design their own poster for a play. Make sure they understand the task. Encourage them to think of a play they know about, if possible. Alternatively, children can choose one of the titles on the page.

2. They use the small poster on the page to write their ideas. If you wish, children may make a much bigger poster with large coloured lettering, etc. and illustrations as a homework or individual project.

3. Alternatively they may use the small poster on the page and do a small version.

Exercise 1

Children create a programme for the play they chose on page 48. If you wish, children can write ideas in the spaces on the page and draw ideas for the cover. They may then use larger paper to make a 4-page folded programme.

Exercise 2

They write a few sentences telling the story in the present tense. Remind them that the present tense is used because the story is a play which actors are going to perform many times.

Any extra individual work that children do may be added to their portfolios.

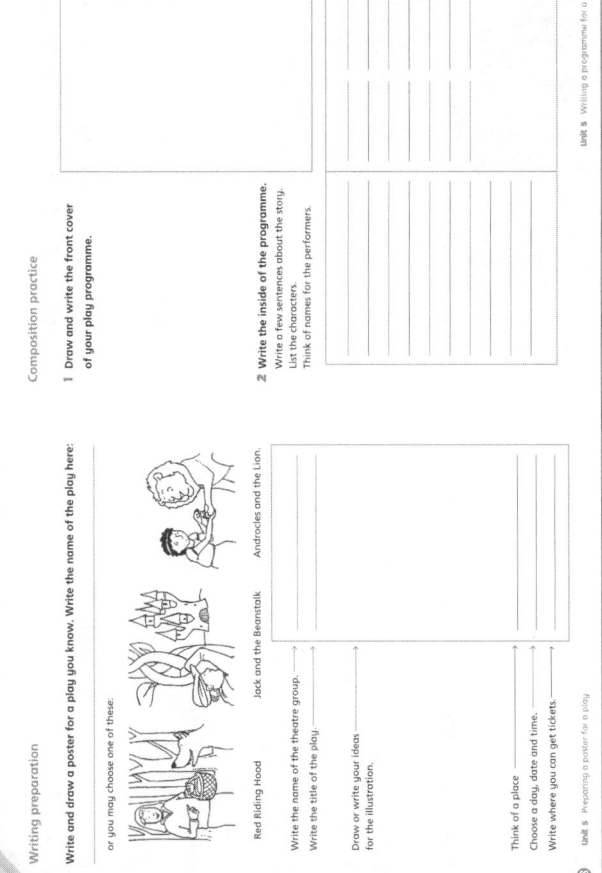

Homework task

Children complete Check-up 5, WB p50. For answers, see p105.

Time division

Session 1
- Class composition writing in books
- Class composition writing in teacher-led board writing
- Warm-up

Session 2
- Composition practice
- Writing preparation
- Warm-up

Portfolio

Children keep posters and programmes if they did them on paper.

Note: For Unit 6 Lesson 1 – ask children to bring in photos of themselves as small babies.

Resource box

Class composition example writing (PB p63)

This play tells the story of the ugly duckling. He is sad because he is ugly. He runs away. He meets beautiful swans and a kind man. He is sad in the winter but in the spring he has a wonderful surprise.

WB answers

Writing preparation: poster (WB p48), Composition practice (WB p49)

No examples are given as work will depend on children's own ideas.

In assessing how well the task has been done the key features to look for are:

Poster	all the required information is included
	the illustration is appropriate for the play
Programme	the front cover has the name of the play and appropriate illustration
	the story is told in a few sentences in the present tense
	the programme has a list of characters and the names of performers

Unit 5 Writing preparation, Composition practice

6 Changes in nature

Lesson 1 Poster 6, Reading

Lesson aim Reading

Text type poems

Lesson targets Children:
- read, understand and practise new vocabulary on the poster
- read, understand and practise reading poems
- answer oral comprehension questions

Key structure *will* future

Key language *It's an egg – it will grow. What will it be?*

Key vocabulary nature

Materials PB pp64–65; poster 6; CD B track 8; Dictionary 4; word cards for poster vocabulary (see poster 6 below or list on p15)

Preparation Make word cards; listen to CD B track 8

Warm-up

Children show photos of themselves as small babies. They talk about what they looked like then and what they are like now. Let them do this in pairs or small groups first, then ask some children to show their photos and speak to the class.

Poster 6

1 Point to the poster. Read out the title.
  Give the class a moment or two to look.

2 Point to the creatures. Read the word/s. Show the word card/s. Class reads and says the word/s.
  Make sure children understand the following words. Use the definitions and example sentences as necessary to ensure understanding:

  dragonfly   an insect with long wings that lives near water
              Dragonflies often have beautiful wings.
  larva   an insect before it grows up and flies
              We looked at a larva in science today.
  tadpole   a baby frog
              Tadpoles are black and have little tails.

  Cover the words on the poster if you wish.
  Point to the creatures at random. Class names them.

3 Ask children *Do you know anything about any of these creatures?* Encourage them to tell you anything they can.

6 Changes in nature

4 Ask *Do you see any of these creatures? Where do you see them?*

5 Ask *Which creatures are beautiful? pretty? What do you like about them? Which creatures are ugly? What don't you like about them?*

Unit 6 Reading

Reading (PB pp64–65)

1 Children look at the pictures.
Ask which creatures they can see on these pages. They should be able to name the butterfly and the bird. They may also remember *chick, caterpillar* and *dragonfly*.
Ask if they know what the writing on these pages is: *poems*. How many? *three*

2 Play track 8. Children listen and follow in their books.

3 Read one poem at a time or play track 8 and pause after each poem.
Use Dictionary 4 to help you to explain new words as necessary. Explain:
pupa – the bag a butterfly grows in before it flies
We drew a picture of a *pupa* in science yesterday.
Help children to find new words. Make up extra sentences for new words if you wish.
Note: Many words in these poems are for understanding only and need not be learned and practised.

4 Ask questions about each poem. See Resource box.

5 Let volunteers read a verse each.
Amazing changes is for two voices so pairs could read this poem.
Play track 8 again.

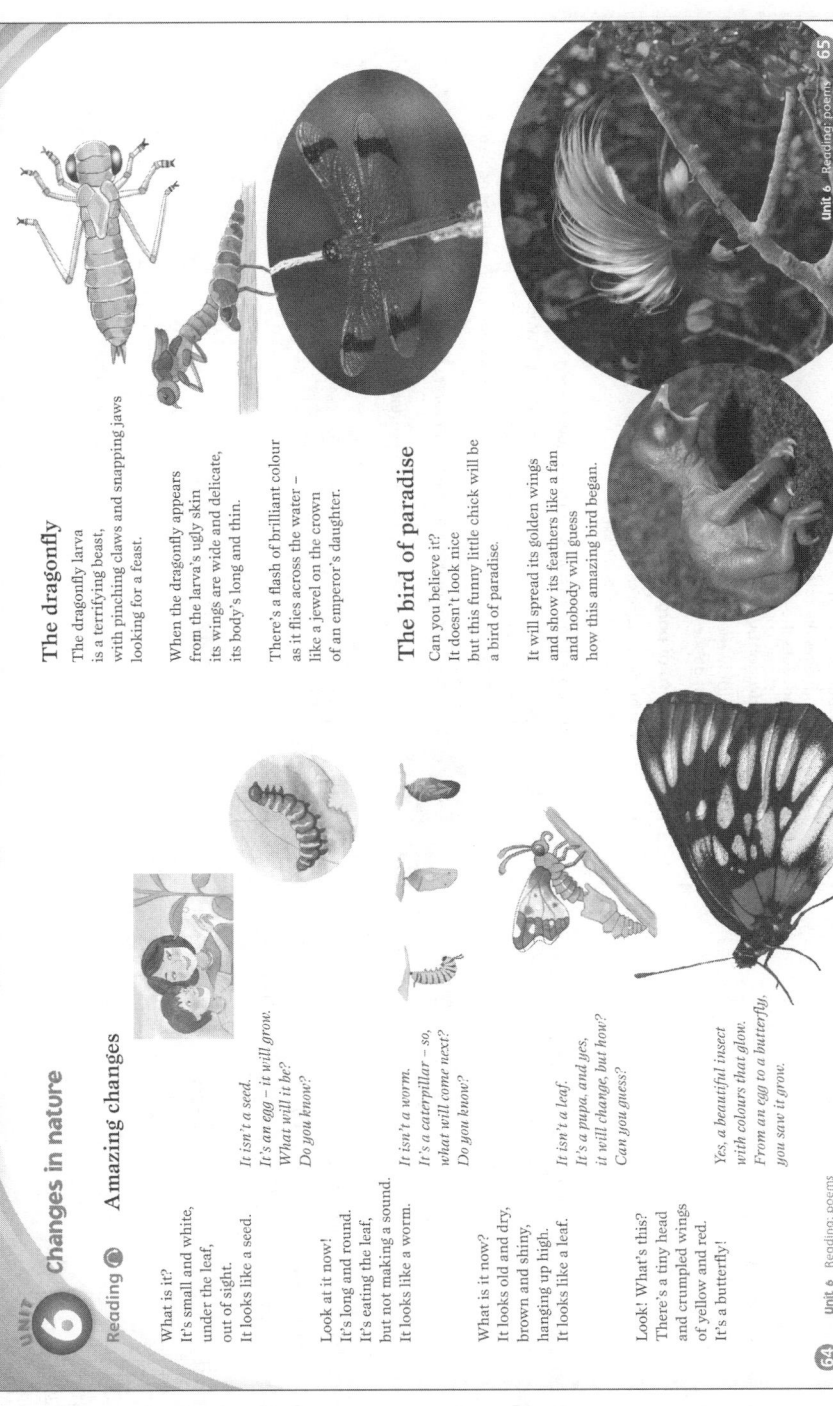

Resource box

Text questions

Amazing changes
What does the egg look like? *a seed*
What does the caterpillar look like? *a worm*
What does the pupa look like? *a leaf*
What colours is the butterfly? *yellow, red*
How many changes are there from the egg to the butterfly? *four – egg, caterpillar, pupa, butterfly*

The dragonfly
Why is the dragonfly terrifying? *It has pinching claws and snapping jaws.*
What is its body like? *long and thin*
What is the colour of a dragonfly like? *a jewel on a crown*

The bird of paradise
Why doesn't the chick look nice? *It does not have feathers and its head is big.*
What do the adult bird's feathers look like? *a fan*

Homework task

Children learn selected vocabulary from Unit 6 Dictionary 4.
See unit word list on pp190–191 for key words, extension words and words for understanding only.

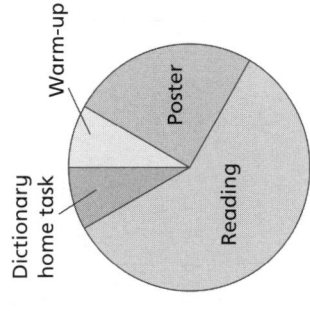

Time division

Poster
Warm-up
Reading
Dictionary home task

Unit 6 Reading

Lesson 2 Reading comprehension and vocabulary (PB p66)

Lesson aim Reading comprehension; vocabulary
Lesson targets Children re-read the poems, then:
- (PB) answer literal and inferential questions
- match words to pictures
- (WB) match words to descriptions
- match words to definitions

Key structure *will* future
Key language *It's an egg – it will grow. What will it be?*
Words vocabulary from Lesson 1
Materials PB p66; CD B track 8 (optional); WB p52; Dictionary 4

Warm-up

Children look at PB pages 64 and 65. Ask them which creature they think changes the most. Let them speak in pairs for a minute then hear ideas from around the class.

Read again

Play track 8, read the poems to the class or let children read them. Class listens and follows in their books.

Activity 1

Ask a volunteer to read the first question. Tell children they put their hands up. Children look back at the poem. Elicit an answer. Check with the class.
Continue in the same way with the other questions.

Activity 2

For question 1, children should look back at the poems to check the detail.
For question 2, children should try to work out what the line *always looking for a feast* means. Children check the meaning of *feast*. They try to decide why the dragonfly larva wants to eat a lot.
For question 3, children should look at the pictures and think of their own ideas.

Activity 3

Ask one or more children to read the words in the box.
Children match the words and the pictures. Elicit the first word.
Check with the class. Children write. Continue with the other words.

Reading comprehension and vocabulary

1 Answer the questions.

Amazing changes
1 What is under the leaf?
2 What does the egg look like?
3 Something is eating the leaf. What does it look like?
4 What is really eating the leaf?
5 What does the caterpillar change into?
6 What does the pupa look like?

The dragonfly
7 Which two words describe the dragonfly's wings?
8 What do the dragonfly's bright colours look like?

The bird of paradise
9 Why does the chick look funny?
10 What colour are its wings?

2 Talk about the answers to these questions.
1 How many times does the butterfly egg change? What are the changes?
2 Why is the dragonfly larva always looking for a feast?
3 What are the differences between the bird of paradise chick and the adult bird?

3 Write the words under the correct pictures.

| jewel | seed | dragonfly | butterfly | tadpole | caterpillar | fan | chick | worm |

66 Unit 6 Reading comprehension: literal questions; deductive questions; word/picture match

Unit 6 Reading comprehension and vocabulary

92

Reading comprehension and vocabulary (WB p52)

If children are doing this page for homework, make sure they understand the tasks. They should be able to read the sentences in exercise 1, but read them with the class as preparation if some children need support.
Remind them to have their dictionaries with them for this work.

Exercise 1
Children read the descriptions and write the word for the creature it matches.

Exercise 2
Children match the words and definitions.

Resource box

PB answers

Activity 1 1 an egg
2 small and white
3 a worm
4 a caterpillar
5 a pupa
6 a leaf
7 wide, delicate
8 a jewel
9 children's own ideas, e.g. it has no feathers, it's pink, its eyes look funny
10 golden

Activity 2 1 three times: the egg changes into a caterpillar, the caterpillar changes into a pupa and the pupa changes into a butterfly.
2 Help the class to think through an answer if they don't think of it themselves. A feast is a big dinner: the larva is going to grow and change a lot so it needs lots of food.
3 Children's own ideas; no feathers, very small

Activity 3 1 caterpillar 2 worm 3 butterfly
4 dragonfly 5 jewel 6 tadpole 7 seed
8 chick 9 fan

WB answers

Exercise 1 1 butterfly 2 chick 3 tadpole
4 worm 5 caterpillar 6 dragonfly

Exercise 2 1 crumpled 2 feast 3 skin 4 seed
5 snap 6 delicate 7 beast

UNIT 6 Reading comprehension and vocabulary

1 Read the description. Write the word.

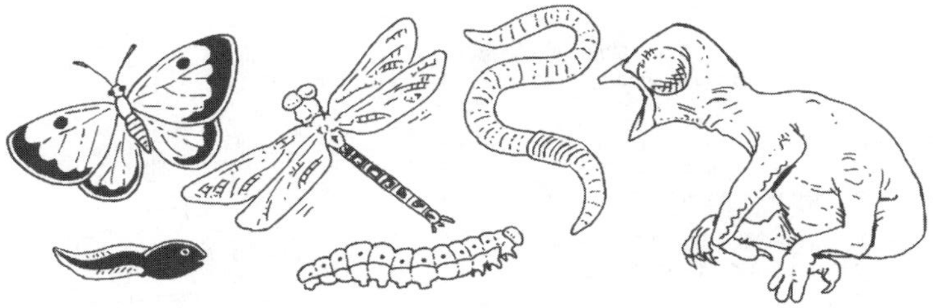

worm   chick   caterpillar   butterfly   tadpole   dragonfly

1 It is an insect. It has large coloured wings. It has a small head _____
2 It does not look pretty. Its eyes are shut. It has no feathers. _____
3 It has no arms or legs. It has a strong tail and it can swim. _____
4 It lives underground. It has no arms, legs or feet. It cannot see. _____
5 It eats leaves. It has a round head and lots of feet. _____
6 It has a long, thin body. It flies over water. Its wings are delicate. _____

2 Match the words in the box to the definitions. Write the word.

crumpled   seed   beast   feast   skin   delicate   snap

1 squashed in an untidy way _____
2 lots of foods for a special occasion _____
3 the outside covering of an animal's body _____
4 the part of a plant that a new plant grows from _____
5 to open and close the mouth quickly _____
6 not strong and looking thin _____
7 an animal _____

Unit 6 Matching words to descriptions and definitions

Time division

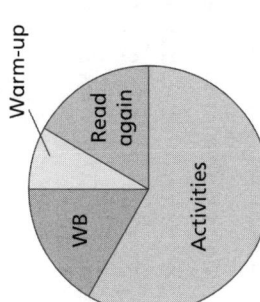

Warm-up
Read again
WB
Activities

Unit 6 Reading comprehension and vocabulary

93

Lesson 3 Speaking (PB p67) Study skills

Lesson aim Speaking, (WB) Study skills

Lesson targets Children:
- listen to a dialogue; listen and repeat the dialogue
- understand the story and answer oral questions
- read and act the dialogue
- (WB) practise matching and dictionary skills

Informal everyday expressions *I hope so. Good luck! Hooray!*

New words *nervous, terrified, ready, hid, true, become*

Materials PB p67; CD B track 9, 10; WB p53; Dictionary 4

Preparation Listen to CD B track 9 before the lesson

Warm-up
Ask the class what happened in Part 5. *What did the children do?* See how much they can remember then let them look back if necessary.

Activity 1
Children look at PB page 67. Read the title of Part 6. Ask *What are the kindergarten children doing?* Tell children to cover the dialogue text and look at the picture. Play track 9. Children listen.

Activity 2
Children look at the dialogue. Play track 9 again. Children listen and follow. Check children understand the new words. Use the dictionary if you wish.

Activity 3
Children close their books. Play track 10. Children listen and repeat in the pauses. Encourage them to use the same expression and intonation.

Activity 4
Ask questions to check understanding of the story. See Resource box.

Activity 5
Children act the dialogue without their books as far as possible. Encourage children to speak without reading their lines word by word.

Study skills (WB p53)

The exercises on this page practise matching and dictionary skills.
Children should be able to do this work independently once the tasks have been explained.

Exercise 1
Children write the words for the animals.

Exercise 2
They match the adult and the baby animals. Some of these words are new but children use the pictures to help them match.

Resource box

Story questions
How were the children feeling before the play? *nervous, terrified*
What did Miss Carey say? *Good luck, everyone.*
Did they forget their lines? *No*
Did the scenery fall down? *No*
Did the kindergarten children like the play? *Yes*
What did they do at the end of the play? *They clapped and they shouted 'Hooray'.*

How do you think Lulu, Max, Molly and Alfie felt after the play?
Children's own answers

WB answers
Exercise 1 1 horse 2 sheep 3 dog 4 duck 5 goose 6 hen
7 swan 8 cat 9 cow 10 wolf
Exercise 2 1 chick 2 lamb 3 kitten 4 cub 5 foal 6 gosling
7 cygnet 8 puppy 9 duckling 10 calf

Time division

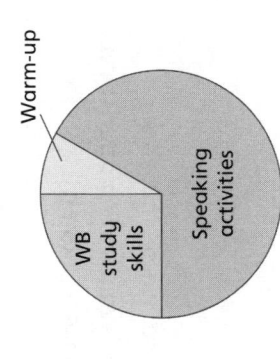

Warm-up
WB study skills
Speaking activities

Unit 6 Study skills

Lesson 4 Grammar (Session 1), Grammar in conversation (Session 2) (PB pp68–69)

Lesson aim Grammar

Lesson targets Children:
- (session 1) understand and practise the key structure
- (session 2) listen to and read a conversation; repeat and practise it
- (session 2) listen to a chant, say it and learn it (optional)

Key structure (session 1) *will* future
Key vocabulary animals and nature
Key language (session 2) *good, better, the best; bad, worse, the worst*
Informal expressions (session 2) *Really? Definitely. What's the matter? Oops!*
Materials PB pp68–69; CD B tracks 11–13; WB pp54–55; poster 6

Session 1 Warm-up

Put up poster 6. Choose two or three creatures. In pairs children write three adjectives to describe each one. They may only list a word once.

Activity 1
Children look at the middle picture. Ask what it is and what is in the thought bubbles.
Ask two children to read the PC kids' bubbles.
Write the sentences on the board. Class reads.
Volunteers read the sentences. Elicit *Yes* or *No* to each one. Children write. For the *No* sentences they say what will happen.

Activity 2
Ask pairs to read the PC kids' bubbles.
Write the first prompt words on the board.
Help the class to compose the question.
Elicit a short answer. Continue with the other prompt words.

Children practise questions and answers in pairs. See Resource box.*

Session 2 Warm-up

Ask about changes. *What will a cygnet, duckling, gosling become? What will a caterpillar, tadpole, chick become?*

Activity 1
Explain that the boy and girl in the photos are looking at the pictures.
Tell the class to listen to them. Play track 11. Children follow in their books.

Activity 2
Children listen to track 12 and repeat in the pauses.

Activity 3
Children practise the conversation in pairs. See Resource box.**

Activity 4
Ask *Do you know what is in the picture?* Explain *cheerleaders* if necessary.
Play track 13. Children listen and follow the first time.
Read the words with the class. Play track 13. Children join in. They may learn the chant, if you wish.

Children complete WB page 54 in class time or for homework.

Unit 6   Grammar, Grammar in conversation

Grammar (Session 1), Grammar in conversation (Session 2) (WB pp54–55)

If this page is for homework, check children understand the tasks.

Exercise 1
Children complete the sentences.

Check they understand all the verbs or remind them to use their dictionaries.

Exercise 2
Children order the words to make sentences.

Exercise 3
Point out the example and the *Remember!* box. Children write negative sentences.

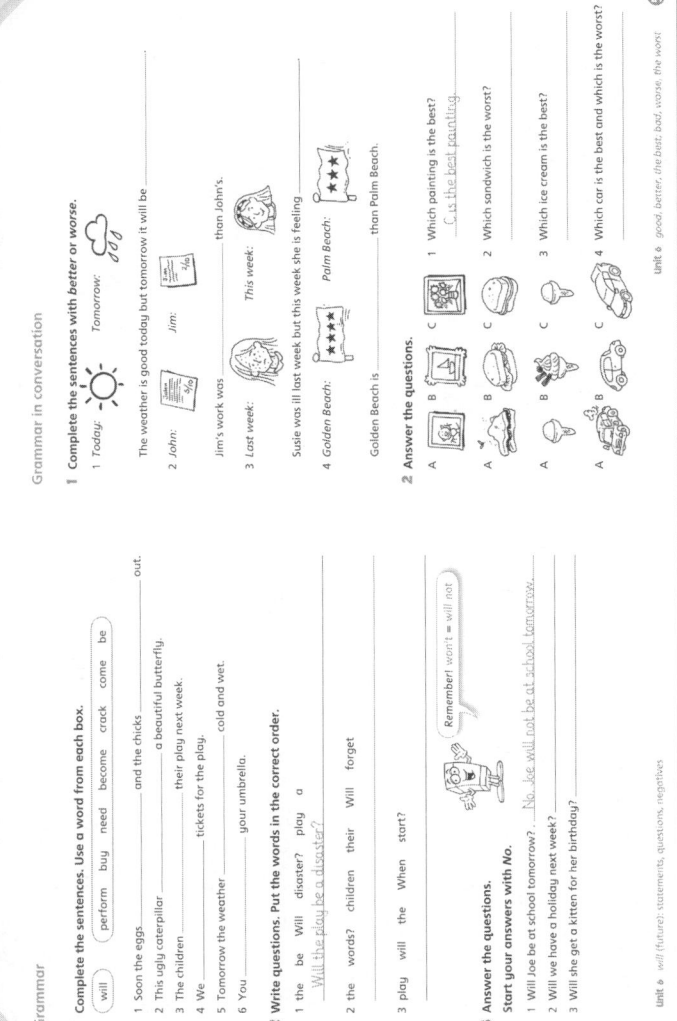

If this page is for homework, check children understand the tasks.

Exercise 1
Children complete the sentences according to the pictures.

Exercise 2
Children find the best or worst object in each line and write a sentence.

Explain that there is one correct answer and they must look at the pictures. They should not answer according to their own opinion.

Resource box

PB answers

*Pair work: Grammar (p68)

Activity 1

Children work in pairs at their desks. They take turns to say the questions and give the short answer. If necessary, bring an able pair forward to demonstrate the activity.

Give the class three minutes to speak in pairs. Then let one or two pairs demonstrate a few questions and answers.

**Pair work: Grammar in conversation (p69)

Activity 3

Children practise the dialogue in pairs at their desks.

Encourage as many children as possible to talk about the pictures using their own ideas and opinions. Make sure they understand they do not need to repeat exactly what the children in the photos said.

Less confident children may work better by keeping to the book dialogue.

Give pairs three minutes to practise the dialogue.

Let one or two pairs stand up and say their conversations while the class listens.

WB answers

Grammar (p54)

Exercise 1 1 will crack, will come 2 will become 3 will perform 4 will buy 5 will be 6 will need

Exercise 2 2 Will the children forget their words? 3 When will the play start?

Exercise 3 2 No, we will not have a holiday next week. 3 No, she will not get a kitten for her birthday.

Grammar in conversation (p55)

Exercise 1 1 worse 2 worse 3 better 4 better

Exercise 2 2 A is the worst sandwich. 3 B is the best ice cream. 4 C is the best car and A is the worst car.

Time division

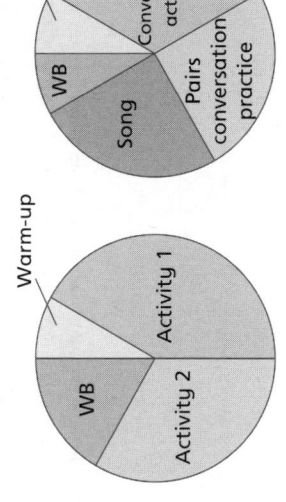

Session 1 — Warm-up, Activity 1, Activity 2, WB

Session 2 — Warm-up, Conversation activities, Pairs conversation practice, Song, WB

Grammar Practice Book

Children may begin Unit 6 when they have completed the PB and WB Grammar pages. They should complete it before the end of PB / WB Unit 6.

Unit 6 Grammar, Grammar in conversation

Lesson 5 Listening, Phonics (PB p70) Use of English

Lesson aim Listening, spelling and pronunciation, Use of English (WB)

Lesson targets Children:
- talk about the scenes in a story
- listen to descriptions of the action in the story and match to pictures
- practise saying, reading and spelling words with aw
- (WB) learn about using the apostrophe for possession

Key structure and language from Unit 6

Target words *claw, jaw, saw, awful, paw, draw*

Materials PB p70; CD B tracks 3, 13, 14; WB pp56–57

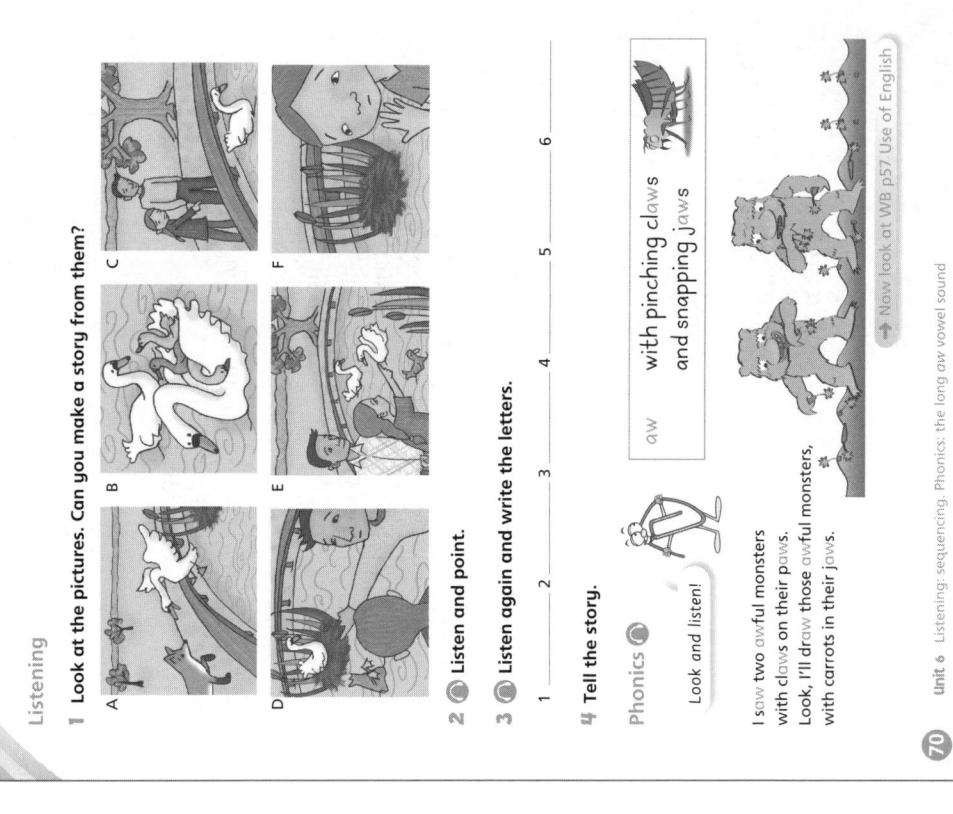

Warm-up

Say the chant from PB page 69, track 3.

Listening

Activity 1

Children look and try to work out the sequence of events. Volunteers suggest what they think the story is.

Activity 2

Children listen to the story on track 14 and point to the pictures that match what they hear.

Activity 3

Play track 14 again. Children listen and write the letters of the pictures in order. Be ready to play track 14 again for them to listen again or check. Check answers together.

Activity 4

Children recount the story in their own words. The aim is not to repeat exactly what they heard on the audio. If you wish, let one child start the story and others continue, saying one or two sentences each.

Phonics

Point out the box. Tell children to follow in their books and repeat in the pauses. Play the first part of track 15. Make sure children repeat accurately. Play the end of track 15. Children listen and follow. Children say the rhyme. They may learn it, if you wish. Children open their WBs at page 56. They complete the Phonics page now or for homework. If it is for homework, make sure they understand the tasks.

Phonics, Use of English (WB pp56–57)

Remind the class of the sound *aw* and *claws, jaws*.

Exercise 1
Children complete the words then write the whole word. Remind them to read what they have written.

Exercises 2 and 3
Children label and complete.

Exercise 4
Encourage children to write interesting sentences.

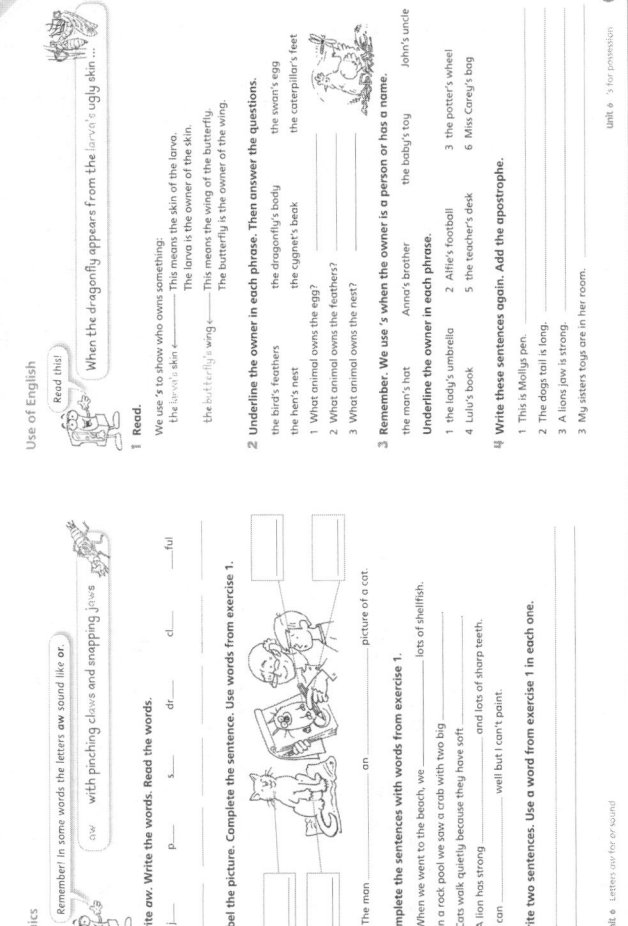

Resource box

Audioscript (CD B track 14) **Listening activities 2-3** (PB p70)
Carly and her father liked to walk in the park. There was a big lake in the park and there were always two beautiful white swans on the water. Carly loved these graceful birds.

One afternoon Carly said to her father, "Look, Dad! There's only one swan today. Where's the other one?"

Dad pointed to the reeds. "Look, Carly," he said. "There's a nest in the reeds. The other swan is sitting on the nest." Carly was excited. "Are there eggs in the nest?" she asked. "Will we see baby swans?" "Yes, we will," said Dad.

The next week, when Carly and her dad went to the park, they saw a fox. It was walking quietly towards the swan's nest. Carly was worried. "Will it steal the eggs?" she asked.

But the swan on the nest saw the fox. It stood up and ran towards the fox angrily. The fox was frightened and ran away.

The next week Carly was sad. The swan's nest was empty and she couldn't see the swans on the lake. "Oh, Dad!" she said quietly. "Did the fox take the eggs? This is the worst day ever."

Dad laughed. "No, the fox didn't take the eggs," he said. "Look!" He pointed across the water. There were the two swans and one of them had three little cygnets sitting on its back! "Three cygnets!" laughed Carly. "This is the best day ever!"

PB answers
Activity 3 1 E 2 C 3 D 4 A 5 F 6 B

WB answers
Phonics (p56)

Exercise 2 saw, awful

Exercise 3 1 saw 2 claws 3 paws 4 jaws 5 draw

Use of English (p57)

Exercise 2 1 the swan 2 the bird 3 the hen

Write up the example sentence. Class reads. Underline *larva's*.

Exercise 1
Go through the presentation with the class. Write up phrases. Underline the possessive noun.

Exercises 2 and 3
Write the phrases on the board. Volunteers underline the owner. Children underline in their books. They answer the questions about the phrases.

Exercise 4
Children rewrite sentences putting in the apostrophe. Write on the board. Volunteers put in the apostrophe. Class checks their work.

Time division

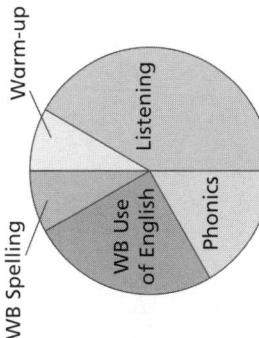

Warm-up · Listening · Phonics · WB Use of English · WB Spelling

Unit 6 Phonics, Use of English

Lesson 6 Class composition (Session 1) (PB p71) Writing preparation, Composition practice (Session 2)

Lesson aim Writing

Lesson targets Children:
- (session 1) complete a poem with teacher support; listen to the poem and read it
- (session 2) (WB) practise identifying adjectives, nouns, verbs and adverbs
- (session 2) (WB) complete a poem; listen to the poem and read it

Key structure and language from Unit 6

Vocabulary nature

Materials PB p71; CD A track 23; CD B track 16; WB pp58–59

Session 1 Warm-up

Sing the seeking song from PB, page 35, CD A track 23.

Class composition

Activity 1

Ask about the pictures. Write notes on the board.

photo 1: *How many eggs are in the nest? How many cygnets are in the nest? Where did it come from? What colour are its features / its beak? Has it got a long neck? Has it got wings? How big are they?*

photo 2: *How many cygnets are there? Are they swimming? What is the adult swan like? What colour is its beak/feathers? What are its wings like? neck like? Is it moving quickly?*

Activity 2

1 Give children a minute or two to look at the first verse. Point out the word bank for the verse. Remind the class of the answers they gave to your questions. Point out the notes on the board. Tell them to think what the best word for each gap might be.

While they are reading and thinking, write the verse on the board with the gaps.

2 Ask for suggestions for the first line. In almost all cases there is only one word that will fit, either grammatically or for sense, but try not to make this a right/wrong exercise. If children suggest a word that does not fit, write it and tell them to read the line. Give them the chance to work out for themselves whether it is the best word or not. Fill in the gap when the class agrees on the best word. Do the same with each line, reminding the class of the answers they gave previously if necessary. They should look in the box for the same word, or a word with a similar meaning.

Ask a volunteer to read each verse as it is completed.

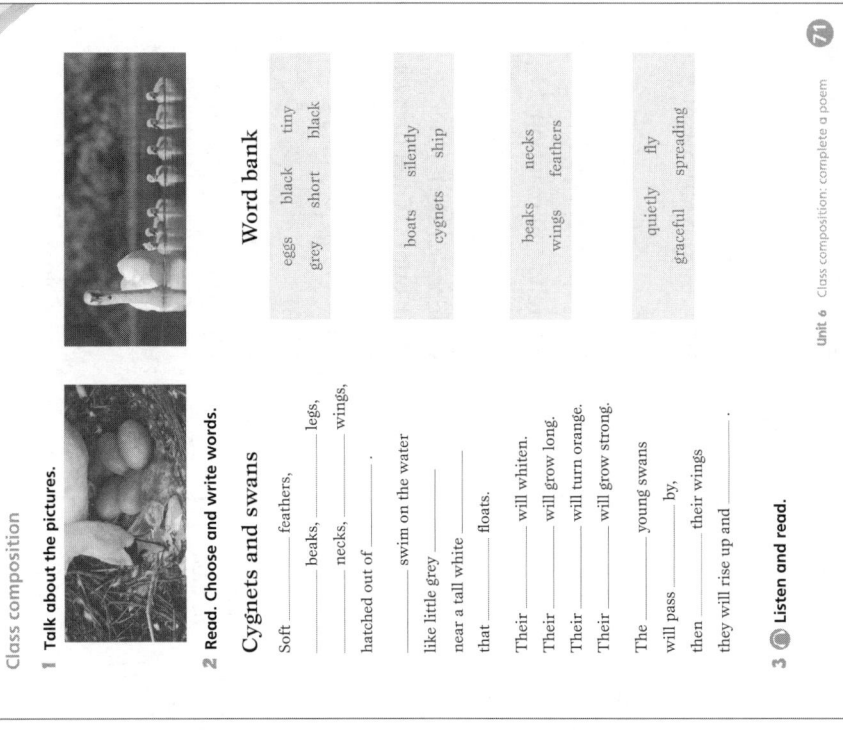

Class composition

1 Talk about the pictures.

2 Read. Choose and write words.

Cygnets and swans

Soft ___ feathers, ___ beaks, ___ legs, ___ necks, ___ wings, hatched out of ___.

___ swim on the water like little grey ___ near a tall white ___ that ___ floats.

Their ___ will whiten.
Their ___ will grow long.
Their ___ will turn orange.
Their ___ will grow strong.

The ___ young swans will pass ___ by,
then ___ their wings
they will rise up and ___.

3 Listen and read.

Word bank

eggs black tiny
grey short black

boats silently
cygnets ship

beaks necks
wings feathers
quietly fly
graceful spreading

Activity 3

Play track 16. Children listen and follow the poem on the board.
Class reads the poem aloud, either individually, in groups or altogether. Encourage them to imitate the intonation they heard on the audio.
Clean the board. Children complete the verses in their books or write the poem in their copy books, in class or for homework.

Unit 6 Class composition

Writing preparation, Composition practice (WB pp58–59)

Session 2 Warm-up

Play *The adverb game* (see Games, page 186).

Exercises 1 and 2

Children should be able to do the work on this page independently (or in pairs) but it is important that they have correct answers before completing the poem on page 59.

Give them a time limit for each exercise and check answers together.

Exercises 1 and 2

Children look at the pictures and use them and the Word Bank to help them complete the poem.

Children should do this work alone or in pairs.

Explain that the word for each space is in the Word Bank but not in any order. They must think about the kind of word they need for each space – e.g. *Is it a noun or an adjective?* – then look for it in the Word Bank.

Give them a time limit to do exercise 2.

Exercise 3

Read the young tadpole poem from the Resource box. Children listen and check their work.

Homework task

Children complete Check-up 6, WB p60. For answers, see p105.

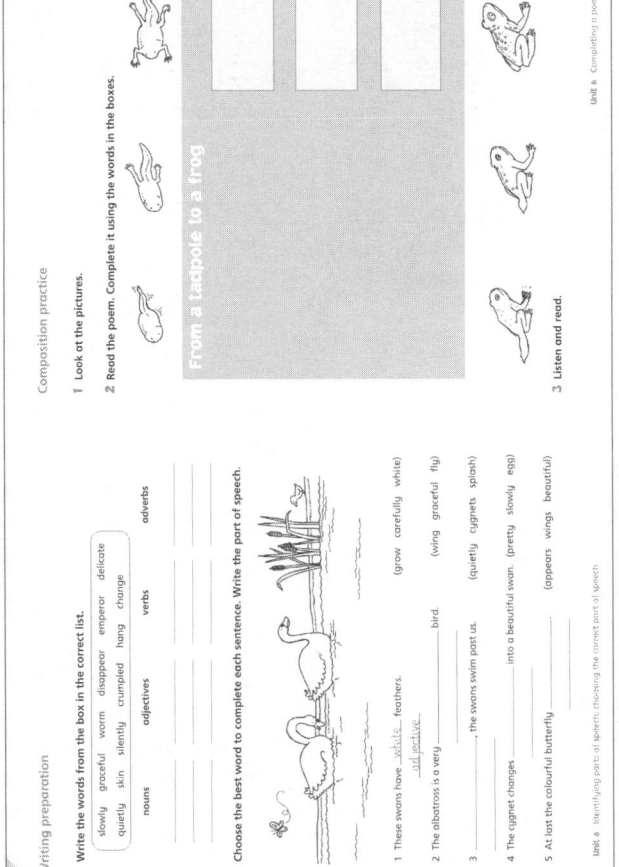

Time division

Session 1: Warm-up, Class composition writing in books, Class composition board writing

Session 2: Warm-up, Writing preparation, Composition practice

Portfolio

Children may make neat copies of their poems.

Resource box

Class composition (p71)

Track 16

Soft grey feathers,
black beaks, black legs,
short necks, tiny wings,
hatched out of eggs.

Cygnets swim on the water
like little grey boats
near a tall white ship
that silently floats.

Their feathers will whiten.
Their necks will grow long.
Their beaks will turn orange.
Their wings will grow strong.

The graceful young swans
will pass quietly by,
then spreading their wings
they will rise up and fly.

If you wish, children may learn some or any of the poems in this unit.

WB answers

Writing preparation (p58)

Exercise 1 nouns: worm, emperor, skin; adjectives: graceful, delicate, crumpled; verbs: disappear, hang, change; adverbs: slowly, quietly, silently

Exercise 2 2 graceful, adjective 3 Quietly, adverb 4 slowly, adverb 5 appears, verb

Composition practice (WB p59)

A young tadpole is round and black
with a funny little tail.
It has no arms, it has no legs.
It's like a tiny whale.

Slowly, little arms appear, with feet and tiny toes.
Then little arms with tiny hands and so the tadpole grows.

It gets fatter, its tail gets shorter
then disappears quite fast.
Its arms are strong, its legs are long.
It's a big green frog at last.

Unit 6 Writing preparation, Composition practice

Revision 2, Project 2

Activity 1

1 Give children a few moments to look at the pictures.
Ask about the first photo. *Is this a rainy place?* Elicit, e.g. **No, there are no trees or plants. It is hot, there are rocks,** etc.
Ask *Who is in the story? two boys, a man and a woman*
Ask about the second photo. *What can you see? flowers and plants What colours are they? purple, yellow, white* Play CD B track 17. Children listen and follow in their books.

2 Ask questions about the story. Children may look back at the text to help them find answers.
Where did Ben go? to America
Who lived there? Ben's Uncle Bob, Aunt Sue and his cousin Joe
What did they do when Ben arrived? **went for a drive**
What did they see? a river
Was there any water? No, there wasn't any water.
Were there any plants? No, there weren't any plants.

3 *What happened when they were driving home?* **there was thunder and lightning**
What happened when they got home? **it started to rain**
Did it rain for a long time? **yes, for hours**
Where did they go a few days later? **to the same valley**
What did they see? **lots of plants and flowers**
Why couldn't Ben believe his eyes? **because it was brown and dry before**
Why did the valley change? **because the rain fell and the plants grew quickly**

Revision 2

1 Listen and read.

Ben went to see Uncle Bob, Aunt Sue and his cousin Joe in America. When he arrived, they went for a drive. It was a hot day and the land was brown, rocky and dry.

They stopped in a wide valley. There was a river in the valley but it was brown and dry, too.

There isn't any water in the river.
There will be water soon. Just wait.

Uncle Bob made coffee over a fire. While they were waiting for the coffee, Ben and Joe explored the valley.

There aren't any plants here.
There will be plants soon. Just wait.

While they were driving home, there was thunder and lightning.

Will it rain soon, Uncle Bob?
It will rain very soon!

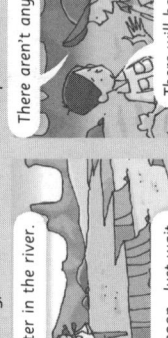

When they got home, it started to rain. It rained for hours.

Will the weather be better tomorrow?
Yes, but it's good for the plants today.

A few days later, they went for a drive again. They went to the same valley. Ben couldn't believe his eyes.

2 Listen again. Act the story.

Activity 2

Children listen to track 17 again.
Let volunteers act the story. If children enjoy this activity, let them practise in groups of five or six (four characters and one or two narrators). Let as many groups as possible act the story for the rest of the class.

Extra activities

Class games

Play in teams. Make statements. Children tell you which of the two photographs it matches – picture 1, picture 2 or pictures 1 and picture 2, e.g.
There aren't any plants. **Picture 1**
There aren't any trees. **Picture 1 and picture 2**
There is a car. **Picture 1**

Use these statements if you wish; add others of your own:
There aren't any clouds. 1, 2
There are people. 1
There are purple flowers. 2
There aren't any people. 2
There isn't any water. 1, 2

Changes

In this project children draw and write about sequences of change.

Children who are interested in science may choose ideas of their own from the natural world. Encourage them to think of their own ideas if they wish.

Alternatively, children choose from the sequences shown on the page.

This project may be done in a group with several children choosing different sequences and putting them on one poster.

2 Do the same with the other sequences. Talk about the things people change. Ask questions. *What does the potter do first? next? then?*, etc. Elicit sentences, e.g. *First a potter takes some clay. Next he makes/shapes it into a pot. Then he paints the pot.*

Do the same with the other sequences, e.g. *First the wool is on the sheep. The weaver gets wool from the sheep*, etc. *First the cook gets some vegetables. He chops/cuts the vegetables*, etc.

3 Children work at their own level. Some will just do the three stages. Other children may wish to put in more stages, e.g. a rainbow after the rain or storm.

Activity 1

Talk with the class about the sequences, e.g. **bright sunny sky, cloudy sky, dark rainy sky.**

Go through the sequence with the class, helping them to form complete sentences. Ask *What happens first, then, after that,* etc. Elicit, e.g. *First the sky is bright and sunny. It is blue and the sun is shining. Then there are clouds. They are white and thick. The sun does not shine always. After that the clouds are thicker and darker. There isn't any sunshine and it rains.*

Activity 2

Children read out their work to the class. Display the work and encourage children to read each other's posters or writing.

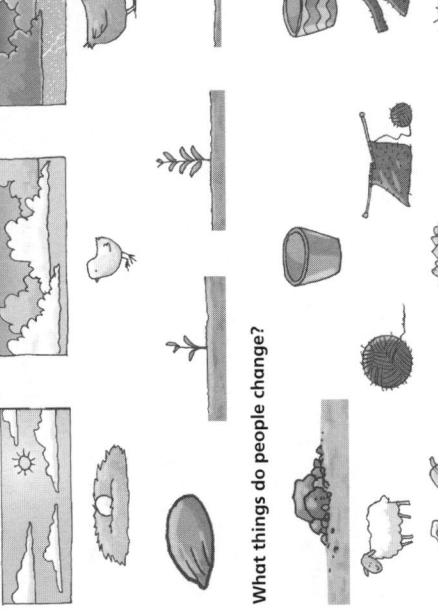

Project 2: Changes

1 What things change?

Find pictures or draw pictures. Arrange them on a poster. Write about them. Here are some ideas. Use two or three of these or find pictures of your own.

What things do people change?

2 Talk about the pictures.

First there is a small nut. It falls onto the ground. Then there is...

First there are some reeds growing. Then a person... Later there is...

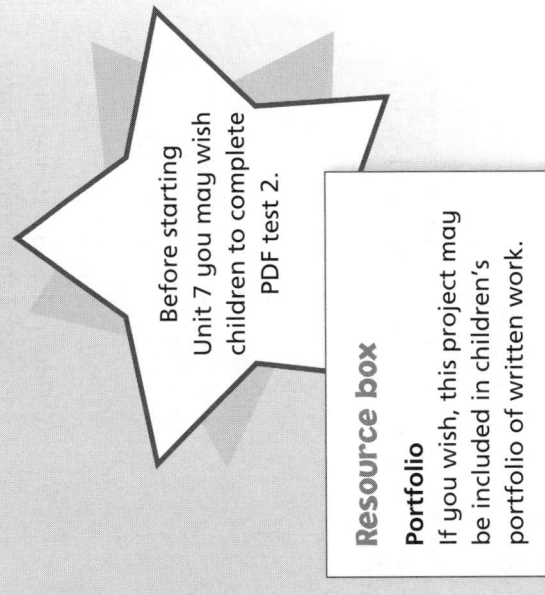

Before starting Unit 7 you may wish children to complete PDF test 2.

Summary box

Lesson aim Revision

Lesson targets Children:
- listen to a story, understand it and act it out
- talk about sequences of change
- draw and write about sequences of change
- show and read out information about changes

Resource box

Portfolio
If you wish, this project may be included in children's portfolio of written work.

Portfolio 2 and Diploma 2: Units 4–6

1 When children have completed all the work in Units 4–6, they turn to page 131 in their WB.

2 This page allows children to make their own assessment of what they have learned in English.

Vocabulary
Tell children to tick each box only when they are confident that they know the key words in each category. Some children may be confident of a wider vocabulary.

Grammar
Make sure children have looked back at all the work they have done.

Phonics
Encourage children to test themselves or test each other in pairs.

3 Check through the completed Portfolio page with each child. Some children may take a little longer to feel confident with the work that has been covered. It is not necessary for the whole class to complete everything on this page before moving on to Unit 7.

1 When children are confident with all the elements of the work on page 131, they may complete the Diploma page.

2 This contains a representative task from each field of work. It is not a formal test.

3 Children receive a sticker for each task completed and one more when they have finished the page.

4 These pages may be taken out of the Workbook and kept in children's individual portfolios of work along with a few examples of children's best work from Units 4–6.

Completed Diploma 2
Exercise 1 cloth, candle, poster, programme, caterpillar, leaves, butterfly, chick
Exercise 2 1 came in, stood up, worked, opened 2 will be, will not rain 3 something, anything, Everything, nothing 4 either ice cream or cake, either apples or bananas 5 baby, lolly, coin, oil, paw, claw

4 Tell children who are not entirely confident to spend extra time learning key words for Units 4–6 in the dictionary. They should also read again the PC kids' speech bubbles on the grammar pages to help them learn and revise the key grammar structures.

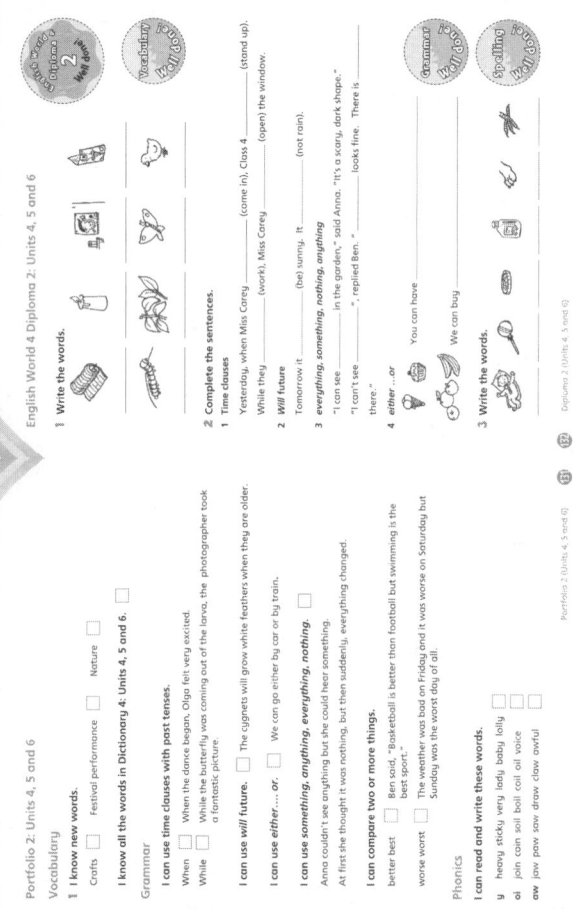

Answers to Check-ups: Units 4–6

Check-up 4 WB pp40–41

Exercise 1 2 When Sally went to the mall, she bought a dress.
3 When Joe came home from school, he had a sandwich.
4 When Lucy opened the box, she found a computer.
5 When the children went to the café, they ate pizzas.
6 When Sam went fishing, he caught a crab.

Exercise 2 1 something
2 anything
3 everything
4 nothing
5 anything

Exercise 3 Children use the pictures and the question in Activity 3 to help them write a complete story in one paragraph. Encourage able children to add in extra detail or extra sentences. Examples are in brackets.

Exercise 4 Children's writing may differ. Example writing:
The (funny) clown was wearing a very big hat. It was enormous. When the children looked in the hat, there was nothing inside. ("It's empty," they said.) The clown put the hat on the table. He put a cloth over the hat. When he put the cloth over the hat, he counted one, two, three. There was something in the hat. When the clown pulled the cloth away, a (beautiful, white) rabbit jumped out of the hat.

Check-up 5 WB pp50–51

Exercise 1 2 were sleeping, was falling.
3 was cooking, was eating (a banana).
4 were playing football, were playing basketball.
5 was picking flowers, was reading.

Exercise 2 2 The boys can either play football or basketball.
3 We can either travel by bus or (by) train.
4 You can choose either a pizza or a burger.

Exercise 3 Children use the pictures and the questions in Activity 3 to help them write the story.

Exercise 4 Example writing: It was half past three. Mum was in the kitchen. She was cooking. While she was cooking the twins were playing football. While the twins were playing football, Grandma and Grandpa were driving to their house. It was four o'clock. The twins were in the bathroom. They were washing their hands. While they were washing their hands, Grandma and Grandpa were knocking at the door. It was quarter past four. Everyone was singing. It was a birthday party for the twins.

Check-up 6 WB pp60–61

Exercise 1 1 will change
2 will sleep
3 will become
4 will have
5 Will … send
6 will … hurt

Exercise 2 1 I think … are better.
2 I think … are worse
3 I think … is the best town in our / my country.
4 I think … is the best pupil in our / my class.
5 I think … is the worse subject at school.
6 I think … is the worst programme on TV.

Exercise 3 Children use the picture and the questions to write a complete paragraph about the weather on the island tomorrow. Children's writing may vary a little. Accept sentences that are accurate and grammatically correct.

Exercise 4 Example writing: The weather will be cold in the north. There will be snow on the mountains. The weather will be better in the east. (It will be warmer.) It will be windy. In the west it will be warm. It will be cloudy and rainy / it will rain. The best weather will be in the south. It will be sunny and hot.

7 People of the world

Lesson 1 Poster 7, Reading

Lesson aim Reading

Text type factual information with captions

Lesson targets Children:
- read, understand and practise new vocabulary on the poster
- read, understand and practise reading the information
- answer oral comprehension questions

Key structure *much, many, a lot of, lots of*

Key language *lots of shops; They do not use much electricity.*

Key vocabulary countries, continents and their people

Materials PB pp74–75; poster 7; CD B track 18; Dictionary 4; word cards for poster vocabulary (see poster 7 below or list on p15)

Preparation Make word cards; listen to CD B track 18

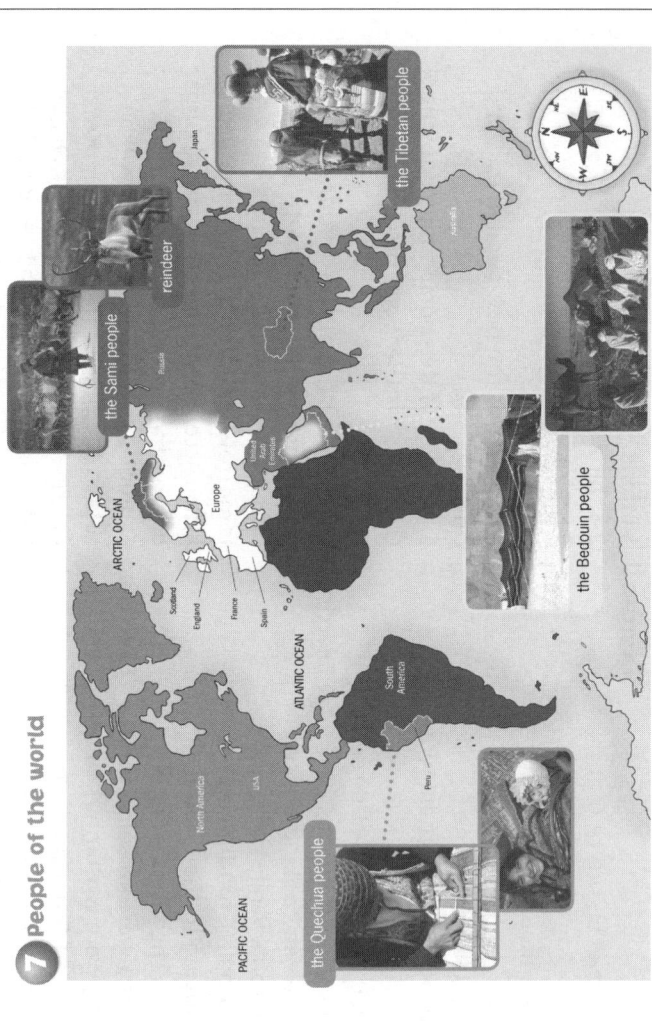

7 People of the world

Warm-up

Ask children to name all the countries and cities they know in English.

Poster 7

1 Point to the poster. Read out the title. Give the class a moment or two to look.

2 Let volunteers come forward and point to and name countries and cities that they recognise.

3 Point to the continents: *North America, South America, Europe, Asia*. Read the word/s. Show the word card/s.

4 Class reads and says the word/s.
Do the same with the new countries and the oceans.

5 Point to the different people shown on the poster and read the names of the people.
Point out and name the reindeer. Show the word card. Class reads.

6 Ask children if they know anything about the countries where the people live. *Is it hot? cold? Are there mountains? rivers?*

The following words are not in Dictionary 4. You may wish to check that children have understood them:

Bedouin	Arab people who live in desert areas of the Middle East
Peru	a country in South America
Sami	people that live in part of northern Europe
South America	the continent that is south of North America
Tibetan	from Tibet, a land near the Himalayan mountains

Unit 7 Reading

Reading (PB pp74–75)

1 Give children time to look at the pictures. Read the title. Ask the class what they can see in the pictures. Encourage them to name and say something about things they know, e.g. weavers, reindeer, dancers, desert, camel, bird.

2 Play track 18. Children listen and follow in their books.

3 Read one paragraph or section of the text at a time.
Use Dictionary 4 to help you to explain new words as necessary. Check children understand *fighter* – a person who fights. Help children to find new words. Make up extra sentences for new words if you wish.

4 Ask questions about each paragraph or a section of the text. See Resource box.

5 Give reading practice around the class. Ask individuals, groups or the class to read sentences or paragraphs. Play track 18 again.

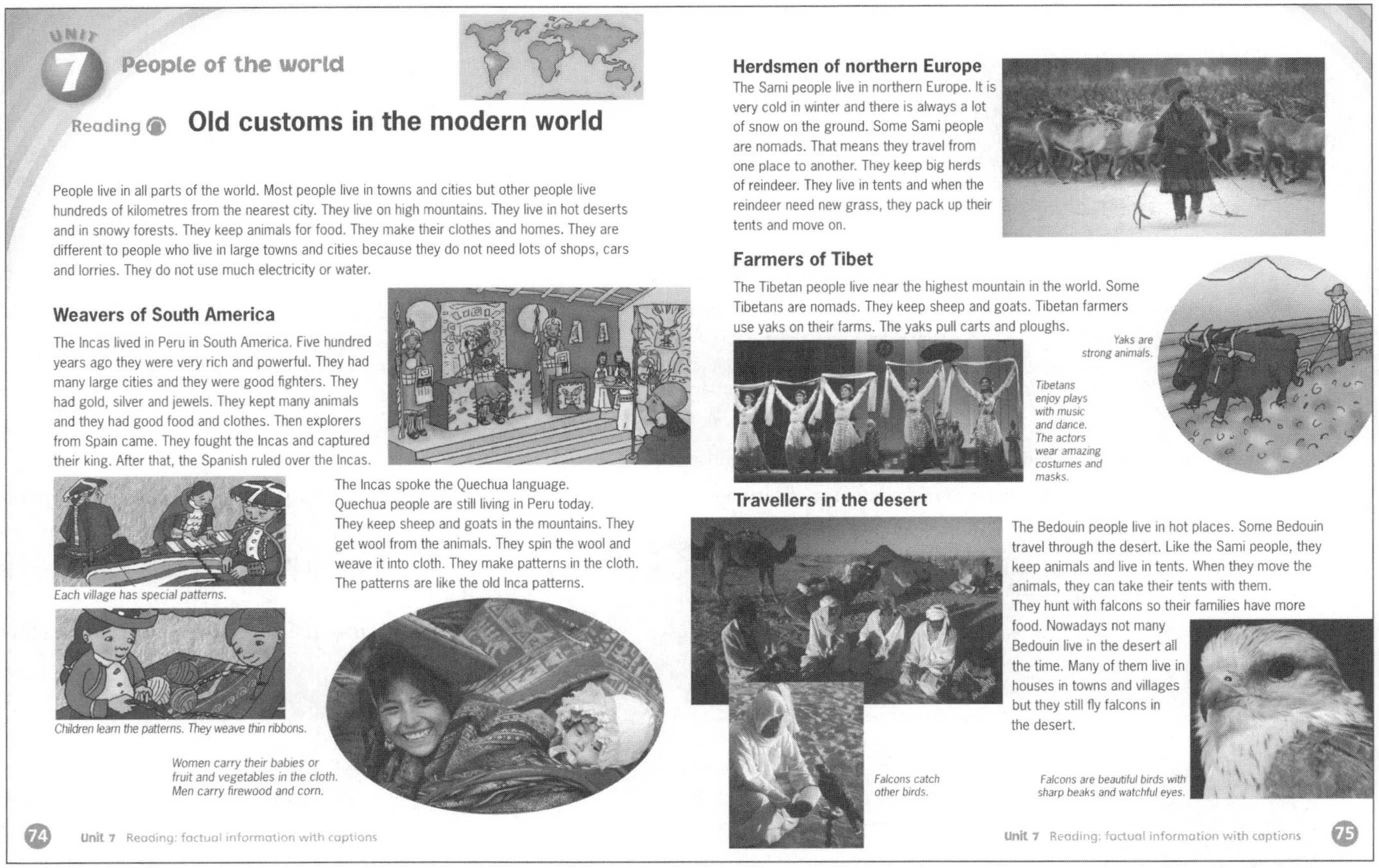

Homework task

Children learn selected vocabulary from Unit 7 Dictionary 4.
See unit word list on pp190–191 for key words, extension words and words for understanding only.

UNIT 7 People of the world

Reading Old customs in the modern world

People live in all parts of the world. Most people live in towns and cities but other people live hundreds of kilometres from the nearest city. They live on high mountains. They live in hot deserts and in snowy forests. They keep animals for food. They make their clothes and homes. They are different to people who live in large towns and cities because they do not need lots of shops, cars and lorries. They do not use much electricity or water.

Weavers of South America
The Incas lived in Peru in South America. Five hundred years ago they were very rich and powerful. They had many large cities and they were good fighters. They had gold, silver and jewels. They kept many animals and they had good food and clothes. Then explorers from Spain came. They fought the Incas and captured their king. After that, the Spanish ruled over the Incas.

The Incas spoke the Quechua language. Quechua people are still living in Peru today. They keep sheep and goats in the mountains. They get wool from the animals. They spin the wool and weave it into cloth. They make patterns in the cloth. The patterns are like the old Inca patterns.

Each village has special patterns.

Women carry their babies or fruit and vegetables in the cloth. Men carry firewood and corn.

Children learn the patterns. They weave thin ribbons.

Herdsmen of northern Europe
The Sami people live in northern Europe. It is very cold in winter and there is always a lot of snow on the ground. Some Sami people are nomads. That means they travel from one place to another. They keep big herds of reindeer. They live in tents and when the reindeer need new grass, they pack up their tents and move on.

Farmers of Tibet
The Tibetan people live near the highest mountain in the world. Some Tibetans are nomads. They keep sheep and goats. Tibetan farmers use yaks on their farms. The yaks pull carts and ploughs.

Tibetans enjoy plays with music and dance. The actors wear amazing costumes and masks.

Yaks are strong animals.

Travellers in the desert
The Bedouin people live in hot places. Some Bedouin travel through the desert. Like the Sami people, they keep animals and live in tents. When they move the animals, they can take their tents with them. They hunt with falcons so their families have more food. Nowadays not many Bedouin live in the desert all the time. Many of them live in houses in towns and villages but they still fly falcons in the desert.

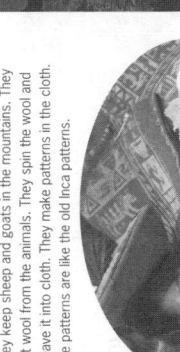

Falcons catch other birds.

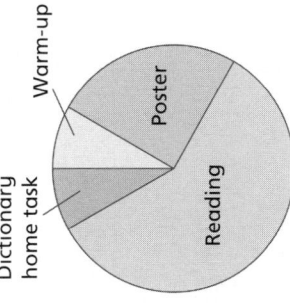

Falcons are beautiful birds with sharp beaks and watchful eyes.

Resource box

Text questions

When people live far away from a city, how do they get food? **They keep animals.**

How do they get clothes and houses? **They make them.**

What were the Incas like five hundred years ago? **rich and powerful**

Where did the explorers come from? **Spain**

Where do the Quechua people get wool from? **their animals**

Where do the Sami people live? **northern Europe**

Which animals do the Sami people keep? **reindeer**

What do the Sami people live in when they travel with the reindeer? **tents**

Which animal pulls the cars and ploughs in Tibet? **yak**

Are some Bedouin people nomads? **Yes, but not many.**

Which bird helps the Bedouin people to hunt? **falcon**

Time division

- Warm-up
- Poster
- Reading
- Dictionary home task

Lesson 2 Reading comprehension and vocabulary (PB p76)

Lesson aim Reading comprehension; vocabulary

Lesson targets Children re-read *People of the world*, then:
- (PB) complete sentences; answer inferential questions
- match words to definitions
- (WB) answer literal questions
- match words to pictures

Key structure *much, many, a lot of, lots of*

Key language *lots of shops; They do not use much electricity.*

Words vocabulary from Lesson 1

Materials PB p76; CD B track 18 (optional); WB p62; Dictionary 4

Warm-up

Play *Opposites* (see Games, page 187).

Read again

Remind children of *Old customs in the modern world*.
Play track 18 or read the text to the class. Children listen and follow in their books.

Activity 1

Give children a minute or two to look at all the sentences. Remind them they should look back to find and check answers.
Ask a volunteer to read and complete the first sentence. Check with the class. Children write in their books.
Where children disagree on answers, tell the class to scan the text and find the sentence.
Continue with the other sentences.

Activity 2

Ask the class the first question. If they cannot answer, tell them to look back at the first paragraph. Help them to think it through if necessary.
Ask the second questions. Help them work out an answer if necessary.

Activity 3

Ask one or more volunteers to read the words in the box.
Give the class a few moments to read the definitions.
Ask a volunteer to read the first definition and give the answer.
Check with the class. Children write.
They may refer to their dictionaries during this activity.

Reading comprehension and vocabulary

1 Complete the sentences.

1 Five hundred years ago the Incas were very _____.
2 The Incas spoke the Quechua _____.
3 The Quechua people _____ the wool and weave it into cloth.
4 They make _____ in the cloth.
5 Some Sami people are _____.
6 The Tibetan people live near the highest _____ in the world
7 Some Bedouin people travel through the _____.
8 Falcons are beautiful birds with sharp beaks and _____ eyes.

2 Talk about the answers to these questions.

Some people live hundreds of kilometres from the nearest city:
1 They do not need lots of shops, cars and lorries. Why not?
2 These people do not use much electricity or water. Why not?

3 Write the words next to the correct definition.

| powerful | explorer | watchful | village | spin | capture | hunt | electricity |

1 strong
2 power that travels along wires and makes lights and machines work
3 seeing everything that is happening
4 to follow and catch
5 person who travels and looks at new places
6 a small group of houses
7 to turn or twist round and round
8 to catch and hold onto

76

Unit 7 Reading comprehension and vocabulary: cloze; personal response; definitions

Unit 7 Reading comprehension and vocabulary

108

Reading comprehension and vocabulary (WB p62)

If children are doing this page for homework, make sure they understand the tasks. You may wish to read the text in exercise 1 with the class as preparation.

Exercise 1
Children read the text and answer the literal questions.

Exercise 2
Children match the pictures to the words.

Resource box

PB answers
Activity 1 1 rich and powerful 2 language
3 spin 4 patterns 5 nomads 6 mountain
7 desert 8 watchful

Activity 2 1 Children should be able to work out: These people keep animals for food. They don't buy all their food so they don't need cars to go to the shops. They don't need so many lorries to bring food. (Explain that there are cars and lorries in these distant places, but a lot fewer than in a city.)
2 The people are a long way from cities and perhaps they live where there is no electricity or only a few houses have it. They probably use water from rivers and lakes nearby. There may not be pipes bringing water into their homes.

Activity 3 1 powerful 2 electricity 3 watchful
4 hunt 5 explorer 6 village 7 spin
8 capture

WB answers
Exercise 1 1 They learned the Inca language.
2 They used Inca money. 3 They grew corn, fruits and vegetables. 4 They built roads and bridges. 5 People could travel through the mountains.

Exercise 2 1c 2e 3f 4a 5b 6d

Reading comprehension and vocabulary

1 Read. Answer the questions.

A long time ago the Incas were the most powerful people in Peru. Other people lived in Peru but the Incas fought against them and won. The other people learned the Inca language. They used Inca money and the Incas ruled over them but it was better than fighting all the time.

The Inca soldiers were brave fighters but they were also good farmers. They grew corn, fruits and vegetables. People were not hungry. They had work and they had homes. The Incas were good builders, too. They built roads and bridges. People could travel through the mountains.

1 When the Incas fought against other people and won, what did the other people learn? _____
2 What money did the other people use? _____
3 What did the Incas grow? _____
4 What did the Incas build? _____
5 Where could people travel? _____

2 Match. Write the letter.

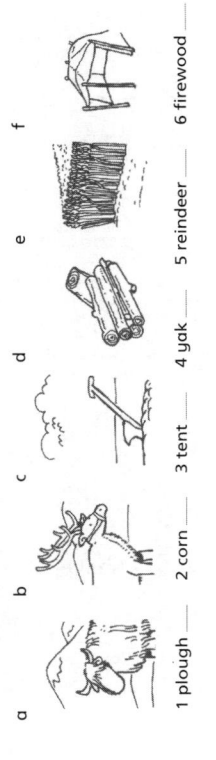

a b c d e f

1 plough ___ 2 corn ___ 3 tent ___ 4 yak ___ 5 reindeer ___ 6 firewood ___

unit 7 Literal questions; matching words to pictures

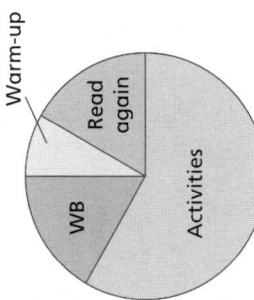

Time division

unit 7 Reading comprehension and vocabulary

109

Lesson 3 Speaking (PB p77) Study skills

Lesson aim Speaking, (WB) Study skills

Lesson targets Children:
- listen to a dialogue; listen and repeat the dialogue
- understand the story and answer oral questions
- read and act the dialogue
- (WB) practise dictionary skills; finding the odd one out

Informal everyday expressions *Come along! Well...*

New words *wonderful, Chinese, invented, rude, suspicious*

Materials PB p77; CD B tracks 19, 20; WB p63; Dictionary 4

Preparation Listen to CD B tracks 19, 20 before the lesson

Warm-up

Play *Words from words* for a minute or two (see Games, page 187). Use, e.g. *farmer, far, farm, arm, me, are*.

Activity 1

Children look at PB page 77. Read the title of the story and the title of Part 1. Ask *Who is in the picture? the children and Miss Carey; a man Are they in school? No, they aren't. What is the man wearing? a long coat, a hat*
Tell children to cover the dialogue text and look at the picture.
Play track 19. Children listen.

Activity 2

Children look at the dialogue. Play track 19 again.
Children listen and follow.
Check children understand the new words. Use the dictionary if you wish.

Activity 3

Children close their books. Play track 20. Children listen and repeat in the pauses. Encourage them to use the same expression and intonation.

Activity 4

Ask questions to check understanding of the story. See Resource box.

Activity 5

Children act the dialogue. Let one or two groups act it out in front of the class or from their desks.
Encourage them to speak out with expression, even if they need to refer to their books.

Study skills (WB p63)

The exercises on this page practise dictionary skills and finding the odd one out. Children should be able to do this work independently once the tasks have been explained.

Exercise 1
Make sure children understand they must look at the third letter to find the order. Do one or two sets with the class if you wish before they do the rest alone.

Exercise 2
Children circle the odd one out.
Look at the example with the class. Ask *Why is 'parrot' the odd one? because the others are all water birds*
Children find the other odd ones in each set. Tell them to think of the reason why the one they chose is odd.

Study skills

a b c d e f g h i j k l m n o p q r s t u v w x y z

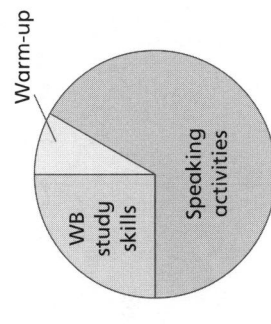

Look at the third letter!

1 Write the words in the correct order.

1	doll	door	dog
	dog	*doll*	*door*
2	brush	bread	brown
3	horse	hot	hope
4	rock	room	road
5	cat	castle	car	came	café

2 Circle the odd one out.

1	duck	swan	goose	(parrot)
2	cow	puppy	sheep	horse
3	wolf	giraffe	penguin	tiger
4	carrot	banana	grape	melon
5	shout	read	sing	speak

Unit 7 Dictionary skills; identifying the odd one out

Resource box

Story questions
What place are the children visiting this afternoon? **the City Museum**
Who wants to see the Incas? **Lulu**
Who wants to see the Chinese room? **Max**
What does Max know about the Chinese? **They invented a lot of things.**
Where does Alfie want to go? **into space**
Who has Alfie noticed? **a man**
What shouldn't Alfie do? **point**
Why not? **It's rude.**
How does the man look? **strange, suspicious**

WB answers
Exercise 1 2 bread brown brush 3 hope horse hot house 4 road rock room rose 5 café came car castle cat

Exercise 2 2 puppy – the others are all adult animals 3 penguin – the others are all land animals 4 carrot – the others are all fruit 5 read – the others are all things you do with your voice

Time division
- Warm-up
- WB study skills
- Speaking activities

Unit 7 Study skills

Lesson 4 Grammar (Session 1), Grammar in conversation (Session 2) (PB pp78–79)

Lesson aim Grammar

Lesson targets Children:
- (session 1) understand and practise the key structure
- (session 2) listen to and read a conversation; repeat and practise it
- (session 2) listen to a song, say it and learn it (optional)

Key structure (session 1) *much, many, a lot of, lots of*
Key vocabulary nature; food and drink
Key language (session 2) *should, shouldn't*
Materials PB pp78–79; CD B tracks 21–24; WB pp64–65

Session 1 Warm-up

Play the *Word chain* game (see Games, page 187).

Activity 1

Ask *What is in the picture? yaks, snow*
Ask four children to read the PC kids' bubbles.
Write up the two questions. Class reads.
Write the first prompt words on the board.
Help the class to compose the question.
Elicit a short answer. Continue with the other prompt words.

Children practise questions and answers in pairs.*

Activity 2

Ask volunteers to read the bubbles.
Point out Pete's reminder. Explain to the class that the two phrases mean the same. Children may use the pictures in Activity 1 to practise the sentences.

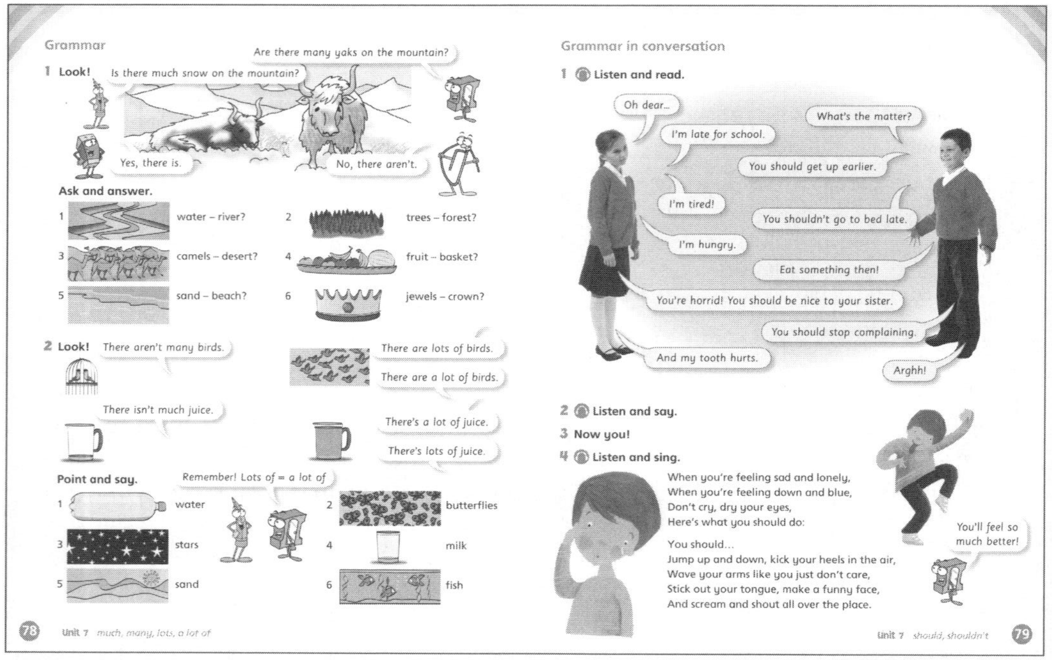

Session 2 Warm-up

Ask children to make five words from *Museum* (*me, us, use, Mum, sum*).

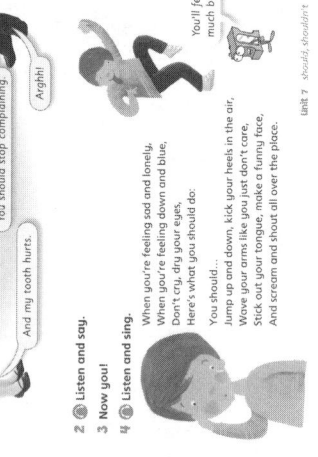

Activity 1

Explain that the boy and girl are talking before they go to school. Tell the class to listen to them. Play track 21. Children follow in their books.

Activity 2

Children listen to track 22 and repeat in the pauses.

Activity 3

Children practise the conversation in pairs. See Resource box.**

Activity 4

Ask *How does the boy look in the first picture? What is Paddy saying?* Play track 23. Children listen and follow the first time. Read the words with the class. Play track 23. Children join in. Play track 24. Children sing with the music. They may learn the song, if you wish.

Homework task

Children complete WB p64 in class time or for homework.

Unit 7 Grammar, Grammar in conversation

Grammar (Session 1), Grammar in conversation (Session 2) (WB pp64–65)

If this page is for homework, check children understand the tasks.

Exercises 1 and 2

Check children know: in questions – *How much* for things that they cannot count; *How many* for plural items. in statements – *much* for things they cannot count; *many* for plural items; *lots of* or *a lot of* for things they cannot count and for plural items.

Exercise 3

Encourage children to write interesting sentences.

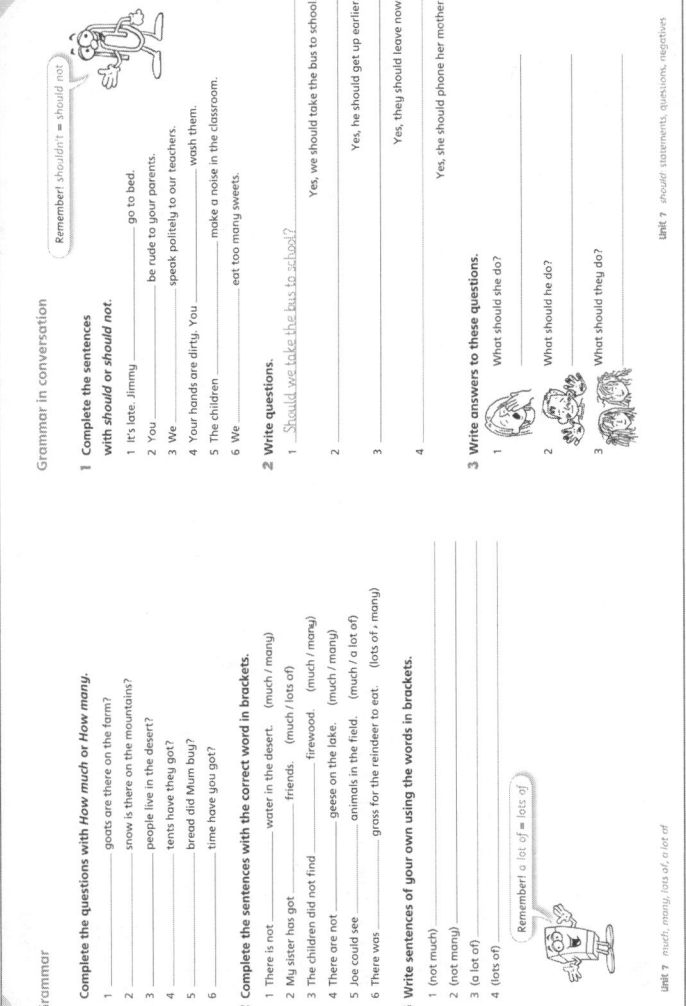

If this page is for homework, check children understand the tasks.

Exercise 1

Point out Pete the Paperclip's bubble. Remind children to use the full form in this written exercise.

Exercise 2

Go through the example before children write.

Exercise 3

Children work out their own answers for these pictures.

Time division

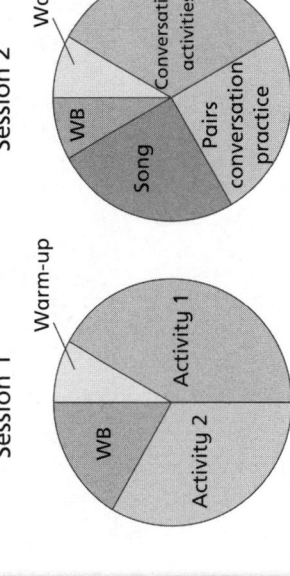

Session 1

Session 2

Grammar Practice Book

Children may begin Unit 7 when they have completed the PB and WB Grammar pages. They should complete it before the end of PB / WB Unit 7.

Resource box

Pair work: Grammar (PB p78)
Activity 1
Children work in pairs at their desks. They take turns to say the questions and give the short answer. If necessary, bring an able pair forward to demonstrate the activity.

Give the class three minutes to speak in pairs. Then let one or two pairs demonstrate a few questions and answers.

Pair work: Grammar in conversation (PB p79)
Activity 3
Children practise the dialogue in pairs at their desks.
Give pairs three minutes to practise the dialogue.
Let one or two pairs stand up and say it.

WB answers

*Grammar (p64)

Exercise 1 1 How many 2 How many 3 How many 4 How many 5 How much 6 How much

Exercise 2 1 much 2 lots of 3 much 4 many 5 a lot of 6 lots of

**Grammar in conversation (p65)

Exercise 1 1 should 2 should not 3 should 4 should 5 should not 6 should not

Exercise 2 2 Should he get up earlier? 3 Should they leave now? 4 Should she phone her mother?

Exercise 3 She should go to bed. 2 He should wash his hands and face. 3 They should do/brush/comb/tidy their hair.

Unit 7 Grammar, Grammar in conversation

113

Lesson 5 Listening, Phonics (PB p80) Use of English

Lesson aim Listening, spelling and pronunciation, Use of English (WB)

Lesson targets Children:
- talk about a world map and people of the world
- listen to a boy talking about people of the world; find his mistakes
- practise saying, reading and spelling words with *ew*
- (WB) learn about pronouns

Key structure and language from Unit 7

Target words *new, grew, flew, blew, jewel, drew, threw*

Materials PB p80; CD B tracks 13, 25, 26; WB pp66–67

Warm-up
Sing the song from PB page 69, track 13.

Listening

Activity 1
Ask *What is the boy in the picture doing? What do you think he is talking about?*

Activity 2
Play track 25. Children listen.
Ask the questions and elicit, e.g. *1 The boy is talking about people around the world. 2 He says a lot but he makes mistakes.*

Activity 3
Play track 25 again. Children listen out for mistakes and write the number.

Activity 4
Play track 25 again. Children tell you the mistakes and correct them.

Phonics
Point out the box. Tell children to follow in their books and repeat in the pauses. Play the first part of track 26. Make sure children repeat accurately.
Play the end of track 26. Children listen and follow.
Children say the rhyme. They may learn it, if you wish.

Children open their WBs at page 66. They complete the Phonics page now or for homework. If it is for homework, make sure they understand the tasks.

Listening
1 Talk about the picture.

2 Listen and answer the questions.
1 What is the boy talking about?
2 How much does he know about this? A lot or not very much?

3 How many mistakes does he make? Listen again.
Write the number.

4 Listen again. Put up your hand when you hear a mistake.
Correct the mistake.

Phonics

Look and listen!
The wind blew.
The little bird flew.
The black clouds grew
and lightning threw
silver flashes, too.
Then we knew –
"It's a storm! Quick! Run inside!"

ew | When the reindeer need new grass, the Sami move on.

Unit 7 Listening: factual information; gist and detail. Phonics: ew long vowel sound

Use of English
Move on to WB page 67.

114

Unit 7 Listening, Phonics

Phonics, Use of English (WB p66–67)

Remind the class of the sound *ew* and *new*.

Exercise 1
Remind children to read the words when they have written them.

Exercise 2
Children circle and write again.

Exercise 3
Remind children the words they need are on the page.

Write the two sentences on the board. Class reads. Circle *Incas* and *They*.

Exercise 1
Go through the presentation with the class. Write sentences on the board and ask children to circle.

Exercise 2
Children circle and write in their books. Write sentences on the board. Volunteers circle and name the noun. Other children check their work.

Exercise 3
Children circle the pronouns. Check answers together. They write the noun in answer to the questions.

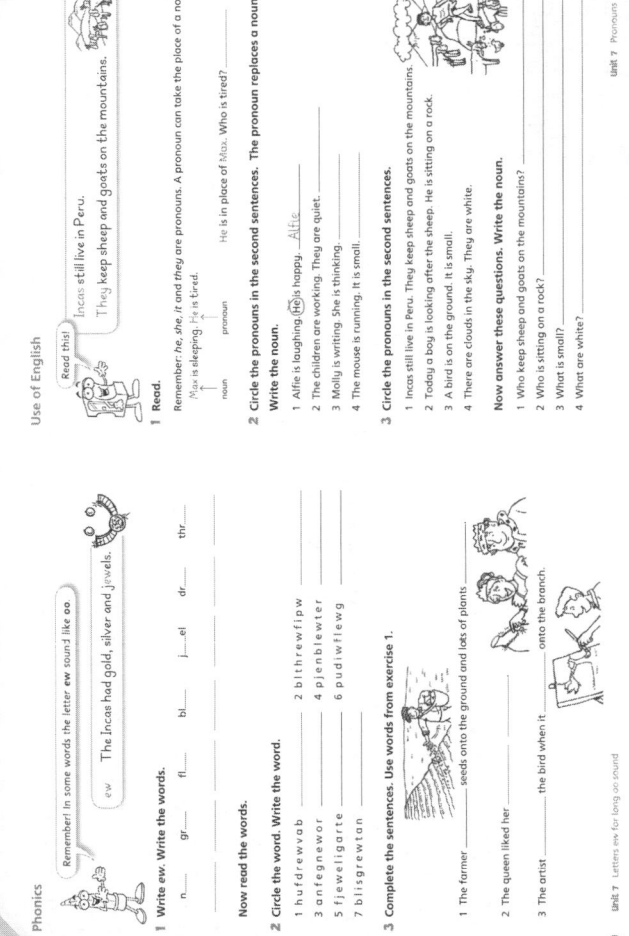

Resource box

Audioscript (CD B track 25) Listening activities 2–4 (PB p80)
Boy:
Here is a map of the world and some pictures. The pictures show some of the people of the world.

First we have the Quechua people. They live in Peru. That's a country in South Africa.

These are the Sami people. They live in the south of Europe. All the Sami are nomads. They travel from one place to another with their yaks.

On the right you can see the Tibetan people. Some Tibetans are nomads and some are farmers.

Finally, here are the Bedouin people. They live in cold countries. Some Bedouin live in the desert but these days many Bedouin live in towns and cities. Sometimes they go to the desert and hunt with albatrosses.

(Incorrect words are underlined.)

PB answers
Activity 3 6
Activity 4 Corrections for incorrect words: America, north, Some, reindeer, hot, falcons

WB answers
Phonics (p66)
Exercise 2 1 drew 2 threw 3 new 4 blew 5 jewel 6 flew 7 grew
Exercise 3 1 threw, grew 2 new, jewel(s) 3 drew, flew

Use of English (p67)
Exercise 2 2 They, the children 3 She, Molly 4 It, the mouse
Exercise 3 1 They 2 He 3 It 4 They; 1 Incas 2 a boy 3 a bird 4 clouds

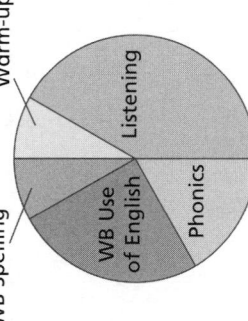

Time division
Warm-up
Listening
Phonics
WB Use of English
WB Spelling

Unit 7 Phonics, Use of English

115

Lesson 6 Class composition (Session 1) (PB p81) Writing preparation, Composition practice (Session 2)

Lesson aim Writing

Lesson targets Children:
- (session 1) compose a description of the customs and life of desert people
- (session 2) (WB) practise verbs and writing statements
- (session 2) (WB) write a description of the customs and life of mountain people

Key structure and language from the unit

Vocabulary desert and mountain features

Materials PB p81; WB pp68–69; CD B track 40

Session 1 Warm-up

Do *Look, write, check* (see Games, page 187).

Class composition

Activity 1

Give children time to look at the pictures. Ask questions and encourage children to say as much as they can. Use these questions and any others as appropriate.
Write notes of the children's answers on one side of the board.
Main picture: *What animals do the Bedouin people keep?*
Why do they keep them?
What do the women do with the wool first?
Photo left: *What do they do with it next?*
Small picture right: *What things do they make with the cloth?*
What colours do they use? What are the patterns like?
Photo right: *What other things do they make? What are they like?*

Activity 2

Help the class to make sentences about the Bedouin people from the notes on the board. Write the sentences. Encourage the class to add extra information as you go through the notes. Add in any new ideas the children think of.
When the paragraph is complete, ask a volunteer to read it to the class.
Ask if there is any more information that they can think of.
Discuss any suggested additions. Make changes to the paragraph that you and the class agree to.
Ask another volunteer to read the final version.
Remove the writing from the board but leave the notes. Children write a paragraph about the Bedouin people in their books.
Encourage them to use their dictionaries to find any words that are not in the notes on the board or to check spelling.
The example writing is a guide and sentences may vary greatly.
Children's own writing may be less detailed and contain fewer sentences.
Encourage children to write to their best level.

Class composition

1 Talk about the pictures.
2 Write about the Bedouin people. Continue in your copy book if necessary.

Unit 7 Class composition

116

Writing preparation, Composition practice (WB pp68–69)

Session 2 Warm-up

Sing the doing better song from PB page 53, track 40.

Exercise 1

Explain the task. Demonstrate by asking *Play. What can you play?* *a guitar* Write *play a guitar* on the board. Children write.

Exercise 2

Ask a child to read the first sentence. Children decide if the sentence is about the Sami people or the Quechua people. Check the class agrees. Go through all the sentences.

Explain that two pictures match two sentences in box A and three pictures match sentences in box B. Explain two pictures do not match any of the sentences.

Exercise 1

Children look at their pictures and write about the Tibetan people. Remind them to look at the noun phrases on WB page 68. Encourage them to look in their dictionaries for words they might need or to check spelling. Go around helping and monitoring as they work.

Exercise 2

Before the end of the lesson, ask one or two children to read their paragraphs to the class.

Children's writing will vary and the example writing is a guide to the highest level of writing that should be expected. Some children will write fewer and simpler sentences.

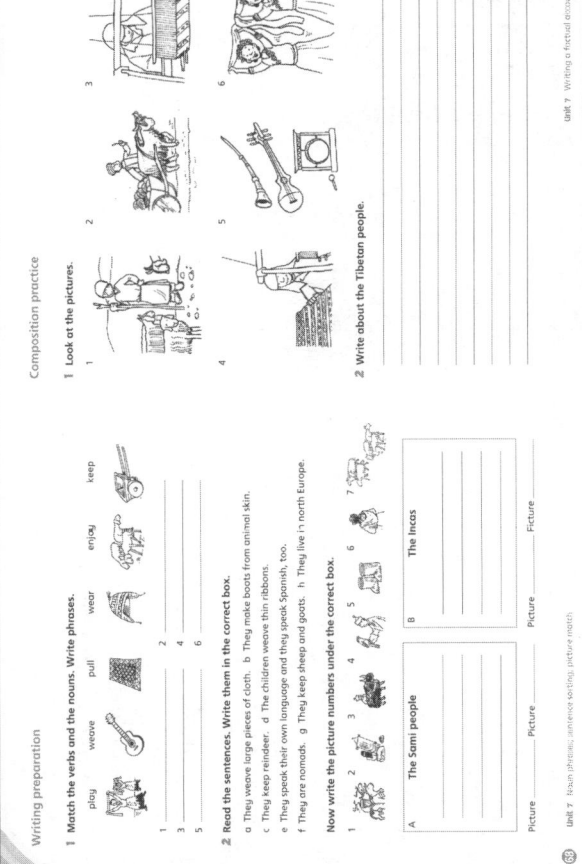

Homework task

Children complete Check-up 7, WB p70. For answers, see p145.

Resource box

Class composition example writing (p81)

Bedouin people keep camels, sheep and goats. They ride the camels through the desert. The camels carry the tents when the people move to a new place. The Bedouin people get meat and wool from the goats and sheep. First, the women spin the wool. Next they weave it (on a loom). They make cushions and clothes. They use red, blue, yellow and green wool. The colours are bright and the women make beautiful patterns. They make rugs, too. They are very big and they have many different colours in them.

WB answers (p68)

Exercise 1 1 play the guitar
2 weave a carpet
3 pull a cart
4 wear a hat
5 enjoy dancing
6 keep sheep and goats

Exercise 2 Sami b, c, f, h; 1, 5
Incas a, d, e, g; 2, 6, 7

Composition practice example writing (WB p69)

Tibetan people keep sheep and goats. Some people are nomads. The farmers use yaks. The yaks pull the carts.
The women get wool from the animals. They weave rugs and carpets. Sometimes the rugs have patterns on them.
Tibetan people enjoy music. They play long guitars with strings. They have drums and they have pipes.
Tibetan women enjoy dancing. When they dance, they wear beautiful clothes.

Time division

Session 1 — Warm-up, Class composition writing in books, Class composition in teacher-led board writing

Session 2 — Warm-up, Writing preparation, Composition practice

Portfolio

Children may make neat copies of their work.

Unit 7 Writing preparation, Composition practice

8 The Incas

Lesson 1 Poster 8, Reading

Lesson aim Reading

Text type A story with a strong setting

Lesson targets Children:
- read, understand and practise new vocabulary on the poster
- read, understand and practise reading the story
- answer oral comprehension questions

Key structure *anybody, nobody, somebody, everybody*

Key language *"Wake up, Poma, wake up!" somebody whispered.*

Key vocabulary the ancient Incas

Materials PB pp82–83; poster 8; CD B track 27; Dictionary 4; word cards for poster vocabulary (see poster 8 below or list on p15)

Preparation Make word cards; listen to CD B track 27

Warm-up

Ask the class what they can remember about the Incas. *Where did they live? What did they have? What did they do?*
Let them look back at paragraph 2 on PB page 74 if they have forgotten.

Poster 8

1 Point to the poster. Read out the title.
   Give the class a moment or two to look.

2 Point to objects and people. Read each word.
   Show the word card/s. Class reads and says the word/s.
   Cover the words on the poster if you wish.
   Point to the objects and people at random. Class names them.

3 Ask the class to say as much as they can about this picture. Tell them to look carefully at it for a few moments.
   Elicit as much from the class as you can.

4 Ask prompt questions if children do not talk about these things, or if they need prompts:
   What kind of building is this? Who do you think lives in it?
   What other people can you see? What kind of clothes are the people wearing? Are these people rich? How do you know?

Reading (PB pp82–83)

1 Give children time to look at the pictures. Read the title. Ask *Who is in this story? Who do you think the people are?* Give children the opportunity to suggest one or two ideas.

2 Play track 27. Children listen and follow.

3 Read one paragraph or section of the text at a time. Use Dictionary 4 to help you to explain new words as necessary.

The following words are not in the dictionary. Children should remember the words from the poster where they are illustrated. If you wish, check that children understand:

headdress a special kind of hat that an important person wears or that somebody wears on a special day The princess's *headdress* had flowers and tiny bells.

throne the special chair a king sits in The king's *throne* was gold and silver.

Help children to find new words. Make up extra sentences for new words if you wish.

4 Ask questions about each paragraph or a section of the text. See Resource box.*

5 Give reading practice. Ask individuals, groups or the class to read sentences or paragraphs. Play track 27 again.

UNIT 8 The Incas

Reading **A message for the Inca king**

It was before dawn when Poma heard a voice. "Wake up, Poma, wake up!" somebody whispered. Poma opened his eyes. In the dim moonlight, he saw the face of his old teacher. Poma sat up in surprise.

"Sh!" said his teacher. "Don't speak. Get dressed and follow me."

Hurriedly, Poma put on his tunic. The other boys were sleeping. He stepped quietly past them and followed the old man outside.

As silent as shadows they crossed the courtyard and entered the great hall. Poma's teacher led him towards a small doorway in one corner. Messengers did not usually go through it. The rooms behind the hall were part of the palace. Suddenly, the old man stopped and spoke.

"Listen, Poma," he said. "You are the youngest messenger in the palace but nobody runs as fast as you. You are not yet seventeen but you are as brave as any man. Now, you have an important task. Come."

Poma followed the old man through the narrow doorway and along a short passage. They entered a large room where lamps burned brightly. The golden walls glowed like the evening sun. Two men stood near the doorway. They were talking quietly. They stopped when they saw Poma. Their tunics were fine wool with delicate patterns of gold. "These are important people," thought Poma.

A table stood in the middle of the room with a gold chair next to it. There were silver cups on the table but the chair was empty. Poma heard his teacher say, "This is the boy, Prince Urco."

A tall man appeared from the shadows. He wore a heavy cloak over his tunic. Bands of gold circled his head and his arms. A collar of gold and rare jewels was around his neck. He beckoned to Poma and the boy stepped forward.

The prince looked carefully at Poma for a moment. "You are strong," he said, "but you must be clever, too. You must take a message to the king. You must remember every word." He leaned forward and spoke clearly. "Repeat," he commanded. Poma repeated the message. The prince nodded. "Now go," he said, "and do not fail."

Poma left the room and ran back through the hall. He crossed the shadowy courtyard and ran out onto the road. Then he ran straight on, out of the city gates and towards the forest. "I must not fail," he repeated. "I must not fail."

Resource box

*Text questions

Who woke Poma? **his teacher**
What time was it? **before dawn**
How did Poma feel when his teacher woke him? **surprised**
Where did they go? across the courtyard and into the hall
What is Poma's work? **messenger**
What can he do? **run fast**
What did his teacher want him to do? **an important task**

Who were in the large room? **two men**
What did Poma think about them? **they were important**
What did they do when Poma and his teacher came in? **stopped talking**
Where did Prince Urco appear from? **the shadows**
What things was he wearing? **a heavy cloak, gold bands, a gold collar**
What did he give Poma? **a message**
Who was the message for? **the king**

Homework task

Children learn selected vocabulary, Unit 8 *Dictionary 4*.

See unit word list on pp190–191 for key words, extension words and words for understanding only.

Time division

Reading / Poster / Warm-up / Dictionary home task

Unit 8 Reading 119

Lesson 2 Reading comprehension and vocabulary (PB p84)

Lesson aim Reading comprehension; vocabulary

Lesson targets Children re-read the story, then:
- (PB) match sentence beginnings / endings
- answer deductive questions
- match pictures to words and definitions
- (WB) order sentences; replace phrases with single words

Key structure *anybody, nobody, somebody, everybody*

Key language *"Wake up, Poma, wake up!" somebody whispered.*

Words vocabulary from Lesson 1

Materials PB p84; CD B track 27 (optional); WB p72; Dictionary 4

Warm-up

Write up adjectives, e.g. *quiet, silent, quick, hurried, bright*. Children make them into adverbs. Ask *Which word means nearly the same as quickly? quietly?*

Read again

Remind children of *A message for the Inca king*. Play track 27 or read the text. Children listen and follow in their books.

Activity 1

Tell children to read all the sentence beginnings and endings silently. Remind the class they should look back to the text to find and check answers. Ask a volunteer to read the first beginning and match it with an ending. Check the answer with the class. Children write.
Continue in the same way, with children referring back to the text to find and check.

Activity 2

There could be a variety of answers to the first two questions. Encourage children to put forward different ideas. Aim to accept children's suggestions as this will build their confidence. If answers are on the wrong lines, ask questions to help them make better suggestions. The last question requires children to imagine.

Activity 3

Children look at the pictures. Ask them to name the objects.
Point out the example. Let a volunteer read the second definition and match it to a word and picture. Check with the class. Children write.

Reading comprehension and vocabulary

1 Match the sentence beginnings with the correct endings.

1 It was before dawn when	a the old man stopped and spoke.
2 Hurriedly,	b the boy stepped forward.
3 As silent as shadows	c from the shadows.
4 Suddenly,	d Poma heard a voice.
5 They entered a large room where	e Poma put on his tunic.
6 A tall man appeared	f ran back through the hall.
7 He beckoned to Poma and	g they crossed the courtyard.
8 Poma left the room and	h lamps burned brightly.

2 Talk about the answers to these questions.
1 Why did Poma's teacher wake him up before dawn?
2 Why did the prince tell Poma to repeat the message?
3 What do you think the message was about?

3 Read. Write the word. Write the letter of the picture.

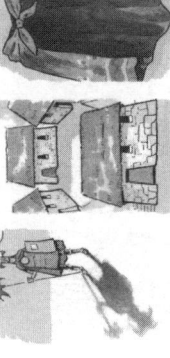

a   b   c   d   e

1 a piece of clothing you wear round your shoulders   cloak c
2 a very large room
3 a loose piece of clothing like a long T-shirt
4 an open space with buildings all round it
5 the dark shape when something is blocking the light

Unit 8 Reading comprehension: sentence beginnings/endings; inferential questions; definitions

Reading comprehension and vocabulary (WB p72)

If children are doing this page for homework, make sure they understand the tasks. You may wish to read the text in exercise 1 with the class as preparation.

Exercise 1
Tell children to read all the sentences carefully before they do this. They should check back to the text as necessary.

Exercise 2
Children choose words to replace words and phrases. They may wish to use their dictionaries to check.

Resource box

PB answers

Activity 1 1d 2e 3g 4a 5h 6c 7b 8f

Activity 2 1 *possible answers*: the message is urgent and Poma has to go early; the message is secret and they don't want anyone to know about Poma taking the message so he must leave in the dark
2 *possible answers*: he wanted to be sure Poma could remember it; he wanted to be sure the message made sense

Activity 3 1 cloak c 2 hall d 3 tunic e 4 courtyard b 5 shadow a

WB answers

Exercise 1 e h j d i b c a f g

Exercise 2 1 whisper 2 hurriedly 3 repeat 4 dawn 5 fail

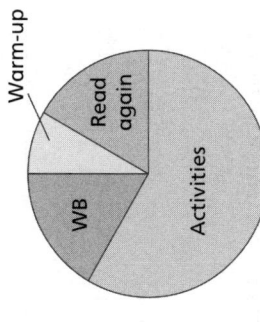

Time division
Warm-up, Read again, WB, Activities

---

1 Read *A Message for the Inca King* again. Number the sentences in order.

a He leaned forward and spoke clearly.
b There were silver cups on the table but the chair was empty.
c The prince looked carefully at Poma for a moment.
d Poma's teacher led him towards a small doorway at the far end.
e Poma heard a voice. 1
f Poma repeated the message.
g Poma left the room and ran back through the hall.
h Poma sat up in surprise.
i They entered a room where the lamps burned brightly.
j The other boys were sleeping.

2 Choose the best word to replace the underlined words.

fail   repeat   hurriedly   dawn   whisper

1 "Sh! Speak quietly," said Molly.
2 Max was late and he packed his school bag in a rush.
3 I didn't hear you, could you say it again, please?
4 We will leave at the moment when the sun comes up.
5 "Oh dear," said Alfie. "I will not pass this test!"

Unit 8 Sequencing sentences from a story; definitions

unit 8 Reading comprehension and vocabulary

Lesson 3 Speaking (PB p85) Study skills

Lesson aim Speaking, (WB) Study skills
Lesson targets Children:
- listen to a dialogue; listen and repeat the dialogue
- understand the story and answer oral questions
- read and act the dialogue
- (WB) practise self correction; spelling and sorting

Informal everyday expressions *What's happening? That's better. Quick! After him!*
New words *jewellery, covered*
Materials PB p85; CD B tracks 28, 29; WB p73; Dictionary 4
Preparation Listen to CD B track 28 before the lesson

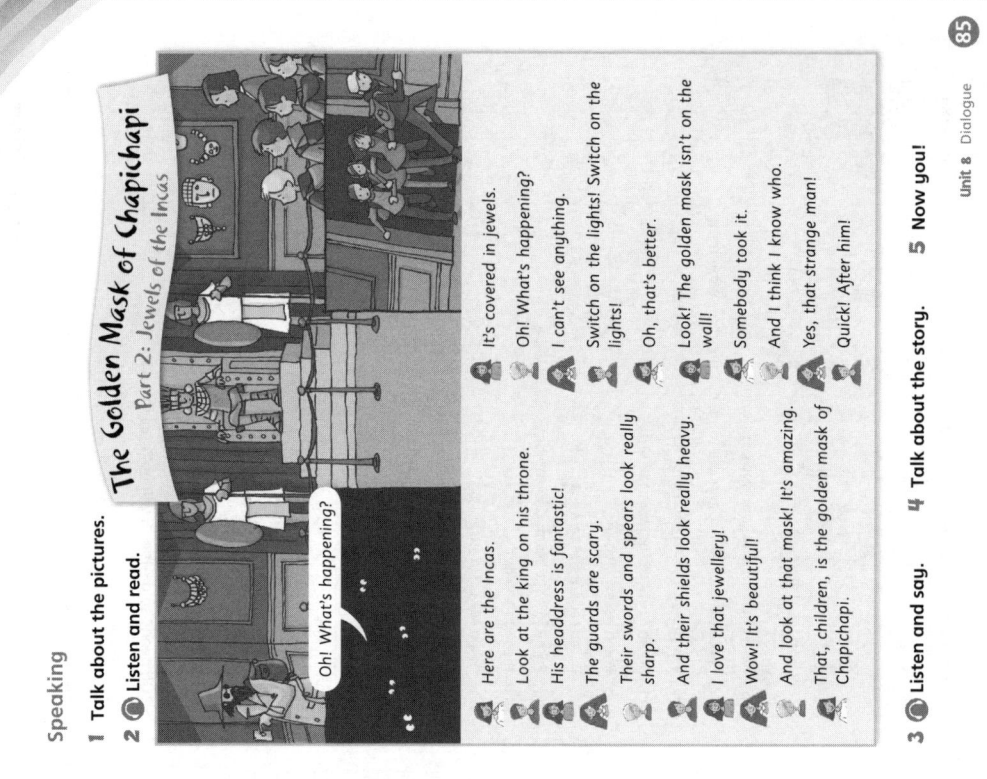

Warm-up
Ask the class what happened in Part 1. *What place are the children visiting? What things are in the museum?*

Activity 1
Children look at PB page 85. Read the title of Part 2. Ask *Which room are they in?* Tell children to cover the dialogue text and look at the picture. Use the dictionary if you wish. Play track 28. Children listen.

Activity 2
Children look at the dialogue. Play track 28 again. Children listen and follow.
Check children understand the new words.

Activity 3
Children close their books. Play track 29. Children listen and repeat in the pauses. Encourage them to use the same expression and intonation.

Activity 4
Ask questions to check understanding of the story. See Resource box.

Activity 5
Children act the dialogue. Encourage them to speak out clearly and to use good expression as they heard on the audio.

Study skills (WB p73)

The exercises on this page practise spelling and sorting into categories. Children should be able to do this work independently once the tasks have been explained.

Exercise 1

Children attempt the spellings. Make sure they understand they should try to spell the word first and check after. The task is not to copy from the dictionary or the book but to attempt accurate spelling independently.

Exercise 2

Children categorise the words.

Resource box

Story questions

Who was sitting on the throne? **the king**
What was he wearing? **a headdress**
What were the guards like? **scary**
What were they carrying? **spears and shields**
What was on the wall? **a mask**
What was it like? **golden**
What happened to the lights while the children were in the room? **They went out.**
What happened to the mask? **Someone took it.**
Who do they think took it? **the strange man**

WB answers

Exercise 1 2 sword 3 throne 4 whisper
5 suddenly 6 palace 7 narrow
8 beckoned

Exercise 2 wear: headdress helmet cloak tunic glasses mask; carry: spear shield umbrella flag sword suitcase

Study skills

1 Read and write. The underlined words are spelt wrong. Try to write the words correctly. Don't look in your dictionary!

1 The prince sent a <u>mesenger</u> to the king. _messenger_
2 The soldier was carrying a <u>sord</u> and a shield. _____
3 The queen was sitting on her <u>thrown</u>. _____
4 Don't speak loudly! You must <u>wisper</u>. _____
5 <u>Sudenly</u> we heard a shout. _____
6 The guards stood at the <u>pallace</u> door. _____
7 He ran along the <u>narow</u> street. _____
8 "Come here!" The man <u>bekoned</u> to the boy. _____

Now check your spelling in your Dictionary.

2 Write the words from the box in the correct list.

| spear | shield | headdress | umbrella | flag | helmet |
| cloak | sword | tunic | glasses | suitcase | mask |

Things we wear	Things we carry

Unit 8 Spelling self correction; sorting vocabulary

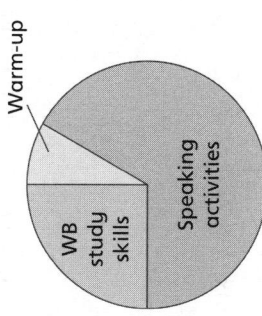

Time division

Unit 8 Study skills

Lesson 4 Grammar (Session 1), Grammar in conversation (Session 2) (PB p86–87)

Lesson aim Grammar

Lesson targets Children:
- (session 1) understand and practise the key structure
- (session 2) look at place on a map and understand the map
- (session 2) listen to and read a conversation; repeat and practise it

Key structure (session 1) *anybody, nobody, somebody, everybody*

Key vocabulary places in a home; general vocabulary

Key language (session 2) asking for and giving directions

Informal expressions *Of course, Uh huh, Mmm, Thank you, Not at all*

Materials PB pp86–87; CD B tracks 30, 31; WB pp74–75

Session 1 Warm-up

Play *What's missing?* (see Games, page 187).

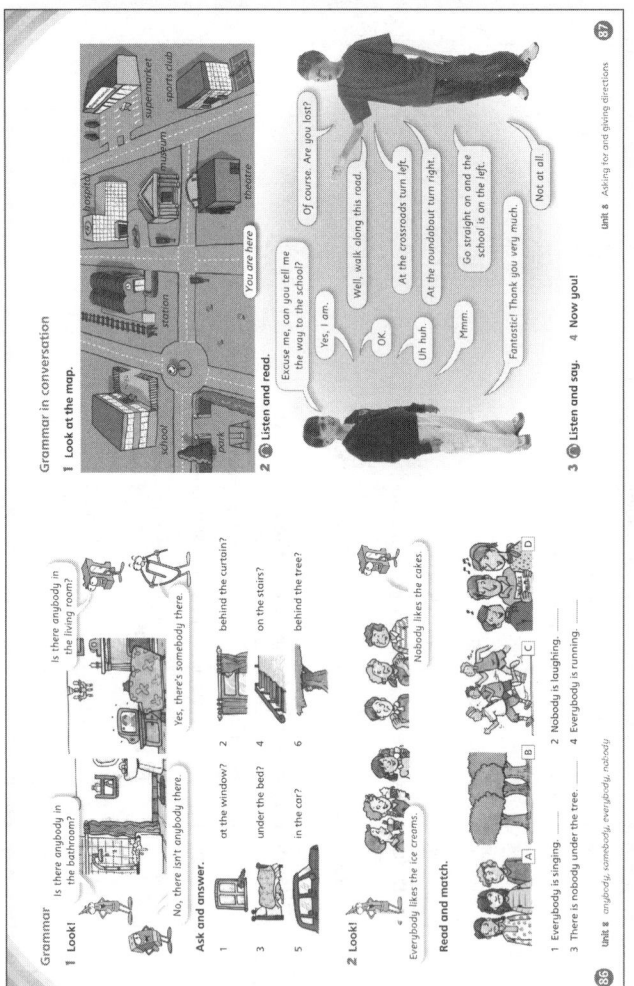

Activity 1

Ask *What are in the pictures?*
Ask four children to read the PC kids' bubbles.
Write up the two questions and answers. Class reads.
Write the first prompt words on the board.
Help the class to compose the question.
Elicit a short answer. Continue with the other prompt words.
See Resource box.*

Activity 2

Children look at the top pictures.
Ask pairs to read the bubbles.
See Resource box.**
Children look at the other pictures.
Ask a volunteer to read the first sentence.
Children match.

In pairs, children take turns to point to a picture and say the sentence.

Session 2 Warm-up

Play *Simon says* to practise left and right with the class (see Games, page 186).

Activity 1

Children look at the map. Explain that it shows places in a town. Ask a volunteer to read out the places.

Activity 2

Point out the boy and girl. Ask where they are: *in the street* Tell the class to listen to them. Play track 30. Children follow in their books.

Activity 3

Children listen to track 31 and repeat in the pauses.

Activity 4

Children use the map and practise the conversation in pairs.
Go around listening to them as they speak. See Resource box.***

Children complete WB page 74 in class time or for homework.

Unit 8 Grammar, Grammar in conversation

Grammar (Session 1), Grammar in conversation (Session 2) (WB pp74–75)

If this page is for homework, check children understand the tasks.

Exercise 1
Children complete the sentences. Point out the singular verb in each sentence.

Exercise 2
Point out the PC kids' box. Write up the information. Remind them of *somebody* and *anybody* in a positive statement and in questions and negative statements.

If this page is for homework, check children understand the tasks.

Exercise 1
Children complete the instructions according to the small maps. Do the first one orally if you like.

Exercise 2
Children complete the dialogue. Let one or two pairs act out the finished conversation.

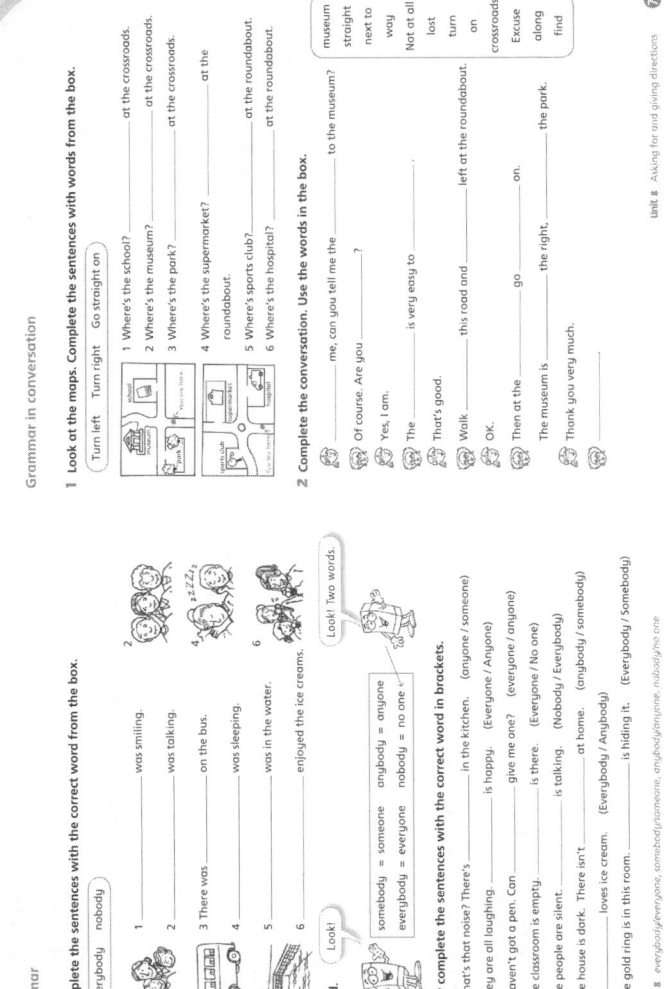

Time division

Session 1: Warm-up, Activity 1, Activity 2, WB

Session 2: Warm-up, Conversation activities, Pairs conversation practice, Conversation, WB

Grammar Practice Book
Children may begin Unit 8 when they have completed the PB and WB Grammar pages. They should complete it before the end of PB / WB Unit 8.

Resource box

Pair work: Grammar (PB p86)

*Activity 1
Children work in pairs at their desks. They take turns to say the questions and give the short answer. If necessary, bring an able pair forward to demonstrate the activity.

Give the class three minutes to speak in pairs. Then let one or two pairs demonstrate a few questions and answers.

**Activity 2
Write the sentences on the board. Point out the singular verb. Explain that *everybody* and *nobody* are singular words.

***Pair work: Grammar in conversation (PB p87)**

Activity 4
Most children should be able to use the map and ask the way to different places. The instructions should always begin from the *You are here* point.

Give pairs three minutes to practise the dialogue.

Let one or two pairs stand up and say their conversations to the class.

Some children might like to act this out as two people meeting and speaking in the street.

WB answers

Grammar (WB p74)

Exercise 1   1 Everybody   2 Nobody   3 nobody   4 Everybody   5 Nobody   6 Everybody

Exercise 2   1 someone   2 Everyone   3 anyone   4 No one   5 Nobody   6 anybody   7 Everybody   8 Somebody

Grammar in conversation (WB p75)

Exercise 1   1 Turn right   2 Go straight on   3 Turn left   4 Go straight on   5 Turn left   6 Turn right

Exercise 2   Excuse, way, lost, museum, find, along, turn, crossroads, straight, on, next to, Not at all

Unit 8   Grammar, Grammar in conversation

Lesson 5 Listening, Phonics (PB p88) Use of English

Lesson aim Listening, spelling and pronunciation, Use of English (WB)

Lesson targets Children:
- talk about Incan objects
- listen to descriptions and match to pictures
- practise saying, reading and spelling words with *air/are*
- (WB) learn about punctuating direct speech

Key structure and language from Unit 8

Target words *chair, fair, hair, pair, air; share, bare, bare, glare, rare, care*

Materials PB p88; CD B tracks 23, 32, 33; WB pp76–77

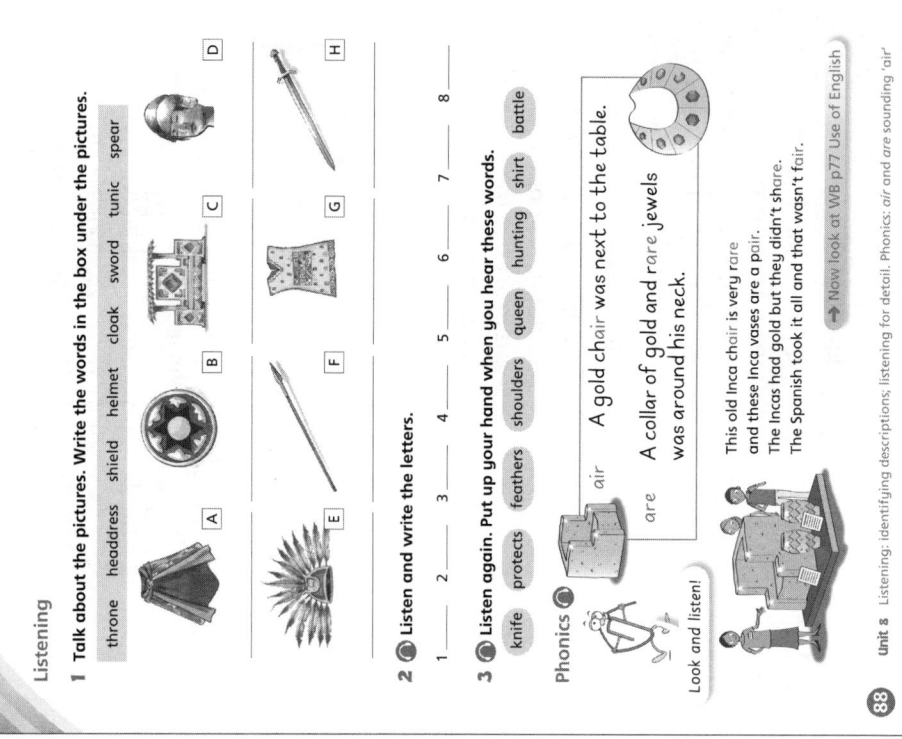

Warm-up
Sing the sad song from PB page 79, track 23.

Listening
Activity 1
Children look at the pictures for a moment.
Ask them to name as many objects as they can.
Ask a volunteer to read the words in the box.
Ask what the objects are like, e.g. *What colour is the headdress? the helmet? the cloak? Is the shield round or square? What colours is the headdress?*, etc.
Children write the words under each picture.

Activity 2
Play track 32. Children listen the first time but do not write.
Play the track again. Children write the letters.
Be prepared to play the track again for them to listen or check.
Check answers together.

Activity 3
Ask one or more children to read the words in the bubbles.
Play track 32 again. Children raise their hands when they hear the words.

Phonics
Point out the box. Tell children to follow in their books and repeat in the pauses. Play the first part of track 33. Make sure children repeat accurately.
Play the end of track 33. Children listen and follow.
Children say the rhyme. They may learn it, if you wish.

Children open their WBs at p76. They complete the Phonics page now or for homework, make sure they understand the tasks.

Phonics, Use of English (WB p76–77)

Remind the class of the sound *air/are* and *chair, rare*.

Exercises 1 and 2

Children complete, write and read all the words.

Exercise 3

Children find the correct word from exercises 1 and 2 to complete each sentence.

Write the sentences on the board in large writing so that the punctuation is clear. Ask individuals to underline the reporting clause in each one. They should find this straightforward as this is revision.

Exercise 1

1 Go through the presentation of the punctuation with the class. Write sentences from the page on the board. Show the class the punctuation for all positions of the reporting clause. Write the sentences to be punctuated on the board. Volunteers write the punctuation.

2 Children write the punctuation in their books. Make up extra example sentences so that they have more practice.

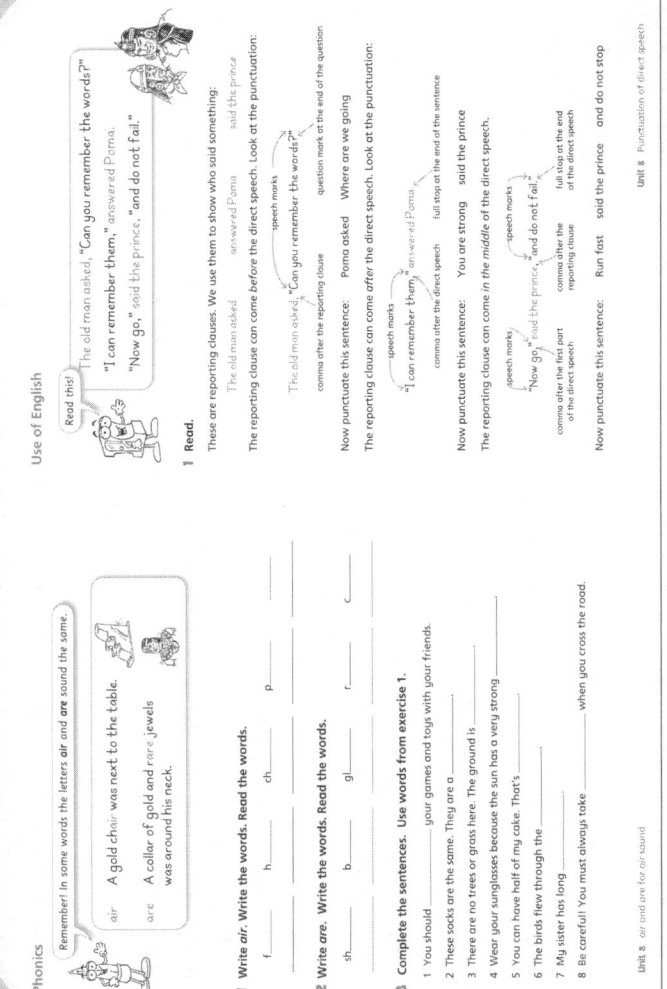

Resource box

PB answers

Activity 2 1H 2B 3E 4A 5C 6F 7G 8D

Audioscript (CD B track 32) Listening activities 2–3 (PB p88)

Number 1: A soldier carries this. He uses it for fighting. It looks like a big <u>knife</u>.

Number 2: A soldier carries this, too. Sometimes it is round; sometimes it is square. It <u>protects</u> him.

Number 3: This is for men or women. They wear it on their heads. It is beautiful. Sometimes it has <u>feathers</u>.

Number 4: A man or a woman can wear this, too. Sometimes it is long; sometimes it is short. You wear it around your <u>shoulders</u> and it can keep you warm.

Number 5: This is a big, beautiful chair. A king or a <u>queen</u> sits on it.

Number 6: A soldier carries this. It is like a long stick. The end is pointed and sharp. In some parts of the world people use these for <u>hunting</u> animals.

Number 7: A man or a woman wears this. It is long and loose, like a <u>shirt</u>.

Number 8: A soldier wears this. It protects his head when he is fighting in a <u>battle</u>.

Note: on the second listening, children put up their hands when they hear the underlined words.

WB answers

Phonics (p76)

Exercise 3 1 share 2 pair 3 bare 4 glare 5 fair 6 air 7 hair 8 care

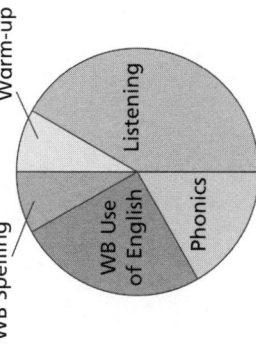

Time division

Unit 8 Phonics, Use of English

127

Lesson 6 Class composition (Session 1) (PB p89) Writing preparation, Composition practice (Session 2)

Lesson aim Writing

Lesson targets Children:
- (session 1) compose a descriptive section of a story with a strong setting
- (session 2) (WB) make notes about events in a story
- (session 2) (WB) write the next part of a story with a strong setting

Key structure and language from Unit 8

Vocabulary the Incas

Materials PB p89; WB pp78–79; poster 8

Session 1 Warm-up

Tell children to look back at PB pages 82 and 83. Talk about the story with the class.
Who was Poma? What did the prince want Poma to do?

Class composition

Activity 1

1 Children look at PB page 89. Ask a volunteer to read the sentences and the questions.
Tell children to look carefully at the picture for a few moments.
Ask them to note in their copy books all the things that Poma could see and the sounds he could hear. Give them a minute or two to do this.

2 Elicit from the class all the sights and sounds they have noted. Write the words and phrases on one side of the board.
When all the ideas have been written up, ask a volunteer to read it to the class.
Help the class to use the notes to compose sentences to continue the story.
This part of the story of Poma is description so the sentences should describe the different things in the scene.
Write sentences the children suggest on the board. Help with grammar.
When the description is complete, ask a volunteer to read it to the class.
Ask if any words need changing. *Are the sentences in the best order? Are there enough adjectives? Should other adjectives or verbs be used?*
Make any changes that you and the class agree make the description better.
Let a child read the paragraph a final time.
Remove the writing from the board. Children continue the story in their books.
Remind them to use the notes on the board and to look at the picture again.

Activity 2

Encourage children to write their own ideas. Make sure they understand that the aim is not to rewrite the class writing exactly. They may write their own sentences in a different order and with different details.

Children's writing can and should vary greatly from the example.

Class composition

1 Read then talk about the picture.

Poma, the Inca messenger, ran through the forest. He came to a pool. What did he see? What did he hear?

2 Continue the story. Write about this place in the forest.

Poma ran along the road through the forest. The sun was high in the sky when he came to a pool. He stopped for a moment because it was so beautiful.

Unit 8 Class composition: continuing a story with a strong setting

Unit 8 Class composition

128

Writing preparation, Composition practice (WB pp78–79)

Session 2 Warm-up
Put up poster 8. Children name the objects

Exercise 1
Go through the questions with the class. Write a few notes on the board.

Exercise 2
1 Ask what they think the message was about. Children may have ideas from Lesson 2.
Children read and answer the questions about what happened.

2 If children find it difficult to put down ideas on their own, do the work with the whole class. Write up several suggestions for the answer to each question. Give children time to choose which answer they like and fill in the writing spaces.

Children write the rest of the story using their answers and notes on WB page 78. Go around helping and monitoring as they work.
Be ready to remind them how to punctuate direct speech. Write an example sentence with direct speech on the board if appropriate.
The example writing is a guide only. Some children will write simpler and shorter sentences. Encourage children to write to their best ability. Before the end of the lesson ask one or two volunteers to read some or all of their writing to the class.

Portfolio
Children may make neat copies of their WB compositions.

Homework task
Children complete Check-up 8, WB p80. For answers, see p145.

Time division

Session 1: Class composition writing in books / Class composition teacher-led board writing / Warm-up

Session 2: Composition practice / Writing preparation / Warm-up

Resource box

Class composition example writing (p89)
He could hear the water. It was falling / running / dropping / splashing into the pool. A small frog was sitting on a rock at the edge of the pool. Two colourful birds flew between the trees. They were red, yellow, green and blue. Flowers were growing all round the pool. There were pink, red and white flowers. More flowers were hanging from the trees. They were red and orange. Brightly coloured butterflies were flying over the water. Poma could not stay. He turned away from the pool and ran on, along the stone road.

WB answers

Composition practice example writing (WB p79)
At last Poma arrived at the king's palace. He felt hot and very tired. The king was in the big hall/room. He felt and very tired. The king was in the big hall/room. When Poma walked into the hall/room he saw the king. He was sitting on a huge gold chair. He wore an enormous headdress of green feathers. His white tunic was long and he had gold bands on his arms. In the room there were lots of gold objects. There was gold on the walls and there were coloured rugs on the floor. Lots of soldiers were standing near the king. They wore helmets and they had shields, spears and swords. They looked frightening.

The king said, "Have you got a message for me?"
"Yes, I have," said Poma. He repeated the message to the king.
The king was excited. "That is very interesting," he said. "I must speak to my soldiers."
Poma was happy. "I remembered the important message," he thought, "but what will happen next?"

Unit 8 Writing preparation, Composition practice

9 Chinese inventions

Lesson 1 Poster 9, Reading

Lesson aim Reading

Text type information and description

Lesson targets Children:
- read, understand and practise new vocabulary on the poster
- read, understand and practise reading information
- answer oral comprehension questions

Key structure first conditional

Key language *If you go to a firework display, you will see Chinese fireworks.*

Key vocabulary early technology

Materials PB pp90–91; poster 9; CD B track 34; Dictionary 4; word cards for poster vocabulary (see poster 9 below or list on p16)

Preparation Make word cards; listen to CD B track 34

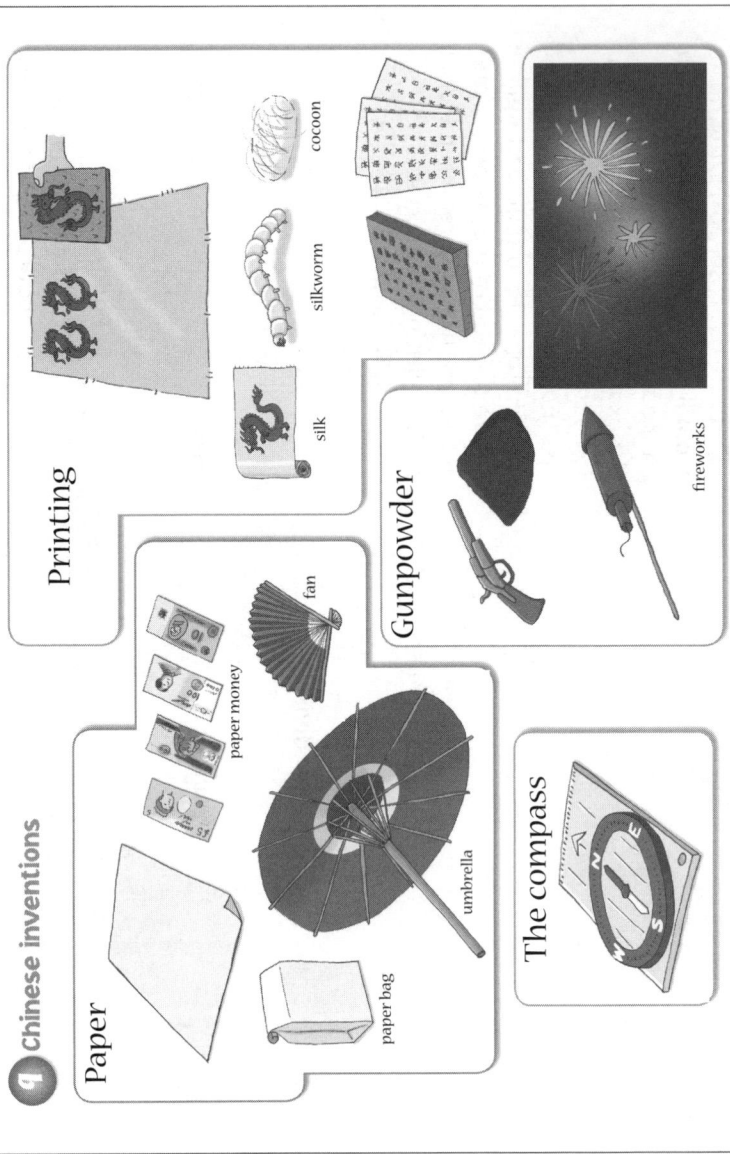

Warm-up

Ask the class to think of things made of paper. Tell them to look around the classroom. Tell them to think of things at home. Make a list on the board, e.g. *books, copy books, maps, posters, bags, money, envelopes, theatre programmes, tickets.*

Poster 9

1 Point to the poster. Read out the title. Give the class a moment or two to look.

2 Point to the headings and labels on the poster. Read them out. For new words, show the word card. Class reads and says the word/s.

3 Use the dictionary to explain new words as necessary. The following words are not in the dictionary. Check that children understand them from the poster. If you wish, explain them using these definitions and example sentences as necessary:

cocoon   the covering a caterpillar makes around it
         The caterpillar is inside the *cocoon*.
gunpowder a white dust that explodes in heat
         People must be careful with *gunpowder* because it is dangerous.
silkworm a kind of caterpillar
         Silkworms make silk threads.

4 Cover the words on the poster if you wish. Point to the new objects at random. Class names them.

5 Make sure children understand all the words on the poster. Take down the poster. Ask *What were the four inventions?* Put the poster back up. Children check.

Unit 9 Reading   130

Reading (PB pp90–91)

1 Give children time to look at the pictures. Read the title. Ask what they can name in them. They should be able to recognise: *writing, a book, paper pictures, cloth, a bowl, fire, fireworks.*

2 Play track 34. Children listen and follow in their books.

3 Read one paragraph or section of the text at a time.
Use Dictionary 4 to help you to explain new words as necessary.
Help children to find new words. Make up extra sentences for new words if you wish.

4 Ask questions about each paragraph or a section of the text. See Resource box.

5 Give reading practice around the class. Ask individuals, groups or the class to read sentences, captions or paragraphs.
Play track 34 again.

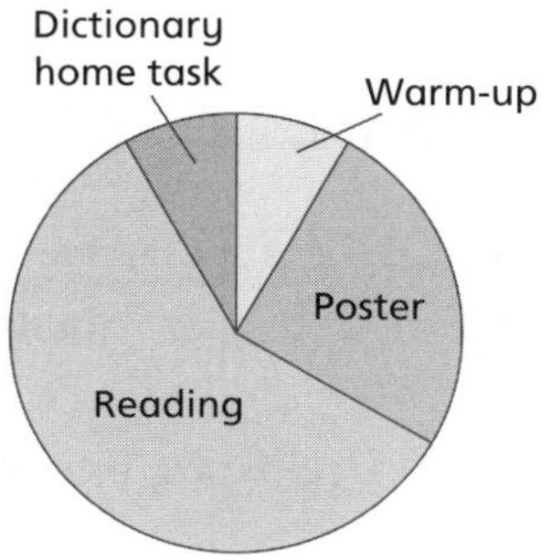

Homework task

Children learn selected vocabulary, Unit 9 *Dictionary* 4.
See unit word list on pp190–191 for key words, extension words and words for understanding only.

UNIT 9 Chinese inventions

Reading A   We use these every day

Paper

The Chinese invented paper about 2,000 years ago. They made it from different plants. At first they used it for wrapping things, then they used it for writing and drawing on. This picture shows leaves and flowers.

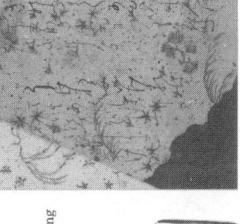

Paper was most useful for books. For hundreds of years, people wrote books. They used pens and ink and it took a long time. Then one of the most important inventions appeared.

Printing

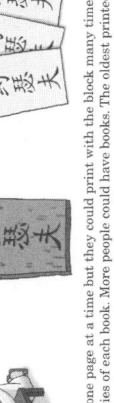

Chinese people first printed on cloth more than 2,000 years ago. They cut a pattern on a block of wood. They put dye on the woodblock then they pressed the block onto the cloth. The block printed the pattern. They could use the block again and again. Sometimes the cloth was silk. The Chinese invented silk, too. This piece of silk is a beautiful curtain.

Later the Chinese printed words on paper. They cut words on the woodblock. This was difficult work. They put ink on the block then they pressed the paper onto it. The woodblock printed the words onto the paper.

Unit 9   Reading: factual information with description

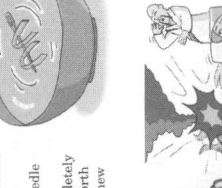

The printers printed one page at a time but they could print with the block many times. They could make many copies of each book. More people could have books. The oldest printed book in the world is from China. It is more than 1,100 years old.

The compass

A long time ago, sailors used the stars at night. They could find north, south, east and west. When it was cloudy, they could not see the stars and sometimes they lost their way.

The Chinese made a discovery. A special stone made a metal needle point to north. They floated the needle in a bowl of water and it pointed to north. It worked at sea when it was cloudy and completely dark. It worked on land in the daytime, too. People could find north and then they could follow a map. They could find their way to new places.

Gunpowder

Chinese scientists discovered gunpowder 1,100 years ago. First they found a kind of salt. It burned with a purple flame. They mixed it with other salts. When they put the mixture in a metal box and heated it, the box exploded. It was a very powerful mixture.

They used the gunpowder to make fireworks. Chinese people still make fireworks. They are the best in the world. If you go to a firework display, you will see Chinese fireworks. They explode in the sky in different shapes and colours.

Unit 9   Reading: factual information with description

Resource box

Text questions

When did the Chinese invent paper? **2000 years ago**

What did they make it from? **plants**

What was it most useful for? **books**

What did the Chinese first print on? **cloth**

What is silk? **a kind of cloth**

What two things did they use for printing on paper? **ink and a woodblock**

How did printing help people? **More people could have books.**

How old is the oldest book? **1,100 years old**

What did sailors first use to find north, south, east and west? **the stars**

What happened if it was cloudy? **They lost their way.**

What was the first compass? **a needle in a bowl of water**

What happened to the mixture of salts when it was heated? **It exploded.**

What did Chinese use gunpowder for? **fireworks**

Time division

- Warm-up
- Poster
- Reading
- Dictionary home task

Unit 9   Reading

131

Lesson 2 Reading comprehension and vocabulary (PB p92)

Lesson aim Reading comprehension; vocabulary

Lesson targets Children re-read *We use these every day*, then:
- (PB) complete a multiple choice activity
- give a personal response; match materials and inventions
- (WB) match words to pictures and definitions
- identify nouns and verbs; complete sentences with verbs

Key structure first conditional

Key language *If you go to a firework display, you will see Chinese fireworks.*

Words vocabulary from Lesson 1

Materials PB p92; CD B track 34 (optional); WB p82; Dictionary 4

Warm-up

Do *Words from words*. Use *discovery*:
disc, cover, very, over, dive, ride, rode.

Read again

Remind children of *We use these every day*.
Play track 34 or read the text to the class. Children listen and follow in their books.

Activity 1

Ask a child to read the first sentence with the alternative endings.
Tell children to think, then to check back to the text. Elicit an answer.
Check that everyone agrees. Children underline.
Continue with the other sentences. Children turn back and scan the text to find and check answers.

Activity 2

These questions require children to think and then to give their opinion.
Children should work in pairs or small groups, putting their ideas together.
Give them a time limit to do this then hear ideas from all the groups.
Note answers on the board. See how much agreement there is.

Activity 3

Children find five pictures that show inventions and five pictures that show materials or tools used in the invention or the process of using it.
Children may need to check back to the text to complete this activity.
They write the letter of the picture and the name of the invention in the first column. They write the letter of the picture and the tool or material in the second column.

Unit 9 Reading comprehension and vocabulary

Reading comprehension and vocabulary (WB p82)

If children are doing this page for homework, make sure they understand the tasks. Remind them to have their dictionaries with them for this work.

Exercise 1
Children match words and pictures then write the word next to the correct definition.

Exercise 2
Children sort the nouns and verbs.

Exercise 3
Children use verbs to complete the sentences. Remind them to make changes to the verb as necessary.

UNIT 4

Reading comprehension and vocabulary

1 Label the pictures.

fan   fireworks   cocoon   flame   ink

Read the definitions. Write the correct word.

1 the threads round a silkworm _____
2 the bright part of a fire _____
3 lights and fire exploding in the sky _____
4 dark liquid you can write with _____
5 something you can move around to cool your face _____

2 Read the words in the box. Write them in the correct list.

mix   discovery   invention   invent   mixture   discover

nouns _____
verbs _____

3 Complete the sentences. Use the verbs from the box in the correct form.

wrap   press   discover   explode   mix

1 Molly _____ Lulu's birthday present in pretty paper.
2 Lulu put dye on the woodblock then she _____ it onto the cloth.
3 The Chinese _____ gunpowder.
4 The scientists _____ different salts together.
5 When they heated the box of gunpowder, it _____.

Unit 4 Definitions; noun/verb recognition; cloze

Resource box

PB answers
Activity 1 1 wrapping 2 books 3 sometimes 4 paper 5 book 6 used 7 point 8 make
Activity 3 Inventions: A gunpowder B silk E compass F printing J paper; Things the Chinese used for their inventions: C plants D woodblock G salt H needle I silkworm

WB answers
Exercise 1 1 fan 2 fireworks 3 cocoon 4 flame 5 ink; 1 silk 2 flame 3 fireworks 4 ink 5 fan
Exercise 2 nouns: discovery invention mixture; verbs: mix invent discover
Exercise 3 1 wrapped 2 pressed 3 discovered 4 mixed 5 exploded

---

Time division

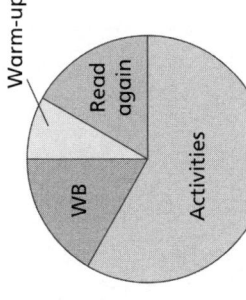

Warm-up, Read again, Activities, WB

Unit 4 Reading comprehension and vocabulary

Lesson 3 Speaking (PB p93) Study skills

Lesson aim Speaking, (WB) Study skills

Lesson targets Children:
- listen to a dialogue; listen and repeat the dialogue
- understand the story and answer oral questions
- read and act the dialogue
- (WB) practise alphabetical order and definitions

Informal everyday expressions *Come on, you two. Hurry up!*

New word *another*

Materials PB p93; CD B track 35, 36; WB p83; Dictionary 4

Preparation Listen to CD B track 35 before the lesson

Warm-up

Ask the class what happened in Part 2 of *The Golden Mask of Chapichapi*. Ask prompt questions if necessary: *Which room were they in? What did they see? What happened to the lights? What happened to the mask?* Let them look back to Part 2 if they have forgotten.

Activity 1

Children look at PB page 93. Read the title of Part 3. Ask what Chinese things they can see in the picture: *a fan, an umbrella, a tall pot, a long dress*. Ask if they know what the animal on the curtain is: *a Chinese dragon*.
Tell children to cover the dialogue text and look at the picture. Play track 35. Children listen.

Activity 2

Children look at the dialogue. Play track 35 again.
Children listen and follow.
Check children understand the new words. Use the dictionary if you wish.

Activity 3

Children close their books. Play track 36. Children listen and repeat in the pauses. Encourage them to use the same expression and intonation.

Activity 4

Ask questions to check understanding of the story. See Resource box.

Activity 5

Children act the dialogue without their books if possible.
Encourage children to remember their lines as much as possible and to speak without reading their lines word by word.

Study skills (WB p83)

The exercises on this page practise dictionary skills.
Children should be able to do this work independently once the tasks have been explained.
If your class has not done exercises on guessing meaning from context, leave time to look at exercise 2 with them.

Exercise 1

Demonstrate the first example on the board. Point out to the class how the first three letters are the same and that it is the fourth letter which tells them the order.
If you wish, do one more example with the class before they complete the rest of the exercise.

Exercise 2

This exercise practises guessing words from their context.
Tell children to read the sentence for general understanding first.
They look at the possible meanings.
They look back to the sentence for clues.
Demonstrate by asking *What is the shop in sentence 1?* ***a baker's***
Which of the three things can you buy in a bakers? ***a cake***

Study skills

a b c d e f g h i j k l m n o p q r s t u v w x y z

Look at the fourth letter!

1 Write the words in the correct order.

1	strong	straight	street
	straight	*street*	*strong*

2	class	clay	clap
3	brilliant	brick	bright
4	horse	horn	horrid
5	flat	flash	flag	flap

2 Read and guess the meaning of the underlined words. Circle your guess.
Don't look in a dictionary!

1 I went to the baker's shop and bought a meringue. (toy   fruit   cake)
2 It was cold so she wore a muffler round her neck. (hat   scarf   gloves)
3 Dad zoomed along the road in his new car. (went quickly   went slowly   stopped)
4 Grandma was tired so she had a little snooze. (biscuit   drink   sleep)
5 The garden was full of lovely red hollyhocks. (insects   flowers   clothes)
6 The play was good but the actors were ghastly. (happy   tired   very bad)

Now check your guesses with your teacher!

Unit 9 Dictionary skills

Resource box

Story questions

Which room are they in? *the Chinese room*
Who likes the fans? *Lulu*
What are they trying to do? *catch a thief*
Where are they going to look next? *in another room*
What kind of clothes can Molly see? *silk*
Who wants to hurry up? *Alfie*
When does Lulu think they'll find the thief? *never*
Who wants to try? *Molly*
Where do you think the thief is now? (*Children may have noticed the pair of feet showing below the curtain.*)

WB answers

Exercise 1 2 clap class clay   3 brick bright brilliant   4 horn horrid horse   5 flag flap flash flat
Exercise 2 1 a cake   2 a scarf   3 went quickly   4 sleep   5 flowers
6 very bad

Time division

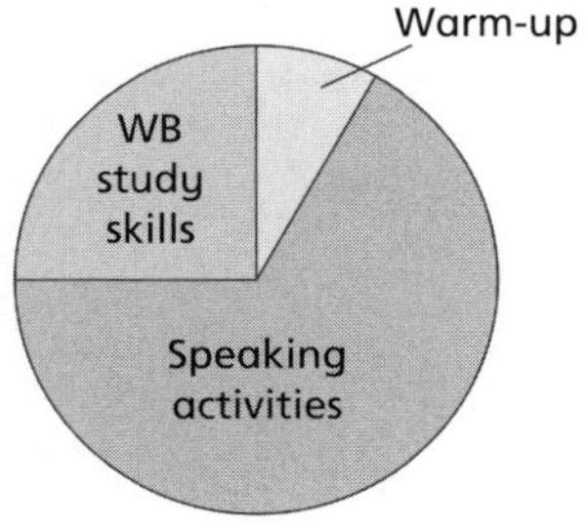

- Warm-up
- WB study skills
- Speaking activities

Unit 9 Study skills

Lesson 4 Grammar (Session 1), Grammar in conversation (Session 2) (PB pp94–95)

Lesson aim Grammar

Lesson targets Children:
- (session 1) understand and practise the key structure
- (session 2) listen to and read a conversation; repeat and practise it
- (session 2) listen to a song, say it and learn it (optional)

Key structure (session 1) first conditional

Key vocabulary recycling of general vocabulary

Key language (session 2) Let's... Shall we...? How about...?

Informal expressions Good idea. That's true.

Materials PB pp94–95; CD B tracks 37–40; WB pp84–85

Session 1 Warm-up

Play *What is it?* See Games, page 187.

Activity 1

Tell the class to look at the PC kids. Ask *What is Paddy thinking about? rain*

Ask a pair to read the bubbles. Write the sentences on the board and underline *if*. Point out the future *will* in both sentences.

Activity 2

Ask different children to read the beginnings then the endings. Write the beginnings while they read.

Ask a volunteer to say the complete first sentence. Check the class agrees. Complete the sentence on the board. Class reads and writes the letter.

Activities 3 and 4

Children work in pairs. See Resource box.*

Children complete WB page 84 in class time or for homework.

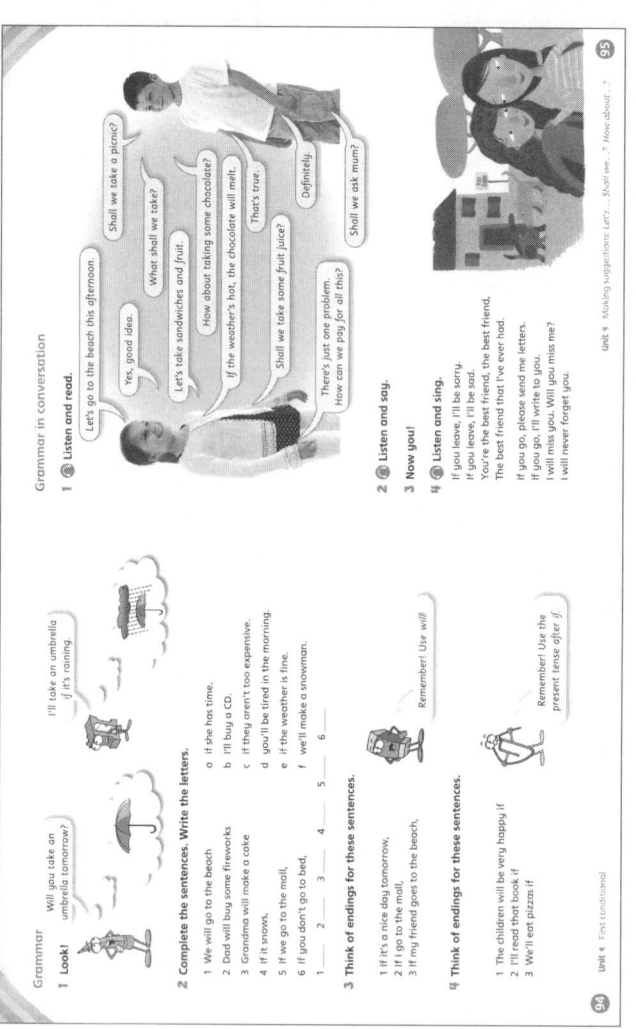

Session 2 Warm-up

Children think of as many words as they can that begin with *r*.

Activity 1

Point out the boy and girl. Ask are they in school or at home? **at home** (they are not wearing school clothes)

Tell the class to listen to the children.

Play track 37. Children follow in their books.

Activity 2

Children listen to track 38 and repeat in the pauses.

Activity 3

Children practise the conversation in pairs. See Resource box.**

Activity 4

Ask children if they can guess what *For sale* in the picture means.

Play track 39. Children listen and follow the first time.

Read the words with the class. Play track 39. Children join in.

Play track 40. Children sing with the music. They may learn the song, if you wish.

Unit 9 Grammar, Grammar in conversation

Grammar (Session 1), Grammar in conversation (Session 2) (WB pp84–85)

If this page is for homework, check children understand the tasks.

Exercise 1
Remind children that the verb in the main clause is future *will*.

Exercise 2
Remind the class that the verb in the *If* clause is in the present tense.

Exercise 3
Encourage the class to think of sentences that are true for them.

If this page is for homework, check children understand the tasks.

Exercise 1
Point out the bubble. Go through another example if you wish.

Exercise 2
Children complete the dialogue. Let one or two pairs read the conversation when this exercise has been completed.

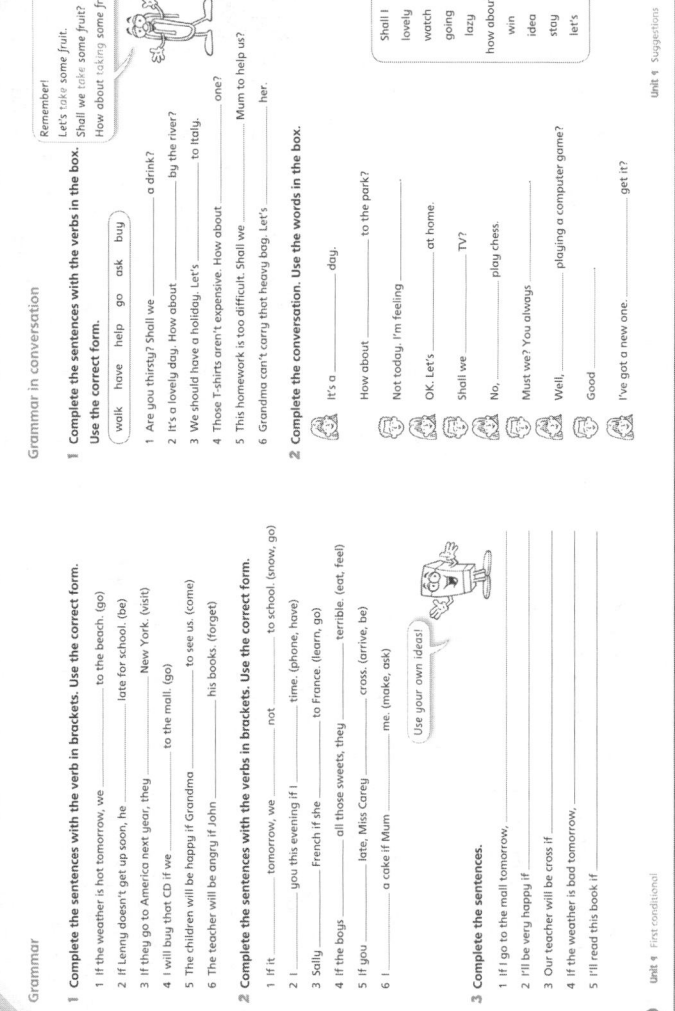

Resource box

PB answers (p94)
*Activities 3 and 4

Before children begin each activity, point out the PC kids' reminders. If you wish, do one example with the whole class before they work in pairs.

Pair work: Grammar (p94)
Children think of ideas for ending the sentence and note them in their copybooks. They practise saying the sentences to each other.

Go around listening as they work. Go through the structure again, if necessary.

Ask several pairs to say sentences for each activity in turn.

**Pair work: Grammar in conversation (p95)

Activity 3
Children practise the dialogue in pairs at their desks.

Encourage able children to suggest different items to take.

Give pairs three minutes to practise the dialogue.

Let one or two pairs stand up and say their conversations while the class listens.

WB answers

Grammar (p84)
Exercise 1 1 will go 2 will be 3 will visit 4 go 5 comes 6 forgets

Exercise 2 1 snows, will, go 2 will phone, have 3 will learn, goes 4 eat, will feel 5 arrive, will be 6 will make, asks

Grammar in conversation (p85)
Exercise 1 1 have 2 walking 3 go 4 buying 5 ask 6 help

Exercise 2 lovely, going, lazy, stay, watch, let's, win, how about, idea, Shall I

Time division

Session 1
- Warm-up
- Activity 1
- Activity 2
- WB

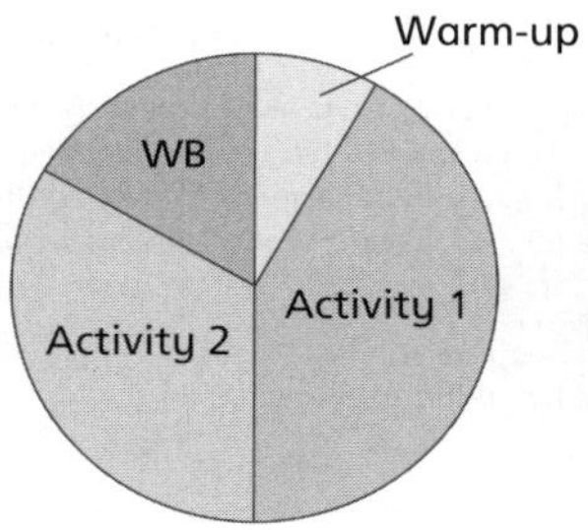

Session 2
- Warm-up
- Conversation activities
- Pairs conversation practice
- Song
- WB

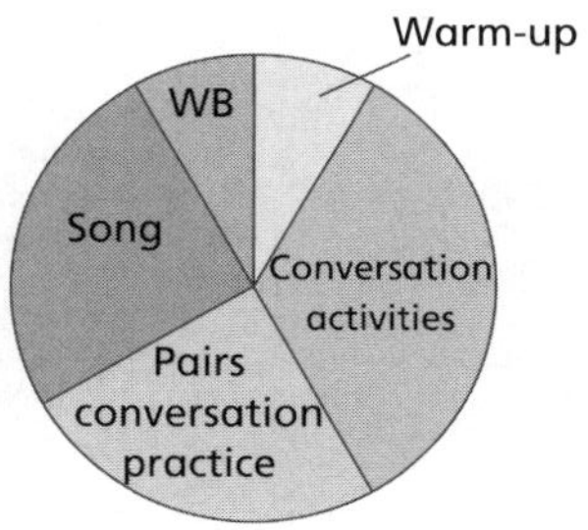

Grammar Practice Book
Children may begin Unit 9 when they have completed the PB and WB Grammar pages. They should complete it before the end of PB / WB Unit 9.

Unit 9 Grammar, Grammar in conversation

137

Lesson 5 Listening, Phonics (PB p96) Use of English

Lesson aim Listening, spelling and pronunciation, Use of English (WB)

Lesson targets Children:
- listen to information about papyrus
- listen to a description of a process; match pictures to the process
- practise saying, reading and spelling words with *igh* /aɪ/
- (WB) learn about subject, verb, object order in a sentence

Key structure and language from Unit 9

Target words *night, high, right, fight, light, bright*

Materials PB p96; CD B tracks 39, 41, 42; WB pp86–87

Warm-up
Sing the sad song from PB page 95, track 39.

Listening

Activity 1
Ask a child to read Ronnie's bubble. Tell the class they are going to hear about papyrus. Read the paragraph to the class. Children listen and follow. Ask different children to read the paragraph again, taking one sentence each.

Activity 2
Children look at the pictures. Ask what is happening in each one or what objects are in the pictures. It is not necessary for children to try to explain the process, just to recognise something about each picture.
Play track 41. Children listen and point to the pictures in order.

Activity 3
Children listen and write the letters of the pictures in order.
Play the track again if necessary for children to listen or check.
Check answers together.

Phonics
Point out the box. Tell children to follow in their books and repeat in the pauses. Play the first part of track 42. Make sure children repeat accurately.
Play the end of track 42. Children listen and follow.
Children say the rhyme. They may learn it, if you wish.

Children open their WBs at page 86. They complete the Phonics page now or for homework. If it is for homework, make sure they understand the tasks.

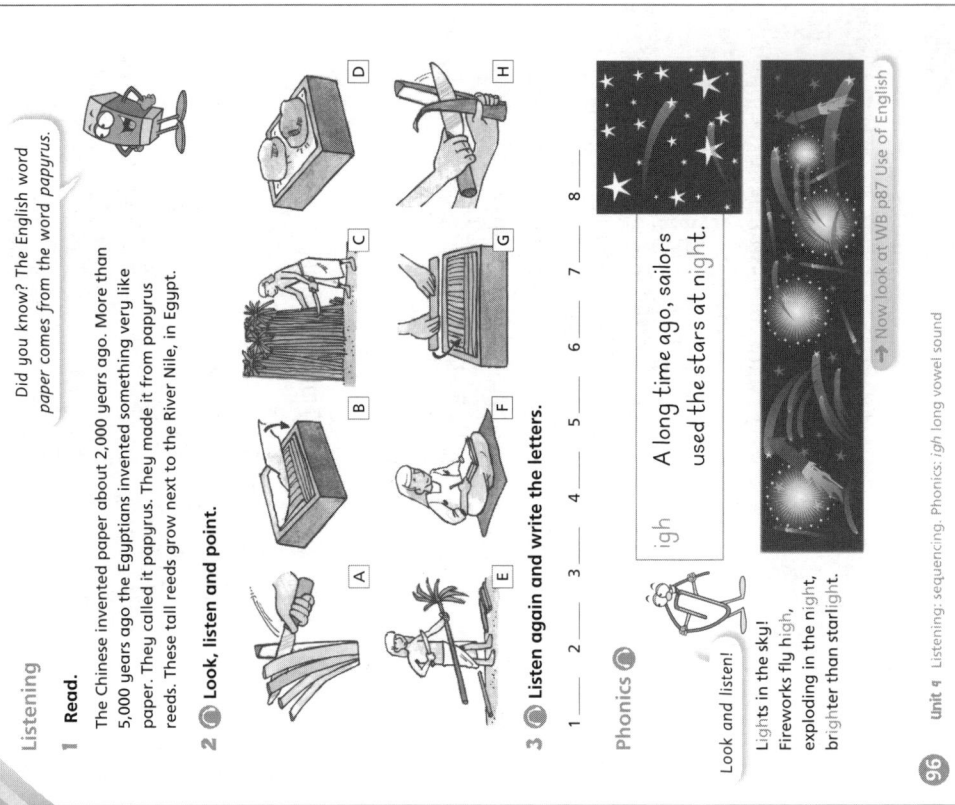

Listening
1 Read.
The Chinese invented paper about 2,000 years ago. More than 5,000 years ago the Egyptians invented something very like paper. They called it papyrus. They made it from papyrus reeds. These tall reeds grow next to the River Nile, in Egypt.

Did you know? The English word paper comes from the word papyrus.

2 Look, listen and point.

3 Listen again and write the letters.
1 __ 2 __ 3 __ 4 __ 5 __ 6 __ 7 __ 8 __

Phonics
igh

A long time ago, sailors used the stars at night.

Look and listen!
Lights in the sky!
Fireworks fly high,
exploding in the night,
brighter than starlight.

→ Now look at WB p87 Use of English

Unit 9 Listening: sequencing. Phonics: *igh* long vowel sound

Use of English
Move on to WB page 87.

Unit 9 Listening, Phonics, Use of English

Phonics, Use of English (WB pp86–87)

Remind the class of the sound *igh* and *night*.

Exercise 1
Remind the class to read the words they have written.

Exercise 2
Children read the clues and complete the crossword.

Exercise 3
Encourage children to do this without copying the word.

Resource box
PB answers (p96)
Audioscript (CD B Track 41) **Listening activities 2–3** (PB p96)
First, the men went to the river. They cut the tall papyrus reeds with sharp knives. Next, they cut the reeds into short pieces. The outside of the reeds, the green part, was very hard, so they cut this off. The inside of the reeds were soft and white. They cut this into long, thin pieces. They took the long, thin pieces and placed them in a box. They placed the pieces side by side: first, top to bottom, and then across. Next, they covered the papyrus with a piece of cloth. Then, they placed heavy stones on the cloth. The stones pressed down on the papyrus. There was sticky juice inside the papyrus, and the stones pushed this juice out. Soon, all the long, thin pieces were sticking together. After a few days, the papyrus was dry. They took it out of the box and used it for writing and drawing. If you go to Egypt, you will see papyrus. Perhaps you will buy a papyrus picture.

Activity 3 1C 2E 3H 4A 5G 6B 7D 8F

WB answers
Phonics (p86)
Exercise 2 1 fight 2 night 3 light 4 right 5 bright 6 high

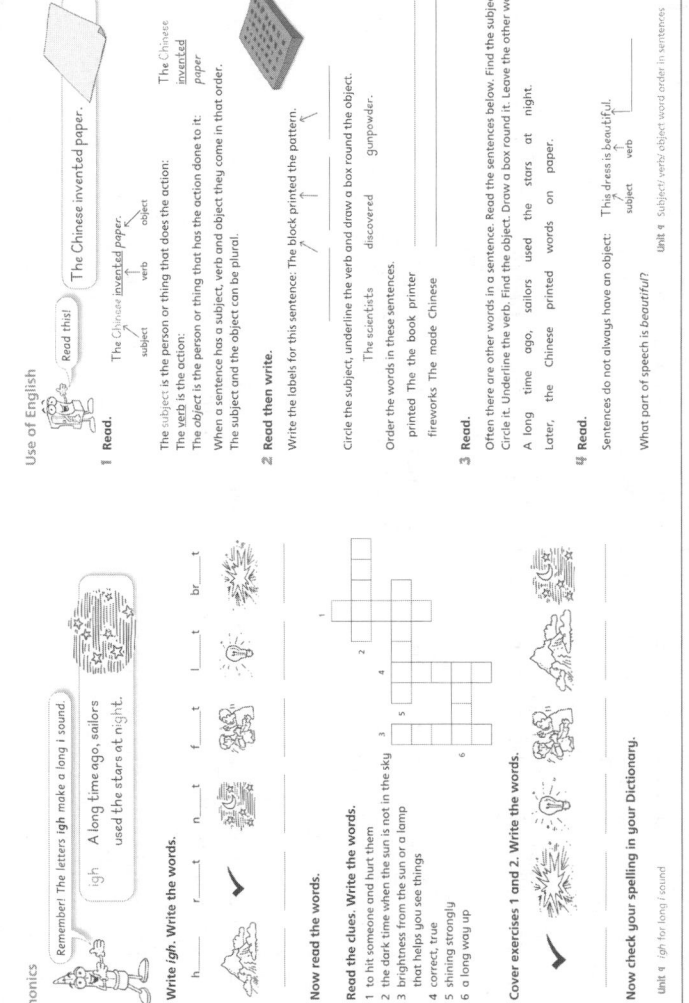

Write the example sentence. Class reads.

Exercise 1
Use the example sentence to go through the presentation. Label it and underline the verb as in the WB. Point out the subject, verb, object order.

Exercise 2
Write up *The block printed the pattern*. Children label it with *subject, verb, object*.
Write up *The scientists discovered gunpowder*. Children circle, underline and draw.
Give children time to read the words in the first sentence. Help the class identify the subject, verb and object, then to order the words. Children write. Do the same with the second sentence.

Exercise 3
Read the information to the class. Write up the example sentences. Children circle in pencil. A volunteer circles, etc. on the board. Children check their work.

Exercise 4
Write up the sentence. A volunteer labels the subject and verb. Ask the question. Label *beautiful: adjective*.

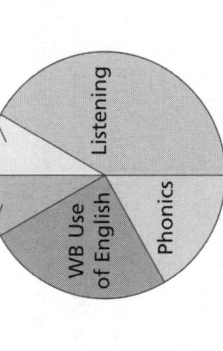

Time division

Unit 9 Phonics, Use of English

Lesson 6 Class composition (Session 1) (PB p97) Writing preparation, Composition practice (Session 2)

Lesson aim Writing

Lesson targets Children:
- (session 1) compose and write information about Chinese paper
- (session 2) (WB) practise writing information and describing a process
- (session 2) (WB) write information about Chinese silk

Key structure and language from Unit 9

Vocabulary the process and materials for making paper and silk

Materials PB p97; WB pp88–89; poster 9

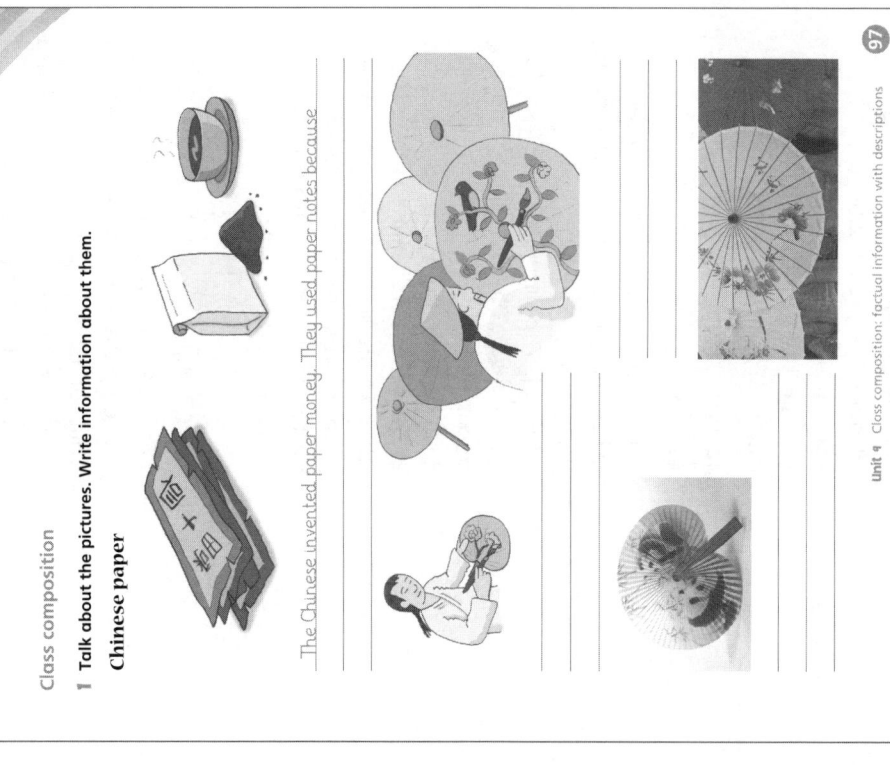

Session 1 Warm-up

Put up poster 9. Remind the class of the four inventions. Ask *Which invention do you think we need most? Which one do we need least?* Hear some ideas.

Class composition

Activity 1

1 Ask a volunteer to read the title. Give the class a minute or two to look at the pictures. Starting from the top, ask what the pictures show. Ask questions about the objects. The example writing is a guide to questions that can be asked but ask any others as appropriate. Encourage the class to say as much as they can about the pictures, from what they can see and from their own knowledge, e.g. *Chinese people use fans because China is a hot country.*

2 When everything on the page has been talked about, ask for suggestions for sentences for each picture.
The writing may vary from the example.
When sentences have been written on the board, ask a volunteer to read them to the class.
Ask if there are any more details that could be added. Make any changes that you and the class agree to.
Let a volunteer read the information a final time.

3 Remove the writing from the board. If any new or unusual words have been used in the composition, you may wish to leave them on the board for children to check spelling.
Children write information in their books.
Writing will vary but children should be able to make two or three statements for each picture, giving accurate information.

Writing preparation, Composition practice (WB pp88–89)

Session 2 Warm-up

Play *Opposites* (see Games, page 187).

Exercises 1–3

Children should be able to complete this page and write information on page 89 with very little help.

If you wish, do the first paragraph with the class. Elicit the answers to exercise 1 and show the class how to write the answers into a paragraph of information.

Children write the first paragraph. Children continue with the other two paragraphs.

Go around helping and monitoring as they work. Make sure children complete each section on WB page 88 and colour the pictures before they try to write the complete paragraph on page 89.

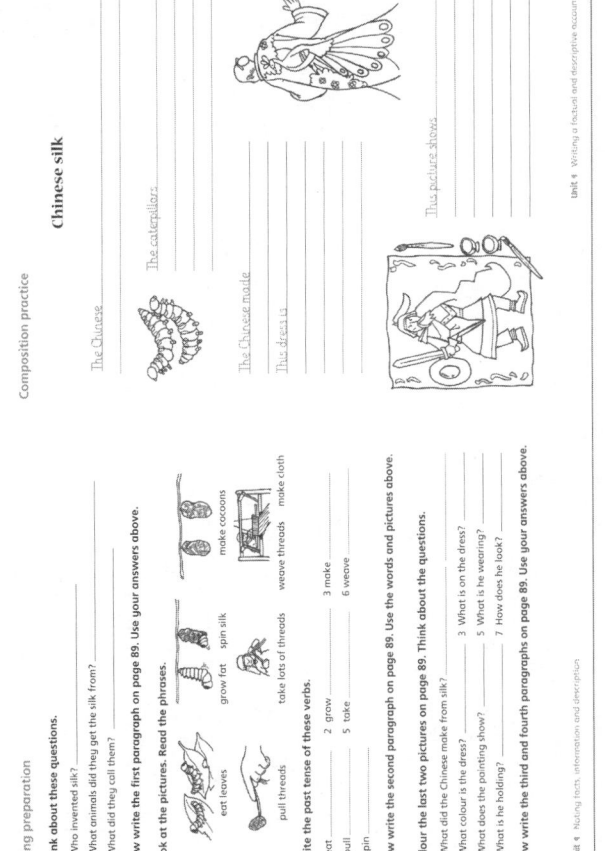

Children should be able to use their answers, the pictures and notes to write clear information and this part of the writing may not vary much. Some children will be able to write detailed descriptions of the dress and the picture. Other children will write shorter sentences. Encourage children to think of adjectives to describe the objects.

Go around helping and monitoring as they work.

Before the end of the lesson, ask volunteers to read some of their work, especially descriptions of the objects that are different to each other. If children make neat copies, encourage them to illustrate their writing.

Homework task

Children complete Check-up 9, WB p90. For answers, see p145. Before they begin WB page 90, read the script on page 145 of this Teacher's Guide.
Children listen and draw before they write.

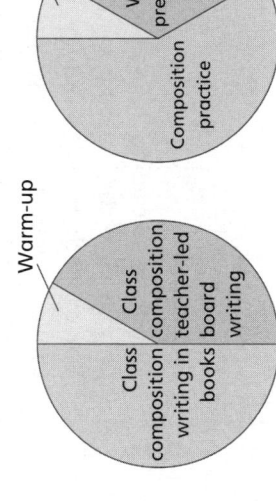

Time division

Session 1 / Session 2

Portfolio

Children may make neat copies to add to their written work.

Resource box

Class composition example writing (p97)

The Chinese invented paper money. They used paper notes because they were lighter than coins. They used paper bags. They kept tea in them.

They made fans and umbrellas from paper. They painted pictures of trees, flowers and birds on them.

This fan has a picture of two animals (bears). They are black and white. They are eating leaves.

These pretty umbrellas are yellow, green and blue. There are pictures of pink flowers and birds on them.

WB answers

Composition practice example writing (p89)

The Chinese invented silk. They got the silk from caterpillars. They called the caterpillars silk worms.

The caterpillars ate mulberry leaves. They grew fat. Then they spun silk. They made cocoons. People took the threads from the cocoons. They took lots of threads. They wove the threads and they made the cloth.

The Chinese made clothes from silk and they made paintings on silk.

This dress is [colour of choice]. It has got a picture on it. the picture is of a bird with a very long tail. The bird is sitting in a tree and there are flowers on the tree. The dress is very beautiful.

This picture shows a soldier. He is wearing a [colour of choice] cloak and a metal helmet. He is holding a sword. He looks fierce / frightening.

Unit 9 Writing preparation, Composition practice

Revision 3, Project 3

Activity 1

Give children a minute to look at the picture.
Ask what the place is: *a museum*
Ask what things they can see in the picture.
Play CD B track 43. Children listen and follow in their books.
Play the track again if children found the text hard to follow.
Ask questions, e.g.
Which room does the man want to go to? *the Russian room*
Which way must he go? *straight on then turn left*
Where do the boy and girl want to go? *the café*
Which display does the boy want to go to? *the Incas*
What does he want to draw? *the soldiers*
Have they got a lot of paper? *No, they haven't got much paper.*
What animal does the girl like? *worms*
Which room will they see them in? *the Chinese room*
Who doesn't like worms? *the boy*
What mustn't the two little children do? *make a lot of noise, touch anything, run in the museum*

Activity 2

Play track 43 again. Children follow.
Choose some children to act out the story.
You could do this by bringing pairs forward for each conversation.
Alternatively, let pairs stand up and read from their places.
Repeat with another group.

Extra activities

Class games

Play in teams. Describe one of the people in the picture, e.g. *He has got a bag. He is wearing long trousers. He is wearing a hat.* Children look for the person who matches the description. They put their hands up when they have found him. Ask *What is he saying?* The child reads out the bubble: *Does anybody know where the café is?* Describe another person. Teams look for the person. The first team to tell you correctly what the person is saying wins a point.
Make the description general at first then give detail to make the answer obvious. Use colour of clothing if there is nothing else particular about the person.

Pair work

In pairs, children do a variation of the class game. Child 1 makes a statement about someone in the picture. Child 2 guesses who is being described and points to the person in the picture. If child 2 cannot guess after the first statement, child 1 must make another statement until child 1 finds the correct person.

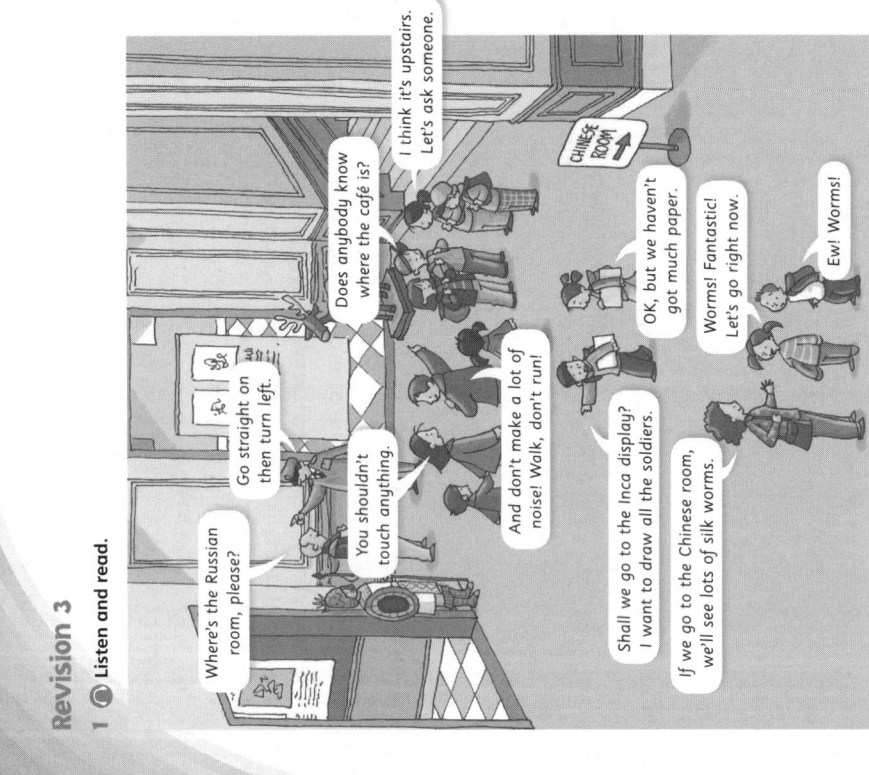

Revision 3

1 🔊 Listen and read.

2 🔊 Listen again. Act the story.

A museum display

In this project children choose a subject or objects that interest them for a display. It can be any subject of their own choice.

1 Read the first four lines to the class.
Make sure they understand all the words in line 2.
Ask what objects are in the pictures.
Explain to the class that they need not only write about old things. They can also choose new things.
Read the rest of the information to the class and explain the task to the class.

2 Explain that they must make the subject interesting for somebody else to look at. They cannot just stick some of their favourite pictures on a poster. They must write information about what is in the display.

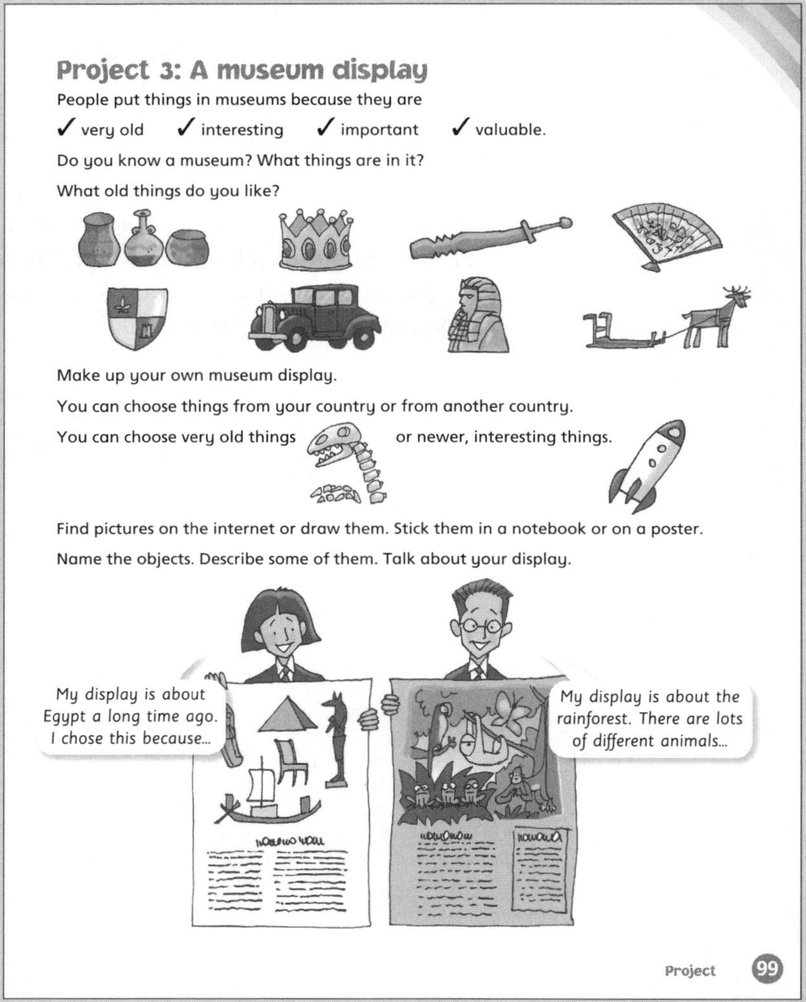

3 All children should be able to complete this project working at their own level. Some children may have a particular interest that they can write about and find pictures of.
Encourage them to find or draw different pictures to create the display.
This project can be done as quickly or slowly as suits your class and they can write a longer or shorter project, as a book or a poster.

4 Children tell the rest of the class about their displays. They tell them what it is about and why they chose it.
If there is not time for all children to read out their information, they could say what their favourite thing in the display is and why.
Put up children's work, if possible, and encourage the class to look at the different ideas.

Project 3: A museum display

People put things in museums because they are
✓ very old   ✓ interesting   ✓ important   ✓ valuable.

Do you know a museum? What things are in it?
What old things do you like?

Make up your own museum display.
You can choose things from your country or from another country.
You can choose very old things or newer, interesting things.
Find pictures on the internet or draw them. Stick them in a notebook or on a poster.
Name the objects. Describe some of them. Talk about your display.

My display is about Egypt a long time ago. I chose this because...

My display is about the rainforest. There are lots of different animals...

Summary box

Lesson aim

Lesson targets
- listen to a dialogue, understand it, read it and act it
- write information for a museum display and illustrate it
- tell the class about the display and what is in it

Resource box

Portfolio
If you wish, this project may be included in children's portfolio of written work.

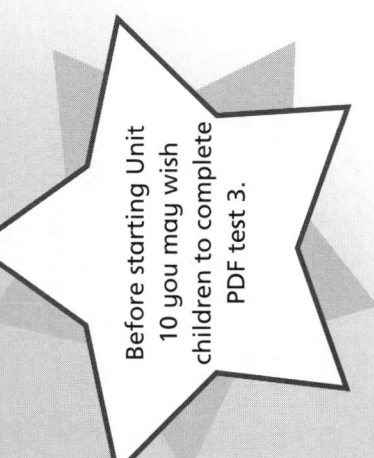

Before starting Unit 10 you may wish children to complete PDF test 3.

Project 3

143

Portfolio 3 and Diploma 3: Units 7–9

1 When children have completed all the work in Units 7–9, they turn to page 133 in their Workbook.

2 This page allows children to make their own assessment of what they have learned in English.

Vocabulary
Tell children to tick each box only when they are confident that they know the key words in each category.

Grammar
Remind children to look at all the grammar they have learned before they tick the boxes.

Phonics
Children tick the boxes when they can read and spell the words accurately. Remind them they may help each other by testing.

3 Check through the completed Portfolio page with each child. Encourage them to work harder on the things they are unsure of. The whole class need not complete everything on this page before moving on to Unit 10 but they should try to revise something from each section.

1 When children are confident with all the elements of the work on page 133, they may complete the Diploma page.

2 This contains a representative task from each field of work.

3 Children receive a sticker for each task completed and one more when they have finished the page.

4 These pages may be taken out of the Workbook and kept in children's individual portfolios of work along with a few examples of children's best work from Units 7–9.

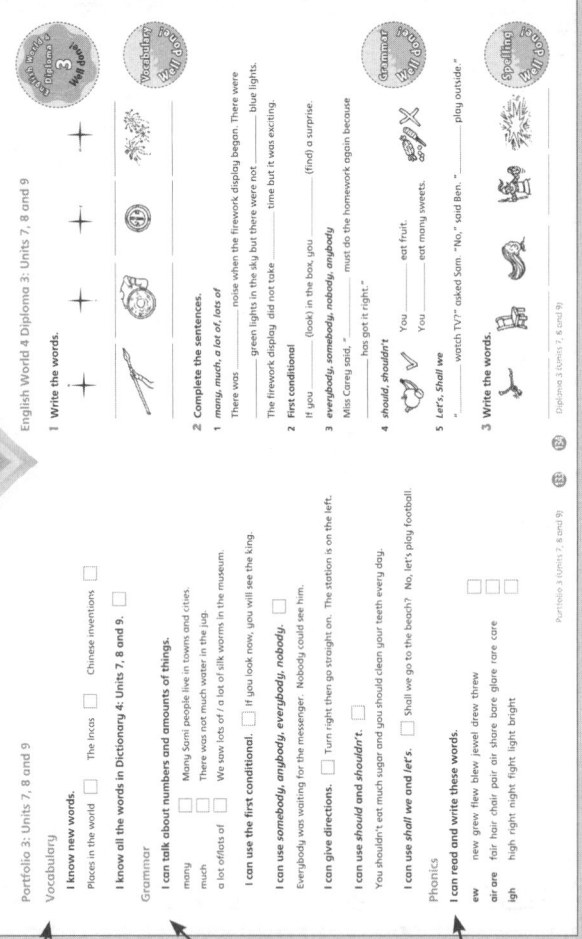

4 Tell children who are not entirely confident (even if they have coloured and ticked everything on the page) to spend extra time learning words for Units 7–9. They may use the Dictionary to help them learn and revise.

Completed Diploma 3
Exercise 1 north, south, east, west, spear, shield, compass, fireworks
Exercise 2 1 a lot of, lots of, many, much
2 look, will find
3 Everybody, nobody
4 should, shouldn't
5 Shall we, Let's
Exercise 3 jewel, chair, hair, fight, bright

Portfolio 3 and Diploma 3: Units 7–9

Answers to Check-ups: Units 7–9

Check-up 7 WB pp70–71

Exercise 1 1 many 2 much 3 a lot of 4 lots of 5 much 6 many

Exercise 2 2 There are not many flowers. 3 There are a lot of birds 4 There is not much water.

Exercise 3 1 should go 2 should make 3 should not play 4 should speak 5 should not wear 6 should not buy

Exercise 4 Children look at the pictures and read the bubbles. They use the questions to help them write the story.

Exercise 5 Example writing: Tom and his mum were in the supermarket. There were lots of people. They needed to buy eggs, bread and milk. There was a lot of milk on the shelves. They bought three bottles. There was not much bread on the shelves. There were not many eggs. They should go shopping earlier next time.

Check-up 8 WB pp80–81

Exercise 1 1 somebody 2 Nobody 3 anyone 4 Everyone 5 anybody

Exercise 2 A Turn right; turn left; on the right B Turn left; go straight on; on the left

Exercise 4 1 Turn left out of the park. At the roundabout turn right. Then go straight on at the crossroads. At the next crossroads turn left and the supermarket is on your right.
2 Turn right out of the school. At the crossroads turn left. Go straight on over the crossroad. At the roundabout turn right. The sports club is on your left.

Check-up 9 WB pp90–91

Exercise 1 1 is 2 will go 3 will travel 4 visits 5 will drive, are 6 look, will see 7 will send, gives 8 drinks, will feel

Exercise 2 1 make 2 do, watch 3 going 4 have 5 playing 6 send 7 listen 8 buying

Exercise 4 Read this script to the class.

Use two colours. With the first colour, draw a line from the box to the map.
Draw a line from the map to the castle.
Draw a line from the castle to the princess.

Draw a line from the princess to the stars. Now use the second colour. Draw a line from the tree to the nest.
Draw a line from the nest to the egg.
Draw a line from the egg to the monster.
Draw a line from the monster to the stars.

Children read each question and follow the lines they have drawn to find the answer and write about the game.

Example writing: If they open the box they will find the map. If they follow the map, they will go to the castle. If they reach the castle, they will meet the princess. If they meet the princess, she will give them three stars.

If they climb the tree, they will find a nest. If they look in the nest, they will see the egg. If they drop the egg, a monster will appear. If the monster catches them, it will take the stars.

10 Space travel

Lesson 1 Poster 10, Reading

Lesson aim Reading
Text type biography
Lesson targets Children:
- read, understand and practise new vocabulary on the poster
- read, understand and practise reading a biography
- answer oral comprehension questions

Key structure *a few, a little*
Key language adjective + *enough*
Key vocabulary space travel
Materials PB pp100–101; poster 10; CD C track 1; Dictionary 4; word cards for poster vocabulary (see poster 10 below or list on p16)
Preparation Make word cards; listen to CD C track 1

Warm-up

Write *space* on the board. Ask children what they know about space travel. Elicit words, e.g. **space rocket, astronaut, planet.** Ask *Can people fly to the moon? Can people live in space? What can they see from space?*

Poster 10

1 Put up the poster. Read out the title. Give the class a moment or two to look.

2 Point to the objects and people. Read the word. For new words show the word card/s. Class reads and says the word/s. Make sure children understand the following words which are not in the dictionary. Use the definitions and example sentences as necessary to ensure understanding:

commander the leader on a space journey
   The *commander* helps the other astronauts to do their work well.

orbit the journey of an object going round a planet or star
   The space craft did two *orbits* of the Earth.

parachute the large piece of cloth that fills with air and helps people and objects to go down to the ground slowly
   The pilot opened his *parachute* as soon as he jumped out of the plane.

satellite a machine that travels in space and sends signals
   There are hundreds of *satellites* in orbit round the Earth.

spacecraft a machine that can travel in space and carry people
   There isn't much room inside a *spacecraft*.

3 Cover the words on the poster if you wish. Point to the objects and people at random. Class names them.

4 Ask children to give their ideas about space and space travel. Ask *Is space travel interesting? Do you want to travel in space? Why or why not?*

5 If children are interested in space travel, ask *Where do you want to go? Find out if children know about any planets or any journeys in space.*

Unit 10 Reading

Reading (PB pp100-101)

1. Give children time to look at the pictures. Read the title. Ask what they can see in the pictures on page 101.
   Do the pictures look exciting? interesting? boring? beautiful?

2. Play CD C track 1. Children listen and follow in their books.

3. Read one paragraph or section of the text at a time.
   Use Dictionary 4 to help you to explain new words as necessary.
   Help children to find new words. Make up extra sentences for new words if you wish.
   Children learned *pioneer* in level 3. Remind them if necessary: someone who does something first.

4. Ask questions about each paragraph or a section of the text. See Resource box.

5. Give reading practice around the class. Ask individuals, groups or the class to read sentences or paragraphs.
   Play track 1 again.

UNIT 10 Space travel

Space pioneers

Valentina Tereshkova
Cosmonaut
The first woman in space

This photograph shows Valentina in her spacesuit.

Key dates

1937	born near Yaroslavl, west Russia
1945	started school
1954	started working in a factory, continued learning in her free time
1959	first parachute jump
1962	joined the space programme
1963	became the first woman in space, married Andrian Nikolayev
1964	her daughter was born, trained as a cosmonaut engineer
1969–97	worked in the Russian Air Force
2007	told her dream: a flight to Mars

Valentina Tereshkova was born on 6th March, 1937 near the city of Yaroslavl in western Russia. Her father was a tractor driver. Her mother worked in a factory.

When she was two years old, her father died in a war-time battle. She started school when she was eight. At seventeen, she started working in a factory. Valentina enjoyed learning so she continued her education in her free time.

There was a flying club in Yaroslavl. Valentina joined and she learned to sky-dive. She made her first parachute jump on 21st May, 1959. She was 22 years old.

She became a spinning engineer at the factory but she parachuted from planes many times.

In 1961 the Russian space engineers had an idea. They wanted a Russian to be the first woman cosmonaut. The woman could not be too tall or too heavy. She had to be young enough and fit enough to fly in space. This was the description:

age – under 30 years old
weight – under 70 kg
height – under 170 cm
important: she **must** be able to parachute.

Valentina fitted this description.

More than 50 young women did the tests but only a few women were good enough. Valentina and four other women joined the space programme in February, 1962.

Valentina trained hard. In November the space engineers chose her for the special flight. "You will be the first woman in space," they told her. Valentina was delighted.

The Vostok 6 spacecraft.

At last the day of the flight arrived. On 16th June, 1963 Valentina took off in the spacecraft Vostok 6. The flight lasted almost three days. During the flight she spoke to people on the ground. Her call sign was Chaika. In English this means seagull. This is the word in Russian: Чайка.

In November she married another cosmonaut. Her husband was Andrian Nikolayev. Their daughter, Elena was born in 1964. Valentina trained as a cosmonaut engineer then she worked in the Russian Air Force until 1997. Valentina Tereshkova became a Hero of the Soviet Union. She received the United Nations Gold Medal of Peace. On her seventieth birthday she told a newspaper reporter: "I still have one dream: a flight to Mars. It is the dream of all cosmonauts."

Vostok 1: the space rocket took Yuri Gagarin into orbit round the Earth.

The first men in space exploration

Yuri Gagarin	Russia	the first man in space, the first orbit of the Earth	12th April, 1961
Alexei Leonov	Russia	the first space walk	18th March, 1965
Neil Armstrong	America	the first man on the moon	21st July, 1969

Resource box

Text questions

Who was Valentina Tereshkova? a Russian cosmonaut, the first woman in space
When was she born? 1937
What did her parents do? father, tractor driver; mother, worked in a factory
What did she like doing? learning
When was her first parachute jump? 21st May 1959
How did she feel when the scientists chose her for the flight? delighted
How long was her flight? 3 days
What did her call sign Chaika mean in English? seagull
What did Valentina work as after her daughter was born? cosmonaut engineer
What was her dream? a flight to Mars
Which country did the first man in space come from? Russia
Who first walked in space? on the moon? Alexei Leonov, Neil Armstrong

Homework task

Children learn selected vocabulary from Unit 10 *Dictionary 4*.
See unit word list on pp190–191 for key words, extension words and words for understanding only.

Time division

Poster / Warm-up / Dictionary home task / Reading

Unit 10 Reading 147

Lesson 2 Reading comprehension and vocabulary (PB p102)

Lesson aim Reading comprehension; vocabulary
Lesson targets Children re-read *Space pioneers*, then:
- (PB) answer literal and inferential questions
- complete a cloze activity
- (WB) match words to pictures
- match words to definitions

Key structure *a few, a little*
Key language adjective + *enough*
Words vocabulary from Lesson 1
Materials PB p102; CD C track 1 (optional); WB p92; Dictionary 4

Warm-up

Do *Look, write, check* with target phonic words from Units 8 and 9 (see Games, page 187).

Read again

Remind children of *Space pioneers*.
Play track 1 or read the text to the class. Children listen and follow in their books.

Activity 1

Go through this activity with the class one question at a time.
Volunteers read each one. Children scan the text to find and check answers.
If children have difficulty or disagree, direct them to the correct paragraph and tell them to read the sentences carefully.

Activity 2

The answers to questions 1 and 2 are not in the text. Encourage children to think of answers for themselves.
For question 3, let children exchange ideas in pairs for a few moments then ask children around the class.

Activity 3

Ask different children to read the words in the box.
Ask a volunteer to read and complete the first sentence. Check with the class. Children write.
Refer children to their dictionaries if they need reminding of what some of the words in the box mean.

Reading comprehension and vocabulary

1 Answer the questions

1 When was Valentina Tereshkova born?
2 Where did she work at seventeen?
3 Where did Valentina learn to sky-dive?
4 What was the Russian space engineers' idea?
5 How many women joined the space programme in February 1962?
6 How long did Valentina's flight last?
7 On her seventieth birthday, what was her one dream?
8 Who was the first man in space?
9 What did Alexei Leonov do first?
10 Who was the first man on the moon?

2 Talk about the answers to these questions.

1 The first woman cosmonaut had to be young and fit. Why?
2 Did the Russian engineers want a small woman or a big woman. Why?
3 Do you have the same dream as Valentina Tereshkova? Why? Why not?

3 Choose the best word to complete each sentence.

lasted   programme   received   education   fit   exploration

1 Your _____ is very important so you must work hard at school.
2 Is space _____ exciting or too dangerous?
3 This year our sports _____ includes football training and swimming lessons.
4 Alfie can run 100 metres in 15 seconds – he is very _____.
5 Last week our school _____ a very important visitor.
6 The children's performance of The Ugly Duckling _____ one hour.

102

Unit 10 Reading comprehension and vocabulary: literal, inferential, personal response; cloze

Unit 10 Reading comprehension and vocabulary

Reading comprehension and vocabulary (WB p92)

If children are doing this page for homework, make sure they understand the tasks. Remind them to have their dictionaries for the second exercise.

Exercise 1
Children match words and pictures.

Exercise 2
Tell children to try to do this without the dictionary first, then to check their work afterwards.

Resource box

PB answers
Activity 1 1 6th March 1937
2 in a factory
3 at the Flying club in Yaroslavl
4 a Russian as the first woman cosmonaut
5 50
6 almost 3 days
7 a flight to Mars
8 Yuri Gagarin
9 walked in space
10 Neil Armstrong

Activity 2 possible answers the children can express: 1 because a long journey makes you tired; the cosmonaut had to stay in space for several days; the scientist did not want the cosmonaut to be ill in the space rocket
2 they wanted a small woman: there is not much room inside a space rocket; a big woman is heavier than a small woman so the rocket takes off more easily with a lighter cosmonaut
3 Children's own answers

Activity 3 1 education 2 exploration
3 programme 4 fit 5 received 6 lasted

WB answers
Exercise 1 1i 2b 3c 4f 5h 6d 7a 8g 9e
Exercise 2 1 delighted 2 become 3 take off
4 hard 5 train 6 battle 7 war-time

Reading comprehension and vocabulary

1 Match the pictures with the words. Write the letters.

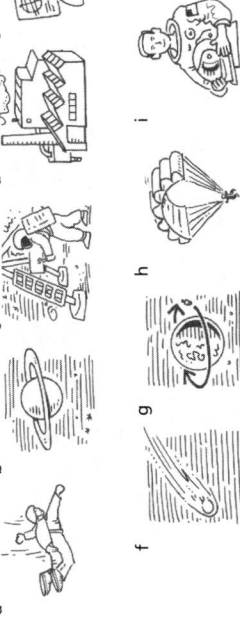

1 astronaut ___ 2 planet ___ 3 space engineer ___ 4 comet ___
5 parachute ___ 6 factory ___ 7 sky-dive ___ 8 orbit ___ 9 commander ___

2 Match the words with the definitions. Write the words. You may check in your Dictionary.

| battle | take off | war-time | become | hard (adverb) |
| delighted | train (verb) |

1 very pleased _____
2 to begin to be something _____
3 leave the ground in flight _____
4 with a lot of effort _____
5 to learn and practise _____
6 a fight between soldiers _____
7 the time when two countries are fighting _____

Unit 10 Matching words and pictures; definitions

Time division

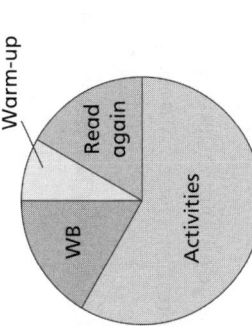

Warm-up
Read again
WB
Activities

Unit 10 Reading comprehension and vocabulary

149

Lesson 3 Speaking (PB p103) Study skills

Lesson aim Speaking, (WB) Study skills
Lesson targets Children:
- listen to a dialogue; listen and repeat the dialogue
- understand the story and answer oral questions
- read and act the dialogue
- (WB) practise dictionary skills and sorting

Informal everyday expressions *Welcome! All right. I suppose.*
New words *return, climb on board, lift off, around, Africa, trip*
Materials PB p103; CD C tracks 2, 3; WB p93; Dictionary 4
Preparation Listen to CD C track 2 before the lesson

Warm-up
Ask the class to tell you what happened in Part 3. Let them look back if necessary.

Activity 1
Children look at PB page 103. Read the title of Part 4. Ask *Which room are they in now? What are they doing? Where are they going?*
Tell children to cover the dialogue text and look at the picture.
Play track 2. Children listen.

Activity 2
Children look at the dialogue. Play track 2 again.
Children listen and follow.
Check children understand the new words. Use the dictionary if you wish.

Activity 3
Children close their books. Play track 3. Children listen and repeat in the pauses. Encourage them to use the same expression and intonation.

Activity 4
Ask questions to check understanding of the story. See Resource box.

Activity 5
Children act the dialogue without their books if possible.
Encourage children to speak without reading their lines word by word if they need their books.

Unit 10 Speaking

Study skills (WB p93)

The exercises on this page practice dictionary skills and sorting.
Children should be able to do this work independently once the tasks have been explained.

Exercise 1
Children match the words and pictures, then check in their dictionaries.

Exercise 2
Children categorise the words.

Study skills

1 Write the words for the pictures.

1. t r o f a c y _____
2. p h a r u c a t e _____
3. s l u g a l e _____
4. s t o m o c a n u _____
5. c a p e s   f r a c t _____
6. m a d e r _____

Now check your spelling in your Dictionary.

2 Write the words from the box in the correct lists.

| space craft | star | seagull | museum | planet | helicopter | parachute |
| moon | factory | fireworks | astronaut | sun |

Things you can see only in the sky	Things you can see only on the ground	Things you can see in both places

Unit 10 Dictionary skills; sorting

Resource box

Story questions
What activity are the children doing in the space room? *going on a journey into space*
Where must they put their bags? *in the box*
Which countries can they see? *China, America*
Which continent can they see? *Africa*
What did the children think of the trip? *fantastic, great – but it wasn't long enough*

WB answers
Exercise 1 1 factory   2 parachute   3 seagull   4 astronaut
5 space craft   6 dream
Exercise 2 sky only: star, planet, moon, sun
ground only: museum, factory
both places: space craft, seagull, helicopter, parachute, fireworks, astronaut

Time division
- Warm-up
- WB study skills
- Speaking activities

Unit 10 Study skills

Lesson 4 Grammar (Session 1), Grammar in conversation (Session 2) (PB pp104–105)

Lesson aim Grammar

Lesson targets Children:
- (session 1) understand and practise the key structure
- (session 2) listen to and read a conversation; repeat and practise it
- (session 2) listen to a song, say it and learn it (optional)

Key structure (session 1) *a few, a little*

Key vocabulary recycling and general vocabulary

Key language (session 2) adjective + *enough*

Informal expressions *Have a look. Exactly.*

Materials PB pp104–105; CD C tracks 4–7; WB pp94–95

Session 1 Warm-up
Do a *Word race* with food and drink (see Games, page 187).

Session 2 Warm-up
Play *The adverb game* (see Games, page 186).

Activity 1
Point out the boy and girl. Explain that they are talking about something that is in the red box. Tell the class to listen to the children. Play track 4. Children follow in their books.

Activity 2
Children listen to track 5 and repeat in the pauses.

Activity 3
Children practise the conversation in pairs. See Resource box.***

Activity 4
Ask what the photo is of: *Earth*. Explain *Someone took the photo from space.* Play track 6. Children listen and follow the first time. Read the words with the class. Play track 6. Children join in. Play track 7. Children sing with the music. They may learn the song, if you wish.

Activity 1
Children look at the pictures. Ask a pair to read the PC kids' bubbles. Write the sentences on the board. Underline *a few* and *a little* and explain the rule. Go through the activity with the class helping them to make correct statements. Then they practice in pairs. See Resource box.*

Activity 2
Ask pairs to read the PC kids' bubbles. Write the questions and answers on the board. Point out and explain the rule. Help the class to compose questions and answers for all the items.

Children complete WB page 94 in class time or for homework.

Children practise questions and answers in pairs. See Resource box.**

Unit 10 Grammar, Grammar in conversation

Grammar (Session 1), Grammar in conversation (Session 2) (WB pp94–95)

If this page is for homework, check children understand the tasks.

Exercise 1
Make sure children have understood the rule for statements.

Exercise 2
Check children have understood the rule for questions and answers.

Exercise 3
Children write complete sentences.

If this page is for homework, check children understand the tasks.

Exercise 1
Check children understand the structure *not (adj.) enough*.

Exercise 2
Children complete the dialogue. Remind them of the structures *not (adj.) enough* and *too + (adj)*. Remind them to read it through to check it makes sense. They should look at it again if it doesn't sound right. Let a pair read their completed dialogue to the class.

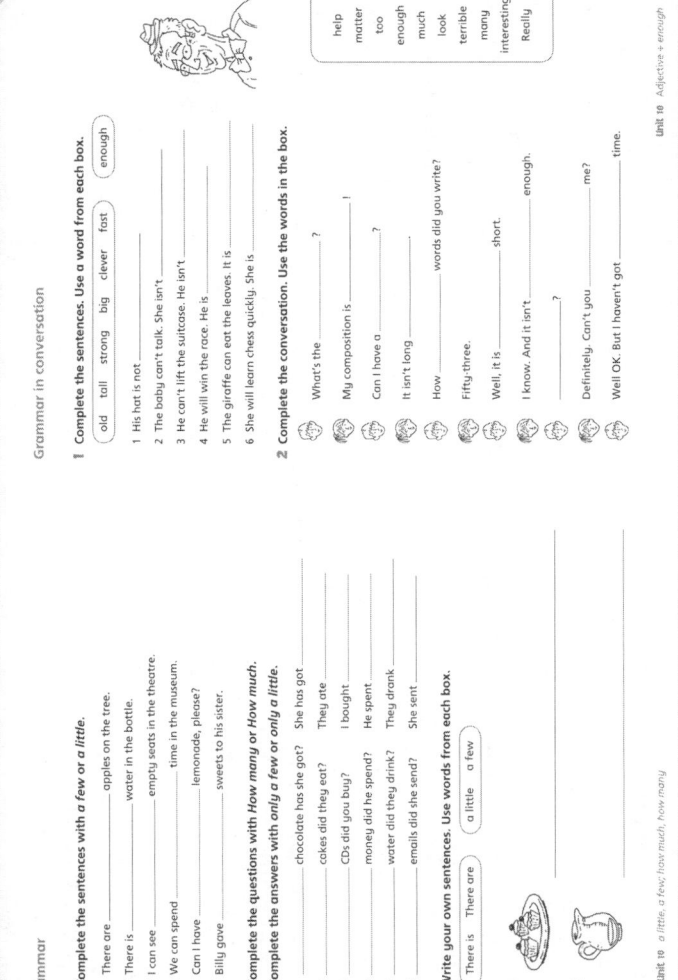

Resource box

Pair work: Grammar (PB p104)

Activity 1
*Children work in pairs at their desks. They take turns to make statements. Go around listening to them as they speak and check for accuracy.

**Activity 2
Children take turns to point to items and ask the question, which the other answers.

If necessary, bring an able pair forward to demonstrate the activity.

Give the class three minutes to speak in pairs. Then let one or two pairs demonstrate a few questions and answers.

***Pair work: Grammar in conversation (PB p105)

Activity 3
Children practise the dialogue in pairs at their desks.

Give pairs three minutes to do this.

Let one or two pairs stand up and say the conversation.

WB answers

Grammar (p94)

Exercise 1 1 a few 2 a little 3 a few 4 a little 5 a little 6 a few

Exercise 2 1 How many, only a little 2 How many, only a few 3 How many, only a little 4 How much, only a little 5 How much, only a little 6 How many, only a few

Exercise 3 1 There are (only) a few cakes (on the plate). 2 There is (only) a little water/juice (in the jug).

Grammar in conversation (p95)

Exercise 1 1 big enough 2 old enough 3 strong enough 4 fast enough 5 tall enough 6 clever enough

Exercise 2 matter, terrible, look, enough, many, too, interesting, Really, help, much

Time division

Session 1

Session 2

Grammar Practice Book
Children may begin Unit 10 when they have completed the PB and WB Grammar pages. They should complete it before the end of PB / WB Unit 10.

Unit 10 Grammar, Grammar in conversation

Lesson 5   Listening, Phonics (PB p106) Use of English

Lesson aim Listening, spelling and pronunciation, Use of English (WB)

Lesson targets Children:
- say what they know about the moon
- listen to a description of the first moon landing and answer questions
- practise saying, reading and spelling words with *ph*
- (WB) learn about the importance of a verb in a sentence

Key structure and language from Unit 10

Target words *photograph, elephant, telephone, alphabet, dolphin*

Materials PB p106; CD C tracks 7–9; WB pp96–97

Warm-up

Sing the song from PB page 105, track 6.

Listening

Activity 1
Ask the class to tell you what they know about the moon. They should remember that a rocket landed on it and Neil Armstrong walked on it in 1969.

Activity 2
Explain to the class that the pictures show the first flight to the moon. Play track 8. Children listen and point to the pictures.

Activity 3
Play track 8 again. Children answer the questions. Pause the track if necessary to note down answers. Play the track again if necessary. Check answers together.

Activity 4
Let a volunteer start the story off, then others continue. Help children to make correct sentences but encourage them to use their own words. They should not try to repeat exactly what they heard on the audio.

Phonics

Point out the box. Tell children to follow in their books and repeat in the pauses. Play the first part of track 9. Make sure children repeat accurately. Play the end of track 9. Children listen and follow. Children say the rhyme. They may learn it, if you wish. Children open their WBs at page 96. They complete the Phonics page now or for homework. If it is for homework, make sure they understand the tasks.

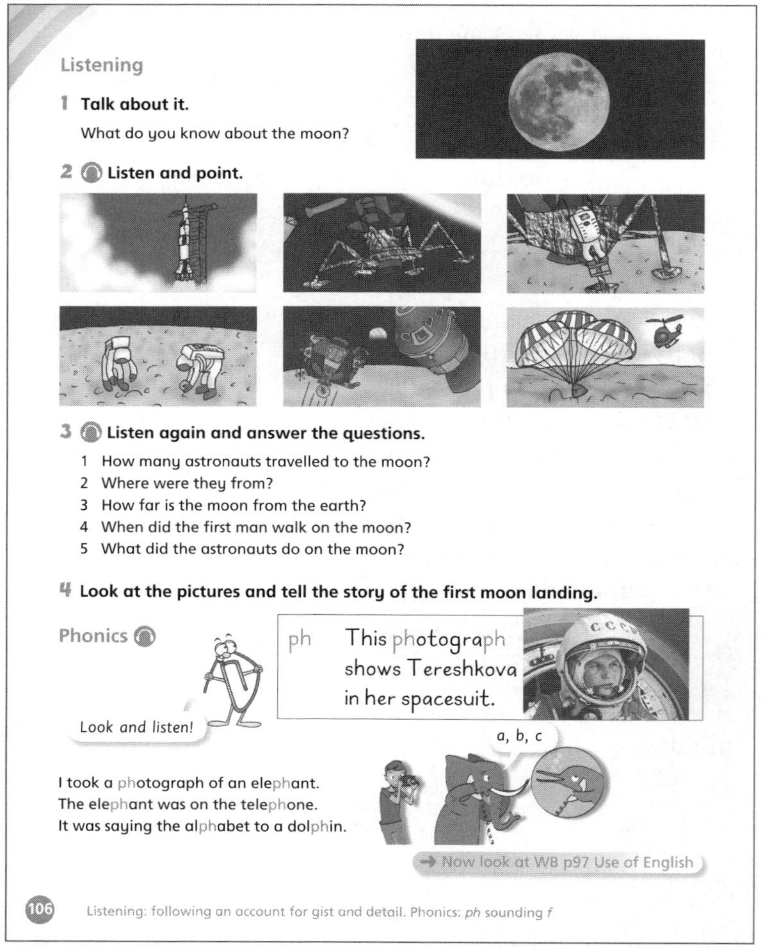

Use of English

Move on to WB page 97.

Unit 10   Listening, Phonics

Phonics, Use of English (WB pp96–97)

Remind the class of the sound *ph* and *photograph*.

Exercises 1–3

Children complete words and read them in the usual way then solve the crossword clues and complete it.

Write the phrase and the sentence on the board. Class reads.

Ask if anyone can say what is wrong with the first one: (not just that a word is missing) the verb is missing.

Exercise 1
Go through the presentation with the class.

Exercise 2
Children underline. Ask volunteers to tell you what they have underlined.

Exercise 3
Children find and circle the groups without verbs. Check answers together.

Exercise 4
Children complete sentences with verbs. Check answers together.

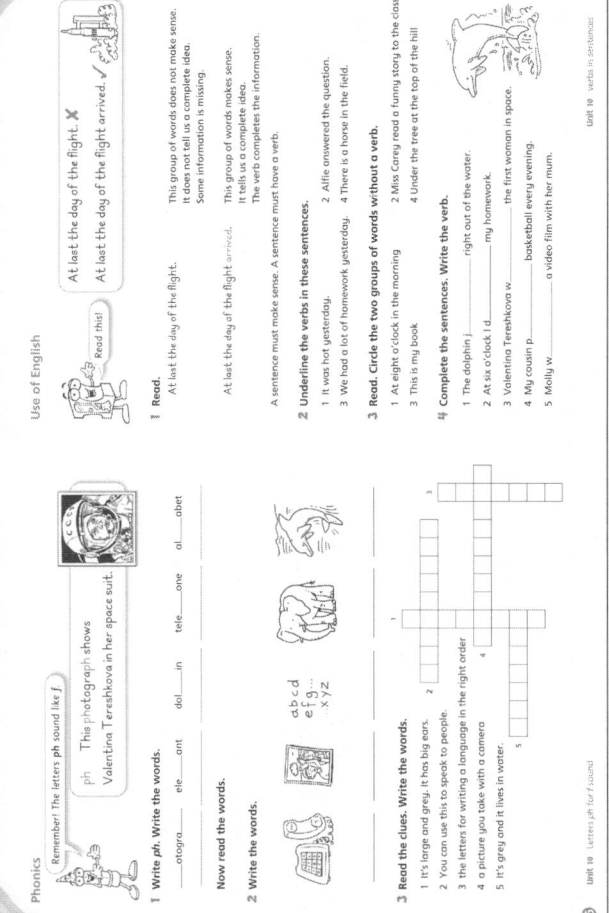

Resource box

Audioscript (CD C track 8) **Listening activities 2–3** (PB p106)

6, 5, 4, 3, 2, 1. Lift off! The huge rocket took off and went up into the sky. Three American astronauts were on board and they were very excited. They were flying to the moon! The moon was 400,000 kilometres away and the journey took three days. (pause)

When they arrived at the moon, the rocket went into orbit around it. Two men went down onto the moon and one man stayed in the rocket. (pause)

The first man to stand on the moon was Neil Armstrong. The date was 21st July, 1969. (pause)

The two astronauts stayed on the moon for about two hours. They picked up rocks to take back to Earth. (pause)

Soon it was time to leave. The two men went back up to the rocket and the three astronauts travelled back to Earth. (pause)

They travelled for three days. Then the rocket's parachutes opened and it dropped into the sea. Soon a helicopter arrived and picked up the three astronauts. (pause)

PB answers

Activity 3 1 three 2 America 3 400,000 km
4 21st July, 1969 5 picked up rocks

WB answers

Phonics (p96)

Exercise 3 1 elephant 2 telephone 3 alphabet
4 photograph 5 dolphin

Use of English (p97)

Exercise 4 1 jumped 2 did 3 was 4 plays
5 watched

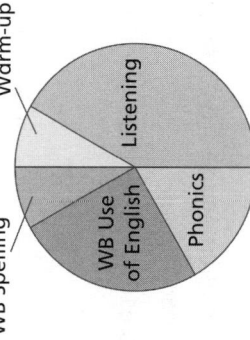

Time division

Warm-up / Listening / Phonics / WB Use of English / WB Spelling

Unit 10 Phonics, Use of English

Lesson 6 Class composition (Session 1) (PB p107) Writing preparation, Composition practice (Session 2)

Lesson aim Writing

Lesson targets Children:
- (session 1) compose a biography from notes with teacher support
- (session 2) (WB) practise vocabulary and writing sentences from notes
- (session 2) (WB) write a biography from notes independently

Key structure and language from Unit 10

Vocabulary space travel

Materials PB p107; WB pp98–99

Session 1 Warm-up

Write *space* on the board. Write these words underneath: *craft train rocket engineer suit medal walk travel*.

Children put *space* in front of six of the words and write a new word or phrase. Children read them out. Ask *Which two words are left over?* **train, medal**

Class composition

Activity 1

Ask the class to look at the picture, the main title and the words at the top of the left column.

Ask questions: *What is the name of this man? What was his job? What did he do?*

Tell the class they are going to use the information in the box on the left to write about Yuri Gagarin.

All the information children need for the biography is given. The task is to write the dates and the facts into sentences and to create a continuous piece of writing.

Ask a volunteer to complete the first sentence using the first piece of information. Write it on the board. Ask the rest of the class if it is correct.

Make any changes necessary.

Continue in the same way with the other dates and information. Help children to compose clear, accurate sentences.

When the biography is complete, ask a volunteer to read it all the way through.

Remove the writing from the board. Children write in their books, continuing in their copy books if necessary.

All the children should be able to complete this task accurately having done the activity once together.

Class composition

1 Read the titles. Read the information. Write about Yuri Gagarin.

Travellers in space

Yuri Gagarin
Cosmonaut
The first man in space

Key dates	
1934	was born near the town of Gzhatsk in west Russia
1950	left secondary school, favourite subject – maths
1951	joined a flying club, learned to fly planes, learned parachuting
1955	joined the Air Force flying school
1957	passed the pilot's test, wanted to be a cosmonaut
1959	started cosmonaut training
1960	joined the space programme
1961	12th April flew in Vostok 1, first man in space, completed the first orbit of the Earth, flight took 1 hr 48 mins
1968	27th March died on test flight when his jet plane crashed, moon crater – Gagarin

Yuri Gagarin was _____

Unit 10 Class composition: biography 107

Unit 10 Class composition 156

Writing preparation, Composition practice (WB pp98–99)

Session 2 Warm-up

Play *What's missing?* (see Games, page 187). Use new words from Unit 10.

Exercise 1

Children should be able to complete this activity independently. Ask a volunteer to read out the words. Children read the sentences and write the jobs. Check answers.

Exercise 2

1 Ask different children to read the dates and facts about Alexei Leonov. Children write complete sentences about him using the information.

2 Check that children are forming clear sentences by asking volunteers to read out their information. Correct any errors. If you wish, write the correct sentences on the board.

Children use the key facts to write paragraphs about Neil Armstrong. All children should be able to use the dates and notes to write clear sentences with accurate information. Remind them they can look back at exercise 2 on page 98 to check how to write the dates into the sentences. Go around helping.
Before the end of the lesson ask one or two volunteers to read all or part of their work to the class. Other children listen and check. Correct any errors.

Homework task

Children complete Check-up 10, WB p100. For answers, see p185.

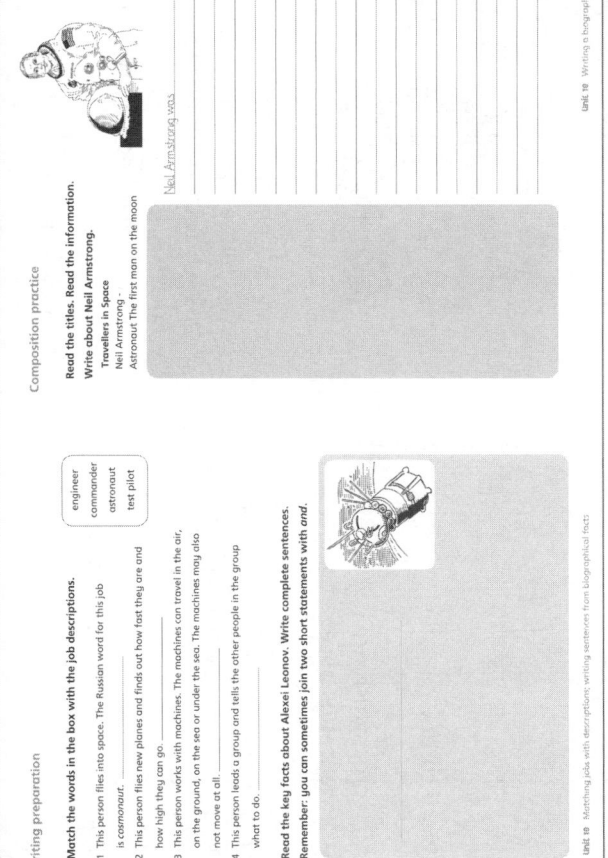

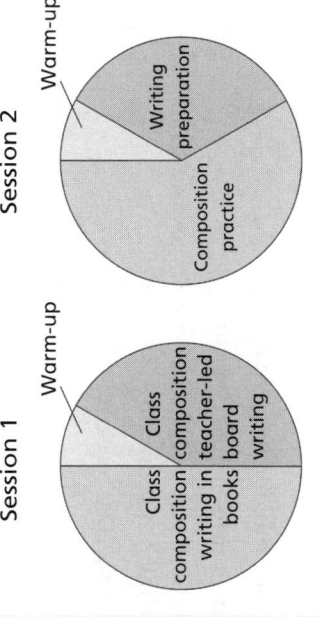

Resource box

Class composition example writing (p107)

Yuri Gagarin was born in 1934 near the town of Gzhatsk in west Russia. In 1950 he left secondary school. His favourite subject was maths.

In 1951 he joined a flying club. He learned to fly planes and he learned parachuting.

In 1955 he joined the Air Force flying school. He passed the pilot's test in 1957. He wanted to be a cosmonaut.

In 1959 he started cosmonaut training and in 1960 he joined the space programme.

On 12th April 1961 he became the first man in space and he completed the first orbit of the Earth. The flight took 1 hour and 48 minutes.

On 27th March 1968 he died on a test flight when his jet plane crashed.

A crater on the moon has the name Gagarin.

WB answers (p98)

Exercise 1 1 astronaut 2 test pilot 3 engineer 4 commander

Exercise 2 born in Kemerova in the south of Russia

In 1960 he joined the Russian space programme and started training to be a cosmonaut.

In 1965 he flew in the Voshkhod 2 spacecraft. On 18th March 1965 he completed the first space walk. The space walk lasted twelve minutes.

Composition practice example writing (p99)

See p185 for example writing.

Time division

Session 1 / Session 2

Portfolio

Children may make neat copies of their WB compositions.

Unit 10 Writing preparation, Composition practice

157

11 Life in the north

Lesson 1 Poster 11, Reading

Lesson aim Reading

Text type Information; description of a person's appearance

Lesson targets Children:
- read, understand and practise new vocabulary on the poster
- read, understand and practise reading the information
- answer oral comprehension questions

Key structure present perfect

Key language *might: … you might see the northern lights…*

Key vocabulary clothing and equipment for a cold climate

Materials PB pp108–109; poster 11; CD C track 10; Dictionary 4; word cards for poster vocabulary (see poster 11 below or list on p16)

Preparation Make word cards, listen to CD C track 10

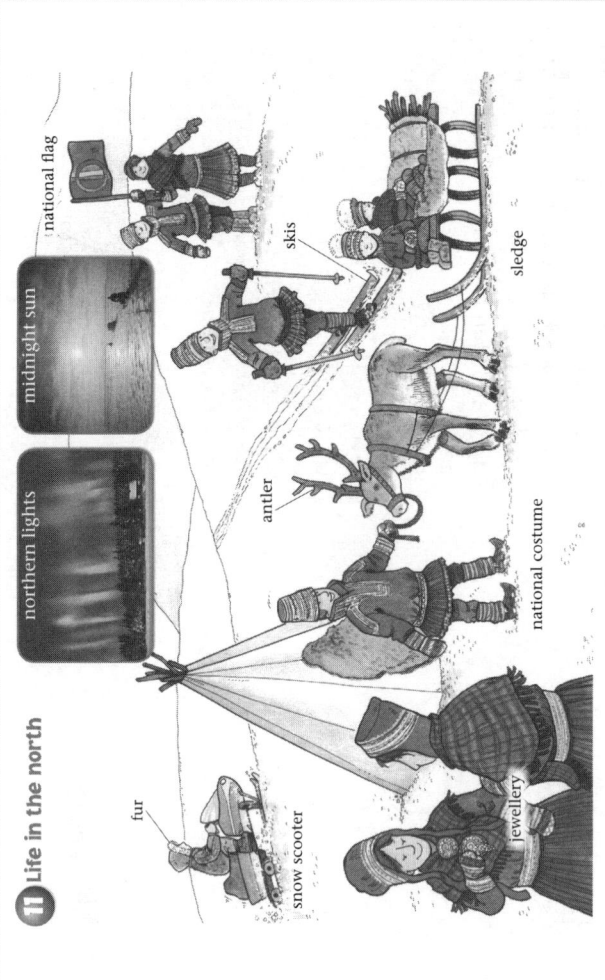

Warm-up

Ask children *Do you like snow?*
Do you see snow sometimes, often or never?
Do you play in the snow? What games do you play?
Do you like cold weather or do you like hot, sunny weather?

Poster 11

1 Point to the poster. Read out the title.
Give the class a moment or two to look.

2 Point to the objects on the poster.
Read the word/s. For new words, show the word card/s.
Class reads and says the word/s.
Make sure children understand the following words which are not in the dictionary. Use the definitions and example sentences as necessary to ensure understanding:

antler   the bone that grows out of a reindeer's head
          Reindeers use their *antlers* to dig in the snow and find grass.
snow scooter   a small vehicle like a motorbike for driving over snow
          Snow scooters can go very fast.

Cover the words on the poster if you wish. Point to the objects at random.
Class names them.

3 Ask children what they think the midnight sun is. Can they explain it?
Ask what they know about the northern lights.
Can they explain them?
If children do not know, use the following explanation if you wish.

4 In the summer, the further north you go, the later the sun sets. In the far north it does not set at all for some weeks, so there is sun at midnight.
The northern lights are made by particles high up above the earth.

Unit 11 Reading

158

Reading (PB pp108–109)

1 Give children time to look at the pictures. Read the title. Ask what things they recognise in the pictures.
Tell them to look at the small map. Remind them that they learned a little about these people in Unit 7.

2 Play track 10. Children listen and follow in their books.

3 Read one paragraph or section of the text at a time.
Use Dictionary 4 to help you to explain new words as necessary.
The following words are not in the dictionary: *Finland, Norway, Sweden*. Check that children understand from the map exactly where these countries are in the world.
Help children to find new words. Make up extra sentences for new words if you wish.

4 Ask questions about each paragraph or a section of the text. See Resource box.

5 Give reading practice around the class. Ask individuals, groups or the class to read sentences or paragraphs.
Play track 10 again.

UNIT 11 Life in the north

Reading

The Sami people

The first Sami people arrived in Europe 7,000 years ago. For thousands of years, they travelled across northern Europe. Today, Sami live in the far north of four countries: Sweden, Norway, Finland and Russia. Sami call this area Sapmi.

The reindeer herds

In the past, the Sami were nomads and they followed the reindeer herds. They used the reindeer for food, clothes and tools. They made tents and boots from reindeer skin. They made coats and hats from their wool. They carved needles, spoons and knives from their antlers.

Later, some Sami people stayed on the coast and became fishermen and farmers but the reindeer have always been important. In the Sami language there are 400 different words that describe the reindeer. Sami still keep reindeer now but very few people follow their herds. They keep them in one large area. Some herders use snow scooters when they herd the reindeer. These are much faster than sledges or skis.

Sami clothes

The Sami people make trousers, skirts and jackets from wool cloth. Usually it is blue. Sometimes it is red or green. Their clothes have colourful borders. They make hats and boots from reindeer fur. Sami people wear this clothing on special days. This is their national costume and they are proud of it. This woman is wearing a red dress. It has a border of green and yellow. There is a long blue, yellow and green fringe on her dress and she is wearing silver jewellery. Her hat is tall with a blue, yellow and green border. She is wearing a belt and there is a small bag on it. She is wearing gloves and she is holding a small white reindeer. She has got long fair hair and she is smiling. She looks very happy and friendly.

The Sami today

The Sami people have changed their lives. Once, they were nomads. Now many Sami live in towns and villages. They work in hospitals, schools and factories. They speak other languages but there are schools where children learn their lessons in Sami. There are newspapers, radio and TV programmes in Sami and they have their own national flag.
More and more people visit Sami towns and villages. They like the Sami crafts and clothes. The land is beautiful in winter. There is snow from November to May. In Sapmi you might see the northern lights and in summer you can see the sun at midnight.

Resource box

Text questions

Which four countries do the Sami people live in? **Norway, Sweden, Finland, Russia**
What is their own area called? **Sapmi**
How did most Sami people live in the past? **They were nomads and they followed the reindeer herds.**
What did they use the reindeer for? **food, clothing and tools**
How many words for reindeer are there? **400**
What is faster than sledges or skis? **a snow scooter**
When do Sami people wear their national costume? **on special days**
What colours are in these costumes? **usually blue, sometimes red and green**
What colour is the woman's dress? **red**
What colours are in the border? **green and yellow**
What colours are the fringe on her dress? **blue, yellow and green**
What is on her belt? **a small bag**
Where do many Sami people live now? **in towns and villages**
When is there snow in Sapmi? **November–May**

Homework task

Children learn selected vocabulary from Unit 11 *Dictionary 4*.
See unit word list on pages 190–191 for key words, extension words and words for understanding only.

Time division

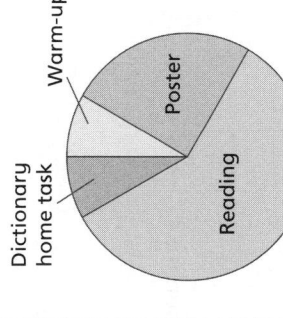

Unit 11 Reading

Lesson 2 Reading comprehension and vocabulary (PB p110)

Lesson aim Reading comprehension, vocabulary
Lesson targets Children re-read *The Sami people*, then:
- (PB) identify true / false sentences; correct the false ones
- talk about national costume / flag; identify parts of clothing
- (WB) match statements to pictures
- complete a cloze exercise

Key structure present perfect
Key language *might: … you might see the northern lights…*
Words vocabulary from Lesson 1
Materials PB p110; CD C track 10 (optional); WB p102; Dictionary 4

Warm-Up
Play *What is it?* (see Games, page 187). Use vocabulary from the unit.

Read again
Remind children of *The Sami people*.
Play track 10 or read the text to the class. Children listen and follow in their books.

Activity 1
Tell children to read through all the sentences silently. Give them a time limit.
Ask a child to read the first sentence. Tell children to think whether it is true or not and to look back and check. Elicit the answer. Check with the class. Children write.
Continue in the same way with the other sentences. Ask for the correct sentence where a statement is false.

Activity 2
Use these questions to talk with the class about national costume or costumes if there is more than one. Encourage children to say as much as they can from their own knowledge and experience.
Children talk about the colours and if appropriate what is on the flag and what it means.

Activity 3
Ask one or more children to read the words in the box.
Children match and write.
They may use their dictionaries to check their ideas.
Check answers together.

Reading comprehension and vocabulary

1 Read the sentences. Write true or false.

1 For thousands of years, the Sami travelled across northern Europe. _____
2 They made tents and boots from reindeer skin. _____
3 They carved needles, spoons and knives from their antlers. _____
4 In the Sami language there are 40 different words for reindeer. _____
5 They made hats and boots from reindeer fur. _____
6 The woman in the photo is wearing a bell. _____
7 Now many Sami live in towns and villages. _____
8 There is snow from December to May. _____

Correct the false sentences.

2 Talk about the answers to these questions.
1 Do you have a national costume in your country? What is it like?
2 Do you wear the national costume? When do you wear it?
3 What colours is your national flag?

3 Write the words under the correct pictures.

jewellery   belt   border   fur   fringe

Unit 11 Reading comprehension and vocabulary: true/false; personal response; words/pictures

110

Unit 11 Reading comprehension and vocabulary

160

Reading comprehension and vocabulary (WB p102)

If children are doing this page for homework, make sure they understand the tasks. You may wish to read the text in exercise 1 with the class as preparation or tell them to read it and check in their dictionaries if they need to.

Exercise 1
Children write the letter of the description next to the person it describes.

Exercise 2
Children complete the sentences. They should check in their dictionaries if they need to.

UNIT 11 Reading comprehension and vocabulary

1 Read the statements. Write the letters.

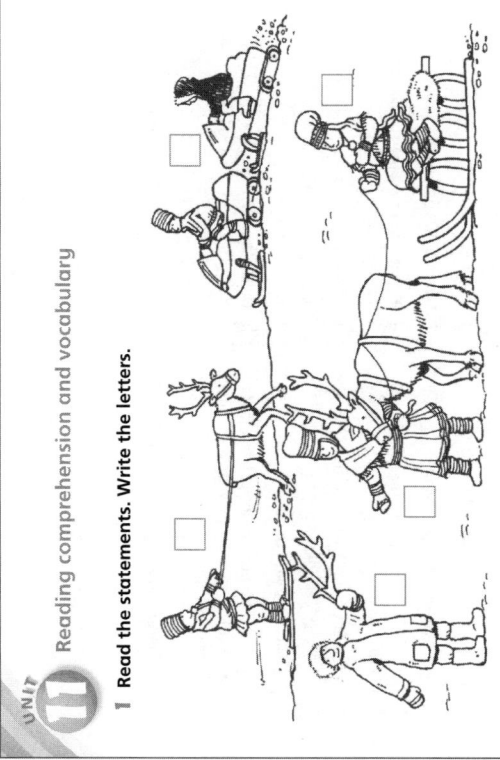

a She is wearing national costume. She is leading a reindeer.
b He is holding antlers. He is wearing a fur coat and a fur hat.
c He is wearing national costume. He is riding a snow scooter.
d She is sitting on a sledge. A reindeer is pulling her along.
e A reindeer is pulling a man. He is on skis.
f He is riding a snow scooter. He is not wearing national costume.

2 Complete the sentences with the correct word from the box.

newspaper   radio   area   carve   coast

1 If you go to the _____, you will see boats on the sea.
2 My dad buys a _____ every morning and he reads it at breakfast.
3 My mum listens to music on the _____.
4 The _____ round our school is very noisy.
5 The Sami could _____ a spoon from an antler.

Unit 11 Matching descriptions and pictures; cloze

102

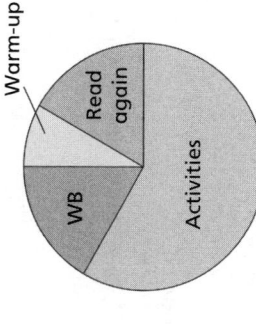

Time division

Warm-up / Read again / WB / Activities

Resource box

PB answers

Activity 1 1 true 2 true 3 true 4 false 5 false 6 false
7 true 8 false
Activity 3 1 fringe 2 fur 3 jewellery 4 border 5 belt

WB answers

Exercise 1 people in top row left to right: e, c, f
people in bottom row left to right: b, a, d
Exercise 2 1 coast 2 newspaper 3 radio 4 area 5 carve

Unit 11 Reading comprehension and vocabulary   161

Lesson 3 Speaking (PB p111) Study skills

Lesson aim Speaking, (WB) Study skills

Lesson targets Children:
- listen to a dialogue; listen and repeat the dialogue
- understand the story and answer oral questions
- read and act the dialogue
- (WB) practise dictionary skills; spelling; definitions

Informal everyday expressions *There you are. Excellent! Wait a minute!*

New words *meat, beard*

Materials PB p111; CD C tracks 11, 12; WB p103; Dictionary 4

Preparation Listen to CD C track 11 before the lesson

Warm-up

Ask what happened in Part 4. *Where did the children go? What did they see?* Let them look back if they have forgotten.

Activity 1

Children look at PB page 111. Read the title of Part 5. Ask *Where are the children now? What are they doing? **The children are in the museum. They are looking at a display about the Sami people.***
Tell children to cover the dialogue text and look at the picture.
Play track 11. Children listen.

Activity 2

Children look at the dialogue. Play track 11 again.
Children listen and follow.
Check children understand the new words. Use the dictionary if you wish.

Activity 3

Children close their books. Play track 12. Children listen and repeat in the pauses. Encourage them to use the same expression and intonation.

Activity 4

Ask questions to check understanding of the story. See Resource box.

Activity 5

Children act the dialogue without their books if possible.

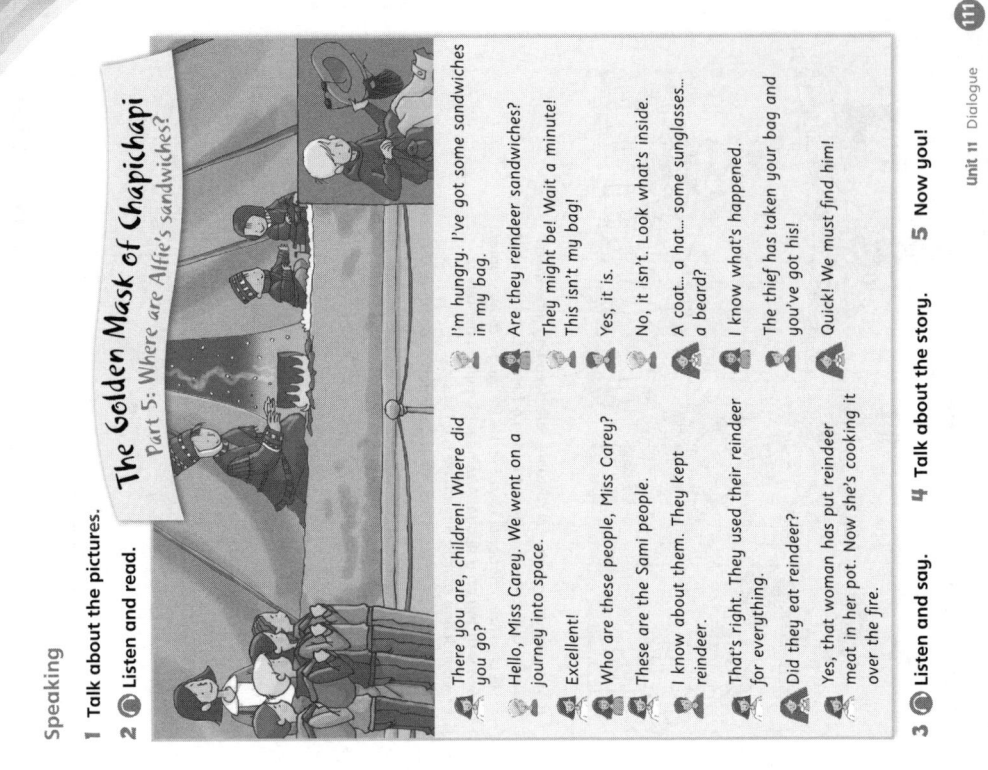

Speaking

The Golden Mask of Chapichapi
Part 5: Where are Alfie's sandwiches?

1 Talk about the pictures.

2 🎧 Listen and read.

- There you are, children! Where did you go?
- Hello, Miss Carey. We went on a journey into space.
- Excellent!
- Who are these people, Miss Carey?
- These are the Sami people.
- I know about them. They kept reindeer.
- That's right. They used their reindeer for everything.
- Did they eat reindeer?
- Yes, that woman has put reindeer meat in her pot. Now she's cooking it over the fire.
- I'm hungry. I've got some sandwiches in my bag.
- Are they reindeer sandwiches?
- They might be! Wait a minute! This isn't my bag!
- Yes, it is.
- No, it isn't. Look what's inside.
- A coat... a hat... some sunglasses... a beard?
- I know what's happened.
- The thief has taken your bag and you've got his!
- Quick! We must find him!

3 🎧 Listen and say.   **4** Talk about the story.   **5** Now you!

Unit 11 Dialogue   111

Unit 11 Speaking   162

Study skills (WB p103)

The exercises on this page practise dictionary skills.
Children should be able to do this work independently once the tasks have been explained.

Exercise 1
Children attempt the correct spelling, then check.

Exercise 2
Children guess meanings. Remind them to look at the choice of words carefully, then to look back at the sentence for clues.

Study skills

1 Read and write. Look at the underlined words. The spelling is wrong. Try to write the words correctly. Don't look in your Dictionary!

1 <u>Ontlers</u> are large horns with many branches.   _Antlers_
2 You can travel over the snow on <u>sludges</u>.
3 <u>Fir</u> hats and boots are warm in winter.
4 The Sami national <u>costum</u> is very colourful.
5 There are many lovely beaches along the <u>cost</u>.
6 It is the land of the <u>midnight</u> sun.
7 We saw a herd of <u>raindeer</u>.
8 Sami women wear silver <u>jevellery</u>.

Now check your spelling in your Dictionary.

2 Read and guess the meaning of the underlined words. Circle the words. Don't look in your Dictionary!

1 I was thirsty so I had a drink of <u>pomegranate</u> juice. (a flower   a fruit   milk)
2 The glass broke into <u>smithereens</u>. (big pieces   tiny pieces   two pieces)
3 After all our hard work we were <u>exhausted</u>. (very tired   very sad   very happy)
4 When she failed her exams, she felt <u>despondent</u>. (happy   sad   hungry)
5 The story was so funny we couldn't stop <u>giggling</u>. (crying   talking   laughing)
6 Her hands felt warm in her new <u>mittens</u>. (boots   gloves   socks)
7 The monkeys <u>clambered</u> through the branches. (climbed   danced   fell)
8 The huge tree fell with a <u>deafening</u> noise. (very quiet   very loud   very funny)

Now check your guesses with your teacher!

Resource box

Story questions
Who are the people in the room? *the Sami people*
What is the woman cooking? *reindeer meat*
What is she using? *a pot and a fire*
Who is hungry? *Alfie*
Has he got reindeer sandwiches? *He might have.*
What is in the bag? *a coat, hat, sunglasses, a beard*
Who has taken Alfie's bag? *the thief*
What must they do now? *find him*

WB answers

Exercise 1 2 sledges   3 Fur   4 costume   5 coast
6 midnight   7 reindeer   8 jewellery
Exercise 2 1 a fruit   2 tiny pieces   3 very tired
4 sad   5 laughing   6 gloves   7 climbed
8 very loud

Time division

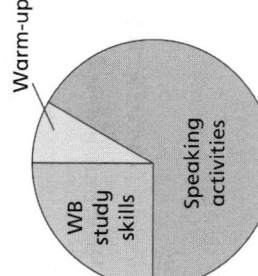

Warm-up
WB study skills
Speaking activities

Unit 11 Study skills

Lesson 4 Grammar (Session 1), Grammar in conversation (Session 2) (PB pp112–113)

Lesson aim Grammar

Lesson targets Children:
- (session 1) understand and practise the key structure
- (session 2) listen to and read a conversation; repeat and practise it
- (session 2) listen to a song, say it and learn it (optional)

Key structure (session 1) present perfect

Key vocabulary revision of general vocabulary

Key language (session 2) *might, might not*

Informal expressions *Not a chance. It's all over. I can always dream.*

Materials PB pp112–113; CD C tracks 13–15; WB pp104–105

Session 1 Warm-up

Play *Word mix* (see Games, page 187).

Activity 1
Children look at the picture. Ask who is in it: *a boy, a girl, a man and a woman*. Ask children to read the PC kids' bubbles. Ask the whole class to read them together.
Write sentences on the board. Underline *have* and *has* and past participles. Class reads. See Resource box.*

Activity 2
Children look at the pictures. Ask a child to read the first sentence. Elicit the answer. Check with the class. Children write.

Activity 3
Ask the questions. Help children to answer correctly.

Children practise questions and answers in pairs. See Resource box.*

Session 2 Warm-up

Play *Action mime* to practise the present perfect (see Games, page 186).

Activity 1
Point out the boy and girl. Ask *What is the boy doing? watching TV* Tell the class to listen to them. Play track 13. Children follow in their books.

Activity 2
Children listen to track 14 and repeat in the pauses.

Activity 3
Children practise the conversation in pairs. See Resource box.**

Activity 4
Ask what jobs the boy is thinking about: *pilot, singer, footballer*. Play track 15. Children listen and follow the first time.
Read the words with the class. Play track 15. Children join in. They may learn this chant if you wish.

Children complete WB page 104 in class time or for homework.

Grammar (Session 1), Grammar in conversation (Session 2) (WB pp104–105)

If this page is for homework, check children understand the tasks.

Exercise 1
Check the class has understood the structure.

Exercise 2
Children order the words. Tell them to look carefully at the example to remind them of the structure.

If this page is for homework, check children understand the tasks.

Exercise 1
Children change the sentences. Make sure they understand that the two sentences have the same meaning.

Exercises 2 and 3
Children write questions and negative sentences. Remind them to look at the examples.

Exercise 4
See Resource box.

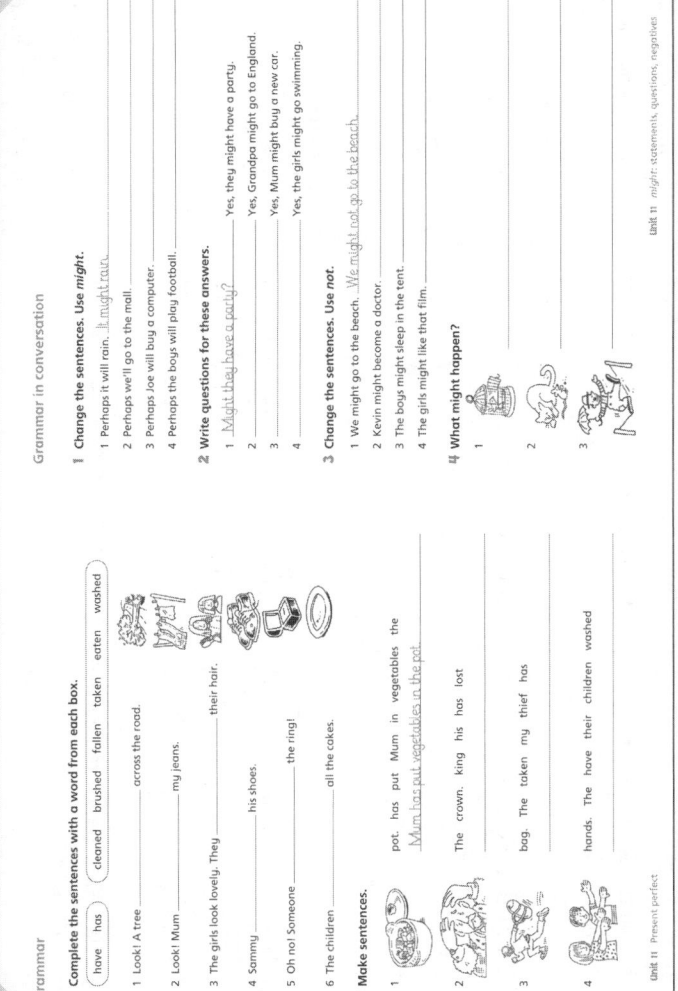

Resource box

PB answers

*Pair work: Grammar (p112)

Activity 1 Make sure children understand that the present perfect is used for something that happened recently.

Activity 3 Children work in pairs at their desks. They take turns to ask the questions and give the answer. If necessary, bring an able pair forward to demonstrate the activity.
Give the class three minutes to speak in pairs. Then let one or two pairs demonstrate a few questions and answers.

**Pair work: Grammar in conversation (p113)

Activity 3
Make sure children understand that *might* expresses something that is possible but not certain.
Children practise the dialogue in pairs at their desks.
Give pairs three minutes to practise the dialogue.
Let one or two pairs stand up and say their conversations to the class.

WB answers

Grammar (p104)

Exercise 1 1 has fallen 2 has washed 3 have brushed 4 has cleaned 5 has taken 6 have eaten

Exercise 2 2 The king has lost his crown. 3 The thief has taken my bag. 4 The children have washed their hands.

Grammar in conversation (p105)
2 We might go to the mall.
3 Joe might buy a computer.
4 The boys might play football.

Exercise 2 Might Mum buy a new car?
3 Might Grandpa go to England?
4 Might the girls go swimming?

Exercise 3 2 Kevin might not become a doctor.
3 They boys might not sleep in the tent.
4 The girls might not like that film.

Exercise 4 Children's own ideas. Accept answers that are grammatically correct and which make sense.

Time division

Session 1 — Warm-up, WB, Activity 2, Activity 1

Session 2 — Warm-up, Conversation activities, Pairs conversation practice, Poem, WB

Grammar Practice Book
- Children may begin Unit 11 when they have completed the PB and WB Grammar pages. They should complete it before the end of PB / WB Unit 11.

Unit 11 Grammar, Grammar in conversation

Lesson 5 Listening, Phonics (PB p114) Use of English

Lesson aim Listening, spelling and pronunciation, Use of English (WB)

Lesson targets Children:
- talk about clothing and objects
- listen to descriptions and match them to pictures
- practise saying, reading and spelling words with *ch* sounding *k*
- (WB) learn about subject and object pronouns

Key structure and language from Unit 11

Target words *school, anchor, choir, stomach*

Materials PB p114; CD C tracks 16, 17; WB pp106–107; poster 11

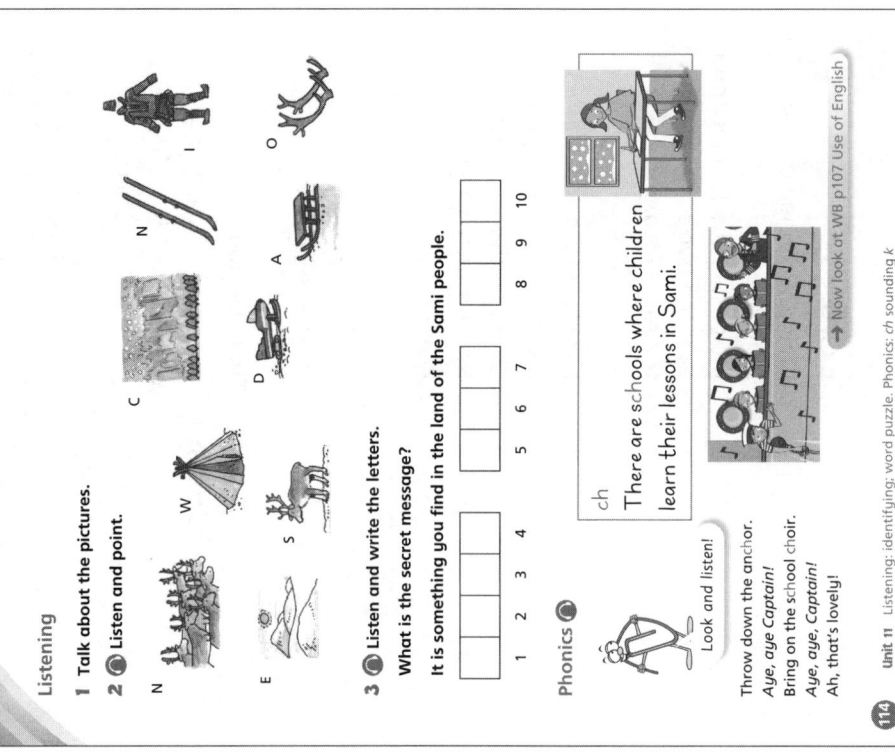

Warm-up

Use poster 11 to revise everything in the picture, including the words for the objects in Activity 1.

Listening

Activity 1
Ask the children to say what is in each of the pictures.

Activity 2
Play track 16. Children listen and point to the pictures as they hear them described.

Activity 3
Play track 16 again. Children write the letters of the pictures as they hear them described.
Play the track a third time if necessary.
Ask what the secret message is: **snow and ice**.

Phonics

Point out the box. Tell children to follow in their books and repeat in the pauses. Play the first part of track 17. Make sure children repeat accurately.
Play the end of track 17. Children listen and follow.
Children say the rhyme. They may learn it, if you wish.

Children open their WBs at page 106. They complete the Phonics page now or for homework. If it is for homework, make sure they understand the tasks.

Use of English

Move on to WB page 107.

Phonics, Use of English (WB pp106–107)

Remind the class of the sound *ch* and *school*.

Exercises 1 and 2
Children practise writing and reading the words.

Exercise 3
Children complete the sentences.

Exercise 4
Children use two of the words in two sentences of their own. Encourage them to write interesting sentences.

Resource box
Audioscript (CD C track 16)
Listening activities 2–3 (PB p114)
Number 1: This is a reindeer. It is the most important animal for the Sami people.
Number 2: When there is a group of many animals all together, we call it a herd. This is a herd of reindeer.
Number 3: These are antlers. They grow on a reindeer's head. They become very big and have many branches.
Number 4: When the Sami are travelling from place to place with their reindeer herds, they live in tents like this one.
Number 5: This is a good way to travel on ice and snow. The Sami put their tents on these and people can sit on them. Reindeer pull them.
Number 6: This is another way to travel.
You put these skis on your feet and slide over the snow.
Number 7: This is much faster than skis or a sledge. One or two people can ride on them.
Number 8: This is the national costume of the Sami people. It is very colourful. They wear these clothes on special days and they are very proud of the costume.
Number 9: The land of the Sami people is in the north of Europe. The winters are very long and dark. Sometimes you can see the Northern Lights in the sky.
Number 10: In the summertime it stays light all day and all night. The sun doesn't go down. In summer the north of Europe is the land of the midnight sun.

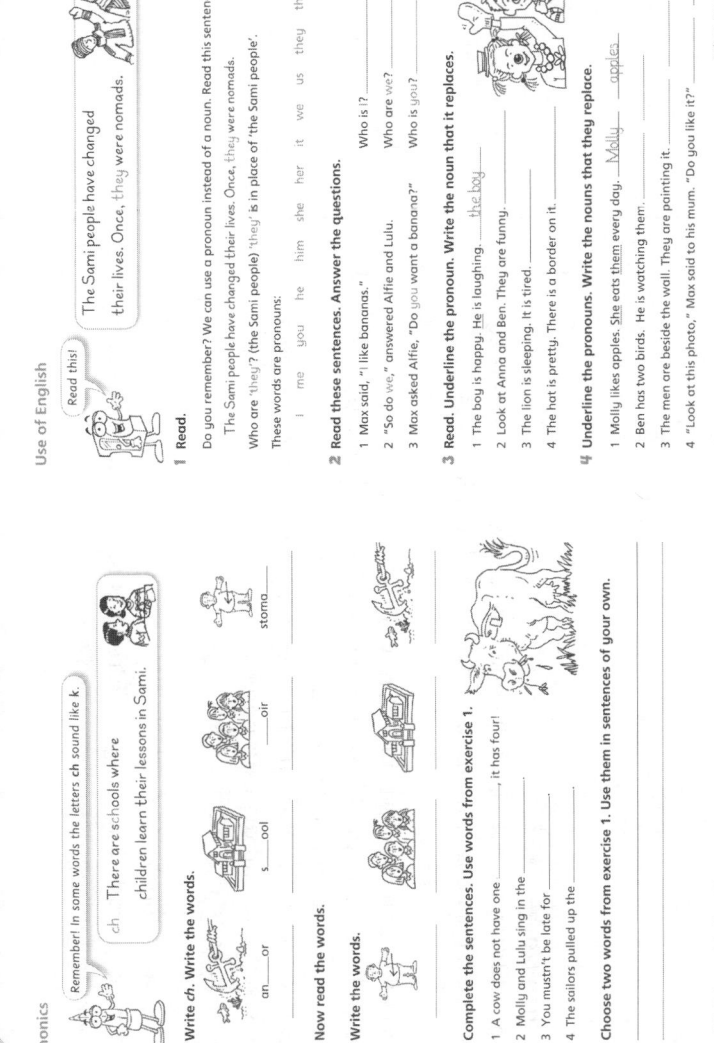

Write the sentences on the board. Class reads. Ask a volunteer to circle the pronoun in the second sentence.

Exercise 1
Go through the revision of personal pronouns with the class. Introduce all the pronouns.

Do exercises 2–4 with the class.

Exercise 2
Children identify the noun/s that the pronouns refer to.

Exercise 3
Children identify the nouns in the first sentences replaced by the pronouns in the second sentences.

Exercise 4
Children identify the subject and object pronouns in the second sentences and write the nouns they replace.

WB answers

Phonics (p106)
Exercise 2 1 stomach 2 choir
3 school 4 anchor

Exercise 3 1 stomach 2 choir
3 school 4 anchor

Use of English (p107)
Exercise 2 1 Max 2 Alfie and Lulu 3 Alfie
Exercise 3 2 They, Anna and Ben 3 It, the lion 4 it, the hat
Exercise 4 2 He, them, Ben, the birds 3 They, it, the men, the wall 4 you, it, Mum, the photo

Time division
Warm-up, Listening, Phonics, WB Use of English, WB Spelling

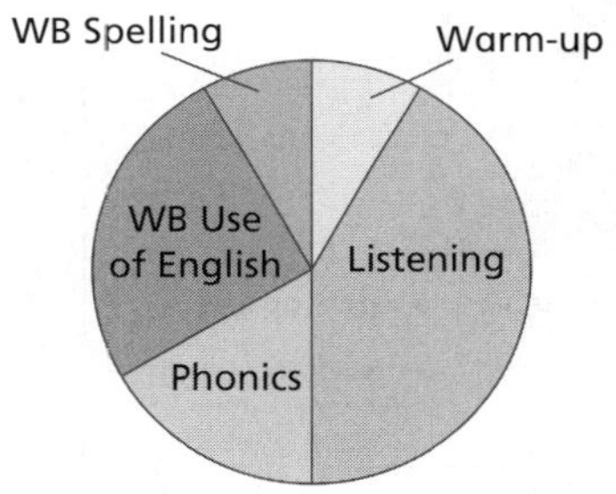

Unit 11 Phonics, Use of English

167

Lesson 6 Class composition (Session 1) (PB p115) Writing preparation, Composition practice (Session 2)

Lesson aim Writing

Lesson targets Children:
- (session 1) compose a description of people with teacher support, then write
- (session 2) (WB) write notes and name objects in preparation for writing
- (session 2) (WB) write descriptions of children independently

Key structure and language from Unit 11

Vocabulary clothing, colours

Materials PB p115; CD C track 15; WB pp108–109

Session 1 Warm-up

Say the rhyme from PB page 113, track 15.

Class composition

Activity 1

1 Give children a minute or two to look at the picture.
Ask questions about the Sami people in general to help children make up a few sentences about them, e.g. *What is the name of these people? Where do they live? What is it like there in winter? Which animals live there?*
Write notes on one side of the board.

2 Ask questions about the photo:
Who is in the picture?
What are they wearing? What are their clothes like?
Write notes on the board. Encourage children to look carefully and give as much detail as they can. Help with any new words they need. Encourage them to think of suitable adjectives.

3 Prompt the class to use the notes to make sentences. On the board write a paragraph of information about the Sami people and a paragraph describing the people in the photograph. When the writing is complete, ask one or more volunteers to read it to the class.
Ask if there are any changes that would make it better. *Are there enough adjectives? Are there any better verbs?* Make any changes that you and the class agree to.
Ask different children to read the composition one more time.
Remove the writing from the board.
Children use the notes to write their own paragraphs.
Go around helping and monitoring as they work. Encourage children to use their dictionaries or the word list at the back of their books to find words or check spelling.

Class composition

1 Talk about the picture. Write about the people. Describe the people.

Unit 11 Class composition: information and description

Unit 11 Class composition

168

Writing preparation, Composition practice (WB pp108–109)

Session 2 Warm-up

Do *Look, write, check* (see Games, page 187) with target phonics words.

Exercise 1
Ask a child to read the labels. Point out the flag. Ask what flag it is.

Exercise 2
Children read out the five questions. Tell the class to look back at exercise 1 to help them answer. Elicit the first answer. Check with the class. Children write the short answer in their books. Continue with the other questions.

Exercise 3
Set a time limit. Talk about appropriate colours for the clothing.

Exercise 4
Children should be able to do this alone. Remind them to use their dictionaries or the word list to check words and spelling.

Read the rubrics with the class (WB page 109). Make sure they understand that they write about the Sami people first. Then they write what the children in the picture are wearing and what they are doing.

Remind them of their answers and the information on WB page 108.

Go around helping and monitoring as they work.

The example writing is a guide only to the level of writing that can be expected. Some children will write fewer sentences than in the example. Remind them to look carefully at all clothing in the pictures and to write as much detail as they can.

Before the end of the lesson let children read work to the class. Descriptions of clothing may vary, especially the colours. Accept sentences that are accurate and correct.

Homework task
Children complete Check-up 11, WB p110. For answers, see p185.

Portfolio
Children may make neat copies of their WB compositions.

Resource box

Class composition example writing (p115)

These are Sami people. They live in northern Europe. It is very cold there in winter and there is a lot of snow. It snows from November to May. There are lots of reindeer in Sapmi.

There is a man and a little child in the photograph. They are wearing special clothes. The clothes are wool. The wool comes from reindeer. The man and the child are wearing blue jackets. The jackets have borders of red, yellow, green and blue. The colours are bright. Their hats are red, too, and they are wearing belts. The child has little white boots.

The man is holding the child. He looks happy. The child is smiling and he/she looks happy, too.

WB answers (p108)

Exercise 2 1 in northern Europe 2 Sapmi 3 four 4 Sweden, Norway, Finland, Russia 5 red, blue, yellow and green

Exercise 4 hat, boots, trousers, jacket, fur, border, gloves, skirt, reindeer, sledge

Composition practice example writing (p109)

See p185 for example writing.

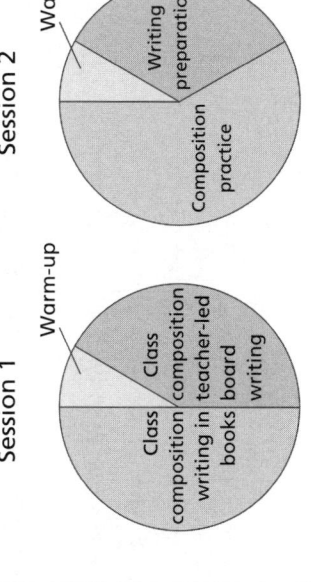

Time division

Session 1 — Class composition writing in books / Class composition writing on teacher-led board / Warm-up

Session 2 — Composition practice / Writing preparation / Warm-up

Unit 11 Writing preparation, Composition practice

12 A desert oasis

Lesson 1 Poster 12, Reading

Lesson aim Reading
Text type Adventure story with a strong opening
Lesson targets Children:
- read, understand and practise new vocabulary on the poster
- read, understand and practise reading the story
- answer oral comprehension questions

Key structure relative clauses with *who*
Key language *Do you remember the two men who were in the 4x4?*
Key vocabulary desert features
Materials PB pp116–117; poster 12; CD C track 18; Dictionary 4; word cards for words on the poster (see poster 12 below or list on p16)
Preparation Make word cards; listen to CD C track 18

12 A desert oasis

[poster image with labels: date palms, sand dune, camel train, oasis, souvenir, tourist, 4 x 4, archaeologist, ruins]

4 Tell children to look at the picture. Ask them to guess or work out the answer to these questions:
What does an archaeologist do? digs up old buildings and objects
What does a tourist do? visits places, buys souvenirs

5 Ask children what they can say about deserts. If necessary, prompt:
How much rain is there? How many different animals are there?
Is there any grass? Are there any trees?

Warm-up

Ask the class to think of words to do with a desert, e.g. *sand, sun, hot, rocks, snake, insect*.

Poster 12

1 Point to the poster. Read out the title. Give the class a moment or two to look.

2 Point to the people and objects. Read the word/s. Show the word card/s. Class reads and says the word/s.
Use *Dictionary 4* to explain new words as necessary.
The following words are not in the dictionary. Check that children understand them from the poster. If you wish, explain them using these definitions and example sentences as necessary:

archaeologist   a person who looks for very old things in the ground *Archaeologists find out about the past.*
camel train   several camels in a line carrying heavy objects from one place to another *Camel trains used to carry silk from China to the Middle East.*
oasis   a place in a desert where there is water *Travellers in the desert often stop at an oasis.*
ruins   parts of old buildings that fell down a long time ago *Archaeologists discovered these ruins last year.*

3 Cover the words on the poster if you wish. Point to the objects and people at random. Class names them.

Unit 12 Reading

Reading (PB pp116–117)

1. Give children time to look at the pictures and the text.
   Read the title. Ask *Is this text a story or is it information? How do you know?*
   Children should recognise from the pictures and direct speech that it is a story.
   Ask *Where does this story happen? in the desert*

2. Play track 18. Children listen and follow in their books.

3. Read one paragraph or section of the text at a time.
   Use Dictionary 4 to help you to explain new words as necessary.
   Help children to find new words. Make up extra sentences for new words if you wish.

4. Ask questions about each paragraph or a section of the text. See Resource box.

5. Give reading practice around the class.
   Ask individuals, groups or the class to read sentences or paragraphs.
   Play track 18 again.

Homework task

Children learn selected vocabulary from *Dictionary 4*, Unit 12.
See unit word list on pages 190–191 for key words, extension words and words for understanding only.

UNIT 12 A desert oasis

Reading

The lost city

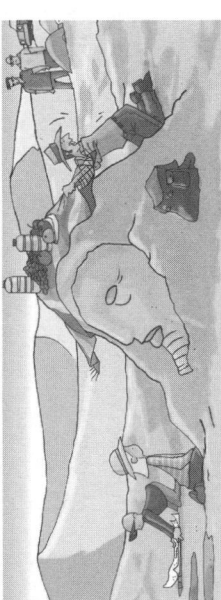

The adventure began when Jenny sat next to a giant ear.
"I'm too hot and tired to go any further!" she said. "We left the oasis hours ago. It's time for a rest." She put her bag on the hot rock beside her and then exclaimed. "Look at this! It's an enormous ear!"
She stood up and brushed a little sand off the rock. "Here's an eye... and down here, there's a nose. It's a huge face!"
Uncle Jim was amazed. "It's the head of a statue," he said. "But why is it here, in the middle of the desert?"
Pete was looking at the ground. "These big flat stones look like a floor," he said. He stepped onto the first stone. It slid away under his foot and he nearly fell over. Uncle Jim grabbed his arm. They stared into a narrow dark hole in the ground.
"What's down there?" asked Pete.
"What can you see?" asked Pete. Uncle Jim was silent.
Uncle Jim knelt down and shone his torch into the hole.
"Oh! Isn't there anything down there?" asked Jenny. She sounded disappointed.
"There's a big room down there," said Uncle Jim. "I can see tall pots and furniture. It might be very valuable. I must phone the city museum."

Unit 12 Reading: a story with a strong beginning

Just then, they heard a distant hum. Jenny looked up. "A car's coming," she said.
"Quick. Let's put this map over the hole," said Uncle Jim. "We shouldn't tell anyone about it. Sometimes people take valuable things and sell them as souvenirs."
"How can we hide the head?" asked Pete.
"I know," said Jenny. "I'll put my big scarf over the head. If we put the water bottles and some fruit on the scarf, it will look like a picnic. Then we'll sit on the head. Hurry!"

A big silver 4 x 4 roared round the sand dunes. Two men got out and walked across the sand.
"Hi," said the first man. "Are you looking for something special?"
"We're not looking for anything at all," said Uncle Jim. "We're just tourists."
The two men looked at them suspiciously. "If you find anything interesting, we will pay you money for it," said the second man.
"We haven't seen anything interesting all day," said Jenny. "No camel trains, no ruins, not even a date palm. It's all very boring."
The two men drove away and Uncle Jim phoned the museum. He spoke to Professor Hamid for a long time.
Professor Hamid was an archaeologist who worked at the museum. When he arrived, he looked into the hole.
"Have we found something exciting?" asked Pete.
Professor Hamid smiled. "Do you remember the two men who were in the 4 x 4?" Pete and Jenny nodded. "Those men are looking for something."
"Treasure?" suggested the children at once.
Professor Hamid nodded. "They are looking for a lost city," he said, "and guess what? I think you have found it!"

Unit 12 Reading: a story with a strong opening

Resource box

Text questions

Why did Jenny want to sit down? **She was hot and tired.**
What did she sit next to? **a giant ear**
Was it a real ear? **No.**
What did the head belong to? **a statue**
What was under the big flat stones? **a dark hole**
What could Uncle Jim see? **tall pots and furniture**

PB (p117)

How did they hide the hole? the head? **with the map / Jenny's scarf**
Who came in the 4 x 4? **two men**
What did they want? **anything interesting**
Where did Professor Hamid work? **at the museum**
What were the two men looking for? **a lost city**
Who has found it? **Jenny and Pete**

Time division

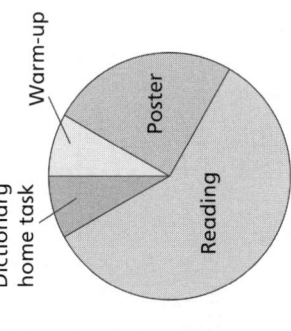

Unit 12 Reading

Lesson 2 Reading comprehension and vocabulary (PB p118)

Lesson aim Reading comprehension; vocabulary

Lesson targets Children re-read *The lost city*, then:
- (PB) write who said different sentences in the story
- answer deductive questions; match words and definitions
- (WB) order sentences from the story
- match words and pictures

Key structure relative clauses with *who*

Key language *Do you remember the two men who were in the 4x4?*

Words vocabulary from Lesson 1

Materials PB p118; CD C track 18 (optional); WB p112; Dictionary 4

Warm-up

Play the *Word mix* game (see Games, page 187). Use vocabulary from Lesson 1.

Read again

Remind children of *The lost city*.
Play track 18 or read the text to the class. Children listen and follow in their books.

Activity 1

Ask a child to read the first sentence.
Ask *Who said it?* Elicit an answer. Check with the class. Children may look back to the text to look for answers if necessary.

Activity 2

The answers to these questions are not found directly in the text.
Children must think and work out an answer.
If necessary, read the appropriate part of the text again.
Ask prompt questions if you wish, e.g. *Can you often find big statues in the desert? Did they want anyone to know about the hole and the room under the stones? Did they want the men to go away or stay with them?*

Activity 3

Ask different children to read out the list of words and the list of definitions.
Give children a few minutes to match. They may find and check definitions in their dictionaries.
Elicit answers. Help the class to check definitions in the dictionary if they do not agree on answers.

Reading comprehension and vocabulary

1 Who said it?

1 It's a huge face! _____
2 It's the head of a statue. _____
3 These big flat stones look like a floor. _____
4 What's down there? _____
5 I must phone the city museum. _____
6 Are you looking for something special? _____
7 It's all very boring. _____
8 Those men are looking for something. _____

2 Discuss the answers to these questions.

1 Why was Uncle Jim amazed?
2 Why did they hide the hole in the ground?
3 Why did Jenny say, "It's all very boring?"

3 Match the words and definitions. Check in your dictionary.

1 amazed ___ a equal to a large amount of money
2 grab ___ b thinking something may not be true
3 valuable ___ c not at all interesting
4 suspiciously ___ d very surprised
5 boring ___ e take hold of something quickly

118

Unit 12 Reading comprehension and vocabulary: identifying the speaker; deduction; definitions

Unit 12 Reading comprehension and vocabulary

172

Reading comprehension and vocabulary (WB p112)

If children are doing this page for homework, make sure they understand the tasks. You may wish to read the text in exercise 1 with the class as preparation. Remind them that they will need their Pupil's Book so that they can read the story again before they attempt exercise 2.

Exercise 1

Children read the story again.
Children read the sentences and work out the correct order.
They should refer back to the text as much as necessary to complete the task correctly.

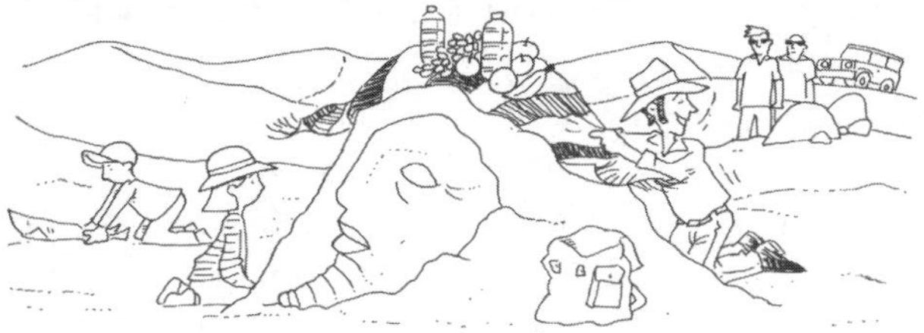

Exercise 2

Children match. Tell them to check in their dictionaries if necessary.

Resource box

PB answers

Activity 1 1 Jenny 2 Uncle Jim 3 Pete 4 Pete 5 Uncle Jim 6 the first man 7 Jenny 8 Professor Hamid

Activity 2 1 Big pieces of statue are not usually found in the middle of the desert.
2 They didn't want anyone to know what was under the stones.
3 She didn't want the men to stay. If she said 'This is an interesting place,' they might find the head and the hole. They might take some things away.

Activity 3 1d 2e 3a 4b 5c

WB answers

Exercise 1 9, 4, 7, 1, 3, 10, 2, 5, 8, 6

Exercise 2 1 furniture 2 treasure 3 archaeologist 4 sand dune 5 torch

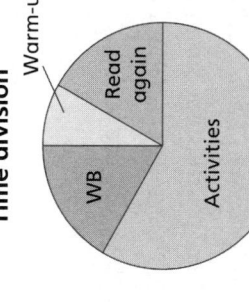

Time division: Warm-up, Read again, WB, Activities

Unit 12 Reading comprehension and vocabulary

Lesson 3 Speaking (PB p119) Study skills

Lesson aim Speaking, Study skills (WB)

Lesson targets Children:
- listen to a dialogue; listen and repeat the dialogue
- understand the story and answer oral questions
- read and act the dialogue
- (WB) practise dictionary skills and sorting

Informal everyday expressions *Are you sure? I don't believe it! It's true.*

New words *palm (tree), pyramid, lid, touch, steal, sure*

Materials PB p119; CD C tracks 19, 20; WB p113; Dictionary 4

Preparation Listen to CD C track 19 before the lesson

Warm-up

Ask the class what happened in Part 5. *Which room were they in? What was in the bag? Was it Alfie's bag?*
Let them look back at Part 5 if they have forgotten.

Activity 1

Children look at PB page 119. Read the title of Part 6. Ask what they think is happening in each picture. *What are the children doing? Why?*
Let children make different suggestions and listen to their ideas.
Tell children to cover the dialogue text and look at the picture.
Play track 19. Children listen.

Activity 2

Children look at the dialogue. Play track 19 again.
Children listen and follow.
Check children understand the new words. Use Dictionary 4 if you wish.

Activity 3

Children close their books. Play track 20. Children listen and repeat in the pauses. Encourage them to use the same expression and intonation.

Activity 4

Ask questions to check understanding of the story. See Resource box.

Activity 5

Children act the dialogue without their books if possible.

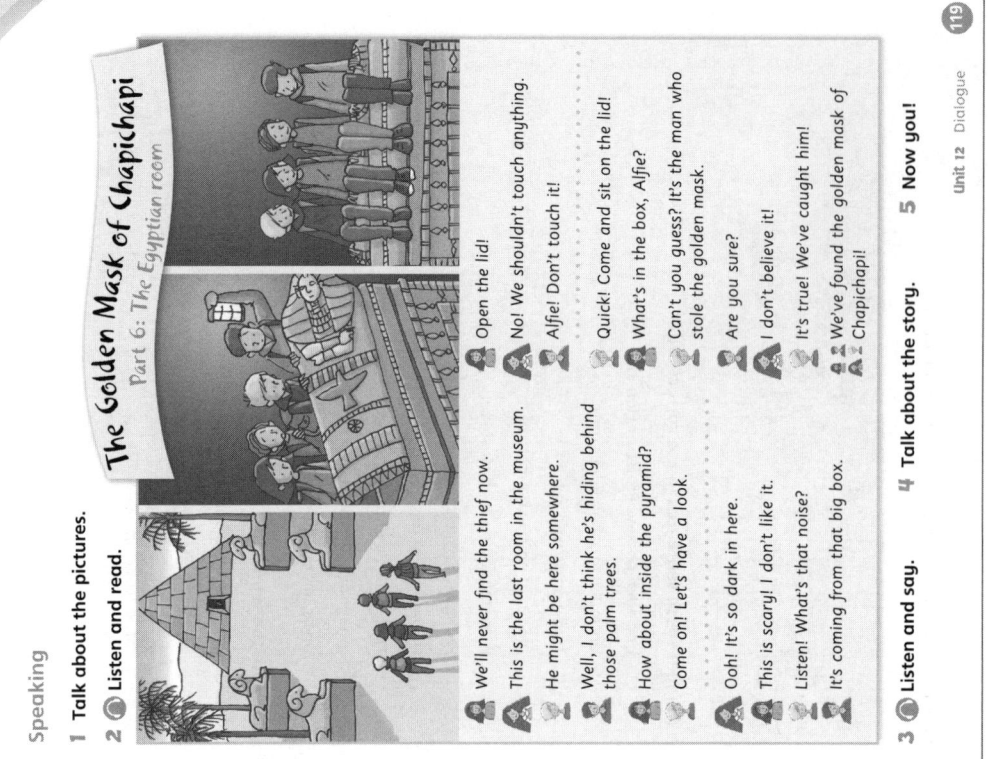

Unit 12 Speaking

174

Study skills (WB p113)

The exercises on this page practise dictionary skills.
Children should be able to do this work independently once the tasks have been explained.

Exercise 1

Children write the words in alphabetical order. Remind them of the dictionary skills they have learned and to watch out for words beginning with the same letter.

Exercise 2

Children match words, definitions and pictures.

Study skills

1 abc Write the words in order.

1	start	desert	statue	camel	treasure	palm
	camel	_desert_				

| 2 | oasis | tourist | dune | stone | torch | sand |

| 3 | huge | disappointed | amazed | flat | valuable | distant |

| 4 | kneel | exclaim | slide | roar | shine | hide |

2 Match. Write the letters.

1 kneel — a You buy this on holiday. It helps you remember your holiday.
2 palm — b A place in the desert. There is water there.
3 souvenir — c A long line of camels
4 dune — d To go down on your knees
5 oasis — e This tree grows in hot places.
6 camel train — f A hill of sand in the desert.

1 dH 2 ___ 3 ___
4 ___ 5 ___ 6 ___

Now check the words in your dictionary!

Unit 12 Dictionary skills

Resource box

Story questions

Is the thief behind the palm trees? **No.**
Where do the children look? **inside the pyramid**
Who is scared? **Molly**
Who hears a noise? **Alfie**
Where is it coming from? **inside the big box**
Who lifts the lid? **Alfie**
What is inside? **the thief**
What do the children do? **sit on the lid**
What have they found? **the golden mask of Chapichapi**

WB answers

Exercise 1 1 camel desert palm start statue treasure
2 dune oasis sand stone torch tourist
3 amazed disappointed distant flat huge valuable
4 exclaim hide kneel roar shine slide

Exercise 2 1 dH 2 eL 3 aK 4 fI 5 bJ 6 cG

Time division

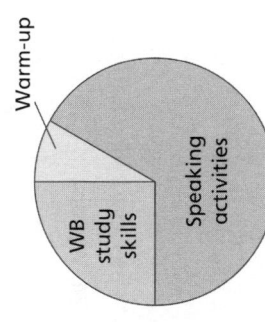

Warm-up
WB study skills
Speaking activities

Unit 12 Study skills

Lesson 4 Grammar (Session 1), Grammar in conversation (Session 2) (PB pp120–121)

Lesson aim Grammar

Lesson targets Children:
- (session 1) understand and practise the key structure
- (session 2) listen to and read a conversation; repeat and practise it
- (session 2) listen to a song, say it and learn it (optional)

Key structure relative clauses with *who*
Key vocabulary jobs and professions
Key language relative clauses with *who*
Informal expressions *Ready? Right. That's easy / tricky. I know!*
Materials PB pp120–121; CD C tracks 21–24; WB pp114–115

Session 1 Warm-up

Do a *Word race* with jobs (see Games, page 187).

Activity 1
Children look at the pictures. Ask a pair to read out the bubbles. Write the sentences on the board. Underline *who*. Class reads. Class reads silently the beginnings / endings. Ask a volunteer to say the first sentence. Check with the class. Children write. Continue with the other sentences.

Activity 2
Ask a pair to read the PC kids' bubbles. Write the sentences. Demonstrate making one sentence. Let a child read the first two sentences. Help children to make one sentence.

Children practise the sentences in pairs. See Resource box.*

Session 2 Warm-up

Ask around the class *Which job is the most interesting? Why?*

Activity 1
Point out the words. Explain the children are using them to play a game. Tell the class to listen to them. Play track 21. Children follow in their books.

Activity 2
Children listen to track 22 and repeat in the pauses.

Activity 3
Children play the game in pairs. See Resource box.**

Activity 4
Ask children how far they think the camel train is going. Play track 23. Children listen and follow the first time. Read the words with the class. Play track 23. Children join in. Play track 24. Children sing with the music. They may learn the song, if you wish.

Children complete WB page 114 in class time or for homework.

Unit 12 Grammar, Grammar in conversation

176

Grammar (Session 1), Grammar in conversation (Session 2) (WB pp114–115)

If this page is for homework, check children understand the tasks.

Exercise 1
Go through the example with the class.

If appropriate, go through the other sentences orally before the class writes.

Exercise 2
Children's own ideas. Encourage them to think about what they look like and what they do. Do an example sentence about yourself to help them, if you wish. Children do the same for a friend.

If this page is for homework, check children understand the tasks.

Exercise 1
Children match sentence beginnings and endings.

Exercise 2
Children use their own ideas to complete sentences. Make sure they understand there is more than one way of completing them correctly.

Exercise 3
Children write their own ideas about what a friend is or does. Go through some ideas with the class before they write, if you wish.

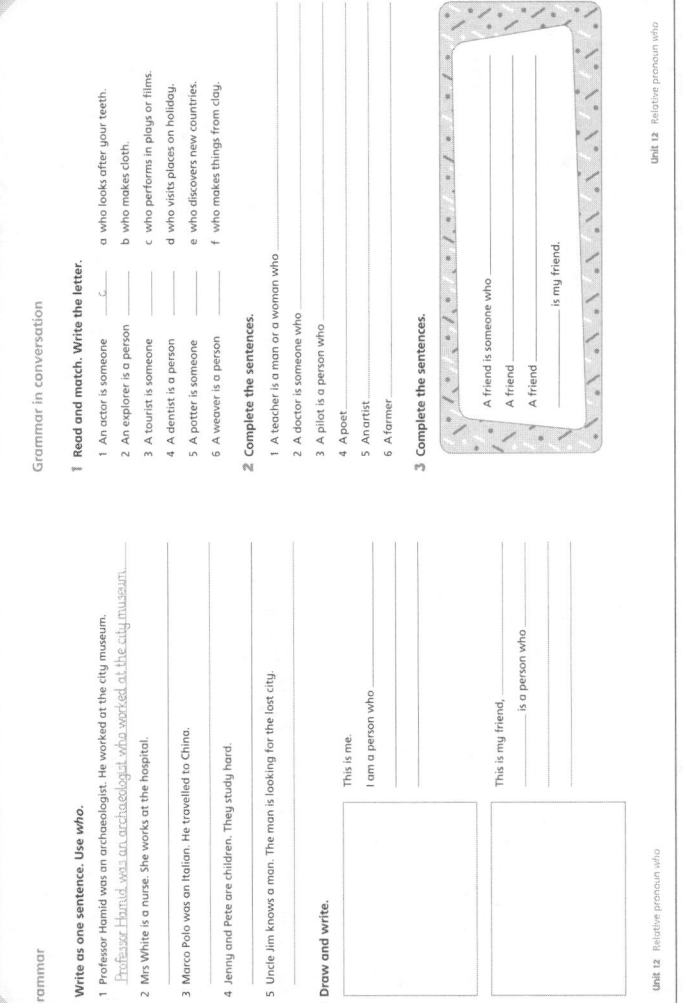

Resource box
*Pair work: Grammar (PB p120)
Activity 2 Children work in pairs at their desks.

**Pair work: Grammar in conversation (PB p121)
Activity 3 Children play the game in pairs at their desks.

Depending on the ability of your class, you may wish to play it altogether first and make sure children know how to describe the people on the cards.

If your class is able, they should be able to play straightaway themselves.

If you wish put one or two more cards on the board.

Give pairs three minutes to practise the game.

Let one or two pairs play it once or twice while other children listen.

WB answers
Grammar (WB p114)
Exercise 1 2 Mrs White is a nurse who works at the hospital.
3 Marco Polo was an Italian who travelled to China.
4 Jenny and Pete are children who study hard.
5 Uncle Jim knows a man who is looking for the lost city.

Exercise 2 Children's own answers.

Grammar in conversation (WB p115)
Exercise 1 1c 2e 3d 4a 5f 6b

Time division

Session 1

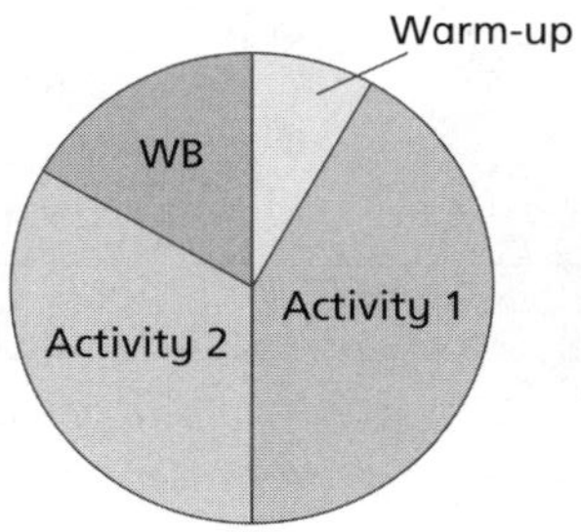

Session 2

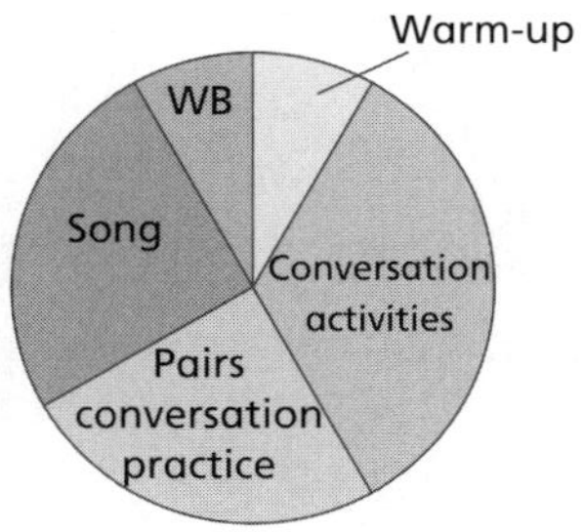

Grammar Practice Book
Children may begin Unit 12 when they have completed the PB and WB Grammar pages. They should complete it before the end of PB / WB Unit 12.

Unit 12 Grammar, Grammar in conversation

Lesson 5 Listening, Phonics (PB p122) Use of English

Lesson aim Listening, spelling and pronunciation, Use of English (WB)

Lesson targets Children:
- talk about places to explore and name items for travelling
- listen to a discussion about a trip to the desert
- practise saying, reading and spelling words with soft c
- (WB) learn about using the exclamation mark

Key structure and language from Unit 12

Target words *face, race, ice cream, mice, dance, juice, prince, princess, pencil, city, circle, bicycle*

Materials PB p122; CD C tracks 24–26; WB pp116–117

Warm-up
Sing the camel song from PB page 121, track 24.

Listening

Activity 1
Ask a volunteer to read the line. Play track 25. Children listen to the conversation and circle the answer: *the desert*.

Activity 2
Ask volunteers to name the different objects.

Activity 3
Play track 25 again. Children tick the ones the explorers mention. Be ready to play the track again for children to listen or check. Check answers together.

Activity 4
Ask children do use their imaginations to answer the questions. Hear some of their ideas. Ask if there is anything else they should take.

Phonics
Point out the box. Tell children to follow in their books and repeat in the pauses. Play the first part of track 26. Make sure children repeat accurately. Play the end of track 26. Children listen and follow. Children say the rhyme. They may learn it, if you wish.

Children open their WBs at page 116. They complete the Phonics page now or for homework. If it is for homework, make sure they understand the tasks.

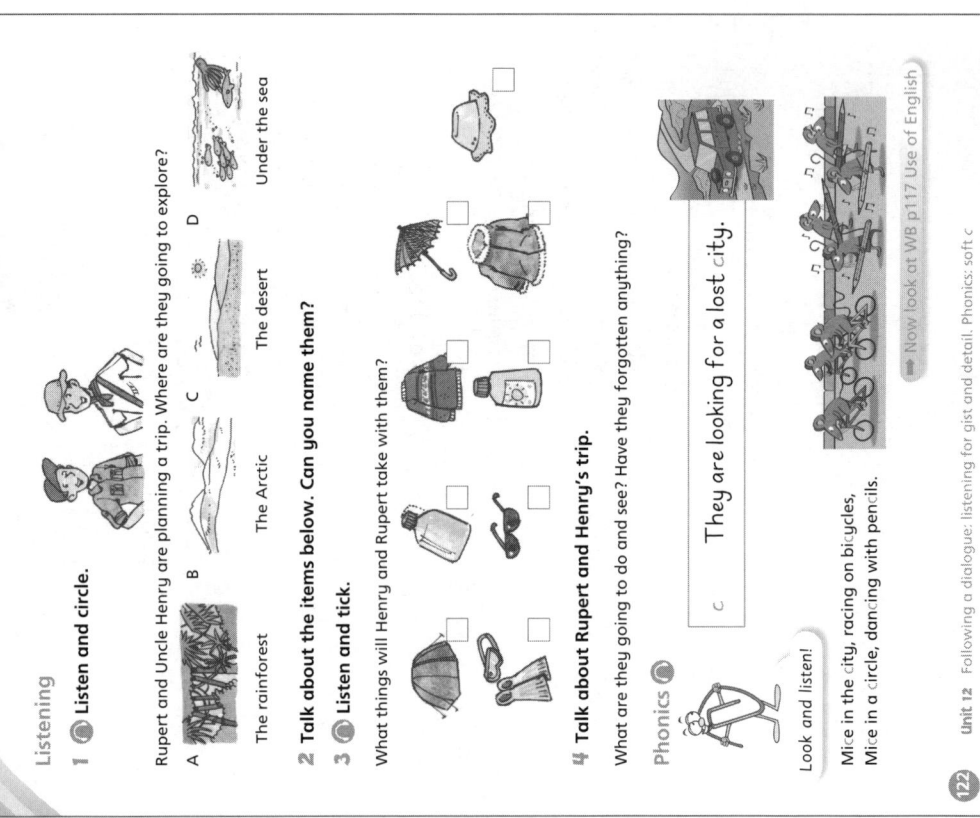

Use of English
Move on to WB page 117.

Unit 12 Listening, Phonics

178

Phonics, Use of English (WB pp116–117)

Remind the class of soft c and city.

Exercises 1 and 2
Children complete, read and write the target words.

Exercise 3
Children complete the sentences.

Write the three sentences on the board.
Point out the punctuation.
Volunteers read with the correct expression for the punctuation.

Exercise 1
Children should be very familiar with punctuation. of statements and questions. They are included here to contrast them with exclamations.
Go through the presentation with the class. Make sure children understand that an exclamation mark usually communicates some feeling from the speaker. They should not be used too often in writing or they lose their effect.

Exercise 2
Tell children to read each sentence carefully and decide what punctuation it needs. The pictures should help them.

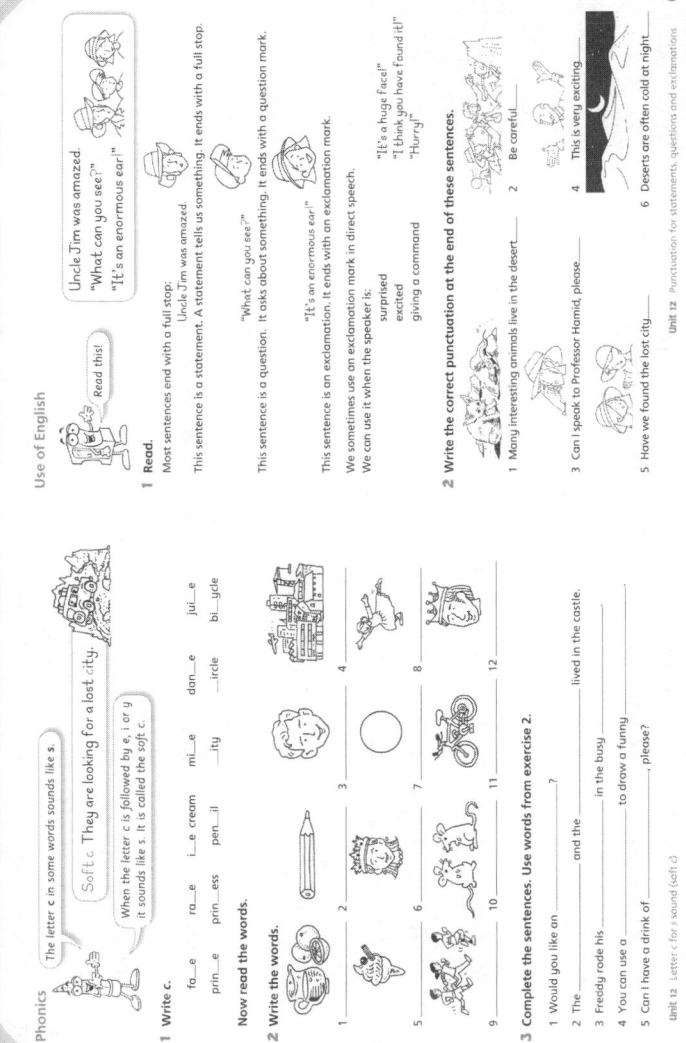

Resource box

Audioscript (CD C track 25) Listening activities 1 & 3 (PB p122)

R: Is it going to be very hot, Uncle Henry?
H: Oh, yes. Very, very hot. So there are lots of things we must take.
R: Really?
H: Well, the sun is very strong so you'll need a hat and a good of pair sunglasses to protect your eyes.
R: And water, too, I suppose.
H: Oh yes, lots of that. We must take plenty of water.
R: How about a tent?
H: Oh, I never take a tent into the desert. I like to sleep under the stars.
R: Really?
H: Yes, and you'll need a warm jumper, too.
R: Why? It's going to be really hot, isn't it?
H: Well, it gets very cold in the desert at night.
R: Really?
H: Wait and see!
R: Will I need a warm jacket, then?
H: No, you won't need one of those. A jumper's fine. And it's not going to rain.
R: Really? I won't take my umbrella then.
H: (Ha, ha, ha.)

PB answers

Activity 3 water, jumper, hat, sunglasses, sleeping bag

WB answers

Phonics (p116)

Exercise 2 1 juice 2 pencil 3 face 4 city
5 ice cream 6 princess 7 circle 8 dance
9 race 10 mice 11 bicycle 12 prince

Exercise 3 1 ice cream 2 prince, princess
3 bicycle, city 4 pencil, face 5 juice

Use of English (p117)

Exercise 1 1 . 2 ! 3 ? 4 ! 5 ? 6 .

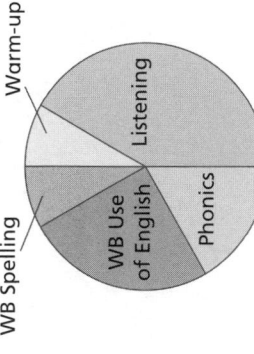

Time division

WB Spelling, Warm-up, Listening, Phonics, WB Use of English

Unit 12 Phonics, Use of English

Lesson 6 Class composition (Session 1) (PB p123) Writing preparation, Composition practice (Session 2)

Lesson aim Writing

Lesson targets Children:
- (session 1) write the next part of the story with teacher support
- (session 2) (WB) make notes about the last part of the story
- (session 2) (WB) complete the story independently

Key structure and language from Unit 12

Vocabulary from this and previous units

Materials PB p123; WB pp118–119; poster 12; CDs A–C

Session 1 Warm-up

Put up poster 12. Remind children of the story *The lost city*.

Class composition

Activity 1

Read, or ask a child to read the short text.
Explain to the class that the pictures show what happened next. They are going to write the story. Give them time to look at the pictures. Make sure they realise that they are in the correct order. Ask different children *What happened in picture 1?* Elicit, e.g. **Professor Hamid found a door.** Write a short note on the board, e.g. *1 found a door*. Continue in the same way, e.g. *2 opened the door; 3 saw inside the room; 4 went inside, looked at the objects; 5 found a chest; 6 opened the chest*.

Activity 2

Ask different children to read each sentence. Ask the class which one is the most interesting opening for the story.
Children should recognise that sentence 2 gives more information than sentence 1. Sentence 4 gives the same information as sentence 2, but in direct speech. Sentence 3 gives the least detail.
Agree on an opening. Write it on the board.

Activity 3

Prompt another sentence for the first picture. Ask, e.g. *What was the door like?*
Ask questions about the other pictures. Use your notes and children's answers to compose two sentences for each one.
Remind them to use direct speech sometimes, e.g. *What did Professor Hamid say when he went into the room?*
When the story is complete, ask one or more volunteers to read it aloud.
Ask whether any further improvements can be made, e.g. *Are there enough adjectives?*
Make any changes that you and the class agree to.
Ask volunteers to read it a final time.

Class composition

1 Read and look at the pictures.

Uncle Jim, Pete and Jenny found a lost city in the desert. They told Professor Hamid about it. Professor Hamid and his men dug in the sand.

1

2

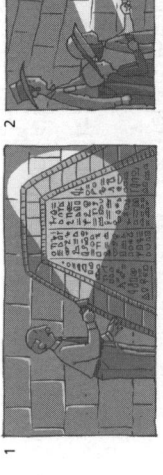
3

4

5

6

2 Choose an opening for the story. Which sentence is the most interesting?
Professor Hamid found a door.
Suddenly, Professor Hamid found a strange door.
There was a door.
"Look," said Professor Hamid, "here is a very strange door."

3 Continue the story. What did Professor Hamid do next?

Unit 12 Writing: a story with a strong opening

Unit 12 Class composition

Writing preparation, Composition practice (WB pp118–119)

Session 2 Warm-up

Class chooses a favourite song to sing.

Exercise 1

Ask the question and ask for suggestions. Write them on the board. Children choose one, or another of their own.

Exercise 2

Ask children to read out the words. Explain they should choose words to describe their object.

Exercise 3

Children tick two things that the professor did. They choose and tick two adverbs.

Exercise 4

Children read the questions that Jenny and Pete asked. They choose Professor Hamid's answers or write their own ideas in the space provided.

Exercise 5

Children think of answers to the questions. If you wish, do this as a whole class and decide on an ending together. Alternatively, let children use their own ideas and write their own ending.

Children write the story working alone (WB page 119). Remind them to use their notes on page 118. Encourage them to add in extra ideas of their own.

Go around helping and monitoring as they work.

Be ready to give any extra words they need. Encourage children to use their dictionaries to find words and check spellings.

Remind children to read through their work when they have finished. They should correct any mistakes they find. Ask one or two children to read their stories to the class.

Homework task

Children complete Check-up 12, WB p120. For answers, see p185.

Resource box

Class composition example writing (p123)

Suddenly, Professor Hamid found a strange door. There were pictures of beautiful birds on it. Professor Hamid opened the door carefully. Jenny and Pete were very excited.

Inside the room they saw a round table and two chairs. There were lots of tall, stone pots.

"This is fantastic," said Professor Hamid. They looked at everything in the room.

"Look at this!" said Pete. He pointed to a large, metal chest.

"Let's open it," said Professor Hamid. Slowly, he lifted the lid.

Composition practice example writing (p119)

See p185 for example writing.

Time division

Session 1 — Warm-up / Class composition writing in books / Class composition in teacher-led board writing

Session 2 — Warm-up / Writing preparation / Composition practice

Portfolio

Children may make neat copies of their WB compositions.

Unit 12 Writing preparation, Composition practice

Revision 4, Project 4

Activity 1

1 Give children a few moments to look at the pictures.
Ask *Who is in this story?* Elicit, e.g. ***a boy, astronauts***
Point out the picture of Ben at the top of the page. *What is he doing?* ***reading a book*** Ask *What is the book called?* ***Fantastic journeys***
Play CD C, track 27. Children listen and follow in their books.

2 Ask questions about the story. Use these or any of your own:
What was Ben's uncle? ***an astronaut***
What did he send to Ben? ***an e-mail***
What was the question in the e-mail? ***Do you want to be the first boy in space?***
How did they go to the space station? ***by snow scooter***
Why couldn't they go by car? ***There was a lot of snow.***
How many men flew with Uncle Jim and Ben? ***three***
Where might they go next week? ***to the moon***
Where did they land? ***in the desert***

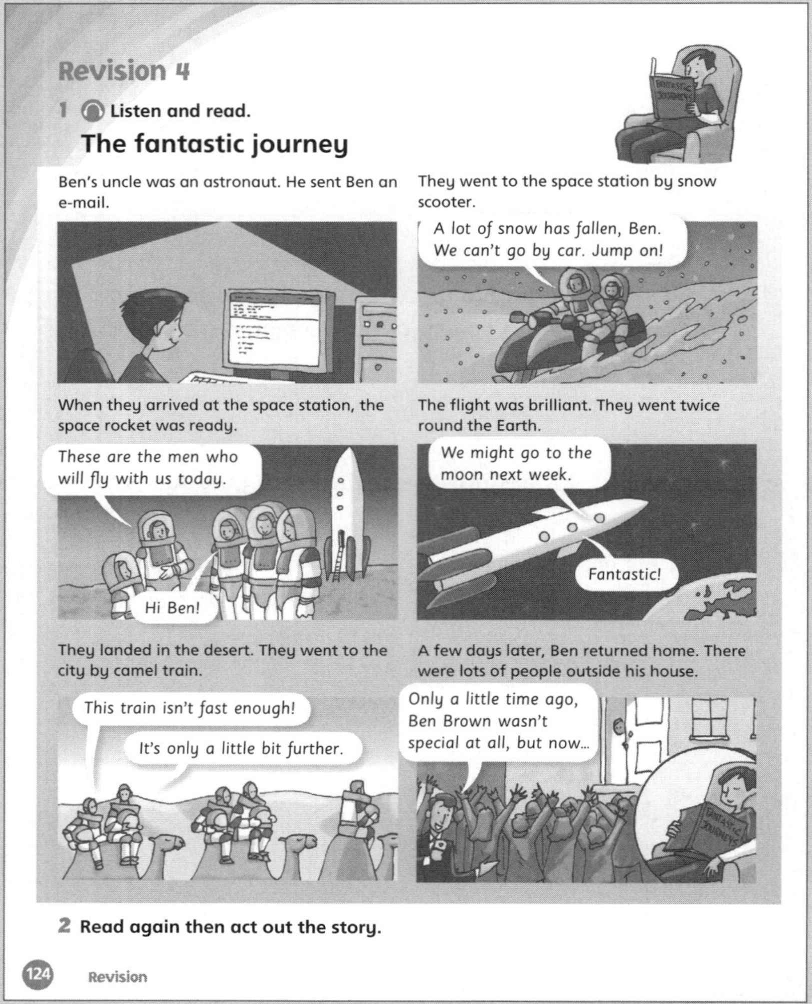

Revision 4

1 Listen and read.

The fantastic journey

Ben's uncle was an astronaut. He sent Ben an e-mail.

They went to the space station by snow scooter.

When they arrived at the space station, the space rocket was ready.

The flight was brilliant. They went twice round the Earth.

They landed in the desert. They went to the city by camel train.

A few days later, Ben returned home. There were lots of people outside his house.

2 Read again then act out the story.

124 Revision

3 *How did they travel to the city?* ***by camel train***
What happened when Ben arrived home? ***There were lots of people outside his house.***
Why was Ben special? ***He was the first boy in space.***
Do you think this story could be true? Why? Why not?

Activity 2

Play track 27 again. Children follow in their books.
Let groups of children act out the story.
If children enjoy the activity let them practise first then let as many groups as possible act for the rest of the class.

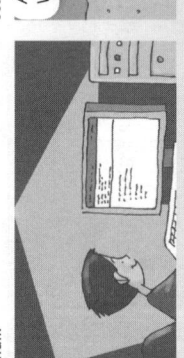

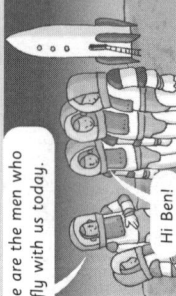

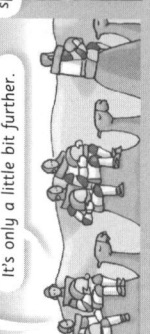

Extra activities

Class game

Children work in teams. Ask them to think of as many different ways of travelling as they can, on land, on the sea, in the air.
Give them a time limit.
They may look through their books for ideas.
Answers can include: *car, bus, lorry, van, truck, bike, motorbike, taxi, train, plane, helicopter, hot air balloon, space rocket, snow scooter, boat, ship, camel, horse, donkey, elephant.*

An amazing journey

In this project children write about an amazing journey that they imagine for themselves.

Activity 1

1 Give children a moment to look at the map. Ask them what they can remember about any of the places that are on the map, e.g. the name of a city; whether the country is hot or cold; what buildings there are there; what people do there.
When you have reminded the class of what they already know, explain the task. Children may choose just one place to write about or they may choose two or three.
The places can be ones they already know something about or ones that are new.
Go through the questions with the class. Make sure they realise they can imagine some parts of the story. Information about real places must be true.

Project 4 - An amazing journey

Look at the map.

Where did you go on your amazing journey? south? north? east? west?
Choose a place or choose two or three places. Find out about the place.

Arctic
North America
Europe
Russia
China
Africa
South America
Australia
Antarctic

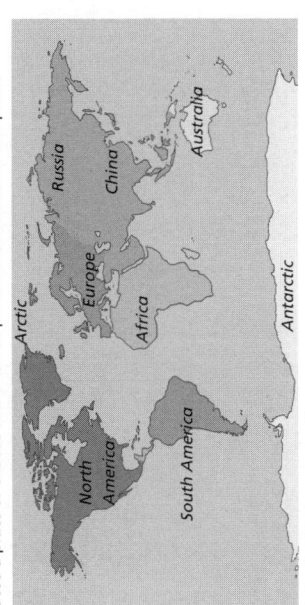

Think about these questions.

Who did you go with? How did you travel?
What did you see? What did you do?
Write about your journey. Draw pictures.

Read your story to the class.

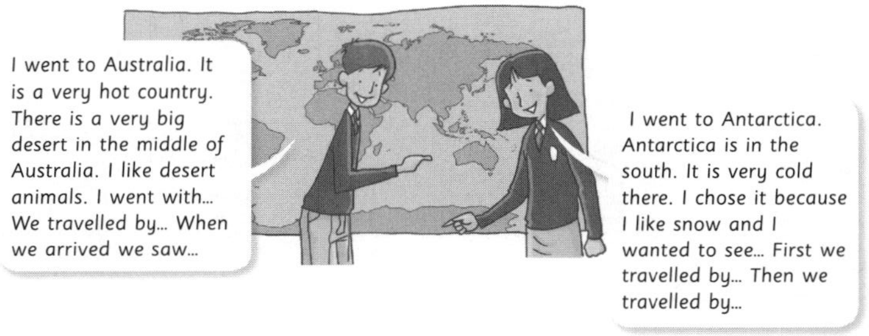

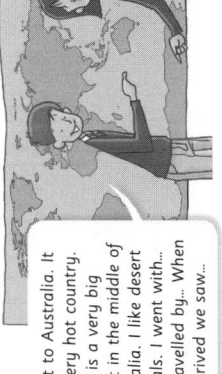

I went to Australia. It is a very hot country. There is a very big desert in the middle of Australia. I like desert animals. I went with… We travelled by… When we arrived we saw…
I went to Antarctica. Antarctica is in the south. It is very cold there. I chose it because I like snow and I wanted to see… First we travelled by… Then we travelled by…

Project 125

2 Children should be able to complete this project working at their own level. All of them should be able to find out a few new things about places they already know of.
Encourage able children to find out more or to write about a completely new place.
Give children some time to find pictures or to draw them.

Activity 2

Let everyone in the class tell the others where they went on the journey and why they chose the place.
If there is time, let them say who they went with and how they travelled.
Count up the number of different destinations. If you wish, mark them on a large map. Find out how many children went to the same place and how many went somewhere that no one else visited.

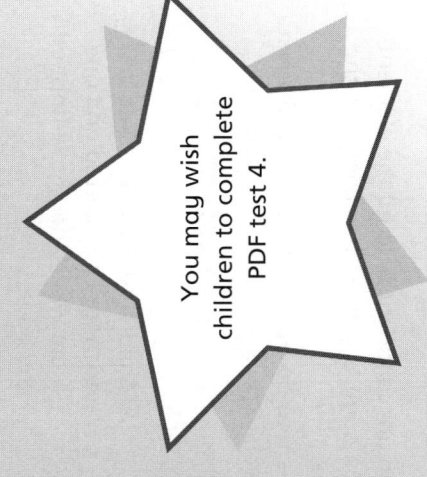

You may wish children to complete PDF test 4.

Summary box

Lesson aim Revision

Lesson targets Children:

- listen to a story and understand it; read it and act it
- write about a journey to one or more places in the world
- tell the class where they went, why and who with

Resource box

Portfolio
If you wish, this project may be included in children's portfolio of written work.

Portfolio 4 and Diploma 4: Units 10–12

1 When children have completed all the work in Units 10–12, they turn to page 135 in their Workbook.

2 This page allows children to make their own assessment of what they have learned in English.

Vocabulary
Children tick each box when they are confident that they know the key words in each category.

Encourage children who know the key words well to learn some of the wider set of words, too.

Grammar
Children should look back at all the grammar pages and check them before they tick the boxes.

Phonics
Encourage children to test each other and practise writing words before they tick them.

3 Check through the completed Portfolio page with each child.

1 When children are confident with all the elements of the work on page 135, they may complete the Diploma page.
Encourage them to do this carefully as it is the last one in this level.

2 Children receive a sticker for each task completed and one more when they have finished the page.

3 These pages may be taken out of the Workbook and kept in children's individual portfolios of work along with a few examples of children's best work from Units 10–12.

4 Encourage them to go back over work they are unsure of. They should do their best to tick everything on the page before they finish English World 4.

Completed Diploma 4
Exercise 1 astronaut, parachute, orbit, antler, sledge, palm tree, ruins, sand dune
Exercise 2 1 a little, a little, a few 2 made, ate 3 enough, make, who
Exercise 3 dolphin, telephone, anchor, circle, mice, pencil

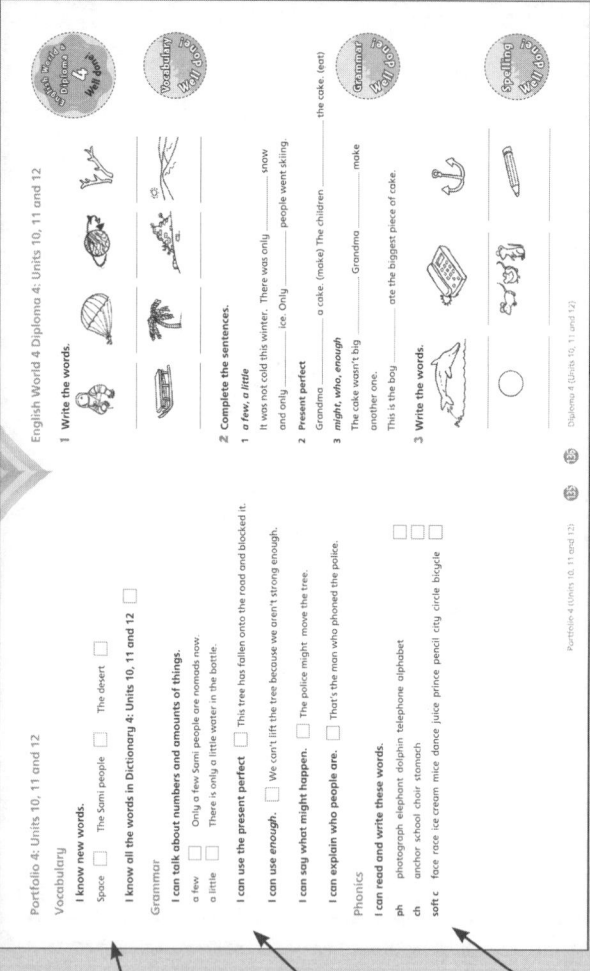

Answers to Check-ups: Units 10–12

Check-up 10 WB pp100–101

Exercise 1
1 There is a little
2 There are a few
3 There are a few
4 There is a little
5 There is a little
6 There are a few

Exercise 2
1 big enough.
2 windy enough.
3 long enough.
4 warm enough.
5 clever enough.
6 fast enough.

Exercise 3 Children use the pictures and the questions to help them write a paragraph about the potter.

Exercise 4 Example writing: The potter took a little clay. It was not wet enough. He added a little water to the clay. He put the clay on the wheel. It took a few minutes to make the pot. Next the potter painted the pot. He used only a little paint. When he finished painting, the pot was beautiful.

Composition practice example writing p99

Neil Armstrong was born in 1930 in Wapakoneta in the State of Ohio, USA. In 1947 he began his studies to be an aeroplane engineer.
In 1949 he learned to fly planes. In 1955 he became a test pilot and he flew new, fast jet places.
In 1962 he flew a plane to 63 kilometres above the ground. Then he joined the US astronaut group and he began training to be an astronaut.
In 1966 he completed his first space flight in the spacecraft, Gemini 8. He flew into space again in Gemini 11.
In 1969 he was the commander of the spacecraft Apollo 11. On 20th July he landed on the moon. He was the first man to walk on the moon. He collected rocks and he took photos. It was his last space flight.

Check-up 11 WB pp110–111

Exercise 1
1 has picked   2 have made   3 has brushed   4 have fallen   5 have eaten
6 has broken

Exercise 2
1 It might snow.
2 The boys might win the match.
3 They might not go to the mall.
4 I might not play basketball.
5 Meg might phone.
6 They might visit Russia.
7 It might not rain tomorrow.
8 Dad might buy a new car.

Exercise 3 Children use the pictures and questions in exercise 3 to help them write the story.

Exercise 4 Example writing: It is a nice day. Mum, Dad, Tom and Meg are having a picnic. When they get home, Mum looks at her hand. She has lost her ring. The ring might be in the picnic box but they can't find it. The next day, Tom is climbing a tree. A nest is in the tree. Tom is surprised. He has found a ring. It might be Mum's ring.

Composition practice example writing p109

There is a father and his child in this picture. They are Sami people. They live in northern Europe. It is very cold there in the winter and there is a lot of snow on the ground. Reindeer live there, too.
The man and the child are wearing blue jackets with red borders. The borders have patterns in them. They are yellow, white and green. The man's hat is very tall. The child has a tall hat, too. He is wearing gloves and he has a belt with a white pattern on.
The man and the child are smiling and they look happy. The weather is cold but their clothes keep them warm. They are wearing their national costume for a special day.

Check-up 12 WB pp120–121

Exercise 1   1 pilot.   2 pupil.   3 actor.   4 tourist.
5 dentist.

Exercise 2   1 writes poems.   2 teaches.
3 looks after people in hospital.
4 mends cars.   5 had lots of gold.
6 live in northern Europe.
(For 5 and 6 there are a number of different answers that could be given; these are suggestions only. Accept answers that are grammatically and factually correct.)

Exercise 4   2 These are the boys who picked the apples.   3 This is the driver who took the apples to market.   4 This is the woman who sold the apples.   5 This is the man who bought the apples.   6 This is the woman who cooked the apples and made a lovely apple cake.   7 These are the children who ate the apple cake.

Composition practice example writing p181

"Look! It's a metal sword!" said Professor Hamid. The sword was long and heavy. It was very dirty, but it was shiny.
Professor Hamid examined it thoughtfully. Then he photographed it carefully.
"How old is it?" asked Jenny.
"It is 3000 years old," said Professor Hamid.
"Who did it belong to?" asked Pete.
"It belonged to a soldier," said Professor Hamid.
"Why was it in the chest?" asked Jenny.
"I think the soldier left it behind," said Professor Hamid.
The professor put the sword into a box. He put the box in his car.
"I am going to take it to the museum," he said. "It is a very special sword."
Jenny and Pete said goodbye to the professor. They were very happy and excited.

Games

Active games

Action verb

To practise the present continuous, write instructions on cards, e.g. *jump up and down; hop; write your name on the board; draw a tree on the board; read a book; walk to the door; open the door.*

Place the cards face down on your desk. Let a child choose a card. As the child does the action, ask the class *What is he / she doing?* Class answers, e.g. **He is jumping.**

Bring pairs forward to choose a card and practise *They are…*

Action mime

This game is played in the same way as the action game but children must mime the action and other children guess what it is.

Write instructions on cards, e.g. wash the windows, brush the floor, throw a ball, catch a ball, kick a ball, clean your teeth, brush your hair, do your homework, watch TV, play the piano, etc.

To practise the present continuous, while the action is happening, ask *What is he / she / are they doing?*

To practise the past continuous, stop the action and ask *What was he/ she / were they doing?*

To practise the simple past, stop the action ask *What did he/ she/they do?*

To practise *While* + past continuous, write *While* on the board to remind the class which word they must begin with.

Bring two children forward. They each choose a card and mime an action. The class watches for a moment. Stop the action. Children guess, e.g. *While Sam was reading, Anna was watching TV.*

Simon says

Give the class instructions, e.g. *Simon says: "Stand up."* The class stands up. *Simon says: "Turn around."* Children turn round. Give an instruction only, e.g. *"Sit down."* The class must not do the action. Anyone who does, is out of the game. Say *Simon says: "Sit down"*. The class sits down.

Use this game to practise left and right. E.g. *Put up your right hand. Touch your left ear, etc.*

The adverb game

Write adverbs on cards, e.g. *quickly, slowly, noisily, loudly, quietly, happily, sadly, hurriedly, angrily.*

Use instructions from the Action game and add others if you wish, e.g. *Open your school bag; Say Hello; Stand up; Wave to your teacher; Clap your hands; Look at the window.*

Write all the adverbs that are on cards in a list on the board.

Give a volunteer an instruction card, e.g. say *Hello*. The child reads the instruction. Give him / her an adverb card, e.g. *slowly*.

The child carries out the instruction according to the adverb. The rest of the class guess which one it is.

Alphabetical order

Use word cards from Lesson 1 (poster work). Divide the class into two or more teams. Stick a group of 6–8 scrambled word cards on the board for each team. Children from each team take turns to come forward and put their group of words in alphabetical order. Children may only place one word at a time. If a team member has made a mistake, another child may correct it but not place a second word as well.

The winning team is the one that has ordered all their words correctly first.

Sentence challenge

Use word cards from Lesson 1 (poster work). Put 6–8 words at the top of the board.

Divide the class into 2–4 teams. Draw a large circle on the board for each team.

Give the teams a few minutes to write sentences using each word on the board.

A child from team 1 takes a word from the board and places it in their circle. Another team member reads out the sentence using the word. If the sentence is correct, the team keeps the word in their circle. If it is not correct, the word must be put back and it is the next team's turn.

The winning team is the one which has the most words in their circle at the end of the game.

You can make this game easier or more difficult according to the words you choose.

If your class is good at the game, put more word cards at the top of the board.

Word games

Word mix
Write a mixture of nouns, verbs, adjectives and adverbs on the board.

Children volunteer to say which of these each word is.

Extension: ask a volunteer to use the word in a sentence.

To make this a team game, team 1 says which word class a word belongs to for one point.

Team 2 may win a point for using the word correctly in a sentence.

Noun chain
This can be a team game or played with the whole class.

Child 1 thinks of a noun and writes it on the board.

Child 2 must write a noun beginning with the last letter of the first word and writes it immediately next to the first word.

Continue like this until the chain stretches across the board, e.g. trainnesttaillionnoisegg.

If children get stuck with thinking of words, they may use their dictionaries.

Word chain
This is the same as the noun chain, but any word can be used.

What's missing?
Put up word cards. Class looks and reads. Take the cards down. Remove one. Put the rest back up. Children tell you which word is missing.

What is it?
Make statements about an object. Children guess what it is, e.g. It's an animal. It's small and quiet. It has a long tail. It's usually grey or brown: a mouse.

Opposites
Put pairs of word cards on the board in scrambled order.

Children volunteer to match a pair.

Use, e.g., north south, east west, left right, up down, light dark, easy difficult, beautiful ugly, old young, fast slow.

Word race
Children write down as many items in a lexical set as they can in one minute, e.g. food, animals, countries, jobs, etc.

I spy...
Choose an object in the classroom and tell the class you are thinking of a word for something in the room.

Tell them to look around them for a moment. Say *I spy with my little eye something beginning with ...* then say the initial letter of the word, e.g. *b*. Children name all the objects they can see in the room. Tell them that they can include objects in pictures on the walls. Children guess, e.g. **book, bag, bottle, boat**. They continue guessing until someone names the correct object.

Variation
Tell the class to look at a picture in one of their books or two pages with pictures that show a lot of different things. Use the picture or pages to play *I spy...*

When children are familiar with this game, they may like to take turns to choose objects and say *I spy with my little eye...*

Spelling games

Words from words
Write a simple word with different vowels and consonants on the board.

Children use the letters in the word to make other words.

Show them how to do this the first time: explain that some letters are in the right order to make a new word, e.g. *farmer*: farm, far, arm, me, are. These can be made by taking three letters and rearranging the order.

Other example words: rainbow: rain, bow, in, no, now, bin, win, on, won, ran; cupboard: cup, board, up, car, bad, drop; feather: eat, the, fat, ate, there, hat, he, rat.

Look, write, check
Write a target phonics word on the board. Children look at the word. Cover the word on the board. Children write it. Uncover the word. Children check their spelling.

Alphabet game
Children think of as many words as they can beginning with a particular letter.

Choose the easier letters, e.g. b, c, d, r, s, t.

This game is best played in pairs or small groups.

Extension: when children have written their list, tell them to write it in alphabetical order

Word list: alphabetical (The number is the unit where you can find the word.)

A act (1)
active (15)
adult (3)
adventure (12)
Africa (10)
against (1)
agree (5)
albatross (3)
alive (5)
almost (10)
alone (2)
amazed (12)
among (7)
animation (1)
another (9)
answer (1)
antler (11)
anyone (2)
appear (3)
Arabian (5)
archaeologist (12)
area (11)
argue (3)
army (5)
around (10)
arrive (10)
astronaut (10)
attack (5)
awful (6)

B baby (3)
back (3
ballet (5)
band (8)
basket (2)
basket maker (4)
battle (5)
beak (3)
beard (11)
beast (6)
beckon (8)
become (6)
Bedouin (7)
before (8)
begin (5)
beside (2)
best (6)
better (6)
bird of paradise (6)
block (9)
board (1)
border (11)
boring (12)
on board (10)

born (10)
both (3)
bottom (4)
bowl (4)
branch (3)
brave (2)
break ((1)
broke (1)
bubble (1)
build (3)
bunch (2)
butterfly (6)
button (2)

C call (5)
call sign (10)
camel train (12)
candle (4)
candlelight (4)
candle maker (4)
captain (1)
capture (7)
carefully (4)
carve (11)
caterpillar (6)
certainly (5)
change into (5)
characters (5)
cheap (10)
chess (1)
chess pieces (1)
chick (3)
Chinese (5)
choir (1)
clay (4)
clearly (8)
clever (3)
click (1)
cloak (2)
closed (2)
cloth (4)
club (1)
coach (1)
coast (11)
cocoon (9)
coil (4)
collar (8)
come in (1)
command (8)
commander (10)
compass (9)
complain (7)
concert (1)
cool (4)

copies (2)
corn (7)
corner (8)
cosmonaut (10)
costume (2)
country (3)
courtyard (8)
cover (5)
covered in (8)
craft (4)
crossroads (8)
crumpled (6)
cupboard (2)
curtain (2)
custom (7)
cygnet (3)

D dancer (5)
danger (3)
date (12)
date palm (12)
daughter (1)
dawn (8)
definitely (9)
delicate (6)
delighted (10)
dentist (12)
description (10
desert (7)
die (3)
dim (8)
dip (4)
disappear (2)
disappointed (12)
disaster (3)
discover (9)
discovery (9)
display (9)
distant (12)
dive (3)
doorway (2)
dragonfly (6)
drama (1)
dream (5)
drive (10)
driver (10)
drown (3)
dry (4)
during (10)
dye (9)

E east (7)
edge (2)
education (10)
electricity (7)

emperor (6)
Emperor penguin (3)
empty (8)
engineer (10)
evil (5)
excellent (1)
excited (5)
exclaim (12)
explode (9)
exploration (10)
explorers (7)

F factory (10)
fail (8)
fair (hair) (11)
falcons (7)
fall off (5)
fall over (12)
fan (6)
feast (6)
feather (3)
feel (2)
felt (2)
fierce (5)
fight (5)
fighters (7)
final (5)
finally (4)
fine (8)
finish (5)
Finland (11)
fireworks (9)
first (5)
fisherman (11)
fit (3)
flame (9)
flash (6)
flight (10)
forest (2)
forget (2)
forwards (8)
free time (10)
frightened (2)
fringe (11)
frozen (7)
fur (11)
furniture (12)
further (12)

G geese (3)
get dressed (8)
gloomy (5)
glow (6)
golden (6)
goose (3)

gosling (3)
grab (3)
graceful (3)
gradually (4)
grass (7)
great (8)
group (1)
grow (6)
guess (6)
gull (3)
gunpowder (9)

H hall (8)
hang (6)
hard (4)
headdress (8)
heat (4)
hero (5)
hide (6)
hood (2)
horrid (7)
hour (5)
hum (12)
hunt (7)
hurriedly (8)
hurt (7)
husband (10)

I important (8)
Incas (7)
ink (9)
intelligent (5)
internet (1)
invented (7)
invention (9)

J Japan (5)
Japanese (5)
jaw (6)
jewel (6)
jewellery (8)
join (1)
journey (10)
just (2)

K kill (5)
kilogram (10)
kilometre (1)
kind (1)
kind of (9)
kindergarten (1)
kneel (12)
knife (4)
knock (2)

Word list: alphabetical

L lake (3)
land (3)
language (7)
larva (6)
last (2)
lay (3)
lazy (1)
lead (8)
leaf (6)
lean (8)
leap (2)
lid (12)
life (3)
lift off (10)
light (2)
look after (12)
look for (6)
loom (4)
lose (1)
lost (adj) (8)
loud (5)
lovely (2)
lump (4)

M map (9)
marry (10)
mask (5)
match (11)
meat (11)
melt (9)
message (8)
messenger (8)
mice (5)
middle (8)
midnight (5)
mix (9)
mixture (9)
modern (7)
moment (8)
money (9)
mould (4)
move (1)
much (3)
museum (7)

n narrow (8)
nation (11)
national (11)
nature (6)
needle (9)
nervous (6)
nets (3)
newspaper (11)
next (1)
nice (6)
nightcap (2)
nil (11)
nod (8)

nomads (7)
north (7)
northern (11)
Norway (11)
nothing (2)
nowadays (7)
nutcracker (5)

O oasis (12)
ocean (3)
once (2)
on time (5)
orbit (10)
orchestra (1)
other (4)
oven (4)
own (6)
owner (6)

P pack up (7)
painting (6)
palace (8)
Palestine (5)
palm tree (12)
pan (4)
paper (9)
papyrus (9
parachute (10)
parent (3)
part (7)
passage (8)
past (10)
patterns (7)
pay (9)
penguin (3)
perform (2)
performers (5)
Peru (7)
photocopier (2)
picnic (9)
pinch (4)
planet (10)
play (1)
ploughs (7)
pocket (4)
politely (2)
poster (5)
pot (4)
potter (4)
pound (2)
pour (4)
powerful (7)
practise (1)
press (2)
prince (5)
printing (9)
problem (9)
professor (12)

program (1)
programme (3)
prop (2)
proud (11)
pupa (6)
put (10)
put on (1)
pyramid (12)

R radio (11)
rare (8)
ready (6)
receive (10)
record (1)
reeds (4)
referee (1)
rehearsal (5)
reindeer (7)
repeat (8)
return (10)
ribbon (7)
ridiculous (3)
roundabout (8)
rude (7)
ruins (12)
rule over (7)
Russian (5)

S safe (2)
salt (9)
Sami (7)
sand dunes (12)
satellite (10)
scenery (2)
scientist (9)
score (11)
scream (2)
script (2)
seaweed (1)
second (1)
seed (6)
set off (2)
shadows (8)
shadowy (8)
shape (4)
shawl (2)
shield (8)
show (5)
sides (4)
sight (6)
silent (5)
silk (9)
silkworm (9)
ski (11)
skin (3)
sky-dive (10)
sledge (11)
slide (12)

smell (2)
smooth (4)
snail (1)
snow scooter (11)
soft (4)
soon (2)
south (7)
South America (7)
souvenirs (12)
space craft (10)
space engineer (10)
space rocket (10)
Spanish (5)
spear (8)
spend (time) (5)
spin (7)
spread (6)
squeak (4)
stage (2)
stare (12)
start (5)
steal (12)
step (8)
still (9)
straight (4)
sure (12)
surprise (8)
suspicious (7)
suspiciously (12)
Sweden (11)
switch on (5)
sword (8)

T tadpole (6)
take back (10)
take off (plane) (10)
task (8)
team (1)
terrible (5)
terrified (6)
terrifying (6)
test (10)
though (6)
thousand (2)
threads (4)
throne (8)
Tibetan (7)
toe (3)
tomorrow (1)
too (1)
tool (11)
torch (12)
total (5)
touch (12)
tourists (12)
train (10)
trap (3)

treasure (12)
tricky (12)
true (6)
try (1)
tunic (8)
twig (3)
twitch (2)

U uncle (3)
unfortunately (3)
usually (3)

V valuable (12)
vase (4)
village (7)

W wake up (8)
warm (3)
war-time (10)
watchful (7)
wax (4)
way (2)
weave (4)
weaver (4)
webbed (3)
website (1)
well (1)
west (7)
wheel (4)
whisper (8)
whistle (11)
wild (3)
winter(3) (11)
wolf (2)
wonderful (7)
work (2)
worm (6)
worse (6)
woodblock (9)
woodcutter (2)
wooden (5)
work (go) (2)
worriedly (2)
worst (6)
wrap (9)
wrinkled (6)

y yak (7)
4x4 (12)

Word list: alphabetical 189

Word list: Unit by unit

bold = key word
normal = *extension word*
grey type = words for understanding

See Introduction, page 9: Lesson 1, *Learning new words*.
See DVD or website for printable lists of key words and extension words for giving out to children to learn during each unit.

Unit 1

act
against
animation
answer
board
break
broke
bubble
captain
chess
chess piece
choir
click
club
coach
come in
concert
daughter
drama
excellent
group
internet
join
kilometre
kind
kindergarten
lazy
lose
move
next
orchestra
play
practise
program
put on
record
referee
seaweed
second
team
tomorrow
too
try
website
well

Unit 2

alone
anyone
basket
beside
brave
bunch
button
cloak
closed
copy
costume
cupboard
curtain
disappear
doorway
edge
feel
felt
first
forest
forget
frightened
hood
just
knock
last
leapt
light
lovely
nightcap
nothing
once
perform
photocopier
politely
pound
press
prop
safe
scenery
scream
script
set off
shawl
smell
soon

stage
thousand
twitch
way
wolf
woodcutter
work
worriedly

Unit 3

adult
albatross
appear
argue
baby
back
beak
both
branch
build
chick
clever
cygnet
danger
die
disaster
dive
drown
Emperor penguin
feather
fit
geese
goose
gosling
grab
graceful
gull
lake
land
lay
life
much
net
ocean
parent
penguin
put on
ridiculous

skin
toe
trap
twig
unfortunately
usually
warm
webbed
wild

Unit 4

basket maker
bowl
bottom
candle
candlelight
candle maker
carefully
clay
cloth
coil
cool
craft
dip
dry
finally
gradually
hard
heat
knife
loom
lump
mould
other
oven
pan
pinch
potter
pour
reeds
shape
side
smooth
soft
squeak
thread
vase
wax

weave
weaver
wheel

Unit 5

active
agree
alive
Arabian
army
attack
ballet
battle
begin
called
certainly
change into
characters
Chinese
country
cover
dancer
dream
excited
evil
fall off
fierce
fight
final
finish
gloomy
hero
hour
intelligent
Japan
Japanese
kill
loud
mask
mice
midnight
nutcracker
on time
Palestine
performers
poster
prince
programme

rehearsal
Russian
show
silent
Spanish
spend
start
switch on
terrible
total
wooden

Unit 6

awful
beast
become
best
better
bird of paradise
butterfly
caterpillar
crumpled
delicate
dragonfly
fan
feast
flash
glow
golden
grow
guess
hang
hide
jaw
jewel
larva
leaf
look for
nature
nervous
nice
own
owner
painting
pupa
seed
sight
spread

190 Word list: Unit by unit

tadpole
terrified
terrifying
true
worm
worse
worst
wrinkled

Unit 7
among
Bedouin
capture
complain
corn
custom
desert
east
electricity
explorer
falcon
fighter
frozen
grass
horrid
hunt
hurt
Incas
language
modern
museum
nomads
north
nowadays
pack up
part
patterns
Peru
plough
powerful
reindeer
ribbon
rude
rule over
Sami
south
South America
spin
suspicious
Tibetan
village
watchful
west
wonderful
yak

Unit 8
band
beckon
before
clearly
collar
command
corner
courtyard
covered in
crossroads
dawn
dim
empty
fail
fine
forwards
get dressed
great
hall
headdress
hurriedly
important
jewellery
lead
lean
lost
message
messenger
middle
moment
narrow
nod
palace
passage
rare
repeat
roundabout
shadowy
shield
spear
step
surprise
sword
task
throne
tunic
wake up
whisper

Unit 9
block
cocoon
compass
completely
definitely

discover
discovery
display
dye
explode
flame
gunpowder
ink
invention
just
kind of
map
melt
mix
mixture
needle
papyrus
picnic
printing
problem
salt
scientist
silk
silkworm
still
woodblock
wrap

Unit 10
Africa
almost
around
arrive
astronaut
board
born
call
call sign
cheap
commander
continue
cosmonaut
delighted
description
drive
driver
during
education
engineer
exploration
factory
fit
flight
free time
hard
husband

journey
kilogram
last
lift off
marry
orbit
parachute
past
planet
receive
return
satellite
sky-dive
spacecraft
take back
take off
test
train
war-time

Unit 11
antler
area
beard
border
carve
coast
fair
Finland
fisherman
fringe
fur
match
meat
nation
national
newspaper
nil
northern
Norway
once
proud
radio
score
ski
sledge
snow scooter
Sweden
tool

Unit 12
4x4
adventure
amazed
archaeologist
boring

camel train
date
date palm
dentist
disappointed
distant
exclaim
fall over
furniture
further
hum
kneel
lid
look after
oasis
palm tree
professor
pyramid
ruins
sand dunes
slide
souvenirs
stare
steal
suspiciously
torch
tourists
treasure
tricky
valuable

Grammar Practice Book Answer Key

Unit 1

page 4
Activity 1: 1 swam 2 didn't swim 3 went 4 didn't go 5 Did, like, did 6 Did, buy, No
Activity 2: 2 Did she go to a concert? Yes, she did. 3 Did she arrive on Friday? No, she didn't. 4 Did she swim on Wednesday? Yes, she did.

page 5
Activity 1: 1 expensive 2 difficult 3 heavy 4 tired
Activity 2: 2 It's too expensive. 3 It's too dangerous. 4 It's too small. 5 It's too big.

page 6
Activity 1: 1 go 2 went 3 Did 4 No, too
Activity 2: 2 I've got a new bike. 3 She doesn't like apples. 5 We are at school. 6 They were not in the house.

Unit 2

page 7
Activity 1: 2 Tamsin and Tina were playing football. They weren't doing homework. 3 Tom was swimming. He wasn't sleeping.
Activity 2: 2 Was Amy reading a book? e 3 Was Tom playing football? d 4 Was Tom sleeping? a 5 Were Tamsin and Tina watching television? c

page 8
Activity 1: 2 It couldn't talk. 3 It could clean the house. 4 It couldn't cook. 5 It couldn't sing.
Activity 2: 2 The old robot couldn't fly. The new robot can fly. 3 The old robot couldn't play the guitar. The new robot can play the guitar. 4 The old robot couldn't swim. The new robot can swim.

page 9
Activity 1: 1 walking 2 Were 3 was. 4 helping 5 wasn't. 6 wearing 7 could 8 couldn't
Activity 2: 1 said Joe 2 asked his sister 3 said Joe 4 His sister said 5 asked Joe 6 said his sister

Unit 3

page 10
Activity 1: The children colour the fish according to the text.
Activity 2: 3 The pink fish is the most expensive. 4 The blue fish is more expensive than the yellow fish. 5 The yellow fish is more dangerous than the red fish. 6 The yellow fish is the most dangerous.

page 11
Activity 1: 1 is as old as 2 isn't as heavy as 3 isn't as beautiful as 4 is as long as
Activity 2: 2 Ping isn't as old as Kitty. 3 Tabby is as thin as Kitty. 4 Ping isn't as big as Kitty. 5 Tabby is as young as Ping.

page 12
Activity 1: 1 more, than 2 most 3 exciting 4 as, as
Activity 2: 1 a 2 b 3 a 4 b 5 b 6 a 7 a 8 b

Review 1

Activity 1: 1 didn't walk 2 bought 3 didn't buy 4 Did, buy, she did 5 Did, buy, No, she
Activity 2: 1 were not 2 was reading 3 wasn't watching 4 Was, eating, was 5 Were, No, they
Activity 3: 1 most expensive 2 more expensive 3 more beautiful than 4 more beautiful than 5 the most beautiful
Activity 4: 1 The sheep isn't as old as the horse. 2 The dog is as big as the sheep. 3 The sheep isn't as big as the horse. 4 The sheep is as heavy as the dog. 5 The dog isn't as heavy as the horse.
Activity 5: 1 I couldn't do the homework. 2 We could hear the birds. 3 The horse was too old. 4 The trousers were too expensive. 5 The homework was too difficult.
Activity 6: 1 cook 2 book 3 wood 4 hook 5 push 6 pull 7 bull 8 head 9 bread 10 thread

Review 1 Writing page
Activity 1: Monday, dress, beautiful, buy, expensive
Activity 2: Example writing: On Wednesday Jack went to the mall. He saw a football game, a car game and a space game. The car game was more exciting than the space game. He couldn't play the car game because he was too young.

Unit 4

page 17
Activity 1: 1 d 2 f 3 e 4 a 5 c 6 b
Activity 2: 2 When he fell on the floor, he kicked the table. 3 When he kicked the table, the food fell on the cat. 4 When the food fell on the cat, the mouse ate some cheese.

page 18
Activity 1: 1 something 2 nothing 3 anything 4 anything 5 something 6 Everything 7 anything 8 nothing
Activity 2: 1 nothing 2 something 3 Everything 4 something 5 anything

page 19
Activity 1: 1 something 2 walked, shouted 3 anything 4 nothing
Activity 2: 2 knives 3 halves 4 leaves 5 thieves 6 wolves

Unit 5

page 20
Activity 1: 2 were reading, were watching television 3 was drinking water, was sleeping
Activity 2: 1 While the young man was talking on the phone, the young woman was working. 2 While the birds were flying, the fish were swimming. 3 While Grandma was cooking, Grandpa was working in the garden.

page 21
Activity 1: 2 I want either a bicycle or a computer. 3 She's going to buy either trainers or a T-shirt. 4 Most people like either apples or pears. 5 In the afternoon my brother either plays football or reads a book. 6 For lunch we have either a sandwich or a salad.
Activity 2: 2 You can either watch television or you can play a computer game. 3 You can either go to the mall or go swimming. 4 You can either take photos or go to the museum.

page 22
Activity 1: 1 was watching, were listening 2 were watching, was listening 3 either, or
Activity 2: in, on, on, at, in, at

Unit 6

page 23
Activity 1: 3 He won't arrive on time at school. 4 He will arrive late at school. 5 His teacher won't be happy. 6 His teacher will be unhappy. 7 It won't be good. 8 It will be horrible.
Activity 2: (answers may vary) 2 It will be sunny. 3 It won't snow. 4 It will be hot. 5 It won't be windy.

page 24
Activity 1: a Lucy b Jack c Sharon d Anita / a Diana b Joe c Ryan d Kate
Activity 2: 1 better than 2 better than 3 the best 4 worse than 5 worse than 6 the worst

page 25
Activity 1: 1 worse, worst 2 won't be 3 will love 4 better, best
Activity 2: 2 They're the baby's shoes. 3 It's the girl's watch. 4 It's the bird's wing. 5 It's the baby's hat. 6 They're the bird's feet.

Review 2

Activity 1: 1 When I got up, I had breakfast. 3 When the girl crossed the road, she fell down.
Activity 2: 1 Everything 2 something 3 nothing 4 anything 5 anything
Activity 3: 1 While the horse was running, the cow was eating. 2 While the boys were talking, the girls were working. 3 While my mother was watching television, my father was working.
Activity 4: 1 I want either trainers or a T-shirt. 2 You can wear either shorts or trousers. 3 We can either read or talk. 4 You will get a good score in this test. 5 It won't be windy tomorrow.
Activity 5: 1 worse 2 the worst 3 the best 4 better than 5 worse than
Activity 6: 1 lady 2 baby 3 lolly 4 coin 5 oil 6 join 7 jaw 8 paw 9 draw 10 claw

Review 2 Writing page
Activity 1: Yesterday, mother and father, watching television, making cakes, best, worst
Activity 2: Example writing: Lucy was at home. While her grandma and grandpa were reading, she was painting with her brother and sister. Her sister's picture was the best. Her picture was the worst.

Unit 7

page 30
Activity 1: 2 There is lots of fruit. 3 There isn't much water. 4 There are a lot of grapes. 5 There aren't many trees. 6 There are lots of camels.
Activity 2: 1 many, lots 2 any, is 3 How much, is, is a lot 4 Is, any, isn't 5 How many, are, aren't many 6 Are, any, aren't

page 31
Activity 1: 2 He should brush his hair. 3 He should clean his clothes. 4 He shouldn't be rude to people. 5 He should eat healthy food. 6 He shouldn't get up late.
Activity 2: 2 Should he go to bed late? No, he shouldn't. 3 Should he eat more sweets? No, he shouldn't. 4 Should he be polite to people? Yes, he should.

page 32
Activity 1: 1 How much 2 much 3 How many 4 many 5 Should 6 lots
Activity 2: 2 They are interesting. 3 It is jumping on the path.
Activity 3: 2 She – their mother 3 they – the songs

Unit 8

page 33
Activity 1: 2 6 o'clock 3 3 o'clock
Activity 2: 1 Someone 2 No one 3 Everyone 4 anyone
Activity 3: 1 somebody 2 nobody 3 somebody 4 anybody

page 34
Activity 1: 2 The school. 3 The museum. 4 The hospital.
Activity 2: 1 along, left, crossroads, right 2 Walk along, left, on the right

page 35
Activity 1: 1 Could, tell, way 2 along, Turn 3 anybody 4 Everybody, Nobody